TRIUMPH
OVER TYRANNY

*The Heroic Campaigns
that Saved
2,000,000 Soviet Jews*

PHILIP SPIEGEL

Foreword by **Natan Sharansky**

DEVORA
PUBLISHING
NEW YORK◆JERUSALEM◆LONDON

Triumph Over Tyranny
Published by Devora Publishing Company
Text Copyright © 2008 Philip Spiegel

COVER DESIGN: Benjie Herskowitz
TYPESETTING: Koren Publishing Services
EDITORIAL AND PRODUCTION MANAGER: Daniella Barak
EDITOR: Sybil Ehrlich

Hard Cover ISBN: 978-1-934440-13-1
Includes index

E-mail: publisher@devorapublishing.com
Web Site: www. devorapublishing.com

Printed in the United States of America

Dedication

This book is dedicated to the memory of eleven courageous individuals who made significant contributions to both the realization of a triumph over tyranny for Soviet Jews and to the author's research for *Triumph Over Tyranny*. Sadly, they did not live to see the book in print.

Rivka Alexandrovich
Yuri Chernyak
Moshe Decter
Michael Dohan
Robert Drinan
Genya Intrator
Tom Lantos
Alexander Lerner
Vladimir Magarik
Yuri Shtern
Lynn Singer

CONTENTS

FOREWORD

*I*n my family we celebrate the Exodus twice. One is the Seder of Passover and the other is day of my release from prison. While all Jews strive on Seder night to feel that they, too, took part in the Exodus from Egypt, for many of the Soviet Jews the story of national liberation requires no imagination.

Indeed, our own personal exodus, from the darkness of Communist totalitarianism to the light of the Jewish state, is a modern retelling of our people's ages-old struggle to overcome tyranny and achieve freedom. But it is more than that. Like the story of the Israelites, the story of the movement to liberate the Soviet Jews is a profound lesson on the power of a people who come together as a community to effect, despite overwhelming odds, positive change in human history.

* * *

Growing up in Communist Russia, the narrative of the Jewish people was almost completely unknown to me. This was not by accident: The Communist regime had declared a decades-long war against Jewish identity in all its forms. There were mass executions of Jewish intellectuals and community leaders. Our synagogues and schools were shut down. Any public expression of Jewish identification was met with swift and savage punishment; any chance of reconnecting with our Jewish brothers and sisters beyond the Iron Curtain seemed as likely as the parting of the Red Sea.

All this changed, however, in June 1967, with Israel's astounding victory in the Six-Day War. The call that went up from Jerusalem, "The Temple Mount is in our hands," penetrated the Iron Curtain, forging an almost mystic link with Soviet Jews. Now, we had a country that wanted us, and a people – strong and courageous – who stood behind us. But it was not just pride that Israel's victory evoked among the Soviet Jews. Our newfound identification with the Jewish state inspired a heroic few among us to break their silence for the first time, and to demand freedom from Soviet oppression and citizenship in Israel.

These bold Soviet Jewish activists prepared to sacrifice their lives in defiance of one of modern history's most powerful and dangerous regimes, and fired the first shot in what was to become a twenty-year war. Our cause was taken up, passionately and tirelessly, by Jews around the world. At the forefront of this global army of Jewish resistance stood a generation of Jews from across the political and religious spectrum, who insisted that no threat to Jewish life and memory go unchallenged.

To be sure, the path to victory was long and hard. But we Soviet Jews knew that we need never go it alone. As we slowly transformed our struggle from an underground movement into overt protest, it was world Jewry which turned the eyes and ears of the world to our plight, and would not let it be ignored. Our perilous protests often in the center of Moscow were matched by marches of ten thousand in New York, Philadelphia, London and Paris. Our slogan was "Let My People Go." Their slogan was "Never again will we be silent about the plight of our brothers." During my interrogations by KGB officials they used to say mockingly, "Who is supporting you?... a bunch of students and housewives?"

Ultimately, it really was an army of Jewish students and

housewives who defeated and the KGB. And what a great and proud moment it was on December 6, 1987, to watch a quarter of a million vanguard troops of this army, American Jews who gathered from all over the country in their final effort to destroy the Iron Curtain.

With the fall of the Iron Curtain, over a million Russian Jews came to Israel and brought with them their boundless energy, ambitions and talent. They enriched every sector of Israeli life profoundly – starting with science, medicine, music, sports etc. It was not only the Jews of the Soviet Union and the State of Israel, however, who benefited from the fruits of the movement's astonishing labors. The liberation of Soviet Jewry, it must be recognized, tore a gaping hole in the Iron Curtain, one that would eventually spell the end of the Soviet empire.

For 3,000 years, we Jews have remembered the great exodus of Israel from Egypt, we keep it alive by telling it anew each time to our children. But the exodus that happened in our lifetime, and which so greatly influenced world history, almost escaped from our collective conscience.

Thus did the Jewish people, a small but determined nation united in its efforts and its vision, make the world a safer and better place for all men and women. And thus may the story of Soviet Jewry teach today's Jewish people that the first step in the vital mission of tikkum olam, repair of the world, must begin with a belief in the responsibility and mutual concern all Jews must share for one another. That is why the efforts being done today to preserve the memory, including this important book by Philip Spiegel, are so crucial to make sure that the story of this struggle and its lessons are kept alive.

Natan Sharansky,
Chairman,
Adelson Institute for Strategic Studies and
Beth Hatefutsoth Board of Directors

ACKNOWLEDGMENTS

My thanks begin with gratitude to my beloved parents, Sol and Helen Spiegel of blessed memory, who immigrated to America from what is now Otyniya, Ukraine, in the 1920s. They instilled in me a feeling of pride to be part of a people who treasure the thousands of years of wisdom embodied in the teachings of the Torah, prophets and great rabbis. I grew up influenced by my parents' concern for social justice and commitment to the State of Israel.

My darling wife, Carolyn Kommel Spiegel, played a primary role in my involvement with Soviet Jewry and in ultimately writing this book. On the first day we met she spoke about the plight of Soviet Jews and I was enthralled to hear her telling about her friends in the Soviet Jewry Action Group who painted "Let the Jews Out!" on a Soviet freighter in San Francisco Bay in 1970. I thank her for bringing me into the Soviet Jewry movement, for encouraging me to write this book, for editing initial drafts of many of its chapters, and most of all, for her patience with me as I elected to spend time on research and writing rather than cleaning the garage or tending the garden.

In 2002, when I contemplated retirement from the electronics industry, I thought back to a question asked of me fifteen years earlier by a student at the University of California during a talk I gave about Soviet Jewry. He asked, "Why do the Soviets oppress the Jews, and if they don't like them, why don't they allow the Jews to emigrate?" It occurred to me that if students were asking such questions in 1987 when the Soviet Jewry campaigns were making front-page headlines it would be likely that young people in the twenty-first century would be unaware that Jews in Russia had been oppressed during the Soviet era.

I decided that my retirement project would be to write a book that would describe the history of the various aspects of the international Soviet Jewry movement. I asked my friends Morey Schapira and David Waksberg about the idea and they enthusiastically gave me lists of people to interview as well as suggestions of literature to read and archives to delve into. Many of the initial interviewees led me to others who also had important stories to tell. Over five years I have interviewed over 200 people in person, by telephone, and by email; they are referenced in the endnotes of each chapter. I appreciate their willingness to share their recollections, memorabilia, and in many cases, edit the chapters that apply to them.

Some of these interviewees went above and beyond the call of duty in their support for my project. Jacob Birnbaum, in New York, was one of the first. Jacob was extremely supportive in discussing his role as founder and director of the Student Struggle for Soviet Jews and the Center for Russian Jewry. He patiently followed up on our initial meeting with countless hours of telephone conversations and emails. His devoted wife, Freda, served as his email and fax conduit, sending me numerous essays and other documents from Jacob's scores of years of dedicated service to Soviet Jewry.

Carolyn and I travel to New York several times each year for family visits – our sons, Ralph and Mike, live there – and no trip to New York would be complete for me without a Sunday morning consultation with Glenn Richter, a veritable encyclopedia of the Soviet Jewry movement.

In Los Angeles Si Frumkin spent considerable time with me and also introduced me to Laura Bialis, the producer/director of the documentary film Refusenik. Together, she and I interviewed Michael Sherbourne and recorded his accounts that appear in Chapter 19. Several years later when Laura's research and filming was complete she was kind enough to send me a compact disk of 150 transcribed interviews which proved valuable in augmenting my own research.

Before traveling to Israel in 2003 and 2006 to interview former refuseniks, prisoners, political leaders and activists, I consulted with Enid Wurtman. She lives in Jerusalem and served as a "411" providing me with numerous email addresses and telephone numbers and graciously offered her office to be used as a venue for some of the meetings .

After I returned from Israel in 2003 Rabbi Yosef Levin of Chabad of the Greater South Bay asked me if I planned to write about Chabad's efforts to keep Judaism alive in Russia during the Soviet era. I replied that I would like to do that, and Levin then put me in touch with his mother, Rachel Liberove, in London, Professor Branover in Israel and Dovid Zaklikowski at Chabad.org in New York. Chapter 2 is the product of Levin's inspiration.

Pamela Cohen and Micah Naftalin, the dynamic duo of Chapter 17, were extremely helpful, spending many hours sharing the histories of their involvement in the movement and their views of the UCSJ philosophy and plans for the future, as well as critically reviewing my initial draft of that chapter.

If Natan Sharansky had been only an inspiring and heroic Prisoner of Zion – dayenu (it would have been sufficient). If he had only allowed me an hour to interview him – dayenu again. But Sharansky did all of this and then also wrote a superb foreword for this book – icing on the cake!

Several friends, Esther Kletter, Dick Roistacher, Charles Wiseman among them, reviewed and edited various chapters of the book. Their questions and insightful comments were beneficial.

I appreciate the enthusiasm Yaacov Peterseil showed in agreeing to have this book published by Devora Publishing. It has been a pleasure working with my editor, Sybil Ehrlich, and finding her emails with expertly revised versions of each chapter attachments in my in-box every morning.

I apologize to all those who helped me bring this book to fruition but who are not mentioned in these paragraphs. Triumph over Tyranny, like the actual triumph over tyranny that resulted from the Soviet Jewry Movement, was a highly collaborative effort. I hope that others will continue to study and write about the events that Elie Wiesel described as a "great moment in Jewish history".

George Shultz, whom I had the pleasure of interviewing in 2003, was the keynote speaker at a fund-raising dinner in 2007 for the American Jewish Historical Society's new archive of the American Soviet Jewry Movement. He declared, "The best reason to record and remember how Soviet Jews were saved is to be prepared to act again when the need arises. If we are ever to live in a civilized world, what was accomplished for the Soviet Jews must become the rule rather than the exception. We must not only preach the doctrine of human rights, we must learn how actually to be our brother's keeper."

In January 2008 the Union of Councils for Soviet Jews, spearheaded by incoming president Larry Lerner, former president Morey Schapira, and national director Micah Naftalin, launched a Soviet Jewry History, Education and Leadership Project (SJ/HELP). The UCSJ plans to create archival and internet opportunities for the thousands of individuals who were part of the movement to memorialize their efforts and activities by providing written histories and recollections. To do this, one can contact UCSJ by email: UCSJ@UCSJ.com, or by writing to:

UCSJ
POB 11676, Cleveland Park
Washington, D.C. 20008

Contributions to support UCSJ's initiative to document and teach
the history of the Soviet Jewry movement can be made on-line
through its website: FSUMonitor.com. Checks can be sent to the
above address, and made out to "UCSJ/SJ-HELP".

Theodor Herzl and the Zionist Dream

"*Wenn Ihr wollt ist es kein Märchen*" (If you will it, it is no dream[1]) are the words Theodor Herzl inscribed in his utopian novel *Altneuland* (*Old-New Land*) in 1902. These words served as a rallying cry for Zionists who strived to create a Jewish homeland during the first half of the twentieth century, and a mantra for Soviet Jews who actively struggled for the right to emigrate during the second half of that century.

Theodor Herzl was born in Budapest, Hungary, in 1860, the only son of a wealthy merchant. Although the family was assimilated and his religious studies ended after his bar mitzvah, he was upset after hearing anti-Semitic remarks in the technical school he attended and wanted to transfer to a gymnasium that emphasized classics rather than mathematics and science.[2] Later when he was a law student at the University of Vienna he joined "Albia," a student union. However, he resigned after the group participated in an anti-Jewish demonstration at a memorial for Richard Wagner, one of the nineteenth century's most influential Jew-haters. Herzl received his doctorate in 1884 and practiced law for a year as a civil servant in Vienna.[3]

In 1886 he moved to Berlin and wrote essays for the *Deutsche Zeitung*, rejecting the editor's proposal that he use a non-Jewish pseudonym. Moving back to Vienna three years later, he achieved moderate success as a playwright and married Julie Naschauer. Their three children, Pauline, Hans and Margarete, were born during the next four years.

Herzl became the Paris correspondent for the *Neue Freie Presse* in 1891 and reported on the court-martial of Capt. Alfred Dreyfus in 1894, which reinforced his conviction that anti-Semitism was a major problem for the Jewish people.[4] He later wrote: "If such things could happen in republican, modern, civilized France, a century after the Declaration of Human Rights, then the Jews need their own country, nation and land."[5] His play *The New Ghetto*, performed in 1896, asserted that even the most assimilated Jew is bound within an invisible ghetto in a gentile world.

Reassigned to the *Neue Freie Presse* home office in 1896, Herzl found Vienna seething with anti-Semitism. Early that year he published a pamphlet, *Der Judenstaat (The Jewish State)* in which he adopted ideas from Leo Pinsker's 1882 pamphlet, *Auto-Emancipation*. Herzl advocated a Jewish homeland in Palestine and traveled to Constantinople in hopes of convincing the Ottoman sultan (who controlled Palestine) to allow Jews to set up a vassal state in return for financing some of the sultan's massive debt.[6]

Although the *Neue Freie Presse* was unsympathetic to Herzl's ambitions for a Jewish state and would not allow the publication of anything he wrote on the subject, he continued to work there as literary editor in order to support his family. On June 4, 1897, he founded *Die Welt*, a weekly that would remain the major Zionist newspaper until World War I.[7]

On August 29, 1897, in an effort to "unite the scattered limbs of Jewry" he convened the First World Zionist Congress in Basel, Switzerland. The term "Zionist" had been coined in 1892 by Nathan Birnbaum, the founder of the *Hovevei Zion* (Lovers of Zion). The 200 attendees represented Zionists from Europe and America and spanned the religious spectrum from atheist to ultra-Orthodox and the political spectrum from socialist to capitalist. Seventy years later the same diversity would be found in the ranks of activists in the cause of Soviet Jewry.

The second congress, again in Basel, drew 400 delegates, including Dr. Chaim Weizmann, a chemist from Russia who would later move to England and develop acetone, a vital ingredient in the manufacture of naval gun propellant that was crucial to British efforts in World War I.[8] At the end of the war Weizmann devoted himself to the Zionist movement and was a leader in the discussions that led to the Balfour Declaration of 1917.

During the fall of 1898 Herzl traveled to Constantinople and Jerusalem to meet Kaiser Wilhelm II of Germany to ask the emperor to intervene with the Ottoman sultan regarding a Jewish state in Palestine. Kaiser Wilhelm was not interested. Undaunted, Herzl met with other world leaders including the pope and the king of Italy, with little to show for his efforts.

Herzl presided over annual congresses until 1903. The Jewish National Fund was established at the fifth congress in 1901 to buy land in Palestine. The seventh congress in 1903 was particularly contentious as the delegates debated an offer from the British Colonial Office to create a Jewish settlement in East Africa. Herzl envisioned it as a temporary emergency solution for Jews who had to emigrate before a Jewish state could be established in Palestine. However the delegates from Russia, led by Weizmann, were furious in their opposition to the scheme.[9] They vowed to consider nothing but Palestine and effectively caused Herzl to drop further consideration of East Africa.[10]

In April 1903 there were massive pogroms in Kishinev (present-day Moldova). Fifty Jews were killed, 600 were injured and more than 1,500 shops and homes were damaged. There was panic among Jews throughout Russia and Herzl decided to travel to St. Petersburg to seek audience with Tsar Nicholas II whose father, Tsar Alexander III, had a solution for the Jewish problem: the government would cause one-third to assimilate, one-third to emigrate and one-third to perish.[11]

Herzl was denied a meeting with the tsar but did procure an interview with Viatscheslav Plehve, the ultra-conservative interior minister, eventually regarded as responsible for inciting the pogroms. Plehve told Herzl that the Russian government would be pleased to see a few million Jews emigrate to an independent Jewish state. "But we don't want to lose all our Jews," Plehve continued. "The very intelligent – and you are the best proof that there are such – we would like to keep." Seventy years later the Soviet government under Leonid Brezhnev would make Plehve's preferences the law of the land as they invoked an "education tax" with the intention of discouraging professionals from applying for exit visas.[12]

The stress of the 1903 congress and his frequent, arduous travel took their toll on Herzl's health. Already he had sacrificed his marriage and his money for the Zionist cause. Six months before his death from pneumonia on July 3, 1904, Herzl revealed to Reuben Brainin, a Hebrew writer, a dream that may have been the motivating force behind his mission. At age twelve Herzl had dreamed that he was taken up into the hands of the Messiah and soared with him to the clouds where they encountered Moses, who pointed to the young Herzl and called out to the Messiah: "This is the child I have been praying for." Moses then said to Herzl: "Go tell the Jews that I shall soon arrive to perform miracles and bestow blessings on my people and on the whole world."[13]

The establishment of the state of Israel on May 14, 1948, was the fulfillment of the vision as noted in Herzl's diary entry after the First Zionist Congress in 1897: "At Basel I founded the Jewish state. If I said this out loud today, I would be answered by universal laughter. Perhaps in five years, certainly in fifty, everyone will know it."[14]

In 1949 a hill in western Jerusalem was renamed Mount Herzl and Theodor Herzl's remains were flown in a airplane painted with the flag of the new State of Israel for reburial in the national cemetery on the top of the hill.

The stages of Herzl's life: growing up in an *assimilated* family, developing an *awareness* of his Jewish identity, choosing to become an *activist* for a Jewish homeland, incurring *antipathy* from his employer and finally, *achieving* his ultimate goal would be replayed a century later by tens of thousands of Jews who chose to leave the Soviet Union and live in a land where they could be safe and proud to be Jews.

Part One

Early Efforts to Save the "Jews of Silence"
1920–1967

CHAPTER ONE

The Bolshevik Campaign to Eradicate Judaism

O n the day that world-famous cyberneticist and former long-term refusenik Professor Alexander Lerner celebrated his ninetieth birthday he was asked, "When did you first decide that you wanted to emigrate from Russia to Israel?" Without hesitation he replied, "I was eight years old at my grandfather's Passover Seder and I heard everyone say, 'L'shana Haba'a B'Yerushalayim' (Next Year in Jerusalem)."[1] That wish was concealed in his heart for the next fifty years while the Soviet regime forbade the observance of Jewish traditions and until he courageously convened a secret meeting of his family and told them of his plan to apply for exit visas. It would be another seventeen years before his dream was allowed to become a reality.

ANTI-SEMITISM UNDER TSAR NICHOLAS II

Lerner was born in 1913 in Vinnitsa, a town in central Ukraine that he described as "known for its huge psychiatric hospital and tasty pickled apples."[2] That year, in nearby Kiev, a Jew named Mendel Beilis was falsely accused of killing a 13-year-old Christian boy to use his blood for the baking of matzah. The Beilis trial drew worldwide attention and outrage. Tsar Nicholas II, who had reigned since 1894, condoned the anti-Semitism inherent in the prosecution. Ever since the "Bloody Sunday" revolution that his troops had put down in 1905, he was fearful that revolutionaries were plotting against him and he believed that over half of the revolutionaries were Jews.

In 1916 Tsar Nicholas appointed himself commander in chief and led an ill-equipped army into war against Germany. By the end of that year Russian soldiers were in mutiny and deserting while the citizens of Russia were freezing and starving. These hardships combined to bring about plots to overthrow the regime, and uncontrollable rioting in early 1917 forced Nicholas to abdicate in favor of his younger brother, Michael, who declined to accept the throne, thereby ending three centuries of Romanov rule.[3]

The provisional government took control and chose Prince George Lvov, a social reformer, to become its leader. He was succeeded in July 1917 by Alexander Kerensky, a leader of the Socialist Revolutionary Party and *Duma* (parliament) member who had been the war minister. The moderate policies of his party and their Menshevik allies were rejected by the Bolsheviks (Communists) led by Vladimir Lenin, who declared Kerensky's government an organ of counterrevolution.[4] The Bolsheviks took control of the government on October 31, 1917, amid cries of "Peace, Land and Bread" and vows of death to the aristocracy.

A BRIEF ALLIANCE OF JEWS AND BOLSHEVIKS

Jews in Russia enthusiastically welcomed the downfall of Tsar Nicholas II as the new provisional government abolished all restrictive laws against Jews. They now had great expectations of an end to the pogroms, confinement in the Pale of Settlement, expulsion from their homes, and exclusion from professions, agriculture and heavy industry.[5] Hebrew and Yiddish schools expanded and the Zionist movement grew to 300,000 members, becoming Russia's largest Jewish political group.[6] The Jewish Workers

Socialist Party, the *Bund*, founded in 1897, had over 33,000 members in 302 branches by the end of 1917. Politically it was aligned with the Mensheviks and favored Yiddish culture over Jewish religion and Zionism.[7]

The expectation of no more pogroms was thwarted as the Bolsheviks struggled to maintain control of the Russian empire while fending off insurrection from the Ukrainian nationalist army and the White Army of tsarist loyalists. There were more than 2,000 pogroms and massacres between 1918 and 1921 perpetrated by the insurrectionists, leaving an estimated 30,000 Jews killed, more than 100,000 dead of illness or wounds resulting from the pogroms, and a million homeless.[8] Most Jews supported the Bolsheviks and, for self-defense, many Zionists and yeshiva students joined the Red Army, which prohibited anti-Semitic violence.[9] Lerner's family was lucky to have survived unscathed as many Jews of the Vinnitsa region suffered greatly during the pogroms of 1919. The most significant disruption the Lerners experienced as the Bolsheviks took over was the upheaval of the elementary education system. In his autobiography, *Change of Heart*, Lerner states:

The new Soviet school system was then only in the process of formation. It as yet had no tried principles for teaching, no qualified teachers, no textbooks. We youngsters of 1920 to 1926 were guinea pigs for experimentation by semiliterate "innovators of pedagogical science."[10]

Lenin, concerned about the problems of the various nationalities in the Russian Empire, appointed Joseph Stalin to a new post: Commissar of Nationalities.[11] Stalin, from Georgia, represented a minority nationality. In 1913 he wrote in his essay *Marxism and the National Question* that he agreed with Lenin that "a nation is a historically evolved, stable community of language, territory, economic life and psychological make-up manifested in a community of culture". Stalin saw Jews as spread all over Russia and not qualifying as a nationality by his definition. He therefore regarded assimilation of the Jews as inevitable and the

Bund's efforts to achieve special rights for Jews, e.g. Saturday as the day of rest, as a step backward and counter to the progress of the proletariat.[12]

JEWS FORCING JEWS INTO ASSIMILATION

In 1918 Stalin set up a Jewish Commissariat as one of 18 national commissariats to serve as an administrative body with clear objectives: to fight the Zionist and Jewish-Socialist parties; to conduct propaganda in Yiddish; to advise the central and local authorities on all Jewish matters; to set up Jewish institutions to carry out Soviet policies; and to help Jewish refugees return to their homes and provide them with economic aid.[13] Within the Communist Party there was a Jewish section, *Yevsektsia*, which worked closely with the Jewish Commissariat. The first commissar for Jewish affairs and a leader of the Yevsektsia was Semion Dimanshtain, who had attended yeshiva and had been ordained as a rabbi in Vilna, Lithuania. He abandoned Judaism when he embraced Marxism. After his arrest at a Bolshevik conference in 1908 he served five years in a Siberian prison, escaped and fled to Paris, where he connected with other emigre Bolsheviks.[14] Several Jews who had been active in the Bund became leaders of the Yevsektsia, but most Jewish workers who had been members of the Bund wanted no role in the Communist Party.[15]

Although Lenin was an ardent atheist he was strongly opposed to anti-Semitism; the Yevsektsia had to persuade him to outlaw all Jewish political parties – especially the Zionists – because they were considered counterrevolutionary. The Zionist offices were closed by September 1919 and most of the 3,000 Zionist leaders were arrested and deported to labor camps in Siberia. Concurrently, synagogues were closed and religious instruction, Christian as well as Jewish, of children under eighteen outside their homes was prohibited. All religious marriage and divorce laws were repealed and only civil marriages were officially recognized. These actions, as well as a campaign of propaganda to promote atheism, were the agenda of the Russian Godless Society whose president, Emelian Yaroslavsky, was a Jewish communist.[16]

As the Bolsheviks solidified their control additional anti-Jewish actions were taken. In Kiev on Rosh Hashanah 1921, in the same auditorium in which the Beilis trial of 1913 had been held, the Jewish religion was put on trial and sentenced to death.[17] The Yevsektsia agitated against observance of the High Holy Days in one of more than 100 campaigns against Jewish religious practices launched in 1922.[18] The secret police could be counted on to arrest violators of the anti-religious laws. A court in Zhitomir sentenced a rabbi to nine months' imprisonment and exile for maintaining a yeshiva where boys younger than 18 were taught Judaism.[19] Alexander Lerner, however, was able to get a Jewish education and became bar mitzvah in 1926, but two years later the Communists started closing synagogues in Vinnitsa, and by 1937 all of them were shuttered. The Communist campaign to eradicate Judaism succeeded in influencing the teenage Lerner to join his friends in abandoning Jewish studies and synagogue attendance.[20]

When Lenin died of a stroke in 1924 he was initially replaced by a "troika" consisting of Stalin, Lev Kamenev, and Grigory Zinoviev. Stalin quickly outmaneuvered Kamenev and Zinoviev as well as his arch-rival, Leon Trotsky, partly by emphasizing their Jewish backgrounds.[21]

In 1930 Stalin decided that the Yevsektsia was no longer useful to his purposes and ordered it dissolved. Most of its leaders were arrested during the purges of 1934.[22] *Yevsektsia*'s legacy prevailed through the second half of the 20th century and was described by Dr. Martin Luther King, Jr. as "a kind of spiritual and cultural genocide". He said:

> While Jews in Russia may not be physically murdered, as they were in Nazi Germany, they are facing every day a kind of spiritual and cultural genocide. The absence of opportunity to associate as Jews in the enjoyment of Jewish culture

and religious experience becomes a severe limitation upon the individual. These deprivations are a part of a person's emotional and intellectual life. They determine whether he is fulfilled as a human being. Blacks as well understand and sympathize with this problem. When you are written out of history, as a people, when you are given no choice but to accept the majority culture, you are denied an aspect of your own identity. Ultimately you suffer a corrosion of your self-understanding and your self-respect.[23]

THE CULT OF STALIN

Alexander Lerner described the people of the Soviet Union in the 1930s under Stalin as "faceless, subservient marionettes, to be manipulated any way the powers saw fit." The cult of Stalin was transforming individuals into a new species, "Homo Sovieticus," that replaced human dignity with a slave mentality under the Communist Party which was as master of the economy, science, culture, arts and mass media.[24]

With the forcible collectivization of Ukrainian peasants, Stalin perpetrated the largest genocide that Europe had ever experienced in peacetime. Starting in 1929 Soviet authorities went through the rural villages of Ukraine rounding up the adult population, compelling them to "voluntarily" join the collective farms. Lerner played the clarinet in an orchestra that was sent to these gatherings to perform the national anthem and festive music to keep the peasants entertained while they signed away their property and freedom. By 1933 whatever they harvested was taken from them and millions starved to death. Lerner recalled the horror of seeing corpses of peasants on the streets of Vinnitsa.[25]

In 1932 the Soviet authorities revived the infamous internal passport that had restricted Jews to the "Pale of Settlement" in tsarist times. This document now had to be carried by all citizens and, in addition to registering their place of residence, it indicated the bearer's nationality. Jews were marked *Yevrei* regardless of where they were born and what republic they lived in. The internal passport effectively limited travel within the Soviet Union and prevented emigration.[26]

Lerner was fortunate at the age of 18 to be allowed to live in Moscow, where he worked as an electrical technician and attended college. Three years later he married Judith Perelman from Vinnitsa and moved with her to a family room in the college hostel where they lived until the beginning of World War II. They spent the war years in Novosibirsk, working in a munitions factory. After the war they returned to Moscow where Lerner's inventions and innovations in automation led to his recognition as a professor and world-class authority in the field of cybernetics in spite of the anti-Semitism prevalent in the Soviet Union. His story continues in Chapter 9, "You Will Never Leave the Soviet Union."

Alexander Lerner at age 90 at home in Rehovot.
Photo by Philip Spiegel.

CHAPTER TWO

Chabad's Clandestine Activities to Keep Judaism Alive

The Cheka agent expected to bring the bearded Jew to his knees by pointing a revolver against his chest and saying, "This little toy has made many a man change his mind." But Rabbi Yosef Yitzchak Schneersohn just stared at his interrogator and retorted, "Your little toy can intimidate only the kind of man who has many gods and lives in only one world. Since I have but one God and live in two worlds [this one and the next] I am not impressed by your little toy!" This encounter with Russian authorities was not Schneersohn's first – he had been arrested and briefly imprisoned four times by tsarist police – and it would not be his last.[1]

REBBE YOSEF YITZCHAK SCHNEERSOHN

In 1920 the 40-year-old Schneersohn succeeded his father as *Rebbe* of the *Chabad Lubavitch Chassidic* Judaism movement. *Chabad* is a Hebrew acronym for *Chochma* (wisdom), *Bina* (understanding) and *Da'at* (knowledge). The movement sprang from the Chassidic (piety) movement founded by Rabbi Israel Ba'al Shem Tov (Master of the Good Name) who lived in Ukraine from 1698 to 1760. Rabbi Schneur Zalman of Liadi, Russia, started the Chabad movement in 1797 and his son, Rabbi Dovber Schneersohn, moved its headquarters to Lubavitch in what is now Belarus in the early 19th century.[2] During tsarist times the movement conducted secret campaigns to prevent Jewish children from being conscripted into the tsar's army. Now under a communist regime the followers of Chabad were absolutely determined to resist the Yevsektsia's restrictions on their faith.[3]

The Rebbe mobilized his envoys to set up underground religious schools for children and to promote Torah observance throughout the Soviet Union. He also worked to improve the economic conditions of the Jews by getting financial support from the American Joint Distribution Committee to establish Jewish agricultural settlements in Ukraine. During World War I his family had moved from Lubavitch to Rostov, where he set up a yeshiva.[4] While other devout Jews were fleeing the Soviet Union, Schneersohn and his followers chose to stay in Russia. He established a Lubavitch Talmudic seminary in Warsaw so that those who found refuge there could continue their studies.[5] In 1924 he was forced to leave Rostov and move to Leningrad.

Three years later Schneersohn organized opposition to a conference of Jewish leaders that the Yevsektsia was promoting in order to facilitate further assimilation of Jews. At the urging of the Yevsektsia, agents of the GPU broke into the Rebbe's apartment and arrested him. Torture, night-long interrogations and cruel beatings in Leningrad's infamous Shpalernaya prison followed, but the Rebbe would not bend. He demanded his *tefillin* and went on a hunger strike until he received them two days later. He spent his days in fervent prayer and used cigarette papers to record his thoughts.[6]

The show trial at which the Rebbe was sentenced to death provoked worldwide outrage. After receiving letters of protests from the German chancellor and the presidents of France and the United States, the Soviet authorities reduced the Rebbe's sentence to three years of exile in Kostroma, in the Urals. When he learned that he would be leaving on a train Thursday and arriving in Ko-stroma on Saturday, the Sabbath, he refused to go and allowed his captors to keep him in Shpalernaya until Sunday. Throngs of Chassidic Jews flocked to the railway station to see him off. Ignoring the armed guards who were to accompany him on the journey, he declared to his followers:

> We must remember that imprisonment and hard labor are only of this physical world and of brief duration, while Torah, mitzvot, and the Jewish people are eternal. May all of you be well and strong physically and spiritually. I pray and hope to God that my temporary punishment will evoke within us might for the everlasting strengthening of Judaism. And there shall be fulfilled in us that God shall be within us as He was with our ancestors to neither forsake nor abandon us; and that there shall be light for all Jewish people in their abodes.[7]

As a result of additional pressure from abroad directed to the highest Soviet officials, on his birthday, ten days later, the Rebbe was released and allowed to leave the country. From a new base in Riga, Latvia (then an independent country) he raised funds to enable his followers to maintain the underground educational network, repair their facilities and bake matzot for Passover.[8] The Rebbe then traveled to Palestine and to the United States where he could warn political leaders, including former President Herbert Hoover, about the evils of Soviet suppression of religion. Taking the last boat out of Riga before the Soviets occupied Latvia in 1940, he moved to New York and directed the establishment of Chabad facilities in America until his death in 1950. His son-in-law, Rabbi Menachem Mendel Schneerson, succeeded him as Rebbe for the next 44 years.[9]

REB SIMCHA GORODETSKY

In 1927 Rebbe Schneersohn dispatched Reb Simcha Gorodetsky to Tashkent, Uzbekistan, to set up a yeshiva to provide Jewish education for the Bukharan Jews whose ancestors had settled in Uzbekistan and Tajikistan in the 14th century. The Soviet authorities had no objection to the building of a new school but they would not permit Gorodetsky, a disciple of the hated Schneersohn, to teach there. Gorodetsky defied the ban, but was arrested in 1944 after a picture of Rebbe Schneersohn and a copy of the *Tanya*, the primary work of Chabad *Chassidut*, were found in his house.[10] Gorodetsky was tried and sentenced to five years in prison, leaving his wife and their three children with no means of support.

Gorodetsky's wife, Raiah, a tall elegant woman, went to the court in Tashkent to protest the harsh sentence. Out of spite, the judge doubled the term to ten years. Raiah left their children with her sister saying, "I can't live without Simcha," and journeyed to Moscow to protest this travesty of justice at a higher level. But Gorodetsky was not known in the West like the Rebbe and there were no protests from heads of state in his behalf, so his sentence was doubled again to twenty years. Raiah was devastated and suffered a debilitating stroke. Gorodetsky toiled in a labor camp until Stalin's death in 1953 when he was released, along with over one million other prisoners, from the *Gulag*. He returned to Tashkent to care for Raiah.[11]

REB YITZCHAK ELCHANON SHAGALOW

Another *Lubavitcher* strongly influenced by Rebbe Schneersohn, Reb Yitzchak Elchanon Shagalow was the last *mohel* in White Russia (now Belarus). Circumcision, the oldest Jewish practice, going back to the time of Abraham, was abhorred by the Soviet Communists who regarded it as a "counter-revolutionary crime and a sinful mutilation of young children." Shagalow would often travel as far as 200 km. from his hometown of Gomel to perform circumcisions secretly throughout White Russia. Occasionally the baby's parents were Communist Party members who maintained a spark of *Yiddishkeit* and wanted to have their newborn son circumcised. In one such case the baby's older brother was a brainwashed *Komsomol* member who threatened to report his parents and Shagalow to the authorities – behavior typical in totalitarian societies where children are taught that loyalty to the state supersedes loyalty to one's parents. The boy screamed, "You will all rot in jail if you circumcise my brother!" The father and Shagalow agreed to perform the *brit* at a hidden location while the father waited outside the room where the "crime" was taking place so that he could claim to be innocent if the police arrested him.

Shagalow, his wife and six children struggled under the Communist regime. They nearly starved in their effort to eat only strictly kosher food. As a Sabbath observer Shagalow could not become a Communist Party member, so in 1931, when private property was being confiscated and converted to collective apartments for party members, his family was evicted from their home. The Shagalows were desperate as no one in Gomel would allow them to share their apartment. Finally they moved their belongings into the Workmen's Synagogue and managed to set up living quarters upstairs in the ladies' gallery. This became their home for seven years.

When their youngest son was born Shagalow performed the brit in front of the older children and taught them all, including the girls, how it should be done, "in case there comes a time when you'll have do this." The concept of a female mohel is not at all new; Moses' wife, Zipporah, circumcised their son Gershom when Moses was rushing back to Egypt for a confrontation with the Pharaoh.[12]

In addition to home-schooling his children, Shagalow taught at the yeshiva he had established in Gomel in 1921. Several years later, when the secret police demanded that he close it, other teachers fled for their lives and students hid in various homes while Shagalow worked out an elaborate plan for teaching them without being discovered. For Passover he found a neighbor with a large oven who was willing to allow Shagalow to secretly bake matzot in it and distribute them to the few faithful Jews of Gomel.

By 1937 the NKVD followed Shagalow every time he boarded a train and returned to Gomel. Finally, two agents came to the

synagogue to arrest him while he was studying Chassidic philosophy from a book of his own handwritten transcriptions. He was
able to stall them while his daughters secured the book and hid
it in the garden. After he was arrested and transported to NKVD
headquarters his family never saw him again.

Nearly 60 years later, following the breakup of the Soviet
Union, his son, Reb Benzion Shagalow, was able to find his file
at the KGB headquarters in Gomel. It revealed that Reb Yitzchak
Elchanon Shagalow had been charged with agitating Soviet citizens to leave Russia and had been shot in prison along with four
other Chassidic rabbis, three months after his arrest.[13]

Shagalow's widow and children survived World War II and
the Holocaust by finding refuge in Uzbekistan. They were able to
emigrate from the Soviet Union in 1946 because one of his daughters had married a Polish citizen who subsequently requested
repatriation for himself and his extended family. In July 1945,
just after Poland established an independent government, Stalin
agreed to repatriation of Polish citizens who had been living in
the Soviet Union during the war.[14]

REB MENDEL FUTERFAS

Like the Shagalows, tens of thousands of Jews escaped from Nazi-
occupied areas of the Soviet Union to Samarkand and Tashkent
in Uzbekistan. Among them was Reb Mendel Futerfas, who knew
exactly what his fellow Jews needed – Jewish education for their
youngsters. He was born near Minsk in 1907, and had studied
and taught in underground yeshivas since 1925. In Samarkand
he established of a network of *cheders* and a yeshiva that served
hundreds of students.

When Polish citizens throughout the Soviet Union were allowed to be repatriated back to Poland at the end of World War II,
Futerfas observed that the Uzbeki authorities were somewhat
cursory in their scrutiny of Polish passports. It appeared that any
scrap of paper written in Polish was acceptable. He organized a
committee of rabbis and launched a campaign to provide Soviet

Jews with Polish documents, and with money and food for the 3,500-mile journey to Poland and religious freedom.

The committee functioned with utmost secrecy because if one of its members had been caught all of the Chassidim would have been in danger. The committee's efforts kept the flow of re-patriates orderly and by mid-1947 Reb Mendel and his associates had rescued 3,000 Jews, including his own wife and children. He then decided that it was time for him to forge a Polish passport and escape to Poland himself. But NKVD agents and armed sol-diers boarded his train at the border, arrested him and took him back to Lvov.

When an NKVD officer gloated, "Now you are in our hands!" Futerfas paraphrased Zechariah 4:6 and declared, "Not with your might you arrested me and not with your power will you release me; God is in charge of everything." For the next three months he was interrogated, tortured and threatened with death, but he would not reveal anything about his co-conspirators or the un-derground religious schools. He was sentenced to eight years of hard labor in Siberia. Upon arrival at the camp he informed the officers that he would not work on the Sabbath. They responded that they would do terrible things to him if he refused to work. He answered, "You can even kill me but on Shabbat I'm not working, no matter what!" The prison guards accepted his demands.[15]

Futerfas also vowed not to eat non-kosher food even if that meant death. During his eight years in the labor camp there were times of extreme hunger and many prisoners died. Futerfas's legs were so swollen that he feared for his life. When a barrel of fish ar-rived all the other prisoners were overjoyed but Futerfas checked to see if the fish were kosher. He noticed that the barrel was shiny and suspected that it might have been covered with non-kosher oil. Deciding whether to eat the fish was a soul-searching experi-ence. His final decision was to not to eat it.[16]

He was able to receive packages from home and use them as bribes to get easier work. Other Chabad rabbis who were im-prisoned also had packages from relatives in the West and bribed guards to allow them to hold High Holy Day services. Chabad Rabbi Moshe Greenberg, put to work building an electric power plant in a Siberian labor camp, befriended a civilian engineer who was Jewish and willing to smuggle a prayer book into the camp and lend it to him until Yom Kippur. Greenberg copied the book by hand and when he was released after Stalin's death, years later, the handwritten prayer book was Greenberg's most prized possession. Ultimately, after emigrating from Russia, he presented it to the Rebbe in New York.[17]

Futerfas had a remarkable Yom Kippur experience in his labor camp. A tall and ferocious-looking guard approached him and asked, "Are you fasting today?" Futerfas couldn't deny it and the guard then said, "So am I. Ten days ago I heard you singing a tune that my father used to sing when he took me to the synagogue. It must have been *Rosh Hashanah* so I counted ten days until today, Yom Kippur, and now I'm fasting too." Futerfas acknowledged his new friend by singing the hymn, *v'Chol Ma'aminim* ("All believe") from the liturgy for Rosh Hashanah and Yom Kippur.[18]

Futerfas was released in 1955 and went to Moscow. Still clad in his prison uniform, he went to the apartment of Reb Moshe Katzenelbogen, an original member of the Samarkand repatriation committee. Futerfas asked Katzenelbogen for money – not to buy clothes, food or housing for himself, but to establish an underground yeshiva in Chernowitz (now Chernivtsi, Ukraine). Futerfas settled in Chernowitz with the funds he needed, established the yeshiva and applied to emigrate to reunite with his family in England.

Eight years later he was allowed to emigrate to England, thanks to an appeal for family repatriation made by prime minister Harold Wilson during his summit meeting in Moscow with Chairman Nikita Khrushchev. Futerfas later settled in Kfar Chabad, Israel, where he taught Chassidut and was referred to as a *mashpiya* (mentor, literally: one who influences). He died there in 1995 at the age of eighty-seven.

RABBIS HILLEL ZALTZMAN AND MOSHE NISSILEVITCH

Hillel Zaltzman grew up in Samarkand and attended underground religious schools established by Futerfas and his associates. Each class had only three or four students but the entire network of such schools in Uzbekistan served 1,500 students. An overriding concern was secrecy about the existence of the network and the identities of students and teachers.

In 1950 the Zaltzman family harbored a fugitive from the NKVD, Reb Berke Chein, in their apartment. Chein and his wife had been involved in supporting the emigration of Soviet Jews with false Polish passports in 1946. Their children had safely traveled to Poland with a couple who had Polish papers. The Cheins were in Lvov preparing for their own escape when the NKVD arrested Reb Berke. They released him after a week of interrogation but a month later they came for him again. As agents banged on the door, he jumped through a window, ran to the railroad station, and traveled to Moscow. He carried no incriminating documents as he was now on the NKVD's most-wanted list. Relatives in Moscow kept him hidden until 1948. When neighbors became suspicious he decided to relocate to Samarkand and stay with Chabad families.

Chein said he was desperate and felt like a dog, with no identity papers, cut off from communication with his wife and children, and unable to do any useful work. The Chabad community leaders in Samarkand decided to find someone sympathetic in the Interior Ministry who could provide legitimate documents bearing a different name. They knew about a deceased man named Goldberg, whose name they could use. Soviet identity papers, however, were in the form of a five- or six-page book including the bearer's complete employment and residence history. Tampering with these papers was both a daunting and criminal act.

To penetrate the Interior Ministry they turned to Zina, a non-observant Jewish woman in her early twenties, very attractive and often seen in the company of local policemen and ministry officials. She was eager to help, saying it would be a *mitzva* to save the life of a Jewish man. Her friends in the ministry agreed to do what they could, but were arrested by the NKVD. Zina, expecting to be arrested too, said to the Chabad leaders, "Tell the Jewish man not to worry. I will not reveal anything even if they tear me to pieces!"

The trial was open to the public and Hillel Zaltzman attended to find out whether Zina's arrest was due to her involvement in support of Chein/Goldberg. Indeed, the name Goldberg did come up, and after a few days Zina and her friends were found guilty. She was sentenced to five years in a labor camp, but was released two years later when Stalin died. Stalin's death also enabled Chein to keep his old name and get new, legitimate papers. When Zina returned to Samarkand, Chein offered her money. She refused to accept anything, saying that she had done it as a mitzva and that she just wanted to return to her prewar home in Vilna. Again, like Shagalow and Futerfas, Zaltzman observed that there is an inextinguishable Jewish spark within even the most secular and assimilated Jew, a spark that fulfills the Talmudic tradition, "*Kol Yisrael arevim zeh bazeh*" (*All Jews are interlinked, responsible for looking after one another*).

When Zaltzman was 18 years old he worked as a commercial artist in a silk screening shop and used his talents to produce materials for teaching the Hebrew alphabet in the underground schools. He worked closely with Rabbi Moshe Nisselevitch, one of the Chabad leaders in Samarkand who had provided Chein with a temporary safe house. Nisselevitch had been educated in an underground yeshiva run by Chabad Rabbi Yosef Goldberg in Kutais, Georgia, during the 1940s. At the time he was also working nights in a sweater factory to support his family, and was being hounded by the local police, who wanted to arrest him for draft evasion. A classmate who had an electric shaver saved Nisselevitch's life by shaving his beard, thus enabling him to become unrecognized by the police and draft officer in Kutais until he moved to Samarkand.[19]

Zaltzman traveled to 35 cities throughout the Soviet Union where Nissilevitch had associates in a network called Chamah, an acronym for *Chavurat Mizakei Harabim* (Society for Meritorious Service to the Masses). Chamah was devoted to supporting Jewish education, delivering food and coal to the needy, and secretly baking matzah for Passover. Additionally, Chamah arranged clandestine Jewish life-cycle events: circumcisions, bar mitzvahs, weddings and funerals hidden from the secret police.[20]

While distributing his materials Zaltzman heard a rumor that the chief rabbi of Moscow, Solomon Schlieffer, had printed a new prayer book – it had been 30 years since the last prayer book was printed in Russia and hand-printed prayer books were so scarce that they sold for $100 each. The rumor was true. Soviet authorities allowed 10,000 copies of the "Shalom Prayer Book" to be printed in Moscow in 1957. Along with permission to print them was the opening of a rabbinical seminary in Moscow with 35 students and eight teachers.[21]

These two manifestations of an apparent relaxation in policy were the direct outcome of an unprecedented visit to the Soviet Union during the summer of 1956 by a delegation of five American Orthodox rabbis, led by Rabbi David Hollander of the Bronx, New York, who was then president of the Rabbinical Council of America. He had conceived the trip the previous year with the blessings of the Soviet Embassy in Washington when it appeared that Khrushchev was seeking a thaw in Cold War relations.

Five decades later, Hollander, at age 90, the world's oldest active pulpit rabbi, recalled how the idea of American rabbis traveling to the Soviet Union in 1956 was "as inconceivable as the possibility of a man walking on the moon!"[22]

The U.S. State Department was well aware of the rabbis' itinerary of four weeks in the Soviet Union followed by three weeks in Poland, Czechoslovakia and Romania. The U.S. Ambassador in Moscow, Charles Bohlen, invited the rabbis to the Fourth of July festivities at the embassy. When Hollander observed that the only Soviet clergymen on the guest list were leaders of the Russian

Orthodox Church, he requested and obtained an invitation for Rabbi Schlieffer. At the embassy the delegation of rabbis met with General Secretary Khrushchev and Chairman Nicolay Bulganin and asked for permission to ship 1,000 prayer books to Russia or to supply a Hebrew linotype machine. The Communist leaders said they were fully capable of printing their own prayer books. Printing the Peace Prayer Book was subsequently used by the Soviet U.N. delegation as an example in support of their statement that "the Jews of Russia enjoy full religious freedom."[23]

Nissilevitch and Zaltzman determined that the underground schools needed 100 copies of the new prayer book, so they went to the gabbai of Moscow's largest synagogue. But anyone trying to buy and transport 100 prayer books on the streets of Moscow in 1957 would have aroused suspicion. Zaltzman remembers that "the *gabbai* was afraid of us and we were afraid of him," so they purchased five or ten at a time and transferred them to trusted associates until they had acquired all 100.

Later that year Zaltzman heard that the new First Secretary of the Communist Party in Poland, Wladyslaw Gomulka, had negotiated an agreement with Khrushchev allowing for the repatriation to Poland of Polish citizens living in the Soviet Union. Zaltzman, seeing this as an opportunity to emigrate, proposed to marry a sixteen-year-old girl who lived in Samarkand and whose mother was Polish. He planned to alter her passport to indicate that she was eighteen. Zaltzman's father was horrified and warned him that the girl was a *Komsomol* member and the proposal was a criminal act for which he could be sent to Siberia. Zaltzman backed off and simply helped the mother and daughter repatriate without him.[24]

On the surface, the Gomulka-Khrushchev repatriation agreement was similar to the one signed by Stalin in 1945. But for Jews there was a significant difference. When Polish Jews were repatriated in 1945–1947 they found communities destroyed and their homes either in ruins or occupied by Poles hostile to the Jews' return. The Jews were forced to find shelter in displaced persons' camps and ultimately settled wherever they could in Europe, Canada, the United States, Latin America or Australia.

Several thousand took the risk of boarding overcrowded boats of questionable seaworthiness for a perilous voyage to Palestine, hoping to evade the British blockade. Most were intercepted by the British and sent to detention camps on the island of Cyprus where they waited until Britain abandoned its mandate of Palestine as Israel declared its independence in May 1948.

The Gomulka-Khrushchev agreement had a third party acting as a secret catalyst – Israel. Under this agreement Jews repatriated to Poland would be transported to Israel.

In his autobiography, *Staying Tuned*, veteran broadcast journalist Daniel Schorr describes how, after filming a documentary at Auschwitz, he accidentally encountered this emigration channel and how his discovery "may have been the greatest ethical dilemma" of his career. He and his cbs film crew had been driving through a small town in eastern Poland, near the Soviet border, when they spotted a caravan of about ten horse-drawn wagons, carrying a few dozen people and piled high with baggage. Schorr stopped his car to investigate and found that he could converse with them in Yiddish. They said that they were Polish Jews and had come from across the border in the Soviet Union and were on their way to a railway station, bound for Vienna and from there to Israel. With the camera rolling Schorr interviewed them but they were unable to tell him how they could be allowed to travel to Israel. Schorr was puzzled because knew that to maintain good relations with Arab states, Russia and its satellites had officially banned emigration to Israel.

When Schorr got back to Warsaw the next day he consulted a chess-playing friend, Shimon Amir, Israel's ambassador to Poland. Shaken by Schorr's report, Amir asked:

'They told you they were on their way to Israel, and you have that on film?'

'Yes. But how is it possible?'

'All right, since you know this much, I will tell you the rest, and you will decide what to do.'

Amir explained that these Jews came from a part of Poland that had been annexed by the Soviet Union, and that there were several thousand more caught on the Soviet side who had survived the war and the Holocaust and were desperately anxious to leave. Israel had negotiated a delicate secret arrangement with the Soviet and Polish governments. The Jews would be "repatriated" to Poland with the understanding that they would almost immediately leave the country – bound for Israel.

Amir then added, "But there was one condition attached to the agreement. The arrangement must remain a secret. If any word becomes public, the Soviets would immediately cancel the arrangement. So you can decide, Mr. Schorr. Put this on television, and you condemn some thousands of Jews to remaining in the Soviet Union."

Schorr held on to the can of film that contained the Yiddish interview and hand-carried it to New York for a confidential meeting with his boss, CBS vice-president Edward R. Murrow. Upon hearing Schorr's story and request to apply "self-censorship for humanitarian reasons", Murrow, a strong supporter of Israel, replied, "I understand."[25]

According to the Association of Jewish Communities and Organizations of Ukraine, 250,000 Polish citizens were repatriated from the USSR between 1956 and 1959. Of them, 20,000 were Jews who continued their journey to Israel. They represented less than one percent of the Jewish population of the Soviet Union.[26] The remaining 99% continued to suffer discrimination, anti-Semitism and persistent disintegration of Jewish religious and community life even though Khrushchev had introduced some liberal reforms. Chamah continued to do what it could to help the Jews of the Soviet Union return to their roots.

The Ezras Achim Society in New York, formed by émigrés from the Soviet Union, sent thousands of packages of clothing that could be sold in Russia to support Chamah projects. In 1960 Chamah members organized Simchat Torah celebrations in the largest synagogues in Moscow and Leningrad. Soon tens of thousands of young Jews were celebrating Simchat Torah annually and demanding the right to emigrate to Israel.

Nissilevitch was allowed to emigrate in 1970 and established a Chamah campus and community center in Kiryat Malachi that reaches out to former Soviet Jews from kindergartners to senior citizens living in Israel. He successfully smuggled out precious manuscripts that he had hidden in jugs and buried for thirty years.[27]

When Zaltzman applied to emigrate the following year he was interrogated by an OVIR officer in Samarkand who argued, "Why do want to go to Israel? It's so dangerous; you'll have to serve in their army. I might be drafted into the Soviet army and may be sent to Egypt. You might kill me." Zaltzman calmly replied, "Don't worry, if I see you, I won't touch you." Reassured, the officer gave Zaltzman his exit visa. In 1973 he moved to the United States to set up Chamah's New York office, where he continues to serve as president. There is also a Chamah office in Moscow that focuses on serving the needy and elderly of Russia; their soup kitchens provide over 300,000 meals each year.

PROFESSOR HERMAN BRANOVER

In Riga rumors of the Gomulka-Khrushchev agreement captured the imaginations of Herman Branover, a 25-year-old physicist, and his fiancée, Fania, with whom he shared Zionist aspirations. They hatched a scheme in which they would break off their engagement, find Poles to marry, travel to Poland, divorce their spouses of convenience, and finally, reunite in holy matrimony in Israel. They found a Polish citizen in Riga who wanted money to buy a car to take to Poland. He agreed to marry Fania and drive to Poland with his new car and to bring his sister to Riga for Herman to marry. The whole plot collapsed when Herman's Polish bride ran away.

Branover was deeply depressed over the failure of the scheme to get to Israel and the gloomy prospects of remaining in the Soviet Union. For solace he turned to Judaism, going to the synagogue every Shabbat and studying Hebrew with Fania. In 1961 they had a Jewish wedding. Branover returned to his scientific pursuits, entering a new field of study – magnetohydrodynamics (MHD) – at the Physics Institute of the Latvian Academy of Sciences, where he earned a Ph.D. In his spare time he wrote philosophical essays questioning atheism and affirming his faith in Judaism. These essays were smuggled to Israel by Fania's Israeli relatives, who were visiting Moscow.

Soon Branover was drawn to learning more about Judaism from a Chassidic Jew named Notke. He was now living a double life – working at the Academy of Sciences by day and studying Torah by night. Eventually he became acquainted with leaders of the Chabad movement and started participating in their gatherings. As a scientist doing classified work he felt that there was also a need to be wary of the omnipresent KGB, so instead of attending High Holy Day services in Riga he would go on vacation to Transcarpathia in southwestern Ukraine. There he would attend traditional services led by underground rabbi Yosef Mordechai Kagan.

The movement for aliyah galvanized in Riga's Jews soon after Israel's victory in the Six-Day War. Notke and his family were among those who successfully emigrated. Branover soon acquired a new role model, Dr. Mendel Gordon, the first Soviet Jew with a Ph.D. to receive an exit visa. Gordon had renounced his Soviet citizenship and sent his Soviet identification papers to Moscow. For this act he lost his job and his apartment and suffered many ordeals. As more Chassidic Jews from Riga were allowed to emigrate there was increasing pressure on Branover to provide more Jewish education for the community. Feeling that Jewish education was vital as the first step in stimulating a desire to seek the right to emigrate to Israel, he used his knowledge of Hebrew to translate fundamental books of Judaism into Russian.

During the summer of 1971, after Branover's siblings and their families arrived in Israel, he received letters of invitation from them. Although he was now a well-paid full professor and noted authority in MHD, with both a well-located apartment, a dacha on Riga Bay and a car, he felt compelled to apply for exit visas for himself, Fania and their son, Geka. Their applications were refused with the comment that because Herman knew state secrets he would have to wait twenty years. Herman and Fania were dismissed from their jobs but they no longer had to hide their Jewish identities and practices.

Since they became known in the West as high-profile refuse-niks they often received phone calls from activists, politicians and rabbis asking what they could do in support of the Branovers. Nobel Prize winners and members of the Nobel Committee in Sweden called to say that Herman's accomplishments in MHD were being considered for a Nobel Prize. He feared that winning the Nobel Prize would further impede the family's efforts to emigrate so he graciously asked the committee not to nominate him. Senator Walter Mondale, who later served as U.S. vice president, called to ask for a statement that could be read on the floor of the Senate. The result of all these calls was the arrival of the KGB to cut off the Branovers' phone. They continued with interrogations and harassment, going so far as to accuse Branover of killing a child in a hit-and-run accident.

Branover found his adoption of Orthodox Jewish observance was somewhat controversial in the refusenik community. Most of them just wanted to get out of the Soviet Union. In his autobiography, *Return, the Spiritual Odyssey of a Soviet Scientist,* Branover offers his reflections on their attitude:

> It seemed strange that these people, who were so decisively breaking away from their past in order to fulfill the important *mitzvah of aliyah to Eretz Yisrael,* were disregarding the other 612 commandments [of the Torah] as well as other Jewish responsibilities. It was painful to see that most of these

people, persecuted and suffering, did not turn their thoughts to God, seeking His help and support. Only rare exceptions among them did what the grandfathers and grandmothers of all of them would not have failed to do.[28]

During the summer of 1972 Branover walked into the post office thinking, "What have I got to lose?" He placed a call to the Lubavitcher Rebbe in New York. Not only did he succeed in reaching the Rebbe, he received a blessing and assurance that the family would soon receive permission to leave for Israel. But soon after the High Holy Days, the KGB put Branover through another round of interrogation and attempts at intimidation.

Suddenly, only a week later, he was invited to the OVIR office and was told that his family had permission to leave as soon as he paid the newly enacted education tax. For Branover, with a Ph.D., this amounted to 31,300 rubles or the equivalent of $40,000, far more money than he had ever had. Unemployed, living off the sale of clothing from Ezras Achim parcels, there was no way in that he could come up with that sum.[29] Miraculously, Branover's telephone became operational again and he could apprise supporters in the West of his new predicament. While some supposedly well-meaning callers suggested that he boycott and protest the onerous tax, others were determined to enable Branover to become the first full professor to emigrate from the Soviet Union. They marshaled their resources and collected funds that were channeled to friends in Riga and Georgia, who lent the money to Branover.

On October 27, the Branovers arrived in Israel to a joyous celebration of Chassidic dancing on the sidewalk outside the airport terminal. They settled in Beersheba, where Branover joined the faculty of Ben-Gurion University. In addition to his role as chair of Magnetohydrodynamics, he heads the Joint Israeli-Russian Laboratory for Energy Research and is also president of SHAMIR, the Association of Religious Professionals from the USSR, and editor-in-chief of SHAMIR's publishing house. He continues to write prolifically on philosophy, religion and ethics, as well as technology.

In April 1985 he received a telephone call from the Rebbe with an accurate prediction that had profound global significance. The Rebbe was asking Branover to tell all his friends that there would soon be an end to the communist regime in Russia and that Jews would be allowed to emigrate to Israel in large numbers.[30]

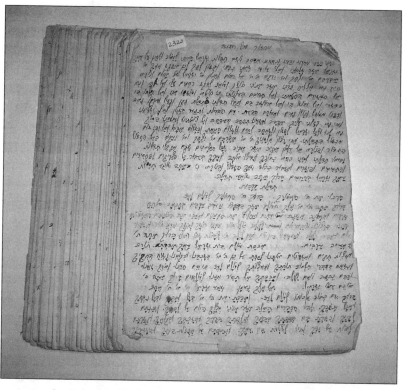

A page from the Machzor that Moshe Greenberg penned and used in Siberia. Greenberg's children are among the over 300 Chabad-Lubavitch emissaries in the former Soviet Union. Photo credit: Chabad.org/Lubavitch Library

Rebbe Yosef Yitzchak Schneersohn.
Photo credit: Chabad.org/Lubavitch Archives

Rabbis Berke Chein (left) and Mendel Futerfas learning in Lubavitch
World Headquarters in 1978. Photo credit: Chabad.org/JEM

CHAPTER THREE

Secret Operations Sponsored by the Israeli Government

*I*n the mid-1980s Israelis were reminded of their kinship with Soviet Jews every time they looked at a 10,000-shekel banknote (then worth about $2). One side had an engraved likeness of their beloved prime minister, Golda Meir, who died in 1978. On the reverse side there was a picture of the crowd of Jews in Moscow who joyously welcomed her arrival in 1948 as Israel's first ambassador to the Soviet Union.

GOLDA MEIR AS MINISTER TO MOSCOW

Golda Meir was born in Kiev in 1898 and immigrated to Milwaukee, Wisconsin, with her parents eight years later. As impassioned Labor Zionists, she and her husband, Morris Meyerson, moved to a kibbutz in Palestine in 1921. After two decades of service in the leadership of the *Histadrut* (General Federation of Jewish Labor) she was appointed by David Ben-Gurion, Israel's first prime minister, as Israel's ambassador to Moscow. She and twenty-five staffers opened a kibbutz-style embassy in the venerable Hotel Metropole on September 3, 1948.

The entire Israeli legation went to the Great Choral Synagogue for Rosh Hashanah services. Normally about 2,000 dour and fearful Jews would attend the High Holy Day services there, but on this occasion a jubilant and exuberant crowd of 50,000 arrived to celebrate the establishment of Israel.[1] They were shouting "Shalom, shalom!" and then at the sight of Golda Meir, they screamed, *"Nasha Golda"* (our Golda), and blew kisses toward her. Meir, overcome with emotion, nearly fainted and could only manage to say one Yiddish sentence to the crowd: *"A dank eich vas ihr seit geblieben Yidden"* (Thank you for having remained Jews). Ten days later, at the close of the Yom Kippur service, a tremor went through the synagogue as the rabbi recited *"L'shana Haba B'Yerushalayim"* (Next Year in Jerusalem). Meir silently prayed, "God, let it happen. If not next year, then let the Jews of Russia come to us soon." But she had doubts that it would happen during her lifetime.[2]

Thousands of Moscow's Jews walked to the Metropole just to gaze at the blue-and-white Israeli flag. Many of them chanted, *"Am Yisrael Chai!"* (The People of Israel lives!)[3] Stalin viewed the Jews' affinity for the new State of Israel and their adulation of Golda Meir as bourgeois and dangerously anti-Soviet.[4] He was furious to learn that Meir was having conversations in Yiddish with Polina Zhemchuzhina, the Jewish wife of foreign minister V.M. Molotov, and with Lena Shtern, a leader of the Jewish Anti-Fascist Committee, the last Jewish organization allowed to promote Jewish culture and maintain relations with Jews outside the USSR.[5] There have been allegations that Meir gave Zhemchuzhina a list of as many as 700 Russian Jews who wanted to join their relatives in Israel, as well as a list of Jews who wanted to fight in the Israeli army.[6]

Reprisals came swiftly: Zhemchuzhina was arrested and exiled to Kazakhstan; Shtern was arrested and the Jewish Anti-Fascist Committee was disbanded; the Yiddish publishing house was shut down and the 700 Jews were tracked down and jailed.[7] In January 1949 dozens of Jewish writers and intellectuals were accused of "rootless cosmopolitanism," fired, purged from the Communist Party and, in many cases, arrested.[8]

Meir and her embassy staff were well aware that they were living in an environment of state-sponsored anti-Semitism. Many of them wanted to visit close relatives in Moscow but were apprehensive that the authorities would arrest any Soviet citizen who met with Israelis, so after what Meir described as "an excruciating dilemma," the decision was made to avoid contact.[9] This decision nullified a pledge made by Meir in August 1948 to the leaders of *Magen* (Shield), an organization of Israelis who tried to assist imprisoned Zionists in the Soviet Union: "If I merit to do something concrete toward the liberating of Prisoners of Zion, I will consider my life's task to have been fulfilled."[10]

DAVID BEN-GURION AND MAGEN

Magen was an informal committee that was established in Tel Aviv in 1928 out of concern for Zionists who were imprisoned in Russia. In 1940 its representative was invited to participate [11]in the Committee for Russian Jewish Affairs within the Jewish Agency for Palestine. After the Soviet Union voted for the UN partition plan that enabled the creation of the State of Israel, Magen leaders wrote to Israel's first foreign minister, Moshe Sharett, and urged him to "seize the opportunity to press the Soviet government to free all Prisoners of Zion and permit them to emigrate to Israel." Sharett's response, "Relations between Israel and the USSR are those of two states, and neither one may interfere in the other's internal affairs in any way," would be used by Soviet leaders to justify their restrictive emigration policies for the next forty years.[12]

Ben-Gurion's public attitude was similar to Sharett's and can be traced to his strong admiration for Lenin and the Soviet system that went back to 1923 when he visited Russia as a Histadrut participant in an agricultural exhibit. In 1932 he sent a contribution to Magen's Tel Aviv office with a note saying, "Sent on condition that you do not carry out activities against Soviet Russia." When Magen leaders approached prime minister Ben-Gurion in

1950 to complain that the Israeli government had not initiated negotiations with the Soviet government to free the Prisoners of Zion and to allow emigration to Israel, he listened attentively but made no promises.[13]

Later that year Ben-Gurion did call upon the Soviet government to allow Soviet Jews to emigrate. The United Nations was the venue for discussions on the subject, with emphasis on family reunification, by Sharett and his Soviet counterpart, Andrei Vishinsky.[14] The talks got nowhere, as Stalin was growing more paranoid and anti-Semitic. In 1952 the Jewish Anti-Fascist Committee was put on trial, and between October 1952 and February 1953 hundreds of doctors, many of them Jewish, were arrested on charges of plotting to kill Soviet leaders. The physicians were alleged to be collaborating with Israeli and Western intelligence. At the same time, plans were made to round up the Jews of the western USSR and transport them to labor camps in Kazakhstan and Siberia. The plans were abandoned and the doctors were freed after Stalin's death in March 1953.[15]

SHAUL AVIGUR AND THE "OFFICE WITH NO NAME"

The Doctors' Plot served as a wake-up call to Israel and the West that Soviet Jewry was in danger, and emigration was a possible solution. Ben-Gurion called upon his intimate confidant, Shaul Avigur, to form a small group called the "Office with No Name" that would nominally be part of the Foreign Ministry, but would actually report to the prime minister.

Shaul Avigur had directed the illegal immigration of European Holocaust survivors to Palestine at the end of World War II. As the Jews of Palestine were preparing for independence he set up *Mossad*, Israel's intelligence service. Golda Meir recalls that "whatever he did, or ordered to have done, was carried out with maximum secrecy, and everyone was suspect, in his eyes, of possible indiscretion." Avigur was described as one of the most influential yet least known men in Israel. Personal anonymity and tight control were hallmarks of his managerial style.[16]

Avigur instructed the Israeli legation in Moscow to carefully make contact with Jews in Russia but to absolutely avoid saying anything that could be construed as anti-Soviet or probes into the plight of Soviet Jews.[17] The staffers were encouraged to hand out literature, including a rudimentary Russian-Hebrew dictionary, and talk about Israel, Jewish history and Jewish culture.[18] In 1955 Avigur's office broadened its scope by seeking travelers to Russia from Western nations who would be willing to bring up the issue of Soviet Jewry with Soviet leaders. Avigur had three goals in mind for Soviet Jews. They should be allowed to express their Jewishness, contact Jews in other countries, and repatriate to Israel. Binyamin Eliav, an Israeli Foreign Ministry official and multilingual publicist, joined the group to disseminate information on Soviet Jewry to appropriate people in the West as a first step in pressuring the Soviet government to achieve these goals.[19] Avigur's group felt the time was right to bring the issue to Western leaders who were confronting a post-Stalin Soviet Union that wanted to improve its image in the free world.[20] However, the World Jewish Congress, headed by Nahum Goldmann, denied that there was discrimination against Jews in the USSR, and advocated improved Israeli-Soviet relations rather than emigration of Soviet Jews.[21]

The Office with No Name took on the code name *Nativ* ("path") and was publicly called *Lishkat HaKesher* (Liaison Bureau), often shortened to "The Lishka."[22] Arie "Lova" Eliav, who served as first secretary of the Israeli Embassy from 1958 to 1960, subsequently headed Nativ operations in the USSR.[23] He traveled throughout the Soviet Union meeting Jews and estimated that over a million of them, especially those residing in republics outside of Russia, would gladly leave for Israel if they could.[24]

In addition to Moscow, Nativ agents operated in Israel's embassies in Bucharest, Budapest, Prague and Warsaw. The main goal was to achieve aliyah of Jews from the Eastern Bloc, in contrast to the Jewish Agency, that promoted aliyah from the West. In 1957, Meir Rosenne, fresh out of the Sorbonne with a Ph.D. in international law, began working in the Paris office of the World Jewish Congress. He was one of a few associates posted by the Lishka in New York, London and Paris with the purpose of publicizing the plight of Soviet Jewry as a moral issue. Their operation outside the Soviet Union was called *Bar* (open field) and was kept separate from *Nativ*.[25]

In 1960 when Binyamin Eliav became Israel's consul general in New York he continued to pursue support for Soviet Jews and asked William Korey, who headed the B'nai B'rith Anti-Defamation League office in Washington, to look into the question of emigration as a human right. Korey worked with Jose Ingles, a Philippine judge and statesman, to prepare a document based on case histories of Jews in the Soviet Union and Eastern Europe who wanted to leave. The document was submitted to the United Nations Commission on Human Rights – the first time the issue of emigration was raised in an international forum.[26] It stated that the right to leave one's country was clearly enunciated in the 1948 Universal Declaration of Human Rights and could be traced back to Magna Carta and the writings of Socrates.[27]

ARYEH KROLL AND HIS ARMY OF TOURISTS

The Universal Declaration of Human Rights also upholds the right of an individual to *return* to his country, and that's exactly what Aryeh Kroll did in 1965 when he boarded a steamer in Istanbul bound for Odessa. He thought he was going on a brief vacation with forty Israelis of Russian origin who wanted to visit their relatives, but what he saw in his native land would change his life forever.

Aryeh Kroll was born in a small town called Kholopinichi, near Minsk in Belarus, in 1923. His father, a rabbi and *shochet* (ritual slaughterer) – two professions that were not valued by Yevsektsia and the Communist regime – managed to emigrate to Palestine in 1933 and was joined there by his wife and Aryeh two years later. The older children remained in the Soviet Union. Aryeh's older brother was killed during the German siege of Leningrad and his sisters integrated into Soviet society; one became a doctor in Minsk and the other an electronics engineer in Leningrad.

Kroll inherited a religious Zionist orientation, in contrast to many young Jews in Palestine who were secular. He became active in Bnei Akiva, an international religious Zionist youth organization, and led its branch in Jerusalem for four years. He later helped rebuild the Biriya settlement (near Safed) that had been demolished by the British in 1946, and then moved to the Negev where he was one of the founders of Kibbutz Sa'ad, ultimately becoming the secretary of this religious kibbutz.

For over thirty years Kroll had not seen his sisters. Having had no contact with them other than occasional letters from Leningrad, he jumped at the chance of traveling to Russia to see them. He described the scene at the Metropole Hotel in Moscow where his sisters and relatives of the Israeli visitors had gathered: "There were people who hadn't seen each other for over forty years. It was a terrible scene, with much weeping. It seemed that even the stone pillars under which we were standing were weeping with us."

One of the Israelis came to Kroll that evening and said with great emotion, "Aryeh, you must help me! My brother traveled for two weeks from Siberia to see me. He carried a tattered, blood-stained *tallit*, and he wants a new one." She related how her brother had this tallit while serving in the Red Army, and how it helped him escape captivity, and enabled him to survive while fighting in the woods. "If he gets a new tallit," she continued, "he will cover himself with it and say to God Almighty: 'Now I am ready to be taken to your place.' All he wants is a clean tallit." Without hesitation Kroll gave her his own tallit.

The next morning Kroll was determined to start acting in support of the deprived Soviet Jews and persuaded the group to go to the Israeli Embassy, where. they were received by Ambassador Yosef Tekoa. Kroll related how he "knew that in Russia walls have ears even in diplomatic missions, and therefore I wrote him a note asking him to collect whatever Israeli souvenirs they had at the embassy, as well as religious objects and Hebrew books, so that we could distribute them to our relatives, and to other Jews we may meet during the trip."

Returning to Israel, Kroll resolved to create networks of support for Soviet Jews. He revealed his plans to interior minister Moshe Chaim Shapira, the leader of *HaPoel HaMizrachi*, a religious party. Shapira replied: "My friend, I am really excited about your story, but it is *Mapai* [the Labor Party] that is in charge of Russian Jews, and only Histadrut members can get jobs there [the Lishka under Avigur]." Not easily discouraged, Kroll simply went to Sde Boker in the Negev, the home of former prime minister Ben-Gurion, who had known and respected Kroll for two decades. Though they differed ideologically they had a common interest in developing the Negev. Kroll told Ben-Gurion, "We must send tourists there [to the Soviet Union] and have them carry Hebrew textbooks, Scriptures, prayer books, song books and records. If we persist in this activity, we will be able to bring about a real revolution; we will stop the assimilation, and then the great aliyah will not be far off." Ben-Gurion replied, "You know that I love you, but in my opinion, your optimism borders on madness."

Disappointed, Kroll returned to his work at the kibbutz. Two weeks later he received a phone call from Shaul Avigur, who said, "You have a great friend. I want you to come see me in Tel Aviv." Avigur then sent Kroll, loaded with books and religious articles, on missions to the Soviet Union. A $25,000 loan from industrialist Yosef Mirelman enabled additional Israeli emissaries to travel to the USSR.

Days after Israel's decisive victory over Egypt, Jordan and Syria in the Six-Day War (June 1967), the Soviet Union branded Israel the aggressor and severed diplomatic relations. Travelers with Israeli passports were no longer welcome in Moscow. Kroll had to change his modus operandi; instead of going to Russia himself and sending Israelis, he would go to Western Europe and the United States to recruit volunteers for missions under cover of innocent tourism. After selecting Jews who were knowledgeable in Hebrew and Jewish religious practices, he trained them on what they should and should not do in their missions to make contact with Soviet Jews. In this new role, Kroll spent about 120 days each year outside Israel. He kept his activities secret, even from his wife and daughters.[28]

He established a hierarchy of recruiters in major cities. Veterans of Bnei Akiva, including Itchie Fuchs in New York and Seth Jacobson in Stockholm, did the initial searches for possible emissaries, but for the first few years Kroll would travel to several cities in one day and book flights with sufficient layovers so that he could meet candidates and recruiters in the airport coffee shops. The candidates who were selected as emissaries would then get more detailed instructions from the recruiters and would often schedule their travel to coincide with holidays when Jews could be found at the few functioning synagogues in the Soviet Union and could be met without creating too much extra attention.[29] In addition to bringing in books and religious articles the emissaries took out the names of Soviet Jews who wanted to emigrate to Israel and needed letters of invitation from "relatives."[30]

In 1969, when he was twenty-one, author and radio talk-show host Dennis Prager was briefed by Kroll and sent on a mission. Because he was fluent in Russian, Prager was sent to Baku, Azerbaijan, in addition to the usual destinations of Moscow and Leningrad. He recalls that it was a harrowing experience. "You knew you were being followed but you didn't know what they would do. I lost eighteen pounds during those four weeks because I never met anyone sitting down; we always walked, usually in public parks."[31]

The emissaries were instructed to avoid involvement in any secret activities initiated by Soviet citizens. They were to avoid acting or speaking against the Soviet regime, contacting dissidents, staying in Jewish homes, taking out incriminating documents, and playing "James Bond". Kroll trained them how to behave during interrogations; if they were asked about the origin of the books and materials they carried, they should just say that the rabbi of their community had asked them to deliver the items to Jews.

Jews whose exit visa applications were rejected by OVIR were summarily fired from their jobs. As refuseniks they were treated as outcasts and lucky to find menial work. Kroll soon learned those out of work were becoming destitute and that it was necessary to provide material help in addition to cultural and spiritual support. Some money from supporters in the West would trickle in to trustworthy refuseniks in the form of bank transfers that could be converted to coupons for use in *"Beriozka"* shops.[32]

Similar to the hierarchy of recruiters in the West, there was a hierarchy of distributors of materials in the Soviet Union. Yuli Kosharovsky, a refusenik Hebrew teacher in Moscow, held a seminar in 1976 for Soviet and foreign visiting Hebrew teachers. Kroll's emissaries attended and then placed Kosharovsky in a key position to channel goods to refuseniks whom he knew and trusted. Similarly, Yosef Radomiselsky (now Yosef Raday) became a coordinator in Leningrad.

Zale Anis of Boston went on a mission in 1977. Upon his return he was able to obtain funding from his colleagues at the Massachusetts Institute of Technology to purchase cameras and sheepskin coats at low cost for distribution to refuseniks. Kroll at first allowed his Nativ travelers to carry these items, but was furious when Anis became active in Boston Action for Soviet Jewry and also started giving the goods to "unauthorized" travelers. These individuals often delivered their valuable hand-carried cargoes to refuseniks outside Kroll's channel of control, some of whom, he suspected, would prefer to emigrate to the United States rather than Israel.[33]

When a refusenik coordinator such as Raday received permission and finally arrived in Israel, he would be brought from the absorption center to a Lishka office, and there Kroll would identify himself and debrief the new immigrant, over glasses of vodka, for an update on the status of the refusenik community.[34]

Looking back on his twenty years in Nativ/Lishkat HaKesher and his role in sending several thousand volunteers to make contact with Soviet Jews, Kroll said: "I thank God Almighty that all the operations ended peacefully. Not a single emissary was imprisoned. Not one of them was killed or died. Some were detained, questioned and expelled, and the things they brought with them were confiscated, but there were no crises that could endanger the entire operation."[35] The story of Kroll's operations was revealed when he was awarded the prestigious Israel Prize for 1999.

NECHEMIA LEVANON

Although Kroll was hired by Avigur, he spent most of his years in Nativ under the guidance of Nechemia Levanon, who took over the Lishka upon Avigur's retirement in 1969. Levanon was born in Latvia in 1915 and grew up in Estonia where he was active in a Socialist-Zionist youth organization. In 1938 he made aliyah and helped organize "The Anglo-Baltic Kibbutz" with members from America, England and the Baltic countries.

This group established Kibbutz Kfar Blum in the northern Galilee, where Levanon was the economic coordinator until early 1953 when Isser Harel, the head of Mossad, and Shaul Avigur told him about ominous reports of Stalin's campaign against "cosmopolitans," a code word meaning Jews, and asked him to go to the Israeli Embassy in Moscow. [36] A few days before Levanon was to leave for Moscow, a group of hot-headed Israelis placed a bomb in the cellars of the Soviet Embassy in Tel Aviv. The Soviets cut off diplomatic relations with Israel and Levanon went to Stockholm to try to find ways of getting in touch with Jews. From Sweden he wrote letters to contacts in Russia and gave them to Finnish and Swedish sailors to put in mailboxes in Russia, as if they had been locally written and mailed. Levanon's memorial website also claims that some Jews successfully escaped from the Soviet Union with Norwegian passports that were forged copies of passports Levanon borrowed from travelers to Sweden.

A few months after Stalin's death diplomatic relations were restored and Levanon went to work in Moscow, officially as agricultural attache in the embassy, unofficially as liaison with Soviet Jews. One night in 1955 about thirty Jews were arrested and

Levanon was found to have supplied them with Jewish prayers books and Yiddish newspapers. He was declared persona non grata and deported to Israel.[37]

For the next thirteen years he alternated between his old job at Kibbutz Kfar Blum and assignments in the Lishka, organizing a public campaign in the West to increase the world's awareness of the plight of Soviet Jewry. From 1965 to 1969 he served as a minister counselor in the Israeli Embassy in Washington, seeking support for Soviet Jewry from American Jewish organizations, the State Department, Congress, and the media. Although, the Soviet Union severed relations with Israel in 1967, an intelligence network with links throughout the West enabled the Lishka to keep tabs on the Soviet Jewry situation, but precious little of that information was passed on to the Soviet Jewry activist organizations that were springing up in America and England.

Prime minister Golda Meir appointed Levanon to succeed Shaul Avigur as director of the Lishka at the end of 1969. Like his predecessor, Levanon has been described as secretive and determined to control. While he acknowledged that American activist groups contributed by bringing awareness of the Soviet Jewry issue to their local communities, Levanon felt that their activities inside the Soviet Union were harmful. He was also fearful that Soviet Jews would be endangered if they had telephone conversations with American or British supporters.[38] When Jews who had recently immigrated to Israel were invited to speak in America, they were admonished by the Lishka to speak only in small "parlor meetings" rather than mass gatherings. This policy of silence was challenged in August 1969 when eighteen families of Georgian Jews who were denied exit visas wrote letters to the UN Human Rights Commission and to prime minister Golda Meir. In their impassioned letter they wrote:

> We will wait months and years, we will wait all our lives if necessary, but we will not renounce our faith or our hopes. We believe: Our prayers have reached God. We know: Our

appeals will reach humanity. For we are asking little – let us go to the land of our forefathers.

They asked Meir to transmit their appeal to the UN, publish it in the press and broadcast it in Russian over the Voice of Israel. After one hundred days with no response, the families sent a more urgent appeal and circulated copies via samizdat (clandestine copying and distribution) to tourists in the Soviet Union. Eventually copies wound up in the hands of new Soviet immigrants to Israel who beseeched Meir to act. Responding to the Soviet olim who convinced her that the Georgian Jews were sincere, she finally read the appeal letter in the Knesset. The Soviets protested that the letter was a forgery but in 1971 allowed the eighteen families to emigrate and then, over the next two years, permitted 20,000 more Georgian Jews to join them in Israel.[39]

Levanon's fears for Soviet Jews in the wake of the Leningrad trials and mass arrests in 1970 helped stimulate the convening of a World Conference on Soviet Jewry in Brussels in February 1971. Jewish establishment organizations in North and South America, Europe and Australia sent representatives.[40] While Levanon described the gathering as a "wonderful demonstration of Jewish solidarity and unity," an activist newsletter in Boston editorialized:

> There was a stench in the crisp Belgian air. It stank of opportunism, organizational self-aggrandizement, bureaucratic buck-passing, cowardice and cynicism. It was the smell of Jewish politics, as the world Jewish establishment bickered in the face of crisis. The world press recorded it all, and despite the hysteria in *Pravda* and *Izvestia*, no doubt the KGB recognized in the Brussels World Conference that same penchant for disunity that paralyzed world Jewry when six million died.[41]

Information flow from the Lishka was a contentious issue during the early 1970s when Colin Shindler in England edited a newsletter

43

called *Jews in the USSR*.[42] Levanon was infuriated to see reports from activists (especially Michael Sherbourne, who was in daily contact with Soviet Jews) along with open discussion of Soviet dissidents, appearing in the newsletter in addition to the official information released by the Lishka.[43] Shindler resigned in 1975 saying, "The Soviet Jewry Office in Israel tried to run a tight ship and frowned on uncontrolled individualism."[44]

Leonard Schroeter's book *The Last Exodus* was an enormous source of information published without Levanon's blessing. Schroeter, an attorney from Seattle with a background in constitutional law, was invited to work in Israel as a principal legal assistant to the attorney-general. He arrived in early 1970 expecting to draft a constitution for the young nation – it was a dream then and still is a dream – but after the arrests in Leningrad and Riga he was assigned to Soviet Jewry issues, reporting to Levanon. For over two years Schroeter interviewed Soviet Jews after they arrived in Israel and served as their ombudsman and advocate. With help from the Mossad and the CIA, he obtained a passport devoid of any indication that he had been to Israel, and used this "clean" passport to travel from London to Moscow where he visited refuseniks and dissidents, including Andrei Sakharov. Schroeter returned to Seattle via London and briefed Foreign Office officials and members of Parliament on the Soviet Jewry situation.[45]

Levanon's tenure as director of the Lishka transcended Israeli party politics; he served under prime ministers Golda Meir and Yitzhak Rabin of the Labor Party, as well as Menachem Begin of the Likud Party, even though he was identified with labor and kibbutz movements. In 1982, he retired to Kibbutz Kfar Blum to write his memoirs and lived there until his death in 2003.[46] When the majority of Soviet Jews opted to emigrate to the United States rather than Israel, Levanon regarded the issue as "a Jewish tragedy."[47] He briefly came out of retirement in 1988 to participate in negotiations in The Hague to express his view that it was "a falsehood for Jews to use a visa for a free country like Israel to obtain refugee status in America."[48]

Levanon traveled to Moscow and had a cordial meeting with Mikhail Gorbachev in 1995. He told the former Soviet leader about his four decades of activity on behalf of Soviet Jews and stated that there were three important events in 20th century Jewish history: the Holocaust, the establishment of the State of Israel, and the emigration of Jews from the Soviet Union. Gorbachev frankly admitted that he did not favor mass emigration of Jews; they contributed a great deal to the Soviet Union as scientists, engineers, doctors, musicians, artists, writers and teachers. He said that he "needed time and serious efforts to clear away all the obstacles in the path of free emigration for all." Gorbachev spoke at length about his visit to Israel and how he was fascinated by "the fact that after thousands of years, free, devoted and bold Jews managed to build a flourishing state, turning deserts into fields and gardens, developing advanced industry and the capability to protect itself against its enemies." He opined that "Israel can serve as an example to Russia in its rehabilitation process."[49]

Aryeh Kroll after receiving the Israel Prize for 1999.
Photo Credit: © Dan Porges photographer.

CHAPTER FOUR

Western Voices for the Jews of Silence

During the 1950s, while most Americans were preoccupied by the Korean War, the Cold War, McCarthyism, economic growth, racial segregation, automobiles and television, two American Jewish organizations were paying attention to the plight of Jews in the Soviet Union.

The Jewish Labor Committee was founded in 1934 in response to the rise of Nazism in Germany by union leaders in New York who were largely Yiddish-speaking, secular, and politically allied with the Jewish Bund of Russia and Poland. After World War II, JLC organized relief and rehabilitation programs for survivors and managed to help some Jews escape from the Soviet Union. During the 1950s and '60s JLC joined the struggles for civil rights and elimination of racism. At the same time it was alone in protesting the anti-Semitic discrimination that was prevalent in the Soviet Union.[1]

The other pioneering group in the United States exposing Soviet anti-Semitic policies in the '50s was the American Jewish Committee (AJC), an organization that had been founded in

1906 by people who were appalled by pogroms in Tsarist Russia.[2] In 1951 they employed Solomon Schwartz, a scholar who wrote *Jews in the Soviet Union*.[3] Since 1908 AJC has been compiling data for the *American Jewish Year Book* which included a summary of news from Russia, and after 1917, the Soviet Union. Their entries from the Fifties include:

> 1950 – 'The last two Jewish schools in the Soviet Union... were closed down.'
> 1952 – 'Jewish servicemen, demobilized from the army and returned to civilian life in Russia, were not reinstated in their former positions as executives, engineers, or doctors, but asked to accept menial jobs.'
> 1953 – The 'Doctors' Plot' – 'Criminal doctors had sabotaged the treatment of their patients...and killed Soviet leaders ... Of nine doctors mentioned in the communiqué, six were Jews.'
> 1954 – 'A strong anti-religious propaganda campaign was waged...'
> 1956 – 'Seven thousand Jews from Grodno and the surrounding area were said to have been deported to Siberia.'
> 1959 – 'State permission was needed to bake matzot.'

MOSHE DECTER

Data on Soviet anti-Semitism revealed by the Jewish Labor Committee and the American Jewish Committee were extremely valuable to Moshe Decter. Born in western Pennsylvania in 1921 to parents who emigrated from a region of Russia that is now Moldova, Decter grew up in a home that revered Zionism and the Hebrew language. He was well aware that the regime in Moscow was viciously anti-Zionist and anti-Hebrew. He was employed by the Anti-Defamation League in the 1950s and one of his tasks was research on Jewish foreign affairs.[4] In 1958 he became managing editor of the *New Leader*, a weekly magazine that was originally an organ of the American Socialist Party but later severed its Socialist ties and became an independent publication which often accepted articles from liberal anti-Communists in America.[5]

The *New Leader* for September 14, 1959, was a special issue entirely devoted to "Jews in the Soviet Union." It contained quotes from Communist Party writers from Canada, England, France and the United States who had visited the Soviet Union and expressed horror at the extent of anti-Semitism they observed. For years under Stalin they covered up what they knew was going on, but after Khrushchev's 1956 denunciation of Stalin's excesses, they felt free to question the issue of Soviet anti-Semitism. Decter pointed out that while Khrushchev had continued Stalin's policy of treating Jews as a potentially disloyal group, the Soviet government would not admit its discriminatory policy toward them, because doing so "would reveal a sharp clash between Soviet constitutional doctrine and the real situation, and more significantly, a profound contradiction of basic ideology." He clearly had his finger on the pulse of Soviet Jewry when he stated that an "unanticipated consequence of Soviet discrimination was a defensive reaction in the form of greater Jewish group consciousness, and an alienation from the regime." Soviet Jews would suffer in silence for another decade before they validated Decter's assessment by openly demanding their rights to live or leave as Jews.

The *New Leader* special issue also provided its readers with examples of anti-Semitic stereotyping, found in recent Soviet scholarly journals, which were reminiscent of the Soviet propaganda published during the "Black Years" of 1948 to 1953. A typical canard was the allegation that international Jewish bankers and oligarchs control world capitalism. Based on reports from clergymen and journalists who visited the Soviet Union, the *New Leader* showed how the Jews were more severely restricted in religious practice than the Russian Orthodox, Baptists and Muslims who had nationwide organizations and were free to print copies of the Bible and Koran. There were only sixty rabbis in all of the Soviet Union and no Hebrew Bible had been printed in the Soviet Union since 1917.

Within days of its appearance B'nai B'rith ordered 60,000 copies of the special issue of the *New Leader* for distribution throughout the United States. Although there was not much immediate attention given to the issue in America, its revelations led to keen reaction in Europe and Latin America, and weakened the Communist parties on those continents.[6]

Decter's article "The Status of the Jews in the Soviet Union" appeared in the January 1963 issue of *Foreign Affairs* and had much more impact. With this article Decter awakened the academic and political communities to the plight of Soviet Jewry.[7] In it he denounced the cultural and religious deprivation imposed on them, citing the fact that from 1959 to 1962 only six Yiddish books were allowed to be published, and in March 1962 a total ban on baking matzah for Passover had been enforced. The article also reminded readers that a popular non-Jewish Soviet poet, Yevgeny Yevtushenko, had published "Babi Yar," a poem indicting the Soviet regime for failure to memorialize the site, near Kiev, where an estimated 100,000 Jews had been slaughtered by the Nazis in 1941.

Decter concluded the article, "In sum, Soviet policy places the Jews in an inextricable vise. They are allowed neither to assimilate, nor live a full Jewish life, nor to emigrate (as many would wish) to Israel or any other place where they might live freely as Jews...Soviet policy as a whole, then, amounts to spiritual strangulation – the deprivation of Soviet Jewry's natural right to know the Jewish past and to participate in the Jewish present. And without a past and a present, the future is precarious indeed."

Soon after publication of the *Foreign Affairs* article, Decter organized a conference on the status of Soviet Jews for academics, intellectuals and theologians at the Carnegie Endowment for International Peace in New York. While Nahum Goldmann, the president of the World Jewish Congress, opposed the event, Decter found a broad range of influential sponsors including Martin Luther King, Jr., Supreme Court Justice William O. Douglas, Bishop James Pike, and Theodore Hesburgh – the president of Notre Dame University and a member of the u.s. Civil Rights Commission – who jointly issued an "Appeal to Conscience for the Jews of the Soviet Union" that called upon Soviet authorities to remedy the inequities suffered by Soviet Jews.[8]

King was particularly supportive of Soviet Jewry and joined Decter's Ad Hoc Commission on the Rights of Soviet Jews that held a day of public hearings on March 18, 1966. Norman Thomas, the American Socialist Party leader and its perennial presidential candidate, was also an influential commission member as a moral force in the country.[9] Getting support from socialists and "fellow-travelers" was in line with a suggestion made by Binyamin Eliav, Israel's consul general in New York. He recommended a strategy of approaching left-wing leaders, rather than staunch anti-Communists, in order to influence the Soviets to change their policies. "We don't have to persuade the already persuaded," he often counseled.[10]

Decter maintained a close relationship with Eliav and with Nechemia Levanon, and financial support from American Zionists who sympathized with their policies enabled Decter to set up his New York-based think tank, Jewish Minorities Research.[11] In his essay "Israel's Role in the Campaign," Levanon praised the "wonderful job" done by Jewish Minorities Research in publicizing the issue of Soviet Jewry. According to Levanon, "By sticking to thoroughly verified material, facts, and figures, Decter was invulnerable to any attempt by the Soviets to discredit him."[12]

RABBI ABRAHAM JOSHUA HESCHEL

The articles that Decter wrote about Soviet Jewry reinforced the ideas of his former teacher, Rabbi Abraham Joshua Heschel, who served as professor of Jewish Ethics and Mysticism at the Jewish Theological Seminary of America from 1945 to 1972. Heschel was born in Poland, a descendent of eminent rabbis, and studied at the University of Berlin and in both Orthodox and Reform yeshivas until 1933, when he escaped the Nazis and moved to England and later to the United States. He is remembered as a man who expressed his passion for social justice and his scholarship in Jewish traditions in the most beautiful and eloquent terms. The philosophy of his books, *Man is Not Alone* and *God in Search of Man*, could be summed up as: "Live your life in such a way that you will remind people of God."[13]

In 1963 Heschel bonded spiritually with Rev. Martin Luther King, Jr. at a meeting of the National Conference of Christians and Jews, and felt it was a privilege to march alongside the great civil rights leader in Alabama two years later.[14] Heschel described that experience as "…the march from Selma to Montgomery was both protest and prayer. Legs are not lips, and walking is not kneeling. And yet our legs uttered songs. Even without words, our march was worship. I felt my legs were praying." Heschel also served as co-chairman of Clergy and Laity Concerned about Vietnam, and crying out for both the people of Vietnam and the soul of America, he encouraged King to take a public stance against the war.[15]

For twenty years Heschel felt burdened with disappointment and shame over the unwillingness of Jewish organizations in America to heed his pleas regarding Jews in the ghettos of Eastern Europe who had been exterminated by the Nazis. Finally on September 3, 1963, he declared at a conference of Conservative rabbis that Soviet Jewry must be the No. 1 priority of American Jews and that they could not remain indifferent to the situation in 1963 as they were in 1943. "East European Jewry vanished. Russian Jewry is the last remnant of a people destroyed in extermination camps, the last remnant of spiritual glory that is no more. We ask for no privilege; all we demand is an end to the massive and systematic liquidation of the religious and cultural heritage of an entire community, and equality with all the other cultural and religious minorities. Let the twentieth century not enter the annals of Jewish history as the century of physical and spiritual destruction!"[16]

Over the next three years Heschel repeatedly decried the failure of American Jewish organizations to make the condition of Soviet Jews a prime concern. At one point he threatened to form his own Soviet Jewry agency if the established national Jewish organizations didn't respond more effectively.[17] For his efforts he was denounced as a demagogue by Conference of Presidents of Major American Jewish Organizations. However, the Rabbinical Assembly, the international association of Conservative rabbis, defended him and rejected the criticism.[18] Heschel continued to chastise American Jews about Soviet Jews, racism and the Vietnam War until he died in 1972. He is fondly remembered as one of the most revered religious leaders of the twentieth century.

ELIE WIESEL

The moral imperative on Soviet Jewry issued by Rabbi Heschel resonated with his friend Elie Wiesel. It was clear to Wiesel that Jews had been abandoned during World War II and no Jew should ever be abandoned. He has said, "If Jews anywhere need my presence, I cannot deny them that presence."[19] Therefore the young writer – *Night* being his sixth book published so far – would travel to Russia to reach out to his brethren during the High Holy Days and Sukkot of 1965. He wished to see with his own eyes whether the reports of a Soviet government campaign to spiritually destroy its Jewish minority were true or exaggerated.

Meir Rosenne, his former classmate at the Sorbonne and a fellow refugee from Romania, was working on Soviet Jewry issues at the Israeli Consulate in New York and briefed Wiesel on what he might expect in Russia. Ephraim Tari was in a similar position in Paris and also advised Wiesel prior to his flight to Moscow. Wiesel's plan was to look for ordinary Jews outside synagogues and avoid meetings with either religious leaders or government officials.[20]

On Wiesel's first evening in Moscow in front of a synagogue a Jew spotted him, assumed from his appearance that he was a foreigner, and in the shadows, asked if he spoke Yiddish. What Wiesel heard were the choked and fearful words, "Do you know what is happening to us? There is no time. We are nearing the end. Impossible to give you details. If I am being watched, I will pay for this conversation. Do not forget."[21] Wiesel encountered this same anguish from Jews in Kiev, Leningrad and Tbilisi. "Fear confronted me like an impenetrable wall in city after city," he wrote in *The Jews of Silence* after he returned to New York. His book also revealed another picture of Jews in Russia, a Simchat Torah celebration on the street outside the synagogue in Moscow, an annual evening of spirited singing and dancing that had attracted huge crowds every year since 1961. To Wiesel it was a sign of Jewish rebirth and resistance.

> This evening gave me new hope and encouragement. We need not despair. The Jews...who had complained to me about the doubtful future of Russian Jewry were wrong. They were too pessimistic, and apparently did not know their own children or the hidden forces which prompt them, at least once a year, to affirm their sense of community. Everyone has judged this generation guilty of denying its God and of being ashamed of its Jewishness. They are said to despise all mention of Israel. But it is a lie. Their love of Israel exceeds that of young Jews anywhere else in the world. If on this night of dancing, gladness finally overcame fear, it was because of them...I am still waiting to see tens of thousands of Jews singing and dancing in Times Square or the Place de l'Etoile as they danced here, in the heart of Moscow on the night of Simchat Torah. They danced until midnight without rest, to let the city know that they are Jews.[22]

Wiesel concluded *The Jews of Silence* by decrying the unresponsiveness of Jews in the free world: "I believe with all my heart that despite the suffering, despite the hardship and the fear, the Jews of Russia will withstand the pressure and emerge victorious...what torments me the most is not the Jews of silence I met in Russia, but the silence of the Jews I live among today."[23]

Two decades later he told an audience of Jews in Moscow that "The 'Jews of Silence' were all those Jews, everywhere, who until the late Sixties, remained complacent and unconcerned and refused to hear your appeal for solidarity and compassion." [24]

Wiesel's book and his participation in countless rallies for the liberation of Soviet Jewry, which he regarded as "my most urgent cause", had a profound impact on the movement.[25] The publication of *While Six Million Died* by Arthur Morse in 1968 had a synergistic effect; readers of both books could grasp the consequences of the previous generation's apathy and the need to avert another Holocaust in their own time.[26]

One of the events that featured Wiesel as the key speaker was at a synagogue in Toronto in 1966. There he was introduced by Rabbi Stuart Rosenberg, who had traveled to Russia himself in 1961, the first Canadian rabbi to visit the USSR, and observed the same government suppression of Judaism, anti-Semitism, and fear that Wiesel was describing. Rosenberg's desire to make the journey stemmed from reading about the 1956 trip by a delegation of American Orthodox rabbis (see Chapter 2). He was one of the first tourists to be briefed by Meir Rosenne, who equipped him with an El Al Israel Airlines flight bag (to identify him as a Jew) and with Russian-Hebrew calendars for distribution to Soviet Jews.[27]

Wiesel returned to Toronto in 1971 for a demonstration when Soviet premier Alexei Kosygin was visiting Canada. Wiesel stood in the back of an open truck and declared: "The Jews of Silence are silent no more. Jewish people, be proud. Be proud of your children in Moscow. Be proud of your children in Toronto. Jewish people, you have found your soul again. The process is irrevocable. The process cannot be stopped. It will go on." [28]

A stirring address by Wiesel to the 1970 meeting of the Council of Jewish Federations and Welfare Funds in Kansas City resulted in the allocation of $100,000 to the American Jewish Conference on Soviet Jewry. For the first time this group had resources to advertise on radio, television and newspapers and launch an educational campaign.[29]

The Soviet government was well aware of Wiesel's book and

subsequent activities on behalf of Soviet Jews. However, he was permitted to return to Moscow in 1979, as chairman of the President's Commission on the Holocaust, and to have a meeting with attorney-general Roman Rudenko, who had been a Soviet prosecutor at the Nuremberg trials. Wiesel presented Rudenko with the names of four Prisoners of Zion that he had obtained from the Lishka. Rudenko initially argued that he didn't know them and that "None of this pertains to me or my department." Suddenly his tone changed and he told Wiesel, "I'll make a deal with you. Two of the four, but not Shcharansky. You choose." Wiesel shrugged, "Who am I to choose?" Rudenko then said, 'Tell them to write me directly." He kept his word.[30]

In his Nobel Peace Prize acceptance speech in 1986 Wiesel expressed outrage at the Soviet government for Andrei Sakharov's isolation, Ida Nudel's exile and Yosef Begun's imprisonment.[31] As a Nobel laureate he spoke at the massive Soviet Jewry rally in Washington on December 6, 1987, the eve of the Gorbachev-Reagan summit meeting.

Forty years after his first journey to the former Soviet Union, Professor Wiesel, in his office at Boston University, reflected on the fall of communism in Eastern Europe, the breakup of the USSR, and the exodus of two million Soviet Jews: "I am convinced that [the events of 1989] would not have happened if not for Russian Jews; they were the first to demonstrate and sing in the streets as Jews. It was a great moment in Jewish history."[32]

ISI LEIBLER

It was not necessary to live in in America to speak out in support of Soviet Jewry in the 1960s. Isi Leibler was born in Antwerp, Belgium, and escaped from the Nazis by sailing to Australia. He graduated from Melbourne University in 1956 with a major in political science, specializing in the Soviet Union. In 1959 he visited Israel and met Shaul Avigur, who put him in touch with Moshe Decter in New York and Emanuel Litvinoff in London. What Leibler learned from them about the distressing condition of Jews in the

USSR, combined with his own realization that passivity on the part of Jews in the free world during the Holocaust had doomed six million, swept him up with a passion to do something to make a difference for Soviet Jews.[33]

Upon his return to Australia, Leibler initiated a campaign within the Australian Jewish community on behalf of Soviet Jewry.[34] Its first achievement was at a committee meeting of the United Nations General Assembly in 1962 when Australian delegate Douglas White raised the question of Soviet Jewry, asserting that "if the Soviet Union had difficulty in giving Jews full freedom to practice their religion, the Universal Declaration of Human Rights placed upon it a moral obligation to permit them to leave the country." This was the first time the issue had been brought up at an international forum. It drew support from u.s. delegate Marietta Tree and Israeli Ambassador to the U.N. Michael Comay, and astonished outrage from the Soviet representatives.[35]

In 1965 Leibler published *Soviet Jewry and Human Rights* which included a letter of endorsement from Rex Mortimer, a leading member of the Central Community of the Australian Communist Party and the editor of the weekly *Guardian*, an organ of the party. Citing every relevant document he could find, Leibler demonstrated that "Jews in the USSR are denied the same rights as other Soviet nationalities and religious denominations...and are blackened by anti-Semitic stereotypes throughout the Soviet mass media."[36] A major part of the book was Leibler's exposé and analysis of the notorious and blatantly anti-Semitic book *Judaism without Embellishment* by T.K. Kichko that had been published in 1963 by the Ukrainian Academy of Sciences. Leibler pointed out how Communist parties in Western countries had immediately and strenuously protested its publication.[37] Mortimer urged that a campaign be launched against anti-Semitism in the Soviet Union. The Communist Party in Australia split into two factions over this issue.[38]

The Lishka encouraged Leibler to go on a worldwide book tour of speaking engagements before Jewish and non-Jewish groups, including many Communist Party meetings. One stop on his tour was a meeting of the World Jewish Congress in Strasbourg, France, where he gave an aggressive speech criticizing the *shtadlanut* (backstairs diplomacy) policy toward Soviet Jewry advocated by the organization's legendary founder and president, Nahum Goldmann. Leibler declared that he got the respect of the left-wingers by confronting them, not by sucking up to them. To his amazement he received a standing ovation from the 120 delegates. But his joy was short-lived, as Goldmann, thoroughly upset, ascended the podium and delivered a two-hour tongue-lashing to the young upstart.

International travel soon became Leibler's day job as he transformed Jetset Tours from a store-front operation to Australia's largest travel company. In 1978 Jetset Tours was appointed by the Australian Olympic Federation to handle its needs for the 1980 Moscow Olympics. This appointment enabled Leibler to get a visa to enter the Soviet Union and he traveled there three times in 1978 and 1979. Whenever he could break away from his business duties in Moscow he would visit refuseniks and developed very close relationships with them. The KGB was aware of his activities and tried to get the Soviet Olympic officials to persuade him to desist, but the Olympic officials didn't want to get involved in politics so the KGB tried to bribe Leibler. He told them, "I'm doing my business and my free time is my time, not your time."

When Soviet tanks rolled into Afghanistan in late 1979, President Jimmy Carter declared that the United States would boycott the 1980 Moscow Olympics and sixty-four nations agreed to do likewise. Leibler was in Moscow when Australia announced that it would support the boycott, so the KGB had its opportunity to get rid of him. Within twenty-four hours he was arrested, detained, prevented from contacting the Australian Embassy, accused of espionage, and expelled with orders never again to set foot on Soviet soil.[39]

Nevertheless, Leibler continued to apply for an entry visa.

With Gorbachev's rise to power and his introduction of glasnost, Leibler and his wife were granted entry visas for a visit in September 1986 and preparations were made for complete logistical support from the Australian Embassy in Moscow. But, in the wake of a heated exchange on the issue of human rights for Soviet Jews between Soviet president (and former foreign minister) Andrei Gromyko and Joan Child, the Speaker of the Australian House of Representatives, the visas were revoked just prior to the Leiblers' departure.[40]

Gromyko's successor as foreign minister, Eduard Shevardnadze, visited Australia in March 1987. He encountered pro-Jewish demonstrations wherever he went. Australian prime minister Bob Hawke, who was very pro-Israel – his daughter spent six weeks on a kibbutz in 1971 – and eager to do whatever he could for Soviet Jews,[41] confronted Shevardnadze on the issues of emigration and anti-Semitism. The press published reminders of Hawke's 1979 humiliating visit to Moscow when he was the president of the Australian Council of Trade Unions. During that visit he had met with refuseniks and tried to intervene on their behalf with Soviet officials, but KGB minders had got him completely drunk. Believing that he had won promises for the refuseniks, Hawke had issued public statements that turned out to be false.[42]

Shevardnadze's interest in Australia was both strategic and commercial; he realized that Australia had a special relationship with China, a leadership role in the South Pacific, and close ties with the United States. Several months later, in a gesture of goodwill, eighty-nine Soviet citizens, many of them Jews, were permitted to emigrate and reunite with relatives in Australia. In August Leibler received a surprise cablegram from Boris Gramm, president of the Moscow Jewish community, inviting the Leiblers to attend Rosh Hashanah services at the synagogue in Moscow. This time their visa applications were granted. Leibler found it "mind-boggling" to be the first political Jewish leader to receive such an invitation. Before leaving for Moscow, he met with Hawke in Canberra and received the prime minister's blessing to "convey to Soviet authorities his great desire to see all long-term refuseniks released."

In Moscow Leibler spoke in broken Yiddish to the elderly worshippers at the synagogue, visited with many refuseniks and met with Soviet officials. He was informed that the Supreme Soviet would soon allow a group of long-term refuseniks to leave for Israel.[43]

Hawke met with Gorbachev in December 1987 in Moscow and presented a list of names of refuseniks that he had obtained from Leibler. Among them were some of the refuseniks he had visited in their apartments in 1979, including Alexander Lerner. This time they were invited to a meeting with him in the grandeur of the Australian Embassy, a building that had been an aristocrat's mansion in Tsarist times. At the conclusion of his official meetings Hawke was jubilant to receive the good news that five of the refuseniks on his list had just been granted permission to leave by Gorbachev and more would soon follow.[44]

Leibler returned to Moscow in October 1988 and negotiated the establishment of a Jewish cultural center within the renovated Moscow Jewish Musical Theater building that would house a library of Hebrew, Russian and Yiddish books, an audiovisual facility, and a social club, as well as being the venue for live performances of Jewish music from all parts of the world.[45] The center would be named for Solomon Mykhoels, the legendary Soviet Jewish actor, director and founder of the Moscow Yiddish Theater.[46] Mykhoels, who had also served as head of the Jewish Anti-Fascist Committee, was assassinated in January 1948 on direct orders from Stalin at the beginning of the dictator's anti-Semitic campaign.[47] The center would be the Soviet Union's first officially approved Jewish center.

Leibler also held meetings with Soviet officials. He reported that emigration rules would be liberalized before the end of 1988 and that the Ministry of Religion had agreed to the opening of a yeshiva in Moscow and the training of a mohel and a ritual slaughterer.[48]

Jews from all over the Soviet Union came to Moscow to attend the Mykhoels Center opening event on February 12, 1989. Elie Wiesel as keynote speaker looked at them and declared, "What a statement of faith you have made! We are proud of you!"[49]

The Leiblers settled in Jerusalem in 1999. Prior to making aliyah Isi Leibler headed the Australian Jewish community and became senior vice president of the World Jewish Congress. He was awarded Commander of the British Empire (CBE) and Officer of the Order of Australia (AO). Like Wiesel, he describes the Soviet Jewry movement as a "great moment in Jewish history" and continues, "The Russian Jews were the yeast that accentuated the inevitability of the breakdown of the [Soviet] system."[50]

Isi Leibler (left) with Australian Prime Minister Bob Hawke prior to departure for Moscow in 1987. Photo credit: Isi Leibler.

CHAPTER FIVE

Sowing the Seeds of a Grassroots Movement

The Cuyahoga River flows right through the middle of Cleveland, Ohio. On its eastern side there is a large and vibrant Jewish community with 30 synagogues. On its western side there is only one synagogue: Beth Israel – The West Temple. It was in the modest brick building of Beth Israel that a study group, formed by three members of the congregation's Social Action Committee in 1962, grew into an international movement that won the support of one superpower and convinced the other superpower to live up to its human rights commitments.[1] These pioneering grassroots activists maintained their determination to accomplish their goal of saving Soviet Jewry, undeterred by the skepticism and, on occasion, opposition they encountered from leaders of established American Jewish organizations and the Israeli government.

The three study group participants were Dr. Herb Caron, a psychologist who did research at the Cleveland v.a. Hospital and taught at Case Western Reserve University; Rabbi Daniel Litt, the temple's spiritual leader; and Dr. Louis Rosenblum, a scientist who was director of the Direct Energy Conversion Division at NASA's

Lewis Research Center. The group participants looked at Jewish population statistics and found that with about three million Jews, the Soviet Union had one quarter of the world's Jewish population. They also knew that there was anti-Jewish discrimination in the Soviet Union and felt that something ought to be done about it. They were concerned that a holocaust could happen again.[2]

The key social action issue in the early '60 s was civil rights, and helping to achieve desegregation was certainly a legitimate Jewish issue. But working for the rights of Soviet Jews was not yet on the front burner. While the study group could not name even one Jew who was being victimized by the Soviet regime, the civil rights movement had martyrs like Emmett Till and Medgar Evers. Civil rights demonstrations and marches were punctuated with slogans like "Jim Crow Must Go" and "One Man, One Vote" and inspired by songs like "We Shall Overcome". Songs and slogans for the Soviet Jewry movement were yet to come.

The study group members felt strongly that their parents' generation of Jews had failed in their response to the events that followed Hitler's rise to power in Germany: the Nuremberg Laws, Kristallnacht and the Holocaust. Rosenblum described the Jewish leadership in the United States as impotent and irrelevant during World War II. He and his fellow activists were determined not to abandon the Jews of the Soviet Union.

Caron, Litt and Rosenblum visited Rabbi Abba Hillel Silver, the dynamic spiritual leader of Cleveland's prominent Congregation Tifereth Israel, who had been president of the Central Conference of American Rabbis and the Zionist Organization of America as well as chairman of the United Jewish Appeal and the American Zionist Emergency Council. He had just returned from a visit to the Soviet Union and the study group was seeking his guidance on how to proceed. To their surprise and disappointment he said that conditions for Jews were improving there, that there really wasn't a Jewish problem and that the study group should go slowly. But they felt that Silver had seen only what Soviet authorities wanted him to see, reminiscent of the experience of International Red Cross observers who had been escorted by the Nazis through a temporary showplace at the Theresienstadt concentration camp.

In October 1963 the group organized the Cleveland Council on Soviet Anti-Semitism. Cleveland's mayor Ralph Locher agreed to be honorary chairman. Other public officials and Christian and Jewish clergymen joined the board of CCSA. In 1965 Abe Silverstein, the director of the NASA Lewis Research Center and an early architect of the Apollo moon landing, became its titular head. Beth Israel converted its choir loft to serve as an office for the council that would be operating on a shoestring because the mainstream Jewish organizations would not provide financial support. Lenore Singer served as volunteer secretary from 1964 until 1978. Beth Israel members and their children volunteered their time and effort to do everything from mimeographing and distributing newsletters and literature to demonstrating in street rallies.

The group was bent on making a difference and showing that concern for Soviet Jews was not just a parochial Jewish issue, so they wrote letters to well-known human rights leaders. The responses were positive and enabled the CCSA to publish an open letter to Soviet leaders that read in part:

> Respected world leaders such as Bertrand Russell, Linus Pauling, François Mauriac, Guy Mollet and Albert Schweitzer, who have devoted their lives to the cause of peace, have urged that you dismantle the frightening apparatus of anti-Jewish persecution. These wise leaders know that peace and persecution cannot coexist. Accordingly, the struggle for world peace and the effort to save Russian Jews are both part of the same struggle directed and inspired by the same leaders.[3]

There was positive, bipartisan response from the U.S. Senate as Jacob Javits and Abraham Ribicoff and 58 other senators co-sponsored a Senate Resolution condemning persecution by the

Soviet Union of persons because of their religion. It was adopted on September 23, 1964, with Senator William Fulbright, the pro-Arab, anti-Israel chairman of the Foreign Relations Committee, casting the only negative vote.[4]

Henry Ford II sent a telegram to the CCSA on November 8, 1963, saying "I share your concern at the reported denial of human and religious rights to Jews in Russia. Your campaign to inform and arouse the public against reprehensible discrimination of this kind should gain sympathetic support from all thinking people."[5] Ironically, a decade later Ford would build the world's largest truck plant on the banks of the Kama River in Russia.

A rally co-sponsored by CCSA and the Jewish Community Federation of Cleveland in 1965 finally brought the problem of Soviet anti-Semitism to the east side of Cleveland, and membership in the CCSA grew to over 600. A year later, Sid Vincent, the executive director of the Cleveland Jewish Federation, agreed to provide some funding for a few specific projects, agreed upon annually. Expenses for CCSA operation and other projects continued to come from dues and the sale of various items. One project for which the Federation provided partial funding was the publication of the "Handbook on Soviet Anti-Semitism" which served as a model of grassroots activism for Soviet Jewry councils that would soon be springing up throughout the country. In his introduction to the handbook, Rosenblum wrote:

> Today in the Soviet Union, anti-Semitism is deliberately cultivated as an instrument of state policy. The situation of the Soviet Jew is desperate. He is allowed neither to live as a Jew nor leave; he is made the scapegoat for Soviet economic and political failures. To ameliorate this situation, world concern must be focused on the plight of the Soviet Jew and continued protests made to the leaders of the USSR. It is our responsibility to cry out for justice; it is our task to redeem the captive. We dare not fail again."

The council attracted media attention by collecting petition signatures at rallies and by picketing visiting Soviets such as a Siberian dance troupe. The *Cleveland Plain Dealer* on April 4, 1966, reported that "more than 1000 persons participated last night in Greater Cleveland protests against anti-Semitism in the Soviet Union."

Later that year the council decided to produce a film on the plight of Soviet Jews to help educate people about the situation. Rosenblum enlisted his friend Mort Epstein, who had some filmmaking experience, as well as some people who produced movies for NASA to volunteer their time and experience. Rosenblum called Elie Wiesel, whose book *The Jews of Silence* had just been released. Wiesel agreed with Rosenblum that there were no recent films about Soviet Jews and that it was indeed time for a new message, so he invited Rosenblum and Epstein to come to New York to talk about it.

When they arrived at Elie Wiesel's office he asked if they had a script.

"No, but we would love it if you could write the script," Rosenblum replied.

"Well, I could write it. Who is going to act in it?"

"We'll have to find people here who would be suitable for the roles."

"No, no, no. That will never work. It has to be authentic, with Soviet Jews in it."

"We can't film in the Soviet Union. We can't do that."

"I can't do anything that isn't authentic."

Epstein and Rosenblum left Wiesel's office and spent an hour walking around Manhattan and thinking about how they could produce the film and who could be the featured spokesperson. Suddenly Rosenblum thought of Rabbi Abraham Joshua Heschel, who said he would be very happy to write a script and appear on camera; it would be in keeping with his philosophy that political acts are just as important as religious deeds. He invited Rosenblum and Epstein to film it at the Jewish Theological Seminary. Everything went smoothly, with Heschel needing only one or two takes for each of the eight scenes.[6] The film opened with Heschel invoking an eloquent moral imperative:

Our age marks the end of moral isolationism. An awareness is spreading in the minds of man that no man is an island, that what happens to a person in another part of the city concerns us directly and deeply, even more what goes on in a distant part of the world, will have a profound effect on all of us right here. It is for this reason that so many of us have become deeply involved, with heart and soul, in the great battle for civil rights, for equal opportunity, for equal rights and for the dignity of all citizens of America. Above all we've also become aware that we cannot detach ourselves from the events that are taking place in other parts of the world. While this great battle is going on in this country for justice and for peace, another drama is being enacted, equally serious, heartrending, agonizing, that is being ignored by so many of us. I mean the drama that is being enacted in Soviet Russia, where there is such a dreadful oppression of Jews and the attempt on the part of Jews to assert their rights to insist upon maintaining and saving their cultural identity and their own inner personality. It is therefore an issue of the greatest importance, a challenge to our conscience to be concerned for this silent drama of the Jews in Soviet Russia.[7]

Copies of the film, called *Before Our Eyes*, were sold and rented to groups throughout the United States and abroad. It helped new Soviet Jewry councils generate interest for this issue in their communities.[8] In Minneapolis Rabbi Moshe Sachs viewed the CCSA as a model for campaigning to bring pressure from abroad to influence Soviet policy. He urged the Minneapolis JCRC to set up a lay-rabbinic committee with initiative and zeal comparable to the Cleveland group to assume responsibility for combating Soviet anti-Semitism.[9]

Rosenblum was in contact with grassroots groups and leaders like Rabbi Sachs, and in May 1968 proposed the establishment of an umbrella organization that would coordinate the activities of the Soviet Jewry movement in the United States and bring the Soviet Jewry issue to national and international attention.[10] Rosenblum's proposal would be realized in 1970 as the Union of Councils for Soviet Jews.

The CCSA started making phone calls to Soviet Jews in 1969 with Sue Somers, a Russian-language student at Oberlin College, acting as translator. The names and phone numbers were obtained from Israel, not from a government source but from Ann Shenkar, an American activist who had made aliyah when she married Israel Shenkar, an Israeli businessman. Ann Shenkar gathered information from Jews who had recently arrived in Israel from the Soviet Union. She compiled lists of names, addresses and phone numbers of Jews they knew who were still trapped in the Soviet Union and were seeking help. The new arrivals in Israel often went to Nechemia Levanon's office to make requests on behalf of their friends and relatives in the Soviet Union but usually got no satisfaction. Somehow they learned that Ann Shenkar was sending a "News Bulletin on Soviet Jewry" to activists in the West so they provided her with the relevant information.[11] Other Soviet Jewry support groups in America also made telephone calls to Jews in the USSR who had been identified by their friends as people who were not afraid to receive calls from America. Rabbi Sachs notes that many of the calls from Minneapolis were in English, but his calls to selected activists who had learned Hebrew in underground *ulpanim* were in Hebrew. This often proved to be an effective way of circumventing the Soviet telephone operators.[12]

These phone contacts with refuseniks played an important role in the passage of the Jackson-Vanik Amendment in 1974 that established, as an integral element of American policy, the principle that trade and credit must be related to the u.s.'s concern for human rights. In April 1973 former President Richard Nixon met in the White House with fourteen members of the Conference of Presidents of Major American Jewish Organizations. Nixon was pressuring them to back off from support of the Jackson-Vanik Amendment. The CPMAJO statement issued after the meeting applauded the Administration and Congress for their efforts on behalf of Soviet Jews but significantly omitted any reference to the Jackson-Vanik Amendment. Rosenblum telephoned Kirill Khenkin in Moscow, a journalist, translator and Jewish activist and, after apprising him of the CPMAJO statement, asked him for a position statement from Soviet Jews. Two days later ten of the leading Soviet Jewish activists sent a message of support for the Jackson-Vanik Amendment to the CPMAJO, which now had no choice other than to publicly endorse Jackson-Vanik. During the next 18 months there were many meetings involving secretary of state Henry Kissinger, senator Henry "Scoop" Jackson and Soviet representatives. A September 1974 report from leading refuseniks Lev Kogan, Alexander Lerner, Alexander Luntz and Vladimir Slepak emphasized the importance of reliable and unimpeded communication by telephone, telegraph and postal service in monitoring Soviet compliance with their commitments on emigration. Recommendations in the report were extremely helpful and were included in one of Jackson's letters of understanding to Kissinger.[13]

Charles Vanik, who spearheaded the Jackson-Vanik Amendment in the House of Representatives, served for 26 years as a Democratic congressman from a district in northeast Ohio. He was briefed by CCSA for a fact-finding trip to the Soviet Union in 1971 and was outraged by the persecution of Soviet Jews described to him by refuseniks he visited. Upon his return he decided to find a legislative solution; one of his staffers, Mark Talisman, discovered that there was a century-old precedent that could apply. During Abraham Lincoln's presidency the United States imposed trade restrictions on Russia because of the pogroms they were conducting against Jews. Vanik was certain that it was once again appropriate to link trade to human rights considerations and asked Talisman to write the House version of Jackson's amendment. That was the easy part. Getting it through the hurdles of Congress, especially the House Ways and Means Committee, was another matter. Wilbur Mills of Arkansas chaired the committee in the early '70s and was under pressure from the Nixon Administration to prevent the bill from coming to a vote. Two factors turned Mills into a supporter. First, Vanik in February 1973 made Mills a co-sponsor, dubbing it the Mills-Vanik Bill. Then Vanik called Cleveland resident Harry Stone, the president of American Greetings, and suggested that Wilbur Mills should be reminded that Stone's company operated a plant in Mills' district.[14]

The years 1962 to 1986 during which the Cleveland Council on Soviet Anti-Semitism functioned (until the local Jewish Community Federation took over activities in support of Soviet Jewry) coincided with the 24 years of Anatoly Dobrynin's tenure in Washington as ambassador of the Soviet Union to the United States. Rosenblum takes great satisfaction in noting that Dobrynin, in his autobiography, described the Soviet Education Tax of 1972 "a stupid political move" and questioned Soviet policies on Jewish emigration.[15]

> I never understood why we did not allow Jews to emigrate. What harm could it have brought to the country? On the contrary, by solving this question we could have ridden ourselves of a serious and permanent source of irritation between us and the West, particularly the United States. Even the members of the Politburo under Khrushchev and Brezhnev could not provide a clear and convincing answer when asked in private to explain their views on emigration. Some were still under the influence of Stalin's view that emigrants were traitors. Others would claim that many Jews in the Soviet Union knew state secrets because of their work on military projects using science and technology or other sensitive

work, or that Jewish emigrants would join noisy anti-Soviet campaigns abroad. Then there was our Middle East policy: the Arab countries were in permanent protest against Jewish emigration, which they thought would strengthen Israel by augmenting its population and skills.

Those reasons were often heard in Moscow. But the most important one was not often heard. In the closed society of the Soviet Union, the Kremlin was afraid of emigration in general (irrespective of nationality or religion) lest an escape hatch from the happy land of socialism seem to offer a degree of liberalization that might destabilize the domestic situation. So the crucial difference in the Soviet and American approaches to the issue was that while the Americans wanted to export its free humanitarian and commercial values, the Soviet government simply wanted the commercial benefits of trade, but not the political values.[16]

Rosenblum, reflecting on his work in the Soviet Jewry Movement said, "We had a special convergence of people and events and a window opened up. If Stalin were still in power we wouldn't have had a ghost of a chance. The Soviet leadership changed and they knew they were falling behind and needed an opening to the West. We recognized that we were at a window of opportunity. We were fortunate to be born at that time and fortunate to have had the *saichel* (good sense) to recognize that we could do something."[17]

An early poster and artwork for stamps distributed by CCSA to other Soviet Jewry groups, on display at Western Reserve Historical Society, Cleveland, Ohio.

Lou Rosenblum at home in Middleburg Heights, Ohio. Photo by Philip Spiegel.

CHAPTER SIX

Mobilizing a Critical Mass in New York

J acob Birnbaum, who has been called the "Father of the Soviet Jewry Movement," vividly remembers August 25, 1939, a day that shaped his life.[1] A lad of twelve, he was walking with his grandfather, Asher Grunwald, to Sabbath eve services in London where the family had taken refuge in 1933 after experiencing anti-Semitic harassment in Nazi Germany. As they approached the synagogue they met an elderly acquaintance of Grunwald's who excitedly asked: "Have you heard the news?"

"What news?"

"Germany and Russia have signed a non-aggression pact."

"Is that true?"

"Yes, yes, I just heard it on the radio. The two foreign ministers, Ribbentrop and Molotov, signed the agreement in Moscow."

Both men then raised their arms and cried out: "*Oy veh*, this is the end! The two Satans of this world have joined together!"

They were not political analysts, scholars or pundits – just two simple Jews who shared a gut feeling of apprehension for their brethren trapped in the lands that were now, or soon could be, controlled by the Jew-hating tyrants Hitler and Stalin. There were nine million Jews in Central and Eastern Europe in 1939, well over half the world Jewish population. And less than a week later, on September 1, the Nazis invaded Poland from the west and the Soviets entered from the east, followed by Britain and France's declaration of war on Germany on September 3.

During the war Birnbaum's father, Solomon, a linguist, worked for the British National Censorship office where he read the terrible letters from the Jews in Europe. The Birnbaum family anguished not only over their own relatives, most of whom did not survive, but over their inability to do anything to alleviate the situation of all Europe's Jews.

They had long been troubled by the fate of Jews in the Soviet Union and recalled how Birnbaum's paternal grandfather, Nathan Birnbaum, the man who coined the term "Zionism," had urged Jews and Christians in Russia to resist the forces of atheistic Communism in the 1920s. Alas, they ignored the foresight of this man, who had served as secretary general of the first Zionist Congress in 1897 and, as a pioneer in the movements for return to Judaism and Jewish renaissance, became Secretary General of the Agudath Israel organization in 1919.

JACOB BIRNBAUM SEEKS GRASSROOTS SUPPORT IN NEW YORK

After the war, while attending the University of London and the Etz Hayim Yeshiva, Jacob Birnbaum became heavily involved in assisting young Holocaust survivors, as well as young Polish Jews exiting the USSR. From them he learned the full extent of the evils of the Soviet system. It became clear to him that something would have to be done for the "lost tribes" remaining in the USSR. Between 1951 and 1962, Birnbaum was involved in three types of activity: in British Jewish communal activities, rising to the position of director of the Jewish Community Council of Manchester, Salford, and Prestwich; on behalf of North African Jews caught in the North African struggle for independence from France; and in a personal quest for Jewish renewal which took him to Europe, Israel, and North America.

His desire to save Soviet Jews became his paramount concern and passion. And so, in 1963 he moved to New York City where he could reach out to a huge Jewish population and create a student movement that would mobilize American grassroots support for the rescue of Soviet Jews. He met Morris Brafman, who had escaped from the Nazis and founded the American League for Russian Jews. In January 1964 Birnbaum persuaded Yavneh, a national Jewish student group, to establish a Soviet-Jewry subcommittee under his direction.

Birnbaum had rented an apartment near Yeshiva University and began knocking on dormitory doors. He told anyone who would listen about the plight of Soviet Jews and how students could launch an activist movement to bring about political action to alleviate the situation. Most refused to hear the message of "a weird guy with a Van Dyke beard and an English accent". It wasn't long before they consulted the directors of the university, who responded that Jews didn't protest; that was for the Blacks who were being segregated down South. The next time Birnbaum appeared on campus, students shook their fists at him saying, "How dare you? You're endangering the lives of our fellow Jews!"

THE STUDENT STRUGGLE FOR SOVIET JEWRY – THE EARLY YEARS

Birnbaum didn't give up and finally did win support from students at other colleges. Under a typewritten letterhead of the "College Students' Struggle for Soviet Jewry" (later shortened to Student Struggle for Soviet Jewry or "Triple S–J"), he invited students to a meeting on April 27, 1964, at Columbia University. In the letter he stated:

There is overwhelming evidence to show that in recent years the Soviet Government has greatly speeded up its attempts at forcible assimilation of Russian Jewry. The screw is being turned swiftly and inexorably tighter. Just one example: in the last few years alone well over 300 synagogues have been closed down, leaving only 60 synagogues for a population of 3,000,000 Jews. Furthermore autonomous cultural life is almost completely banned. By contrast, tiny Soviet minorities of less than half a million have flourishing cultural institutions of every kind, and most other religious denominations continue to lead a viable, if limited, existence.

We are able to document a concerted effort at spiritual and cultural strangulation, very often shot through with vicious 'anti-Semitism'. The net result is that masses of Jews are in an increasingly ambiguous position, neither assimilating nor living self-respecting Jewish lives, nor yet being able to emigrate.

This is an intolerable situation and a moral blot on humanity. Justice is indivisible. Just as we, as human beings and as Jews, are conscious of the wrongs suffered by the Negro and we fight for his betterment, so must we come to feel in ourselves the silent, strangulated pain of so many of our Russian brethren.

We who condemn silence and inaction during the Nazi Holocaust, dare we keep silent now?

The time has come for a mass grassroots movement – spearheaded by the student youth. A ferment is indeed at work at this time. Groups of students all over New York are spontaneously coming together and hundreds of signatures have been collected.

There is a time to be passive and a time to act. We believe most emphatically that this is *not* a time for quietism. We believe that a bold, well-planned campaign, to include some very active measures, can create a climate of opinion, a moral power, which will become a force to be reckoned with.

About 200 students of varied backgrounds from throughout the metropolitan area came to the meeting and were addressed by Brafman and Birnbaum, who urged them to recognize the Holocaust as a warning and the civil rights movement as a model for grassroots action. Referring to the ineffective American Jewish Conference on Soviet Jewry, he declared that a "Struggle" not a "Conference" was needed to convince Washington to intervene with Moscow on behalf of Soviet Jewry. He received emotional and enthusiastic response. One student stood up and sang a song he had just composed: "History Shall Not Repeat".[2]

Rabbi Irving "Yitz" Greenberg, then a professor of history at Yeshiva University, felt that Birnbaum was a unique person who had caught the tail of the tiger on the issue of Soviet Jewry. Greenberg was one of the "Young Turks" on the YU faculty who were convinced that it was time for action.[3] Rabbi Steven (now Shlomo) Riskin, a lecturer in Bible and Talmud at YU, was another vocal proponent of activism who had marched for civil rights with Dr. Martin Luther King and Rabbi Abraham Joshua Heschel. Both Greenberg and Riskin had first met Birnbaum in Israel in 1962 and had spoken about Soviet Jews being in danger.[4] Opposed to them were YU's senior rabbinic leaders, more than half of them elderly and European-born, who believed in a tradition of *Shtadlanut*. Greenberg characterized this tradition as begging the authorities rather than demonstrating or threatening, hoping that out of goodwill they would throw you a bone.[5]

Several students called for immediate action. Birnbaum proposed a rally at the Soviet Mission to the United Nations on May 1, a major Soviet holiday. Although they had only four days to plan and organize the rally, Birnbaum was able to enlist 1,000 students to march for four hours across the street from the mission.[6]

Under headlines of "UN Reds Picketed on Anti-Semitism" and "1,000 Students March Against Soviet Persecution" New York's daily newspapers carried stories about the May Day demonstration. They noted that the young men and women who marched for four hours at the Soviet Mission to the UN were from 13 colleges. *The New York Times*, whose reporter was impressed with the fervent yet orderly spirit of the marchers, reported that "Although silent protest was the keynote of the picketing, singing was frequently heard. Among the selections was 'Ani Ma'amin,' the Hebrew chant 'I Believe,' which was sung by Jews being marched to Nazi concentration camps and gas chambers." A photo in the *New York Daily News* showed the local congressman, Leonard Farbstein, at the head of the line, carrying a sign that read "Let My People Pray". With a month to go before the primary election, Farbstein, in his bid for reelection, placed a banner advertisement in the paper urging voters to "Support Congressman Farbstein's Fight Against Soviet Anti-Semitism."[7]

This was not the first time that students had protested in front of the Soviet Mission on behalf of Soviet Jews. A few days before Passover in 1962 scores of students assembled there to protest the ban on the baking of matzah in the Soviet Union. This protest had been initially organized by Yeshiva University students, but the leadership of the demonstration was turned over to Bernie Kabak, a Columbia University student who was president of the student Zionist organization, after the YU students were threatened with disciplinary action by YU administrators. Letters were sent to the parents of Yeshiva University High School students who had joined the demonstration stating that they were "absent from classes without excuse". Yeshiva University administrators were acting in support of Rabbi Pinchas Teitz of Elizabeth, New Jersey, who frequently traveled to the Soviet Union, had good relations with Soviet officials and covertly brought religious articles to rabbis in Russia. He feared that protests by activists in America would antagonize Soviet authorities and undermine his efforts to keep Judaism alive in the USSR. Although protests continued they apparently had no effect on Rabbi Teitz's campaign; he was able to make 22 trips to the Soviet Union before his death in 1995.

Kabak recalls that an official at the Soviet mission was willing to talk with the demonstrators and acknowledged that the

Soviet authorities had made an error in policy regarding the ban on matzah. A reporter from the *New York Herald-Tribune* found it noteworthy that the official would deviate from the typical Soviet image of infallibility.[8]

Several years later Birnbaum and Teitz discussed their differing strategies for saving Soviet Jewry. Birnbaum said, "I have no objection to your conducting behind-the-scenes discussions with Soviet officials but these will never be truly effective without our massive public pressure from the West." Teitz responded, "I have to admit that the Talmud brings instances of the combination of internal and external pressures, but one has to be very careful, Reb Yaakov."[9]

Although the 1962 matzah demonstration was an ad-hoc event with no plans for follow-up, news items about it attracted the attention of a high-school student named Glenn Richter, who devoured whatever information he could find about Soviet Jews and attended Riskin's seminars on Jewish studies. Two years later as a Queens College political science major, Richter, who had been active in civil rights organizations, mused, "If we Jews can work for others, we can also work for ourselves". At a meeting of the American League for Russian Jews, he met Birnbaum and two like-minded college students, Arthur Green and Jimmy Torczyner. In early 1964 the three students started working with Birnbaum and recruited other students to participate in the meeting at Columbia University and the May Day rally at the Soviet mission.[10] Torczyner, a Yeshiva University student, was put on probation for his activism,[11] while just four miles down Broadway, at the more liberal Jewish Theological Seminary, Green was encouraged by Rabbi Abraham Joshua Heschel to continue his civil rights and Soviet Jewry pursuits.[12]

Soon after the May Day rally Birnbaum received both negative and positive phone calls from the parents of students who participated. The negative callers typically berated Birnbaum saying, "I saw my kid on TV last night demonstrating for Soviet Jewry. How dare you put Jewish youth in danger!" The positive callers thanked Birnbaum for steering their sons and daughters away from what they perceived as the escalating violence of the civil rights movement. Additionally, they were happy that their children were being diverted to a Jewish cause.[13]

Birnbaum wanted to work with the American Jewish Conference for Soviet Jewry, and soon after the May Day rally had a meeting with George Maislen, who chaired AJCSJ's steering committee. Birnbaum said, "Let's send out information kits to summer camps and share the cost." Maislen's fuming reply was, "Aha, that's why you're here; all you're here for is to get money." Birnbaum retorted, "No, I don't want your money; I want you to do your duty and send out this kit." Maislen terminated the meeting by suggesting that Birnbaum send a proposal to Jerry Goodman, the American Jewish Committee's representative to the AJCSJ.

The AJCSJ was an amalgam of representatives from 24 national Jewish organizations and this interaction was typical of the reaction Birnbaum received from the Jewish establishment. Skeptics in those Jewish organizations could come up with a long list of pessimistic questions:

"Are Soviet Jews really being persecuted?"

"Are Jews in the Soviet Union at greater risk than Jews in Israel or Arab lands?"

"If there is a Soviet Jewry problem shouldn't it be handled by AJCSJ rather than a maverick group like the SSSJ?"

"Will public protest, as advocated by the SSSJ, result in a backlash with more anti-Semitic and anti-Israel measures promulgated by the Soviet government?"

The summer of 1964 was one of intense activity for the SSSJ. Jewish, Catholic, and Protestant clergymen joined SSSJ activists at the Soviet Mission in June for a week-long protest fast and prayers culminating in an "all-faith appeal to the conscience of the world." Information kits developed by Arthur Green were distributed to Jewish summer camps throughout America without any support from AJCSJ. There was extensive lobbying at the Democratic National Convention in Atlantic City, New Jersey. Although meetings with party officials did not result in a Soviet Jewry plank becoming part of the Democratic platform for the 1964 presidential election campaign, Robert Kennedy climbed on to a car roof and spoke out earnestly about the plight of Soviet Jewry.[14]

Two months later over 2,000 people gathered in New York's Lower East Side for a rally organized by the SSSJ and featuring New York's senators Jacob Javits and Kenneth Keating, along with other local political figures.[15] The rally demanded an end to Soviet anti-Semitism and launched a petition that was sent to former President Lyndon Johnson.[16]

By the end of 1964 the SSSJ was coordinating activities, disseminating materials and dispatching speakers in support of Soviet Jewry to communities throughout the United States and Canada. Some of their literature wound up at Hillel facilities in England and Australia. Birnbaum and Richter set up a temporary office on Whitehall Street in lower Manhattan, near the U.S. Army recruiting office.[17] They later moved to an office in an old Jewish Theological Seminary building, thanks to support from rabbis Abraham Joshua Heschel and Wolf Kelman, the executive director of the Rabbinical Assembly. It was a definite improvement over the cramped conditions of Birnbaum's bedroom that had been the SSSJ's initial headquarters. While this was the world's only full-time organization in support of Soviet Jewry, neither Birnbaum nor Richter received any salary for their work. Eventually, Richter gave up his projected law studies to devote himself full-time to the SSSJ.[18] He would continue in his role as national coordinator of the SSSJ for the next quarter century. Membership dues of $3 per year, occasional donations from synagogue men's clubs, contributions at rallies and proceeds from the sale of buttons and literature barely covered daily operating expenses.[19]

There was a feeling of accomplishment as Birnbaum revealed news that the Soviet authorities would allow the baking of matzah in Moscow and Leningrad for Passover in 1965. Nevertheless, a huge rally at the Soviet Mission was planned for Passover.[20] This would be the first of many rallies with a Jewish theme organized by SSSJ. As a symbolic reminder of the collapse of the wall at the Battle of Jericho, seven *shofars* were sounded seven times. More than 2,000 people, many of them students, turned out to parade from the Soviet Mission to the United Nations at Dag Hammarskjold Plaza.

Birnbaum wanted to highlight the event with an appearance by the popular Rabbi Shlomo Carlebach. He wrote to Carlebach asking him to compose a melody for *"Am Yisrael Chai"* (The Jewish People Live), the words that had been chanted by Soviet Jews in 1948 upon Golda Meir's arrival in Moscow. Carlebach read the letter while flying to Prague for a "Behind the Iron Curtain" concert tour. He observed that the letter was on Student Struggle for Soviet Jewry letterhead and feared that a KGB agent might be on board the plane looking over his shoulder, so he leaped out of his seat, ran to the lavatory and flushed the letter down the toilet. Carlebach's concert in Prague drew only 25 youngsters who had received no Jewish education and could not be motivated to sing or dance. Carlebach felt heartbroken and after four hours trying excite the audience, he jumped onto a table and began chanting *"Am Yisrael Chai"* to a melody he had made up spontaneously. The youngsters quickly responded by clapping and singing and dancing with Carlebach. Immediately after returning to New York a jetlagged Carlebach phoned Birnbaum saying, "Yankele, I've got it for you!" and agreed to sing it at the April 4, 1965, rally. The song soon became not only the organizational anthem of SSSJ but the anthem of young Jews in the Soviet Union. At last the movement had its own "We Shall Overcome".

Six weeks later, the SSSJ held its first demonstration at the Soviet Embassy in Washington, D.C. Again it was punctuated by the sounding of *shofars*. The *Washington Post* reported that the symbolic purpose of the protesters was to "cause the walls of hate and separation and prejudice to tumble down."[21]

When he wasn't in the sssj office or at Queens College, Richter could be found on street corners giving out leaflets or setting up a sound truck. In *Memoirs of a Jewish Extremist* Yossi Klein Halevi describes how he met Richter in Brooklyn during the summer of 1965. It didn't matter that Halevi was in sixth grade; Richter appointed him Borough Park Elementary School chairman of the sssj and presented him with a stack of leaflets. The son of Holocaust survivors, Halevi could relate to sssj slogans like "I Am My Brother's Keeper" and "This Time We Won't Be Silent". He was inspired when Richter told him, "In my understanding of Jewish history, someone always came along to help. So now it's my turn. No great soul-searching stuff; you just do what you gotta do, man." Halevi readily became an activist and recruiter for the sssj and participated in the Menorah March on a bitterly cold evening in December 1965, walking with 1,000 people in a torchlight procession across Central Park and up Fifth Avenue to the Soviet Mission for the lighting of a giant 10-foot, 200-pound Chanukah menorah carried by alternating teams of *shtarkers* (strong men).

Speakers at the demonstration called upon Soviet officials to keep their promises to allow matzah baking, publication of Yiddish books and emigration of Jews who wanted to be reunited with their families, separated since 1917.[22] By April 1966 there had been no easing of the restrictions on Jews in the Soviet Union so the sssj organized its *Geula* (Redemption) March from the Soviet Mission to the UN. Some 15,000 marchers – the largest gathering at a Soviet Jewry event up to that time – heard Javits demand "complete equality [for Jews] with other minorities in the Soviet Union". At the head of the march there was a huge mural painted by Morris Katz, who is listed in Guinness World Records as the world's fastest artist, depicting the opening of the Red Sea with the words, "As the Red Sea parted for the Israelites, So will the Iron Curtain part for Soviet Jews."

The concept of the Iron Curtain parting for Soviet Jews implied a call for free emigration, which was in conflict with some establishment leaders who wanted to focus exclusively on easing

Soviet restrictions on Jewish life and were willing to accept emigration limited to the reunification of families. Nevertheless, the SSSJ continued to include "Let My People Go" as a fundamental demand on its agenda.[23] A series of events in 1967 would not only prove that the Student Struggle for Soviet Jewry had the right idea; it would alter the course of Jewish history.

SSSJ *marchers assembling for New York Menorah March across Central Park, December 1965. Photo credit: Archives of Jacob Birnbaum.*

Discussing a petition in 1964. Left to right: Senator Jacob Javits, Jacob Birnbaum, Senator Kenneth Keating. Photo Credit: Archives of Jacob Birnbaum.

Leaders of SSSJ's historic May Day 1964 protest, the first public confrontation with the Kremlin. Jimmy Torczyner is holding the "Why No Prayer Books?" placard, to his left is Glenn Richter holding "Reopen the Synagogues" placard and to his left is SSSJ founder Jacob Birnbaum. Photo Credit: Archives of Jacob Birnbaum.

Banner created for the 1966 Geula March by Morris Katz. Photo credit: Archives of Jacob Birnbaum.

Part Two

Soviet Jewish Resistance
and Renaissance
1967–1990

CHAPTER SEVEN

I am a Jew and Israel is My Homeland

During the spring of 1967 the entire Jewish world was apprehensive about the survival of the State of Israel. Egypt's former President Gamal Abdel Nasser, bellicose in declaring his aim to eradicate Israel, ordered the withdrawal of the United Nations Emergency Force that had been stationed in the Sinai to enforce a cease-fire since 1956. On May 15, 1967, Israel's Independence Day, Egyptian troops moved into the Sinai and started massing near the Israeli border. A week later, in violation of international agreements, Egypt blockaded the Straits of Tiran to all Israeli shipping and all ships bound for Eilat, cutting off Israel's oil supply. Meanwhile Syria stepped up its shelling of Israeli farms and villages from its bases in the Golan Heights that tower 3,000 feet above the Galilee. The number of Arab terrorist raids into Israel from territory occupied by Jordan more than doubled compared with 1966. Finally, on June 4, former President Abdel-Rahman Aref of Iraq joined in a military alliance with his Arab neighbors saying, "Our goal is clear – to wipe Israel off the map."

The region erupted into a three-front war – Egypt, Jordan and Syria – on June 5, 1967. The Soviet leadership was quick to blame Israel as the aggressor and predicted that the Arab states with their superior numbers and Soviet-supplied weaponry would annihilate the Jewish state. Many Soviet Jews doubted the propaganda of concocted Arab victories and exaggerated Israeli losses that were spewed out by Radio Moscow and *Pravda*; instead they turned to friends who had shortwave radios and could, during gaps in the jamming, hear the real news from Radio Liberty, Voice of America, the BBC, Deutsche Welle or, in some locations, even the Voice of Israel.[1] Those who were listening on the night of June 7 would have heard General Chaim Herzog, military commentator for the Voice of Israel (and from 1983 to 1993, Israel's president), speaking on the most decisive day of the Six-Day War:

> The miracle of our generation continues as does the brilliant campaign, the like of which there is no record in the history of Israel, and perhaps in the history of the nations, and which has achieved today what millions of Jews throughout the generations have prayed for.

Herzog was reporting the liberation of Jerusalem and the destruction of the retreating Egyptian forces. Two days later the West Bank was taken from the Jordanians and there was quiet along the Northern front as the Syrians agreed to a cease-fire. Israeli flags flew from the Golan Heights (formerly Syria) to Sharm el-Sheikh (formerly Egypt at the southern tip of the Sinai Peninsula).[2]

Meanwhile the leaders in the Kremlin wrung their hands in utter disbelief and dismay as vast arrays of tanks and planes that they had squandered on their Arab clients were turned to twisted, burned-out hulks. In time, they would also learn that they had suffered another loss in the Six-Day War – the hearts and minds of their Jewish people.

Of course, many Soviet Jews had become disillusioned about the Soviet system and government well before the Six-Day War, but kept their views to themselves. Israel's victory refuted the often repeated canard that Jews are cowards and serve only in the rear of the armed forces. Feelings of Jewish pride swelled throughout the Soviet Union.[3] General Moshe Dayan became the hero of young Soviet Jews, who would greet each other by saying "Shalom" while covering one eye to emulate Dayan's signature eye patch.[4] A handful of Soviet Jews began asking themselves: "If Israelis are willing to fight and die for their country, how can I sit by quietly? Am I not willing to stand up and express my solidarity with them?"

BORIS KOCHUBIEVSKY DARES TO STAND UP FOR ISRAEL

Boris Kochubievsky was one of the first to come out of the closet of silence and openly announce his support for Israel. He was born in Zhitomir, Ukraine, in 1936 and lived with his father after his parents' divorce two years later. He was sent to an orphanage after his father, a Red Army major, was murdered at Babi Yar in 1941, and his mother fled the Nazis. He had no idea that he was Jewish until his mother located him after the war and told him how his grandparents had been buried alive by Ukrainian collaborators and how, before World War II, other relatives had been murdered by Ukrainian nationalists and Stalin's henchmen. He grew up with no knowledge of Judaism or Jewish culture, attended trade school, and became a radio engineer. But he harbored deep resentment against the Ukrainians for what they had done to his grandparents, and for almost ten years before the Six-Day War he wished that he could emigrate from the USSR. But Israel was not the Promised Land to him; he thought of it as just a "desert with camels and donkeys." He felt completely nihilistic, not believing in religion, socialism or capitalism.[5]

After the Six-Day War, trade union members throughout the USSR were called into factory meetings to approve resolutions denouncing Israel. The Communist Party leaders expected unanimous consent; however, they didn't get it at Kochubievsky's workplace in Kiev. He shocked his fellow workers by declaring, "I want the record to show that I disagree. I do not consider Israel an aggressor. This was a necessary measure of protection of the Jewish people from total physical annihilation." The trade union committee demanded his resignation. He refused but was ostracized and harassed for months. Finally, in May 1968, he did resign and wrote an essay, "Why I Am a Zionist," which was circulated in *samizdat* form, smuggled to the West, and published in *The New York Times*. He clearly expressed the feelings of Soviet Jews of his generation:

> Why is it that the most active sector of Jewish youth, raised and educated in the USSR, still retains a feeling of Jewish national unity and national identity? How is it possible that Jewish boys and girls who know nothing about Jewish culture and language, who are mostly atheists, continue to feel so acutely and to be so proud of their national affiliation? The answer is simple: Thanks for that, in large measure, can be given to anti-Semitism – the new brand which was implanted from above and, as a means of camouflage, is called anti-Zionism…We are convinced that there can no longer be room for Jewish patience. Silence is equivalent to death… If we remain silent today, tomorrow will be too late…. More and more Jews are coming to understand that endless silence and patience lead straight down the road to Auschwitz. That is why the leaders of the Soviet Union have anathematized Zionism. That is why I am a Zionist.[6]

A month later he married Larissa Alexandrovna, who shared his Zionist passion even though her father was a Ukrainian KGB agent. The couple soon went through the arduous procedure of submitting applications for exit visas to OVIR, so that they could emigrate from the USSR to Israel. Their applications were denied and Larissa was dismissed from the Kiev Pedagogical Institute where she was a fourth-year student.

They attended a state-sponsored official memorial gathering at Babi Yar on September 29, 1968, the anniversary of the 1941 murders. Boris Kochubievsky overheard a man asking someone, "What's going on here?" and the reply, "At this ravine the Germans murdered a hundred thousand Jews." Then he heard the man comment, "That wasn't enough." At that point Kochubievsky expressed his outrage and protested to authorities, insisting that Babi Yar be memorialized as a uniquely Jewish tragedy, in contrast to Soviet dogma that referred to "Soviet citizens, Russians, Ukrainians and others who were slaughtered by the Nazi barbarians."

Two months later Boris and Larissa were invited to the OVIR office to pick up their exit visas. When they arrived they were held in a small room for three hours and told that they could not leave the country. Meanwhile KGB agents ransacked their apartment. Boris sent a letter of protest to general secretary Leonid Brezhnev in which he asserted, "I am a Jew. I want to live in the Jewish State…Let me go! As long as I live, as long as I am capable of feeling, I shall devote all my strength to obtaining an exit visa for Israel."

Nine days later Kochubievsky was arrested and charged with anti-Soviet slander. Warned that he could be sentenced to ten years at hard labor, he told his interrogator, "Just go ahead and shoot me; I don't want to live with you!"[7] He was committed to a mental hospital for two months and then put on trial – a four-day sham with no opportunity to have defense witnesses or friends present – found guilty and sentenced to three years' hard labor. There were vigils in the West protesting his imprisonment, but they were to no avail as Kochubievsky soon found himself in a "severe regime" labor camp. He was the only political prisoner among a gang of criminals who were encouraged by the guards to beat him.[8] Fortunately he was not forgotten in the West and was hailed as the first hero of the Soviet Jewry movement.

He was certain that his samizdat documents would reach the West and inspire Americans to work for his freedom. This belief strengthened his determination to survive.[9] Upon his release in December 1971, Boris received an exit visa and immigrated to Israel, whereas Larissa chose to stay in the USSR with their daughter.[10] Boris found employment as a radio engineer developing equipment for the Israel Defense Forces, and also traveled to the West and spoke out on behalf of other Prisoners of Zion. In 1974 he remarried, and changed his name to Baruch Ashi, an abbreviation of his father's, grandfather's and great-grandfather's names.

Nearly forty years after the Six-Day War, he looks back with a smile, "When I started to fight for emigration, the Jewish people around me thought I was a complete idiot and that I was doing them wrong. Now they are all here!"[11]

RUTA ALEXANDROVICH – THE ROCKY ROAD FROM RUMBULA

Just as Babi Yar was sanctified for Kochubievsky and the Jews of Kiev, the Rumbula Forest, near Riga, Latvia, was revered by the Jews of that city. It was the site of the murder of over 20,000 Jews from the Riga Ghetto by Germans and their Latvian collaborators on November 30 and December 8, 1941. After twenty years had elapsed with no memorial to mark the mass grave, Rivka Alexandrovich and other Riga Jews walked through the forest to search for the site. Attracted to spots where there were flowers in bloom that seemed unnatural in a pine forest, they started digging and found bones. They dug in the forest every Sunday for three years and eventually built a makeshift memorial. The authorities tried to prohibit the activity and briefly arrested some of the activists. Nevertheless, Rumbula became established as the meeting place for the young Jews of Riga, a city that had been home to a vibrant Jewish community until 1941. It should be noted that Latvia, Lithuania and Estonia did not become part of the Soviet Union until 1945 so the Jews of these three republics were more familiar with Judaism and Jewish culture than Jews in the rest of the USSR.

There were strong Zionist aspirations among the Jews of Riga, and the Alexandrovich family submitted applications to emigrate to Israel in 1965.[12] They were refused and Rivka's teenage daughter, Ruta, was expelled from the Young Communist

League. Undeterred, Ruta became active in collecting, duplicating and distributing leaflets on Jewish history. In 1969 she, along with twenty-one other Jews whose exit visas had been refused, signed a letter to UN secretary general U Thant. The letter invoked the Universal Declaration of Human Rights: "Everyone has the right to leave any country, including their own." It further stated:

> We are being kept forcibly. We are not allowed to go. Such treatment is an act of lawlessness. It is an open violation of the rights of man. We consider that to hold us forcibly is against the most elementary concepts of humanity and morality. We demand free exit from the USSR![13]

On June 15, 1970, Ruta's twenty-third birthday, the homes of Jewish activists in Riga and other parts of the Soviet Union were searched by KGB agents. Hebrew books and dictionaries, Israeli postcards, copies of petitions, letters and personal correspondence were confiscated from the Alexandrovich apartment. Ruta was called in for interrogation but she refused to cooperate.[14] On October 7 she was arrested and whisked off to an isolation cell on the pretext that she had just returned from Odessa where there had been a cholera epidemic.[15]

Ruta was put on trial at a workers' building outside Riga on May 24, 1971, along with three young men who were active in the Riga Zionist community. The Riga Four, as they were called, were accused of producing anti-Soviet literature and working to undermine the Soviet regime. Ruta admitted her role in distributing literature about Israel and Jewish culture, but denied that she had acted to undermine or weaken the Soviet regime. All four were found guilty and Ruta was sentenced to a year in prison.

Her fiancé, Sanya Averbukh, and her mother launched a campaign of writing letters and getting support from the BBC and other Western media.[16] The authorities gave Rivka Alexandrovich an exit visa for Israel to get rid of her because they knew she had been frequently communicating in fluent English with supporters in Israel, the United States and Europe. One treasure she brought to Israel was a matchbox filled with tiny bones from Rumbula that she turned over to Yad Vashem. Rivka, an articulate English teacher, then embarked on a speaking tour of the United States asking Americans to write to officials in Latvia requesting amnesty and an early release for Ruta.

Ruta was forced to serve her entire term but was allowed to emigrate with her fiancé and her father in October 1971. Sanya and Ruta were married in Tel Aviv a month later in a huge wedding attended by prime minister Golda Meir, Israeli government officials and hundreds of immigrants from the Soviet Union.[17]

YASHA KAZAKOV – EVOLUTION TO JEWISH IDENTITY AND ZIONISM

A year before her arrest Ruta Alexandrovich wrote a letter renouncing her Soviet citizenship. She arranged for the letter to be smuggled to her aunt, Leah Slovin, who was already in Israel. Slovin, seeking Israeli support and publicity for Ruta, brought it to the attention of officials in the Lishka, citing the precedent of Yasha Kazakov, a college student who had gained notoriety by renouncing his citizenship in Moscow shortly after the end of the Six-Day War.[18]

Kazakov recalls that there was nothing Jewish in his family's home in Moscow when he was growing up. When he was three years old, friends in the street started making references to his being a Jew. He had no idea what they meant. Three years later he heard about the doctors' trials (Chapter 4) and that Jews were traitors. He couldn't understand how all Jews could be bad. As he grew older he wanted to know what made Jews different, and starting searching for sources. He went from library to library looking at whatever books he could find that mentioned Judaism, Israel or Palestine. Finally he concluded that: "I belong to something special, something great…and I want to live in Israel."[19]

In January 1967 nineteen-year-old Kazakov, an engineering

student, decided to visit the Israeli Embassy in Moscow. He carefully observed the movements of the militia officers guarding the embassy. As soon as the officer closest to the entrance turned his back, Kazakov entered and asked a clerk how he could emigrate to Israel. He was told to get a *vyzov*, fill out an application, and take it to OVIR. Kazakov was surrounded by militia men as he opened the door to leave. When they questioned him he made up a story about wanting to find out about his grandfather, who was missing after World War II and may have wound up in Israel. Kazakov revisited the embassy several times over the next few months, and was always stopped and harassed by the militia officers. Embassy personnel gave him Hebrew textbooks and Israeli literature, and when it became clear that he had no relatives in Israel who could send him a vyzov, the embassy presented him with an entry permit guaranteeing that if he were granted an exit visa, Israel would allow him to enter.

Kazakov submitted the Israeli entry permit in lieu of a vyzov with his application to OVIR but it was refused because he had no relatives in Israel. He continued visiting the embassy in search of Hebrew literature until June 9, 1967, when a militia officer informed him that the Soviet Union had just severed diplomatic relations with Israel and the embassy would be closed indefinitely. Kazakov then went to the reception room of the Supreme Soviet in Moscow and spent two hours filling out a request for renunciation of Soviet citizenship. He submitted it on his twentieth birthday, four days later.

He wanted Americans to know about his situation so he headed for the U.S. Embassy, which was more difficult to penetrate than the Israeli Embassy. The militia officer on duty threatened to break his hands and arms if he didn't leave, and when he finally exited the building he was taken to a militia station, strip-searched, and questioned for several hours. He was dismissed with a warning not to go there again, and the KGB was informed of his activity. This resulted in his expulsion from Moscow State University.

Meanwhile Kazakov launched a campaign to publicize his renunciation. He gave copies of it to American journalists, West German tourists and personnel at the British Embassy.

Kazakov's parents were aware of his activities and were apprehensive, but his mother said, "It's better for you to leave because you have no future here." Kazakov himself felt that he had a ninety percent chance of being sent to jail instead of Israel: "I knew I would be going east, but I didn't know whether it would be the Far East (Siberia) or the Middle East (Israel)."[20]

After a year went by with no positive response to his application for an exit visa or his renunciation of Soviet citizenship, Kazakov wrote a letter to the Supreme Soviet demanding his right to emigrate. The letter reiterated his renunciation and declared:

> I am a Jew, I was born a Jew, and I want to live out my life as a Jew. With all my respect for the Russian people, I do not consider my people in any way to be inferior to the Russian, or any other people, and I do not want to be assimilated by any people.... I consider the State of Israel my fatherland, the fatherland of my people, the only place on earth where there exists an independent Jewish state, and I, like any other Jew, have an indubitable right to live in that state.

One of the copies of the letter that Kazakov gave to Western tourists wound up in the hands of Nechemia Levanon, who then was in charge of the Soviet Jewry desk at the Israeli Embassy in Washington. Levanon sent the letter to the editor of the *Washington Post* and it was published on December 19, 1968. Other media around the free world, fascinated by the courage of a twenty-year-old student who would challenge a superpower, reprinted and broadcast the letter. Throughout the USSR samizdat copies of Kazakov's letter circulated among the Jewish community.[21] Soviet authorities realized they had a potential troublemaker on their hands so they granted him an exit visa the following month. On February 15, 1969, Kazakov left Moscow for Vienna on his way to Israel.

With a good knowledge of Hebrew, Kazakov quickly acclimated to Israeli life.[22] He, along with a few other immigrants from
the Soviet Union who believed that Israel should be campaigning for free emigration and also should be broadcasting Jewish
cultural information in Russian over the Voice of Israel, met with
Shaul Avigur to bring their ideas to his attention with the hope
of getting the Lishka (Chapter 3) to change its policy of avoiding
any action that could be deemed anti-Soviet. "Why is it," Kazakov
asked, "that Russian Jews are not afraid to risk their lives by sending letters and petitions to the West, yet the Israelis, living in safety
and freedom, are fearful of publishing them?" Avigur would not
budge; he maintained his position that secret negotiations with
the Soviets had resulted in a trickle of Jews reaching Israel – about
twenty per month in 1968 – but open endorsement of free emigration might lead to a complete cessation of the flow.[23]

Ignoring the Lishka's fears, Kazakov appealed, in an advertisement placed by the sssj, in *The New York Times* on March 26,
1970, for a world protest against "the Soviet government's spiritual annihilation and forced detention of Soviet Jews." On a visit
to New York he declared a hunger strike at the Isaiah Wall of the
un to call attention to his family's refusal status.[24]

Despite his differences with Lishka's strategy two decades
earlier, Kazakov became its director in 1992. This followed exem-
plary service in the Israel Defense Forces and employment in the
Israeli Foreign Service. During the Yom Kippur War of October
1973 he was one of several new soldiers in a tank unit commanded
by Ehud Barak, who later became prime minister (1999–2001).
Barak recalled how Kazakov was not only the best gunner in the
brigade, but that he would also take two 25-kilogram shells un-
derarm and carry them to his tank. At that time the Soviet Union
was supporting Egypt in the war and Barak worried about what
would happen if Soviet troops were deployed to fight against Israel.
He commented to other commanders, "If all Red Army soldiers
are like Kazakov, we're in big trouble!"[25]

Kazakov joined the Israeli Foreign Service in 1978 and was

posted to the embassy in Vienna. In keeping with Foreign Service protocol he took a Hebrew name, Yaakov Kedmi. He directed the Lishka from 1992 until 1999 when he resigned in a policy dispute with prime minister Benjamin Netanyahu.[26] Although Kedmi has retired from public service, he remains an outspoken advocate for the rights of immigrants to Israel.

Baruch Ashi (né Boris Kochubievsky) at home in Jerusalem, 2006. Photo by Philip Spiegel.

CHAPTER EIGHT

The Foiled Hijacking that Launched an International Movement

Mark Dymshitz was born to fly. Perhaps there was something auspicious about his birth date, May 10, 1927, for on that day Charles A. Lindbergh was setting a transcontinental speed record as he flew his *Spirit of St. Louis* from San Diego to New York in preparation for his monumental New York to Paris flight ten days later.[1]

Dymshitz entered the Soviet Air Force at the end of World War II and was trained as a pilot. This was a time when the Soviet military, decimated by four years of the "Great Patriotic War" against the Nazis, could ill-afford the luxury of anti-Semitism. Dymshitz's skill and leadership abilities were recognized and he advanced to the rank of major at age 30.

But by 1960 anti-Semitism was rampant and even though he was a thoroughly assimilated Communist Party member, married to a Russian woman and with two daughters whose nationalities were registered as Russian, Dymshitz was offered a choice:

demobilization or a demeaning assignment. He chose to leave the Air Force and sought a job in civil aviation in Leningrad where he and his family resided, but his Jewish nationality was a barrier. The only work open to him as a pilot was in Uzbekistan piloting 12-seater AN-2 planes. In 1966 he moved back to Leningrad and studied agricultural engineering but kept looking for opportunities to fly, even in Uzbekistan.[2]

Israel's victory in the Six-Day War stirred up pride in his Jewishness. He joined an *ulpan* in Leningrad and learned about Zionism. Getting to Israel became his obsession but he realized that a former major in the Soviet Air Force was hardly a candidate for an exit visa.[3] He knew he would have to escape. Should he climb over mountains? Swim under water to Turkey using home-built scuba gear? Fly over a border in a hot-air balloon or a small plane? Yes, a small plane! He would, with other Jews who were also desperate to escape to Israel, hijack a plane! However, there would be no violence and innocent people must not be harmed; unlike the hijackings that occurred in the following decades.

PLANS FOR A WEDDING

In December 1969 Dymshitz broached his idea to Hillel Butman, with whom he studied Hebrew. Dymshitz proposed to buy tickets for an AN-2 flight to Yerevan, Armenia, and order the pilot to divert to Turkey. If the pilot refused, the other passengers would overpower him and Dymshitz would take over the controls. Butman did not laugh at Dymshitz's wild scenario; instead he considered expanding it to enable a larger number of Jews to get out of Russia. This meant a larger plane rather than one flying to Yerevan. Why not fly from Leningrad? The closest country that might be amenable to giving asylum would be Sweden. Landing there represented an opportunity to publicize the plight of Soviet Jews and impact world opinion. Dymshitz and Butman agreed upon a 52-passenger TU-124 flying between Leningrad and Murmansk as their target. They worked out plans for avoiding Soviet radar and communicating with air traffic controllers.

Butman discussed the plan in a secret meeting of his "Committee" and they voted unanimously to allocate money to investigate whether the hijacking would be feasible. Dymshits used 75 rubles from Butman to buy himself a ticket on a flight to Moscow.

While on board he was invited into the cockpit by an old friend from Uzbekistan. Dymshits thus familiarized himself with the plane's layout and equipment. Over dinner with his old friend, Dymshits learned that the crew usually didn't carry the weapons they had been issued.

During the first three months of 1970 Butman discussed the plan with forty of his closest associates and hid the list of their names. One of them, Misha Korenblit, went to Kishinev to recruit additional passengers. Butman flew to Riga to see Sylva Zalmanson, who had been helping Butman publish samizdat. Sylva was one of the signers of the 1969 letter to U Thant. Her application for an exit visa was refused because the moped factory where she worked would not provide a character reference. She told Butman that she had just married Edik Kuznetsov, from Moscow, who had served seven years in prison for anti-Soviet propaganda and that he was now working as an English translator in a psychiatric hospital in Riga. As they walked together Butman disclosed the hijack plan. She was excited about it but questioned whether it was feasible. She assured Butman that he could trust her husband and that she was determined to reach Israel by any means, however impossible they might seem.

The next day Butman and Kuznetsov went to the Rumbula memorial site and talked about the plot. Butman observed that for Sylva Zalmanson the operative word was *Israel*; while for Kuznetsov it was *freedom*. Kuznetsov emphasized the importance of having trustworthy people involved in the operation and recommended two non-Jewish dissidents who had served prison time with him and were completely reliable – Yuri Fedorov and Alexsey Murzhenko.[4] As a student in Moscow, Fedorov had participated in "Freedom for Intellect", a human rights group that distributed denunciations of the Soviet regime. At nineteen he had been arrested by the KGB and sentenced to five years in prison. Murzhenko, a Ukrainian human rights activist, was also nineteen when he was arrested for anti-Soviet propaganda. He served six years in prison and, like Fedorov and Kuznetsov, had a deep yearning for freedom.

Another member of the Riga Zionists who worked on *samizdat* publications with Butman was Yosef Mendelevich. He had been an electronics student at Riga Polytechnic Institute but dropped out in his final year, 1968, in order to apply for an exit visa, which was denied. He reapplied and was sent to a mental institution. However, he was found "sane but not to be trusted with weapons" so he was exempted from military service and spent most of his time as editor of *Iton*, the national Zionist samizdat newspaper. On one of Mendelevich's frequent trips to Leningrad he learned of the plot from Butman.[5] Mendelevich's sister, Meri, and her husband, Leib Khnokh, were also active among the Riga Zionists and eager to participate.[6] Mendelevich himself thought that the plotters had an 80 percent chance of being killed or arrested, but felt that it was worth trying and that there would be support from the West on their behalf.[7]

There were enough potential passengers to fill a TU-124 airliner, but Butman feared that so many Jews flying on the same plane from Leningrad to Murmansk would arouse suspicion and a possible KGB investigation. So he suggested that everyone involved pretend that they were going to a wedding in Murmansk. The operation then took the code name "Wedding". May 2, 1970, was set as the wedding date. May Day was a major holiday in the Soviet Union so the participants would be off work and radar operators who had been partying might be less vigilant the following day. The conspirators also agreed that they would not use weapons to overtake the crew, and they would be careful to avoid injuring anyone. They would fly on the 1 P.M. flight on May 2.[8]

SECOND THOUGHTS

In early April some of the people who were in on Operation Wedding were beginning to doubt whether it was a good idea. They feared reprisals, including the shutting down of the ulpanim. A secret conference was convened and two of the conspirators, David Chernoglaz and Vladik Mogilever, asked Butman to abandon the plan. Butman felt strongly that if Operation Wedding succeeded in enabling aliyah for fifty refuseniks it would be well worth the expected reprisals. On the other hand, if the hopes and dreams of thousands of Jews would be forever shattered, he could never forgive himself. The dilemma was resolved with the suggestion from ulpan member Grisha Vertlib, who said, "Let's ask Israel." Butman agreed to put Operation Wedding on hold until they could obtain input from the Israeli government.[9]

A few days later at a Passover Seder in Mogilever's apartment, Butman was introduced to Dr. Rami Aronzon, a Jewish tourist from Norway who had shown up at the Leningrad synagogue for services on the previous Sabbath.

Aronzon's family had moved to Israel when Rami was fifteen, and Aronzon's father served briefly as the rabbi at Kibbutz Sa'ad where Aryeh Kroll lived (see Chapter 3). Two years later Rami returned to Norway to attend college and medical school. What his *Seder* hosts did not know was that Aronzon was in Russia on a mission sponsored by Kroll, who knew that Aronzon was an observant Jew who had been a member of Bnei Akiva, a religious Zionist youth movement.

Aronzon actually conducted the Seder for several hours, proving to everyone that he was not a KGB agent. He recalls there was matzah and that he brought some kosher wine. But for *maror* (bitter herbs) someone remarked: "Just open a window and inhale the air of oppression." Mogilever and Butman arranged a secret rendezvous with Aronzon in a park the following day, and in Hebrew, almost drowned out by fireworks celebrating Lenin's birthday, Butman told Aronzon about the underground ulpan and the organization behind it. Then he disclosed Operation Wedding and the dispute within the organization, and finally the need to get an opinion from Israel. Aronzon was horrified at what he considered to be a suicidal scheme and advised against it, but he agreed to memorize what he had just heard and from outside the Soviet Union he would write a letter to Dr. Asher Blank, who had been a Leningrad ulpan member until he immigrated to Israel in 1969.

Blank would be asked to call Butman and advise "what Israeli doctors think is the best treatment for Butman's mother." "Take her on a trip" was code for hijack an airplane; "fresh air in the park" would mean stage a demonstration; "consultation" would represent the option to hold a press conference.

Aronzon traveled by train from Moscow to Finland on May 2 and continued to Stockholm where he stayed at the home of Seth Jacobson, a friend from his Bnei Akiva days and, until November 1972, coordinator of Kroll's operations in Scandinavia. Aronzon wrote an 18-page report in English that included everything he had learned about the Zionists in Leningrad and the proposed hijacking. Jacobson arranged for the delivery of the report to Kroll in Israel. Later that month, Aronzon, back in the small Norwegian town where he worked as a medical intern, received an urgent phone call requesting that he meet someone from Israel at an airport in London the next day. He complied and met Kroll's boss Nechemia Levanon, who was returning from meetings in the United States and had just received and read Aronzon's report. Levanon was incredulous. Over and over he asked, "Do you stand by what you wrote in this report?" and "Is there really a Zionist organization in Leningrad?" He couldn't believe that there were more than a handful of people who organized Hebrew schools, mimeographed Jewish cultural materials and had connections to like-minded Jews in Moscow and Riga.[10]

On May 25 Dr. Blank in Israel telephoned Butman and told him that "taking your mother on a trip" would be harmful. Butman told Dymshitz about the call and Dymshitz said, "If Israel is against the plan then I agree to abandon it." Thus all of the Leningrad participants withdrew from the operation. But the attitude in Riga was different. When Mogilever phoned Sylva Zalmanson and told her that the advice from Israel was against "taking a trip," she replied: "In any case the patient is better," implying acquiescence with the agreement to cancel Operation Wedding. Actually the Riga group and Dymshitz had a new plan.[11]

THE WEDDING IS DOWNSIZED

Dymshitz had learned of a newly scheduled flight route, using an AN-2, from Smolny Airport, outside Leningrad, to Priozersk, a small town on Lake Ladoga. It is now believed that this new route was actually devised by the KGB as a trap for the would-be hijackers.[12] In fact, Yuri Andropov, who would, twelve years later, become general secretary of the Soviet Union, wrote a memorandum on April 30, 1970, to the Central Committee of the Communist Party of the Soviet Union in his capacity as chairman of the Committee for State Security, i.e.: head of the KGB, that named Butman and Chernoglaz as leaders of a "Zionist organization in Leningrad consisting of…nationalistically minded citizens." The memorandum concluded:

> Unconfirmed sources report that at the meeting of the committee on 26 April of this year an action was proposed, the nature of which is being kept in strictest confidence and for the implementation of which Jewish nationalists living in Riga are being enlisted. The majority of the members of the committee spoke out against this action, fearing that it could pose a threat to their organization and to its members. Thus, they considered it necessary to receive sanction from Israel's ruling circles. The Committee for State Security is taking measures to verify the information received and to prevent the realization of possible hostile actions on the part of the Jewish nationalists.[13]

The new version of Operation Wedding would involve 12 conspirators buying tickets for all the seats on a flight from Smolny to Priozersk. Upon landing they would overpower the pilot and co-pilot, tie them up and leave them in a nearby forest. Then other conspirators who were waiting in Priozersk would board the plane and Dymshits, in the pilot's seat, would immediately take off for Sweden. The scaled-down wedding was set for June 15.[14]

On the evening of June 14 Leib and Meri Khnokh, Sylva Zalmanson and a new recruit, Boris Penson, boarded a train from Leningrad to a station close to Priozersk. They walked to the forest near Priozersk Airport and camped there for the night to await the arrival of the plane from Leningrad. The next morning at Smolny Airport there were twelve passengers bearing wedding gifts at the gate for the Priozersk-bound plane. In this group were Dymshits and his wife and daughters, plus Kuznetsov, Mendelevich, Fedorov, Murzhenko, Israel and Wulf Zalmanson (Sylva's brothers) and new recruits Anatoly Altman and Mendel Bodnya.[15]

ARRESTS AND SEARCHES

The group in the Priozersk forest thought they were safe. But at 3 A.M. a uniformed man appeared in the forest near the sleepers, fired a shot over Sylva Zalmanson's head and shouted: "Hands up!" Soon dogs and twenty officers arrived, spraying tear gas into the eyes of the four would-be hijackers, who were then tied up, handcuffed and loaded into trucks headed for a jail in Leningrad. This was just the beginning of a long day of anti-Zionist arrests and searches throughout the Soviet Union.

At 8 A.M. the group of twelve at Smolny Airport who were ready to board the flight to Priozersk with their wedding gifts were arrested and roughed up by KGB officers from Moscow and Leningrad. Other Leningrad activists including Butman, Mogilever and Vertlib were arrested at their homes or workplaces. Some of the Zionist committee members from Leningrad were arrested in other cities where they were vacationing or on business trips. Additional suspects and their materials pertaining to Israel were seized during KGB raids in Moscow, Riga, Kiev, Kharkov and Kishinev.

The Priozersk and Smolny defendants were held incommunicado and interrogated. Meri Khnokh was released because she was pregnant. Wulf Zalmanson, a lieutenant in the Soviet Army, was turned over to military authorities to face a tribunal for desertion, in addition to other charges. Dymshits's wife and daughters were released when it was determined that they were not conspirators but were just going along for the ride.

The West first learned of the case from a Page 1 story in *The New York Times* of June 22, 1970, that was based on a report that was published in *Leningradskaya Pravda* the morning after the arrests. It said that "all those apprehended were being detained pending investigation under Article 64-A of the Russian Federation Criminal Code, which is the article for treason. Among the crimes listed as treasonous are 'flight abroad'. Punishment under that article ranges from 10 years' confinement to death."[16]

Five days later the *Times* published a story headlined "Leningrad Jew Says 8 Held Are Innocent." It told of a letter written to Soviet attorney general Roman Rudenko by Viktor Boguslavsky, one of the dozens of Jews whose homes were searched on June 15, which asserted: "They never planned to steal an airplane, but they would be happy if they could buy a ticket to Vienna, even if they had to sell their last shirt."

Referring to the Jews who were not in Leningrad on the day they were arrested, Boguslavsky asks:

> What connection could they have had with the incident at Smolny Airport? Their only guilt is that they were born Jews and sought to remain such. They thirstily devoured rare information about the history of their people. They studied their mother tongue. The fate of their relatives and friends in Israel concerned them. They were not indifferent to the fate of the State of Israel, recalling the great tragedy in the history of their people.[17]

For writing this letter Boguslavsky was charged with anti-Soviet agitation and propaganda and sentenced to three years in prison.

THE FIRST LENINGRAD TRIAL

After over four months of investigations a trial was set to begin on December 15 in Leningrad City Court.[18] Although it was announced as an open trial only 200 seats were available and special passes were given to Communist Party functionaries who were hostile to the defendants. Fewer than thirty of seats were occupied by relatives of the defendants.[19] The highly successful and controversial American defense attorney, F. Lee Bailey, and Telford Taylor, who as chief U.S. prosecutor at Nuremberg had established the guidelines for trying German war criminals after World War II, requested permission to attend the trial but the Soviets refused to admit them.

The case would be heard by a panel of three – a chief judge and two laymen. The prosecutor, S.Y. Solovyiev, was regarded by Leningrad Jews as anti-Semitic. Each defendant had a lawyer but defense attorneys in Soviet courtrooms were never known for aggressively supporting their clients.[20]

Human rights activist Elena Bonner, a friend of Kuznetsov's, claiming to be his aunt and effectively his next-of-kin, was given a pass to the trial. She recorded each day's proceedings and either she or a friend would take the report to Moscow for copying and distribution to Western journalists and to her friend, famed physicist and human rights leader Andrei Sakharov, who viewed the affair as "yet another tragic consequence of the USSR's failure to permit emigration."[21] All of the defendants except Fedorov and Murzhenko entered guilty pleas and stated that their goal was to emigrate to Israel.[22]

The prosecution would not permit introduction of a document written by Mendelevich and signed by eight of his co-conspirators that had been found by the KGB. The "Testament" could be regarded as a possible suicide note, declaring the group's intentions if they were to perish in their daring action. It stated: "We, nine Jews living in the Soviet Union, are attempting to leave the territory of the state without requesting the permission of the authorities…Being an alien element in that country, we are constantly threatened with a recurrence of the events of the '40s and '50s when the policy of spiritual genocide reached its apotheosis in the physical annihilation of the Jews..." It included a plea to UN Secretary General U Thant to "take steps to put an end to the violation of elementary human liberties," and a challenge to world Jewry: "Jews of the world! It is your holy duty to struggle for the freedom of your brothers in the USSR. Know that, to a great extent, the fate of the Jews of Russia depends on you..." The "Testament" closed with a pledge of nonviolence: "It should be stressed that our actions represent no danger for outsiders; when the plane takes off, we will be the only ones on board."[23]

After a week of testimony and cross-examination Solovyiev delivered his summation, which included a harangue about the "intrigues of international Zionism" and then stated his request for penalties: death by firing squad for Dymshitz and Kuznetsov, fifteen years for Fedorov and Mendelevich, fourteen for Murzhenko, thirteen for Khnokh, twelve for Altman, Penson and Israel Zalmanson, ten for Sylva Zalmanson and five for Bodnya.[24] The defendants were then given the opportunity to make their final statements. Of these, Sylva Zalmanson's was the most memorable with a stirring and haunting effect not heard since the publication of Anne Frank's *Diary of a Young Girl*:

> I am completely overwhelmed. I am stunned by the sentences the prosecution has demanded for us. The procurator has just demanded the death penalty for something that has not been done. If the court agrees to this then such outstanding men as Dymshitz and Kuznetsov will perish. I do not think that Soviet law can possibly regard someone's intention to live in another country as treason, and I am convinced that those who unlawfully violate our right to live where we wish ought themselves to stand trial. Let the court at least note that, had we been permitted to leave, this 'criminal conspiracy', which has caused us – not to mention our relatives – so much pain, would never have happened. Israel is a country

to which we, as Jews, are tied both spiritually and historically. It is my hope that the Soviet government will decide this question positively in the near future. The dream of returning to our ancient homeland will never desert us. Several of us did not believe that our undertaking would be successful, or had little confidence in it. Even when we were at Finland Station we noticed we were being followed. But it was too late to turn back – to return to the past, to continue to wait and to live on our suitcases. Our dream of living in Israel was not to be compared with the fear of the pain it might cause us. By leaving this country we would have harmed no one. I wanted to live there as part of a family and work. I would not have been involved in politics. My entire interest in political matters was exhausted by my simple desire to leave. Not even now do I doubt for one moment that I will one day live in Israel, whatever happens. This dream of mine, consecrated by 2,000 years of waiting and hoping will never desert me. Next year in Jerusalem! 'If I forget thee, O Jerusalem, may my right hand wither!'

On Christmas Eve the court announced the sentences. They were exactly what Solovyiev requested except for ten years for Penson, eight for Israel Zalmanson and four for Bodnya[25]. The hostile spectators applauded the verdict, and when Elena Bonner stood up and screamed: "Fascists, how dare you applaud death?" they shouted back: "It serves them right!" Other defendants' relatives exclaimed: "Good lads!" "Don't give up!" "We'll see you in Israel!"[26]

Israel Zalmanson could not understand why the relatives were so positive; to him the operation was a total failure, leading to the arrest of others and the confiscation of fifteen typewriters. He sat next to Kuznetsov, who indicated that he expected to be executed because he said "Goodbye" to well-wishers who were saying *"L'Hitraot"* (Hebrew for "see you later") to all the prisoners.

Kuznetsov then lightened up a bit and told Zalmanson that his lawyer told him about people in Riga who had just obtained exit visas.[27]

Sakharov was shocked by the severity of the sentences and immediately sent a telegram to Brezhnev asking for commutation of the death sentences. As soon as news of the verdicts reached the West the Kremlin was flooded with messages of outrage.[28] The pope and other religious and civil rights leaders worldwide urged clemency. Thousands in Israel protested and demonstrated. Even the Communist parties in France and Italy expressed their indignation. Referring to the sentencing to death in Spain of six Basque separatists earlier that year, a European newspaper cartoon showed Brezhnev and Spain's dictator, Francisco Franco, dancing around a Christmas tree decorated with hanged men.

Franco actually commuted the Basques' death sentences on Christmas Day, and Brezhnev became convinced that the Kremlin was in an embarrassing situation because the Soviet press had denounced those death sentences when they were first imposed by their Fascist enemy. Suddenly the Russian Supreme Court announced that an appeal hearing would be held on December 30. On New Year's Eve the court commuted the two death sentences to fifteen years' imprisonment for Dymshitz and Kuznetsov. Mendelevich's sentence was reduced to twelve years and the sentences for Altman and Khnokh were reduced to ten years.

ACTIVISTS IN THE WEST JOINS RANKS
TO SUPPORT SOVIET JEWRY

Even though the death sentences were commuted, countless individuals in the West considered the trial a wake-up call to protest Soviet anti-Semitism.[29] The sssj held emotional demonstrations every day during the trial. When the trial was over people made and kept New Year's resolutions to support Soviet Jews.[30]

As a law student at McGill University, Irwin Cotler organized the first Canadian branch of sssj in 1964. Recently as Canada's minister of justice he recalls that: "The demonstrations worldwide on behalf of the Leningrad prisoners served to solidify public advocacy, not only as a strategy, but as a medium of redress."[31]

In an editorial on December 31, 1970, *The New York Times* declared: "until Moscow takes the bonds off these unhappy people by recognizing the legitimacy of their desire to emigrate, it will be subject to embarrassment and justified world censure of the type that now besets it." In New York the sssj staged a "Stalin Lives Again" rally on January 7, 1971. The Jewish Defense League, led by the charismatic and militant Rabbi Meir Kahane, deviated from the non-violence of the sssj. Their tactics included harassment of Soviet officials, detonation of bombs at Soviet buildings in New York and holding a demonstration in Washington that led to 1,300 arrests.[32]

THE SECOND LENINGRAD TRIAL

On May 11, 1971, nine prisoners who were arrested at locations other than Smolny Airport and Priozersk and actually opposed the hijacking scheme were put on trial in Leningrad. Butman and Korenblit were charged with treason because they had participated in the early meetings of the hijack planners. All the defendants were charged with anti-Soviet agitation and propaganda and found guilty. Butman and Korenblit were sentenced to ten and seven years in prison respectively. The others received sentences of from one to four years. As in response to the first Leningrad trial, there were outcries of protest from the West against the Soviet regime and support for the "Leningrad Nine." The Jesuit weekly *America* summed up the prevailing concern of the Roman Catholic clergy in the United States:

> Catholics have in the past decades ample reason to know what persecution means and, by the same token, to appreciate the helping hand of a friend. The plight of the Jews in the Soviet Union should and does concern Catholics – and not Jews only. Human liberty is indivisible.[33]

In the U.S. Congress the Brock-Jackson resolution, passed on July 12, 1971, called upon the State Department to raise the issue of Soviet violations of the Universal Declaration of Human Rights in the General Assembly of the United Nations.

Soviet leaders responded to the criticism and also attempted to rid themselves of Zionist troublemakers by increasing the number of exit visas issued in 1971 by tenfold over any previous year. Thirteen thousand Soviet Jews were allowed to emigrate to Israel.[34]

Dymshitz, Kuznetsov, Mendelevich and Sylva Zalmanson remained in a Leningrad jail until the end of May 1971 so that they could testify in the Second Leningrad Trial. When the trial was over they were sent to a labor camp for political prisoners in Potma, a desolate swampy area 335 miles east of Moscow. Sylva Zalmanson quickly learned about the rigors of life in the Gulag where prisoners would be given extra food if they informed on other inmates, anti-Semitism was unbridled and the temperature in the unheated cells went down to 40 degrees below zero. She was prepared, having been briefed by Kuznetsov, her ex-con husband, to get out of bed and jump up and down in order to speed up blood circulation. Working at sewing canvas work gloves under poor light with unreliable machines trying to meet unrealistic production quotas made her ill.

Word of Sylva Zalmanson's prison conditions reached the West from another Potma prisoner who was released and allowed to emigrate to Israel. Ruta Alexandrovich graphically described Sylva's plight during a press conference in London. Sylva became the martyr of the Leningrad hijackers and Meir Kahane warned that if "anything happens to her or another Jew, Soviet diplomats around the world will be targets for Jewish militants."[35]

RELEASE, ALIYAH AND CAMPAIGNING

In the spring of 1974 when Yuri Linov, a colonel in Soviet intelligence, had been caught red-handed spying in Tel Aviv, prime minister Yitzhak Rabin secretly arranged a deal with Soviet leaders whereby Linov would be freed in exchange for Sylva Zalmanson as well as a Jew sentenced to death in Bulgaria on charges of spying for the United States. Sylva initially said she would not leave Russia until her husband and brothers were freed, but had to settle for meetings with them in Moscow, and on August 23, 1974, she flew to Israel. From Israel she immediately launched a campaign to win freedom for her family and friends. In the fall of 1974 she went on a speaking tour of the United States and a year later she returned to stage a hunger strike at the Isaiah Wall opposite the United Nations building to demand the release of her husband and brothers, and to demand that she be allowed to visit them in Soviet prisons. Thousands of New Yorkers including elected officials maintained the vigil with her and signed a petition on her behalf. On the sixteenth day of the strike Sylva collapsed and was taken to Beth Israel Hospital. She was released after five days and held a press conference to thank all her supporters and to announce plans to continue her efforts.[36]

Sylva tirelessly campaigned for the next four years and finally on April 27, 1979, while she was in London, she received a telephone call from Jerry Goodman, the executive director of the National Conference on Soviet Jewry: "Fly to New York immediately! Edik is here, freed in a prisoner exchange! Dymshitz is here too." Goodman had just been informed of the exchange by Carter's security advisor, Zbigniew Brzezinski, who said some Soviet spies had been caught on the New Jersey Turnpike and, after secret negotiations, the Soviets swapped Dymshitz and Kuznetsov along with a political dissident and an Orthodox priest for them. Sylva and Edik had a private reunion in New York and flew to Israel. Dymshitz flew on an El Al plane and was the captain's guest of honor in the cockpit. During the flight he chatted with the pilot about how to qualify for an Israeli civilian pilot's license. A few days earlier the Soviets had released Altman, Butman, Khnokh, Penson and Wulf Zalmanson and allowed them to fly to Israel. Of the original desperate dozen only Fedorov, Mendelevich and Murzhenko remained in prison.[37]

INCREDIBLE FAITH

Mendelevich entered prison with a deep commitment to observe every aspect of Judaism that he possibly could. His determination was reminiscent of the courageous dedication and unwillingness to bend displayed by rabbis Schneersohn and Futerfas decades earlier. As soon as Mendelevich arrived at the labor camp in Perm, in the Ural Mountains, the KGB colonel in charge threatened to punish him if he didn't uncover his head. Mendelevich refused to remove his *kippah* and said he was not afraid of punishment or even dying, and furthermore, he said he would not work on the Sabbath. He told the colonel, "Those who will die by the commands of Brezhnev are afraid of death. However, those who believe that our death will be by the command of God are not afraid of His command."

By November 1980 Mendelevich had acquired a suitcase full of Jewish books left behind by prisoners who had been released. KGB officers confiscated the books. Mendelevich demanded their return and the right to teach Hebrew to other inmates. When the authorities turned him down he went on a hunger strike. He felt it was important to let supporters in the West know about his hunger strike and counted on Ida Nudel, the "guardian angel" of prisoners of conscience, to be his communications link. Mendelevich gave the wife of a friendly Ukrainian nationalist prisoner visiting her husband a detailed message to send to Nudel.

Nudel earned her nickname by corresponding with prisoners, sending them parcels of food, medicine and books, visiting them in the camps, prisons and transport points, and advocating for them regarding violations of prisoners' rights.[38] She was relentless in pursuing her own demand to emigrate to Israel. In 1978, after seven years of waiting, she hung a banner from her balcony in Moscow reading, "KGB: GIVE ME A VISA TO ISRAEL." For this she was arrested, convicted of "malicious hooliganism" and sentenced to four years of exile in Siberia. In 1982 she was allowed to leave Siberia but instead of returning to Moscow, she was forced to reside in Bendery, Moldavia.[39]

A postcard from Nudel with a picture of Lenin's statue was handed to Mendelevich six weeks later. It was the one piece of mail the KGB was happy to deliver to him; it confirmed that Nudel had received his message. For fifty-six days he drank water but ate no food and his weight dropped from 176 to 121 pounds.[40] Word of the hunger strike reached the United States and Mendelevich's books were returned after ambassador Max Kampelman protested to Soviet officials during the Madrid conference for review of the Helsinki Accords.[41]

After years in prison Mendelevich was determined to celebrate *Chanukah*. To do so he fashioned a menorah out of stale bread and used forty-four matches, obtained from another prisoner in exchange for some food, as candles. Each night when the guards were out of sight he lit the requisite number of matches and, although they burned for only a few seconds, Mendelevich reveled in fulfilling a *mitzvah* in the depths of Vladimir Prison.

After nearly eleven years in Soviet prisons, he was released and told: "By decision of the Supreme Soviet you do not deserve to be a Soviet citizen and you can no longer stay on this sacred soil." This was music to his ears as he boarded a plane for Vienna on his way to a his new life as a rabbi in Israel.

Once in Israel Mendelevich launched a campaign for the release of the last two Leningrad hijack prisoners, Yuri Fedorov and Aleksei Murchenko.[42] Because they were not Jewish the KGB had particularly resented their participation in the plot to help Jews escape from Russia and at the trial they were told, "It will be worse for you." No pleas or pressure could get them released early, especially during the early 1980s when the top Kremlin leadership was going through the succession of Brezhnev to Andropov to Chernenko and there was little interest in détente with the West. Murzhenko was finally released in 1984 but rearrested briefly in 1985 for a parole violation. He died on December 31, 1999.

Fedorov, the only defendant in the group who refused to plead guilty to any charge, served his entire fifteen-year term and was released in 1985. A year later he applied for an exit visa and flew to New York, where he worked for the New York Association for New Americans helping Russian-speaking immigrants start new lives in America. In 1998 he returned to Russia to visit friends and relatives and was appalled at the miserable conditions of poverty under which former prison camp inmates were living, so he founded the Gratitude Fund to provide assistance to "veterans of the struggle for freedom whose imprisonment lasted more than fifteen years and who are more than sixty years old." Fedorov, a selfless, saintly man, unchanged by years in the Gulag, says in the Gratitude Fund prospectus: "Soviet power collapsed and the ideas of communism came tumbling down. None of it would have happened if it weren't for the many people who sacrificed their personal freedom and their lives for democracy."[43]

*Sylva Zalmanson on hunger strike in New York demanding
the right to visit her husband, Edward Kuznetsov. Photo
from Yeshiva University Archives, SSSJ Collection.*

CHAPTER NINE

You Will Never Leave
the Soviet Union

R efusenik: Why was my application refused?
KGB Officer: State secrecy.

Refusenik: But I quit doing classified work years ago and our technology was ten years behind the West.

KGB Officer: Aha, that's the secret![1]

The refusenik in this often-told joke could have been Alexander Lerner, Vladimir Slepak or Yuli Kosharovsky. All of them were electrified by Israel's victory in the Six-Day War and dreamed of making aliyah, but they knew that their access to state secrets would prevent them from obtaining exit visas. All transferred to non-classified work, waited three years, and then expected to be part of the growing number of Jews who were emigrating in 1970 and 1971.

Their applications were refused and they were dismissed from their jobs. In 1976 they were part of a delegation who met with Comrade Albert Ivanov, chief of the Administrative Department of the Central Committee, to express their grievances, and to ask to speak to whoever made decisions about refusals for security reasons. Ivanov replied, "Nobody will be allowed to see the committee that made these decisions. It would be unthinkable to dispute a policy determined by one of our Soviet scientific institutes.[2] Moreover, the reasons for establishing such a policy are always confidential."[3] In fact, as they would learn later, their KGB files were marked "Never to leave Soviet Union." Nevertheless, they never stopped believing that they would emigrate someday.[4]

VLADIMIR SLEPAK

Life in Moscow for the Slepaks in the early 1960s was just about as good it could be for a Jewish family. Vladimir, nicknamed Volodya, was in charge of a secret laboratory developing radar display screens for the Ministry of Defense. His wife, Masha, was a radiologist at a city hospital where most of the doctors were Jewish. Their older son, Alexander, was attending a "Special English School" for children of the ruling elite. After Leonid was born in 1959, they moved into the relatively luxurious apartment on Gorky Street that Volodya's father, Semyon, graciously turned over to the growing family.

The Slepaks enjoyed summer vacations in the forests near Moscow where they could camp, hike, fish and swim. They often went on camping and sailing expeditions with friends who were also Jewish professionals. Volodya had a shortwave radio, and in these remote locations he was able to tune in to unjammed Russian-language broadcasts from America, Britain, Germany and Israel. News of Israel's victory in the Six-Day War exhilarated the Slepaks, Drapkins, Polskys and Prestins as they sat around campfires after a day of kayaking on Lake Tzesarka in Lithuania.

The conversations were guarded and the children were warned to say nothing about them to anyone when they returned to Moscow. Masha reminded Volodya that she had dreamed of emigrating to Israel two years earlier but Volodya thought she was being capricious. When friends asked if he would come to the Simchat Torah celebration at Moscow's synagogue Volodya declined, fearing that his security clearance could be jeopardized if the KGB or militia observed him there.

Masha's desire to emigrate stemmed from her experience as an intern in 1952, working with Jewish doctors who had been arrested in the Doctors' Plot.[5] She knew the plot was a fraud and returned home from work every evening with horrifying stories of honest doctors accused of being spies and traitors.[6] Her father-in-law brushed off her concerns with a Stalinesque declaration, "It is better to prosecute one hundred innocent people than to let one traitor go free." Volodya defended his wife and shouted at his father, "I will never accept such a philosophy. I will never join your party!"

With those words Volodya distanced himself from his father just as Semyon had rebelled against his own father.[7] In 1913 Semyon, then named Solomon, had refused to become a rabbi and instead ran away to New York, where he washed skyscraper windows, studied medicine and learned English by reading newspapers. He became a Marxist revolutionary and as soon as he read about the abdication of tsar Nicholas II he returned to Russia via Canada, sailing from Vancouver to Vladivostok. There he fought in the Bolshevik army and was almost killed. As the Bolsheviks took control throughout Russia, Semyon advanced in the Soviet regime, ultimately becoming responsible for support of the Communist insurgency in China, and later serving as a Politburo aide in Moscow who summarized the foreign press for Stalin's top echelon of leadership. Though he had narrowly escaped arrest and death during Stalin's purges, Semyon wept when Stalin died.[8] Several years later Volodya asked Semyon if he knew about the mass deportation of Jews that had been planned just prior to Stalin's death. Semyon admitted having known about it and doing nothing to prevent the family from being shipped off to a labor camp. Volodya was incredulous to hear that his own father, after the horrors of Auschwitz, could allow such evil and said, "You must have been crazy to help them do this against you." Semyon walked out silently, and never again discussed politics with his son.[9]

For their vacation in 1968 the Slepaks and their friends found an uninhabited island in the Dnieper River where they could sail, camp and listen to news from the West on Voldoya's short-wave radio. They were appalled to learn of the Soviet invasion of Czechoslovakia. It was a devastating blow to anyone who thought that liberalization was coming any time soon. Some spoke about emigrating.

Soon after returning to Moscow the Drapkins invited their friends to meet a group of Jews from Riga who had received exit visas and were in Moscow to get their Israeli entry visas from the Dutch Embassy. One of the Riga contingent offered to help the Moscow Jews find relatives in Israel who would provide official letters of invitation. Masha looked at Volodya and said, "This is a special opportunity. Are you ready to do it?" Volodya didn't respond at first, so she reiterated, "Who knows when it might happen again? We must use this opportunity." Volodya nodded in agreement, "Let's do it!"

Four months later the Slepaks received an invitation from a woman in Israel who claimed to be a relative. Volodya knew that such letters were routinely opened and read by KGB agents who would inform employers of their contents. He took the first step and told his boss that he wished to resign because he had found another job. The boss offered to promote him to head of the department with a higher salary, but Volodya refused and started working for an oil prospecting and mapping organization at a lower salary. In March 1970 the Slepaks were ready to submit their application for exit visas. Only one document was missing: a signed statement from Semyon Slepak that he had no objection to his son's emigration. Volodya telephoned his father and asked him for the statement. Semyon was adamant, "I will never write or sign such a statement! Do not call me again! I will not have anything to do with an enemy of the people!" Volodya was crushed. However, he was able to convince the OVIR official to forgo the required statement from his father, but his new employer provided a character reference for him only on condition that he quit his position.

After many weeks of waiting, Volodya was informed that OVIR had refused his application due to secrecy and that he could reapply after five years. The Slepaks were now refuseniks and a visit from Major Nosov and four KGB officers made clear what their new status really meant. Nosov came with a search warrant in connection with the case of Yuri Fedorov and the foiled Leningrad hijacking. Volodya stated that he didn't know Fedorov and had no anti-Soviet material. Nevertheless, after more than twelve hours of meticulous searching, every foreign-language book in the Slepak library, his tape recorder, shortwave radio (his only connection to the free world), and a broken typewriter were put into sacks and taken away.[10]

During the spring of 1971 a committee called the Women for Soviet Jewry was organized in Canada and started making telephone calls to refuseniks. Russian-born Genya Intrator of Toronto acted as coordinator and interpreter. Volodya Slepak was one of the people they called and his descriptions of refusenik life and emigration trends were circulated to like-minded support groups in the West.[11]

Slepak was sure his apartment was bugged by the KGB and he had to be careful to never make any anti-Soviet statements. Vladimir Bukovsky, a leading dissident, visited the Slepak apartment and introduced Volodya to journalists from Reuters and UPI. To circumvent the bugging Bukovsky pulled out a child's magic slate and passed it around for their conversation. The very next day these journalists had stories to report to the West. Slepak and fifteen other refuseniks staged a sit-in at the Office of the General Procurator to protest their refusals. They had to be forcibly removed and were given fifteen days in jail. During this time they took a leaf from Mahatma Gandhi's notebook and staged a hunger strike, taking water but no food. After thirteen days the militia broke the strike by force-feeding one of the prisoners.[12]

A well-publicized hunger strike could be highly effective in galvanizing support from the West. The Slepaks and other refuseniks staged another one in October 1973 to show solidarity with Israel during the Yom Kippur War. In June 1975, to protest their five years in refusal, Volodya fasted for twenty-four days and Masha fasted for fourteen. Their final hunger strike took place in 1987, after seventeen years of refusal, and lasted for seventeen days. While Masha and Volodya were fasting in Moscow, their sons, who had been able to emigrate in 1977 and 1979, staged their seventeen-day hunger strike on the steps of the U.S. Capitol in Washington.[13]

Refuseniks were extremely excited when they heard the announcement that Nixon would visit Moscow in the spring of 1972 for summit meetings with Brezhnev. Slepak was one of a committee that issued a statement to the press offering to apprise Nixon of the situation of the Jews in Moscow who had been "long unsuccessful in obtaining permission to emigrate to Israel." The last thing the KGB wanted was any kind of demonstration during Nixon's visit, so they disconnected the telephones of refusenik leaders, arrested them for "preventive confinement," and took them to towns outside of Moscow where they were held incommunicado for the duration of the summit.[14]

Volodya's next arrest was in 1978 for displaying a banner that read, "LET US GO TO OUR SON IN ISRAEL" from the balcony of the Slepak apartment. He was sentenced to five years of internal exile for "malicious hooliganism." Masha was also arrested and tried but her sentence was suspended due to her poor health. Volodya was sent to a *kolkhoz* in Eastern Siberia, close to the Chinese border. Masha managed to travel there and spend some time with him.[15]

Despite the freezing cold and the isolation, Slepak found some advantages in his exile. During the harvest season there was no one working in the town's telephone station so the chairman of the collective farm asked Slepak if he could work as the operator. "Of course," Slepak replied, "Nothing is too difficult for me."[16] For several months, until the KGB found out, he had a window of opportunity to speak to friends all over the world and told people in Moscow that he could hear unjammed broadcasts of the BBC.[17]

Masha and Volodya returned to their Gorky Street apartment when Volodya was released from exile at the end of 1982. They had an eleven-month wait to get their internal passports and residency permits reinstated and during that time Volodya was unable to work. Once he had these documents he reapplied for an exit visa, but again it was refused for secrecy reasons. To avoid arrest for violation of the anti-parasitism statute, he took a job as elevator operator in a hospital and morgue.[18]

Working nights, he was able to be visited at his apartment by supporters from the West during the day. One of them, congressman James Scheuer of New York, took a strong interest in his case and brought the matter up during a meeting with newly installed general secretary Mikhail Gorbachev in 1985. Gorbachev was adamant, "The Slepaks will never leave the Soviet Union." Scheuer met again with Gorbachev in 1987 and again asked about the Slepaks. Cynically, Gorbachev replied, "If we have agreement on disarmament, they can leave, if not, they will stay here."[19]

Two months later, with a Reagan-Gorbachev summit in sight, the Slepaks received a surprise phone call from OVIR, "You are granted permission to leave the USSR. Please come to the OVIR office tomorrow." They received their cards and proudly brought them to the farewell party for Ida Nudel. Pandemonium and tears of joy filled the room and all the other refuseniks had a single thought, "If the Slepaks are getting out, we'll get out too!"[20]

ALEXANDER LERNER

Professor Lerner carefully disconnected the telephone in his apartment, made sure all the doors were locked, drew the window shades and convened a family meeting that was spoken in whispers. It was the spring of 1971 and he said that some daring people had applied for permission to emigrate to Israel, and some had actually gotten out. He wondered if "we would be able to leave this land of 'advanced socialism' – the workers' paradise." All five members of the family agreed that they had had enough of "slavish submission to a brutal, hypocritical system." It was time to fulfill Lerner's half-century-old dream of "Next Year in Jerusalem."

Lerner was highly respected and privileged as deputy director of a major scientific institute and Russia's foremost expert in cybernetics. He was one of very few Soviet scientists and engineers allowed to travel to international conferences and had two cars, a large apartment and a country house.[21] His application for an exit visa – the first from a professional of his stature – sent shock waves throughout the Soviet scientific establishment.[22] The first indication of his intention to emigrate was discovered by the KGB when they intercepted a letter of invitation from his relatives in Israel. The KGB immediately contacted Lerner's boss, academician Y.A. Trapeznikov, who then summoned Lerner to his office and said, "This is Zionist propaganda and I'm sure you will give it a deserving answer." Lerner replied, "I am sorry but that letter is my invitation and I do want to go to Israel." Trapeznikov angrily called all of his laboratory and department directors to a special meeting and acknowledged that Lerner's mail had been seized and warned them that such letters were taken very seriously. Undeterred by Trapeznikov's threats, Lerner submitted his application for an exit visa.

In December 1971 he was not surprised when his application was refused and he was dismissed from all his professional posts and expelled from the Communist Party.

The pretext of his refusal was that he had worked on control systems for nuclear submarines, but that work had ended in 1962 and was already well known in the West.[23] Reflecting on his initial refusal, Lerner asserted that "the authorities strongly wanted to make an example of me." His approach to counter the refusal, dismissal and ostracism was to participate in as many protests and contact as many friends in the West as possible.[24] He joined other Moscow refuseniks in street demonstrations and in protesting anti-Semitic editorials that had been published in *Pravda*.[25]

Lerner invited refuseniks to his apartment for weekly semi-nars so they could keep abreast of the latest developments in their fields despite having been dismissed from their jobs. Refuseniks and, occasionally, foreign visiting scientists would discuss both technical issues and Jewish culture. Eventually, non-Jewish dissi-dents would attend and some, like Andrei Sakharov, would be the lecturers. The KGB ignored the seminars for about two years and then in 1981 started harassing participants, preventing them from entering Lerner's apartment and other seminar venues. Scientists from abroad wishing to travel to Russia and suspected of planning to attend refusenik seminars were denied entry visas.[26]

During the summer of 1975 a group of U.S. senators, includ-ing Hubert Humphrey (D-MN), Patrick Leahy (D-VT), Jacob Javits (R-NY) and Abraham Ribicoff (D-CT) were in Moscow for meetings with Brezhnev. They wanted to meet with refuseniks and managed to contact Lerner and some of the regular seminar attendees. At a meeting the next day the senators were shocked when they were shown a series of rabidly anti-Semitic articles from recent editions of a Ukrainian newspaper. One senator asked, "My God, that's unbelievable! Tell me, do you think we'll make things worse by taking a hard line with the Soviets?" Lerner and his colleagues, Mark Azbel, Victor Brailovsky and Benjamin Fain, answered, "We certainly do not. We're speaking for all re-fuseniks when we say that we believe economic pressures are the only means the United States can use to improve this situation. We support the policy of America's holding this line, not retreat-ing a single step."[27]

Lerner had additional meetings with visiting senators. In 1978 Hubert Humphrey and Ted Kennedy (D-MA) came to Lerner's apartment to discuss how the U.S. Congress could help refuseniks be granted the right to emigrate. When Kennedy returned two years later, Lerner invited Andrei Sakharov and Elena Bonner to join the discussion focusing on the plight of dissidents in jails, labor camps and psychiatric hospitals.

Isi Leibler, who in the 1960s had alerted Australia to the

injustices of the Soviet regime with regard to its Jewish minority, was able to visit Russia in 1978 as an executive of Australian Jewish organizations and as a board member of the World Jewish Congress. He was accompanied by Robert Hawke, a leader of Australia's trade unions and a man with strong sympathies for Soviet Jews, who had been invited to Moscow by Soviet trade unions. Hawke and Leibler met with Lerner to devise a strategy that might force the Soviets to allow free emigration. They proposed that if the Soviets agreed to three demands they would arrange for the American government to ease restrictions on trade with the Soviet Union. The three demands were (1) a five-year time limit on refusing permission to emigrate for any reason including secrecy; (2) immediate permission for all refuseniks who had already been waiting for five years or more; and (3) removal of all deliberate restrictions on applications to emigrate. Hawke presented the proposal to the chairman of the Soviet National Trade Union Council, who claimed to be negotiating on behalf of the Soviet government. He was assured that the proposal had been accepted by the government and would be honored. Sadly, it was all a shameless deception. None of the restrictive emigration policies were modified.

Several years later Hawke led the Australian Labor Party to victory in parliamentary elections and became prime minister. As such he worked actively for the release of Prisoners of Zion and refuseniks, and upon visiting Moscow for meetings with Gorbachev in 1987, he asked the Soviet leader to allow Lerner and several other refuseniks to emigrate.[28]

Lerner's wife, Judith, died of a sudden heart attack in 1981 after ten years of tension and uncertainty about the family's future.[29] Their daughter, Sonya, who was living in Israel, was allowed to return to Moscow to attend the funeral, an unprecedented gesture thanks to an appeal from West German chancellor Willy Brandt to Soviet foreign minister Gromyko. During her five-day visit she asked the head of OVIR if the authorities were willing to allow her father and brother to leave and join her in Israel. The bureaucrat curtly replied, "This is not a case of reunification and we are not prepared at this stage to consider it." Again, their hopes were dashed.[30]

Several months later two KGB men dressed in police uniforms barged into Lerner's apartment while he was meeting with other leading refuseniks to draft the latest annual report on emigration for dissemination to friends in the West. Lerner was taken to the police station where two other KGB agents were waiting. One of them grimaced at Lerner, uttered a few obscenities and then the following dialogue took place:

KGB: What a traitor and scoundrel you have to be to pull such a trick after everything you've been given – an education, position, high pay, and the devil knows what else. Now you want to emigrate. Like hell!

Lerner: I won't be spoken to in such terms. I won't answer any questions. Please behave decently.

KGB: We know all about your dirty deals. Don't try to be too smart or we'll talk about sexual dirt that you'd rather not hear about. It'll be worse for you.

Lerner: Don't try to provoke me with threats. No one will believe any dirt your superiors try to heap on me.

KGB: We'll find people to believe it, and we'll give you what you deserve, you promiscuous bastard. You deserve it!

Lerner: I don't know what you are driving at or what you want of me. I know you can curse anyone up and down, but what do you want of me?

KGB: Better give up your stupid idea and announce that you have no intention of going anywhere.

Lerner: I won't, ever, under any circumstances. I'd rather hang myself than stay here and live among the likes of you.

KGB: You won't make us cry by hanging yourself. Maybe it will do some good. Your kind doesn't commit suicide. You don't want to die. You want a sweet life, living as a parasite on decent Russians, on working people, on patriots.

Lerner: I've said everything I want to. Can I go?

KGB: It's not clear yet if you'll get out of here tonight or where you'll go from here. Maybe you won't be going home so soon. I've got to draw up a case against you for resisting arrest and for spoiling our man's suit when you pushed him. You broke a pen in his pocket and the ink spotted his new suit. It cost 300 rubles.

Lerner: You're inventing all that. I have ten witnesses to what happened, so you can't prove any of your fabrications.

KGB: Your witnesses, every one of them, are your accomplices. Nothing they can say will carry weight.

Lerner: As things stand today, you can't do anything to me without a trial, and any trial will produce such a noise in the West that it won't foster trust or respect for Soviet justice. You realize, of course, that my friends won't leave me in the lurch.

At this point a "good cop" KGB agent took over and tried to negotiate an agreement in which Lerner would get permission to emigrate with his son if he would agree to cease "all contacts with foreign correspondents, tourists and congressmen."

A week later a KGB general confirmed the offer to Lerner, who now was faced with a major dilemma. Three questions kept coming up in his mind. "What would my friends in the aliyah movement think? What about all my supporters in America and Europe? What would Israelis say about it?" He resolved it by stopping contacts with foreigners, but since meeting with other Russians was not covered by the ban, he would continue his customary activities with fellow refuseniks.

A year passed with Lerner isolated from the world outside the USSR and not a word was spoken about permission to emigrate. He ended his year of abstinence by walking to the U.S. Embassy, presenting his documents to a KGB agent, and meeting with ambassador Arthur Hartman.

At the end of 1987 Lerner's daughter-in-law, Tanya, received a telephone call from the OVIR office with a message for Prof. Lerner that the family was being given permission to emigrate! Gorbachev had finally decided to yield to Robert Hawke's request that he heard again in London from prime minister Margaret Thatcher and in Washington from Reagan.

A month later the Lerner family was warmly welcomed to Israel and a new life in Rehovot where Lerner, his daughter, Sonya, and his son, Vladimir, would all be on the staff of the Weizmann Institute.[31] Lerner celebrated his ninetieth birthday there in October 2003 but passed away on April 6, 2004, remembered as the "de-facto patriarch of the Soviet refusenik movement."[32]

YULI KOSHAROVSKY

"It was a race between the United States and the Soviet Union and we were working like hell; sometimes twenty, twenty-five hours a day!" Yuli Kosharovsky was describing his first job as an electronics engineer designing the control system for an intercontinental ballistic missile that could carry nuclear warheads. The facility where he worked was in Sverdlovsk, an industrial city about 1,200 miles from Moscow, known as the Pittsburgh of Russia. Like many other Jews, Kosharovsky's parents fled there during World War II as their hometowns in Ukraine were being overrun by the Nazis. Thousands of them remained to attend its universities, work in the growing postwar industries, assimilated, and married non-Jews.

Kosharovsky knew of his Jewish identity only from his grandparents. He often wondered about what it meant to be a Jew. During the Six-Day War he strongly sympathized with Israel and was incredulous when he heard the lies and propaganda in the Soviet media. He began to have doubts about his loyalty to the Soviet Union, and a recurring thought was: "It is not my country. I don't want to work for it." He told his supervisor that he no longer wanted to work in the missile facility. There were no immediate repercussions but eight months passed before he could be released from his assignment and all that time his heart was burning with a passion for Zionism and resentment for the blatant anti-Semitism that was endemic in Russian society.

Kosharovsky's father died in 1968 and was buried in a Jewish cemetery. A year later Yuli visited his father's grave and was accosted by eight boisterous Russian youths who were drinking vodka and telling anti-Semitic jokes. When he expressed outrage at their behavior one of them said, "Let's put this little Jew in the grave with his father." Kosharovsky flew into a rage, picked up a shovel, and was ready to ferociously attack all of them. The rowdies apologized and left but Kosharovsky was convinced that he could no longer live in Russia.

For the three-year interval before he could apply for an exit visa because of his previous secret work, Kosharovsky worked at a medical institute at one-third the salary he had received when he was designing the ICBM control system. The new job did, however, give him free time to study Hebrew. He and some Zionist friends found that there was no information on Jewish history or culture to be readily found in Sverdlovsk. They did find a Hebrew-Russian dictionary compiled by Felix Shapiro. The presence of the group in the library was reported to the KGB and those who were students risked being forced to end their studies.

Kosharovsky located a self-teaching Hebrew book and as soon as he completed eight of its lessons he started teaching Hebrew to a group of forty friends who were interested in learning about their Jewish heritage. Other members of the group taught Jewish songs and told stories of their backgrounds. There were no outside materials brought in by tourists as in Moscow and Leningrad because Sverdlovsk was a military region, closed to foreign visitors.[33]

The group soon began to prepare and circulate samizdat documents and on December 26, 1970, Kosharovsky and his friend Valery Kukuy issued a sharply worded denunciation of the harsh sentences meted out to the defendants in the Leningrad hijack trial. It was signed by ten Jews of Sverdlovsk and sent to Soviet leaders and to the president of Israel. The KGB questioned the signers and tried to intimidate them by searching their apartments. Kukuy and Kosharovsky were vilified in the local newspaper, lost their jobs, and were arrested. Kosharovsky was detained under wretched conditions for twenty-seven days on charges of hooliganism, but Kukuy was put on trial for anti-Soviet slander and sentenced to three years in prison.[34]

On March 10, 1971, Kosharovsky submitted his first application for an exit visa. His wife, Sonya, who was not Jewish, was willing to go to Israel with him and their five-year-old daughter, but Sonya's mother fainted upon learning the plans. Sonya declared, "I cannot kill my mother!" and then agreed to an amicable divorce. It was difficult for them. Kosharovsky recalls how Sonya was his first love and she was not only faithful to him but tried to be more Jewish than he was.

Kosharovsky moved to Moscow where he could join a support group of other people who were refused for secrecy reasons. But he didn't have a residence permit to live in Moscow so he initially slept in a railway station. Within a month his contacts in Moscow arranged a fictitious short-term marriage for him and Nora Kornblum, a Moscow resident, enabling him to get properly documented. He lived with friends, taught Hebrew, copied Jewish books, studied English and organized seminars for unemployed engineers.

In the process of teaching Hebrew and learning English, Kosharovsky developed some highly efficient techniques for language acquisition and shared them with other underground Hebrew teachers in Moscow and, eventually, in twenty-five other cities, even conducting teaching seminars on tours of the Caucasus Mountains and on riverboat cruises during the summers.

He also served as a consultant to individuals who needed assistance in preparing documents for their exit visa applications. Inna Genis, a widow who had studied statistics at Moscow State University, visited him with some questions. He liked her at first glance and in a month they were married.[35] Their religious ceremony, in 1975, was officiated by Rabbi Haskel Lookstein who was visiting from New York.[36] Seventy-five people crowded into a tiny apartment to see the *chuppah* and participate in what refusenik activist Mark Azbel described as "one of the high points of the year." The guests included some of the most prominent refuseniks and Jewish culture activists in Russia. For nearly all of them it was the first time they had seen a Jewish wedding, and for some, it was a reinforcement of their personal decisions to return to Judaism.[37]

Kosharovsky wrote to Brezhnev on March 10, 1978, the seventh anniversary of his first application for an exit visa, describing his long wait as "an act of tyranny." He also applied to pay taxes on the income he earned from his Hebrew classes but was told that teaching Hebrew was not legitimate work and he would be charged with parasitism if he didn't obtain a proper job. Kosharovsky then became the janitor in a kindergarten, earning 70 rubles per month, about one-tenth his former salary as an engineer.[38]

He did continue to teach Hebrew on Sundays, and in March 1979 he convened a week-long seminar on "Hebrew and Jewish Cultural Heritage" for fifty activists. Later that year police inspectors came to his apartment and stated that they had received complaints from neighbors that drunken orgies were going on and that they were being disturbed by Kosharovsky's visitors.[39] In 1980 Kosharovsky was warned by the KGB that if he didn't stop teaching Hebrew within two months they would create incriminating evidence against him. Exactly two months later he was out jogging when a man who appeared to be drunk waving a wine bottle approached him and dropped the bottle. Members of the *druzhinniki* appeared and took Kosharovsky and the drunkard to the police station and asserted that there had been a quarrel. Both were sentenced to thirteen days in jail but the drunkard disappeared and Kosharovsky served his sentence alone.

The prison sentence, a twelve-hour search of his apartment, and subsequent KGB threats to "break his hands and feet" didn't deter him from teaching Hebrew.[40] However he had to be extremely careful, and in 1984, which he described as a "most difficult year," Kosharovsky organized a committee of leading activists called the "*Mashka*," a Russian-sounding acronym of three

Hebrew words: *Moadon Leshtiya Kabira,* meaning "club for strong drinking". This was the secret umbrella group that coordinated the movement in Moscow and functioned until the collapse of the Soviet Union. Meetings were held in various places using coded messages to communicate the time and place. There were always bottles of strong liquor on the table to make the gathering look like someone's birthday party in case the apartment were invaded by neighbors, police or KGB.[41]

Many of Kosharovsky's former students were now teachers and went on secret missions outside of Moscow. Some were arrested, and their wives, sometimes hysterical, came to Kosharovsky screaming, "You sent my husband on the mission and he was arrested there. Now get him out!" Nevertheless, Kosharovsky felt it was vital to keep the network highly motivated to be able to resist the pressure of the authorities and their illegal anti-Semitic attacks.

One of the most successful activities of Kosharovsky and his associates was the dissemination of thousands of books of Jewish content, mostly from Israel and America, during the biennial Moscow International Book Fairs. Delegates from the Association of American Jewish Book Publishers brought hundreds of books on Jewish themes as well as free handouts with Jewish information.[42] During the fair thousands of Soviet Jews lined up to view them. It was a rare opportunity for parents to instill in their children a sense of Jewish pride and identity.[43] Every night during Book Fair week Yuri Chernyak, a Mashka activist, loaded his car, a prized possession from his days as a high-ranking theoretical physicist, with bulky bags of books that had been brought to his apartment by tourists and drove the bags to the apartments of other activists and friendly gentiles for storage and distribution to Jews throughout the Soviet Union. When Chernyak observed KGB agents outside his apartment building he made a daring getaway and evaded them. Nearly 10,000 books were smuggled in this manner; Soviet authorities expected the foreign visitors who exhibited at the fair to depart with all of their books.[44] Each book was a potentially positive influence on the recipient to consider emigration as Gorbachev's policy of *glasnost* was coming into vogue in the late 1980s and exit visas rose from fewer than 1000 in 1986 to 8,563 in 1987 and 26,183 in 1988.[45]

But Kosharovsky's reapplications for an exit visa continued to be in vain and on December 6, 1987, the day of massive Soviet Jewry rallies in Washington and Tel Aviv, on the eve of the Gorbachev-Reagan summit meeting, Kosharovsky and other refuseniks tried to demonstrate and hold a hunger strike in Moscow but were surrounded by KGB and detained outside the city for several hours. Kosharovsky was able to speak by telephone to the Tel Aviv rally that was attended by former President Chaim Herzog, prime minister Yitzhak Shamir and foreign minister Shimon Peres. His message was, "In the era of glasnost, we can see not only a great gap between the promises and our reality, but signs of a return to our previous situation."

To mark the seventeenth anniversary of his first application for an exit visa, Kosharovsky issued a statement to the press that he and Inna would begin a hunger strike on March 10, 1988. On that day U.S. Senator Dennis DeConcini (D-AZ), a co-chairman of the Commission on Security and Cooperation in Europe, took to the Senate floor to issue a plea for the Kosharovskys and rebuked the Soviet Union for disregarding their international commitments. Inna and Yuli ate no food for seventeen days while receiving as many as 100 telephone calls of support each day. In April Kosharovsky had recovered and was back to his routine of jogging each morning. He said that "running opened up my mind."[46]

When the Bay Area Council for Soviet Jews learned that Kosharovsky was a runner they publicized his case by carrying "Free Yuli Kosharovsky" signs during the 77th annual Bay to Breakers Race across the city of San Francisco, an event that attracts over 100,000 runners, walkers and observers. He ran with other refuseniks on the same day in Moscow while his friend and former refusenik Alex Ioffe, in Haifa, Israel, ran simultaneously "as a free Jew in a free land." Among the runners in the San Francisco race was a new arrival, Benjamin Bogomolny. The *Guinness Book of World Records* created a category of "most patient" and awarded the honor to Bogomolny, who had applied for an exit visa in 1966 and was not permitted to emigrate until 1986.[47]

At the end of May 1988 Reagan came to Moscow for his last summit meeting with Gorbachev. He invited several dozen human rights advocates, refuseniks and intellectuals for a reception and discussion at the u.s. ambassador's residence. Kosharovsky was asked by the refuseniks to be their spokesman and he eloquently addressed the president and Mrs. Reagan, summarizing his case and the major grievances of the Jewish community, and expressed the disappointment they were feeling about the slow pace of emigration under "the more liberal government" of Gorbachev.[48]

This reception was followed by meetings with Richard Schifter, undersecretary of state for humanitarian affairs, at the American Embassy that led to Kosharovsky being placed on a shortlist of refuseniks whose cases would be brought up before the Soviet Foreign Ministry.[49] Finally on December 14, 1988, he was notified in writing that he could emigrate.[50] He, Inna and their three children arrived in Israel on March 12, 1989, ending his eighteen years as a refusenik. They were greeted at Ben-Gurion Airport by premier Yitzhak Shamir and went directly to their new home in Alon Shvut.[51] A month later he was working as an engineer for a company that was producing cable TV products and he felt like he "was beginning to put roots into this ground...in a country created just for me."[52]

Yuli Kosharovsky in Moscow, 1987.
Photo Credit: BACSJ/Marshall Platt.

CHAPTER TEN

Teach Hebrew, Go to Prison

H is parents severely discouraged him from studying Russian, that *goyisher loshen* (gentile language), so Felix Shapiro, born in 1879, sought refuge in a quiet forest outside their *shtetl* near Bobrusk, Belarus, to read Russian books. Under the birch trees, immersed in the poetry of Pushkin or the novels of Dosto-evsky, Shapiro could hardly imagine that in the next century his grandson would also find a forest the venue for practicing another forbidden language – Hebrew.

After attending yeshiva, attaining a rabbinical certificate and helping his father teach in a *cheder*, Shapiro parlayed his knowledge of Russian into admission to the prestigious University of St. Petersburg where he was trained as a dentist.[1] He remained in St. Petersburg until 1915 but preferred to teach Hebrew rather than pull teeth.[2] With his ailing wife, Mina, he moved to Baku, Azerbaijan, for its therapeutic climate where he became the principal of a Jewish school. After the revolution Soviet authorities closed the school, leaving Shapiro unemployed until he opened a shelter for the homeless. Lenin's wife, who was minister of education, heard about Shapiro's work and invited him to assist her in

Moscow, which he did from 1924 until 1941. He survived the war in the Ural Mountains.

When the State of Israel was established there was a need for diplomats in the Soviet Embassy there to have knowledge of Hebrew. Shapiro began teaching Hebrew in the diplomatic school in Moscow and in the city's School of Oriental Languages. He also had private students, including a KGB officer who lived in Shapiro's communal apartment. After Stalin's death Shapiro began work on a Russian-Hebrew dictionary, the most exciting project of his life. While others his age were retiring on pensions, Shapiro had an explosion of energy. The KGB supported his efforts in compiling the dictionary because it would be a valuable tool in their activities. But they were not in favor of his repeated requests to have it published and accessible. Finally, in 1963, two years after his death, it was published and 25,000 copies were sold throughout the Soviet Union and Poland.[3]

The dictionary included up-to-date idiomatic expressions from Israel, grammar, and examples of conversational usage. It became a favorite of clandestine Hebrew teachers in the Soviet Union and was utilized by them for the next thirty years.[4] In 2005, to commemorate the 125th anniversary of Shapiro's birth, his daughter, Leah Prestin-Shapiro, living in Beersheba, published *Dictionary of Forbidden Language*, a collection of his works and memoirs.[5]

VLADIMIR PRESTIN

Shapiro's grandson, Vladimir Prestin, showed no interest in learning Hebrew during Shapiro's lifetime, and the only *Yiddishkeit* imparted by Shapiro to the lad were a few Bible stories. Prestin's attitude changed after the Six-Day War and several holiday camping trips with the Drapkin, Polsky, and Slepak families, who started whispering about living in Israel as early as 1964. Five years later, Prestin picked up his grandfather's dictionary and starting learning Hebrew. Soon after that he taught others what he was learning himself and applied for exit visas for himself, his wife, Elena, and their six-year-old son, Misha. The applications were refused due to the secret nature of Prestin's computer work.[6]

Ida Nudel became one of Prestin's first Hebrew students in 1970. She credits him with teaching her "more than just Hebrew." When she became apprehensive about being summoned by the KGB, he explained to her, "You are not obligated to talk to them. Every citizen has rights as well as obligations. From childhood they indoctrinate us only about our responsibilities but they never speak about our rights. You have the right not to inform on a friend. You have the right *not* to speak with them at all. If they serve you a summons officially, that's one thing, but if they do it unofficially, as they say, 'for a conversation,' then you don't have to talk. You can say, 'I don't want to. I have the right.'"

Prestin soon discovered that in addition to summoning activist refuseniks for questioning, the KGB had other methods of intimidation. They disconnected his telephone.[7] Nudel allowed him to use hers; day and night there were calls for him from Jews who had been dismissed from their jobs, refused exit visas, or threatened by the KGB. This experience sparked her determination to do whatever she could to help refuseniks who were in prison or in danger of being arrested.[8]

Prestin was arrested along with Polsky, Slepak, and other refuseniks and dissidents on the morning that Nixon arrived in Moscow for his 1972 summit meeting with Brezhnev. The arrests were preventive measures to ensure that there would be no embarrassing demonstrations during Nixon's visit. Without explanation, police officers removed the activists from their homes and kept them incommunicado outside the city until Nixon was out of the Soviet Union. Prestin was held for fifteen days on trumped-up charges of "pestering a woman."[9] Upon returning home he continued teaching Hebrew and maintaining contacts with supporters who visited from the West. He would regularly join other refuseniks who gathered in forests near Moscow for picnics to celebrate Jewish holidays and study Hebrew and Jewish culture together.

However, Prestin chose to maintain a lower profile from 1981 to 1986 while Misha was a university student. His son could be subject to expulsion and subsequently drafted in the military if the KGB wanted to subject the Prestins to further reprisals for their activities. Like the Lerners and Slepaks, the Prestins received permission to emigrate in late 1987 after Gorbachev heeded requests from Reagan and prime ministers Thatcher and Hawke.[10]

YOSEF BEGUN

Yosef Begun was a thirty-five-year-old electrical engineer working on radar at a Moscow aviation factory when he heard news of the Six-Day War from the Voice of America and BBC. He quit his job in 1969 and applied for an exit visa two years later. When he was refused he was told, "If you're quiet you'll get a visa in two or three years." Keeping quiet was not Begun's style; he joined every refusenik group he could find and became accustomed to enduring KGB harassment for his activities.

He supported himself by working as a mathematics teacher, night watchman and fireman, all the while becoming increasingly interested in studying Jewish culture and the Hebrew language. As soon as he acquired a working knowledge of Hebrew at a secret *ulpan* in Moscow he began conducting Hebrew classes for private students. But he was at risk of being arrested for parasitism. He tried to convince the authorities that teaching Hebrew was a legitimate occupation and offered to pay income tax on his earnings as teachers of other languages did, but the Ministry of Finance retorted that Hebrew was not taught in schools of the USSR.[11]

In 1972 Begun's name appeared on a memo from KGB chief Yuri Andropov to the Communist Party of the Soviet Union Central Committee as one of nine prominent refuseniks, including Lerner, Polsky, Slepak, and Prestin, who "are privy to state secrets" and "temporarily refused exit visas to Israel." The memo described them as individuals "who have fallen under the influence of Zionist propaganda and are pursuing their own selfish goals, pass themselves off as 'victims of anti-Semitism', organize various kinds of anti-social actions, and prepare and distribute collective letters, appeals, etc."[12]

Begun organized a Purim party at his apartment in 1977 and had some unwelcome guests – police officers who arrested him on charges of parasitism and anti-Soviet agitation. He was held in a Moscow prison for three months awaiting trial and during this time he embarked on a hunger strike but was force-fed every three days.[13] He showed amazing fortitude and left an inscription on the wall of his cell that was discovered by Natan Sharansky when he became a prisoner in the same cell. It was a *Magen David*, with the Hebrew words: *Asir Tsiyon Yosef Begun. Chazak ve'ematz!* (Prisoner of Zion Yosef Begun. Be strong and courageous!)

The trial was rescheduled several times and finally took place, lasting only nine hours, with the prosecution reiterating that teaching Hebrew was not an acceptable profession and Begun arguing that he was not a parasite and had sufficient means to support himself. Nevertheless he was sentenced to two years in exile, including time already served in prison. Begun's appeal was dismissed, and without any medical attention, he was transported 10,000 kilometers from Moscow to a camp in Magadan, a frigid area of Siberia that is washed by the Arctic and Pacific oceans.[14] Although he was in such a remote part of the Far East, Begun was not forgotten in the West. His case was brought up by ambassador Arthur Goldberg at the Belgrade follow-up meeting of the Conference on Security and Cooperation in Europe.[15]

The one bright moment for Begun during the Magadan winter was the arrival of his fiancée, Dr. Alla Drugova, and their marriage there. When she complained to the camp commandant that it was 40 degrees below zero and Begun's room and bed were full of snow due to a leaky roof, he curtly replied, "Conditions are suitable for someone of his character."[16]

Begun was released from the camp and returned to Moscow at the end of February 1978, but the Moscow spring was stormy for him. He was immediately informed that anyone who had served a sentence for parasitism was not eligible to reside in Moscow. His protests led to another arrest, a psychiatric examination, a hunger strike, and another trial in which he had to be dragged into the courthouse because he was too fatigued to stand. The sentence was three years in exile, and after an arduous 52-day journey with stops at horrendous transit prisons Begun was back in Magadan, where he remained until August 1980. Alla was able to visit him and reported his deplorable conditions to supporters in the West.

Again Begun was denied permission to live in Moscow, so he found lodging and a job as a fireman about 100 kilometers outside the city. Alla was offered an exit visa, but only if she were willing to divorce Begun and emigrate without him. She agreed and soon after arriving in Israel in November 1981 initiated a campaign on behalf of Begun.

A year later the apartment of his third wife, Inna, was searched and many books were confiscated.[17] Within a week he was arrested, carrying a bag of Hebrew texts and Jewish history books, at a railroad station in Moscow after visiting friends in Leningrad, and he was taken to the infamous Vladimir Prison where he was held incommunicado and charged with anti-Soviet agitation and propaganda. For nearly a year he was interrogated as the authorities built up a case against him. It would be anti-Soviet agitation and slander, subject to a maximum term of seven years in prison followed by five years in exile.[18] A KGB major who interrogated Begun tried to negotiate: "You're so old to be a prisoner for twelve years; maybe you'll make some statement of remorse and you'll be freed."[19] Begun would not bend.

A day after Begun's arrest Brezhnev died and Yuri Andropov, Begun's nemesis, became general secretary. Andropov declared his opposition to "the festering sore of false cultural demands by those bad elements."[20] Viktor Chebrikov, Andropov's successor as head of the KGB, sent a memo to the CPSU Central Committee a week before Begun's trial asserting that "Under cover of distributing textbooks for the study of Hebrew and bringing Jews into contact with their 'national culture', Begun illegally prepared anti-Soviet literature and other materials containing slanderous fabrications defaming the Soviet state and social order...Begun's hostile activity was continually directed and stimulated by established foreign Zionist centers, which transferred to him pertinent instructions, literature and monetary and material resources..."[21]

The trial in Vladimir was another mockery of justice with Begun unable to call witnesses, have an attorney of his own choosing, or have his friends and relatives in court during the trial proceedings. When he received the expected verdict and sentence, seven years in prison followed by five years in exile, he shouted *Am Yisrael Chai!* (The people of Israel live!).[22]

There was a storm of protest in the West. The *Washington Post* reported, "The recent arrests and trials of human rights advocates and Jewish activists have created a deepening chill here and suggested that the authorities are mounting a new campaign to eliminate remaining stirrings of dissent.[23] Jacob Birnbaum and the Student Struggle for Soviet Jews who had been leading a "Let My People Know" campaign to promote the study of Hebrew and Jewish culture in the USSR, placed a full page ad in the *New York Times* headlined: "In America you have to kill someone to get 12 years in prison. In Russia you may just have to teach Hebrew."[24] Reagan issued a statement describing Begun as a "courageous Jewish believer" and condemning the Soviet Union's "illegal and inhumane acts."[25]

All the protests from the West had no effect on the Kremlin and Begun was transferred from Vladimir Prison to the Perm labor camp in the Ural Mountains. In 1985 the Netherlands Embassy in Moscow, which had been representing Israel's interest in the USSR since 1967, started taking a more active role in support of dissidents and refuseniks. They sent a diplomatic note about Begun and his prison conditions to the Soviet Ministry of Foreign Affairs. An embassy official visited Inna Begun's apartment when she and Yosef's son, Boris, were preparing to start a hunger strike to protest the refusal of camp officials to deliver letters from

Begun to his family. The hunger strike and its publicity apparently worked because two months after it began a letter arrived from Begun saying that he was now in the Chistopol prison camp and his health was "not bad."[26]

As Gorbachev solidified his power and began a new regime, political prisoners were being released from Chistopol but Begun was not among them. He had been offered a release if he were to ask for a pardon and sign a statement saying that, once freed, he would not become involved in anti-Soviet activity. He refused, insisting that "my activity had never been anti-Soviet."[27] He was put on "strict regime" which meant reduced rations to about 1,000 calories per day consisting of nothing but coarse black bread, potatoes and cabbage, and also no visitors or mail.[28] Finally on February 20, 1987, he received an unconditional release after having served four and a half years, including 200 days in solitary confinement. He was greeted with a hero's welcome at a snowy railroad station in Moscow by Inna, Boris and many other refuseniks and journalists.[29]

Begun received an exit visa in September 1987 but, as he told Isi Leibler who visited him, he felt he needed to remain in Moscow until all of his family could leave, and to demand rehabilitation, rather than a pardon, because as long as his crime remained on the books, other activists and Hebrew teachers could be subject to the same injustice that was inflicted upon him. He also told Leibler, "I survived only because I had faith as a Jew. If I had not been a Jew I would be a dead man."[30] On January 19, 1988, Begun and his family flew out of Moscow, bound for Israel, telling reporters and well-wishers, "Now that I'm going, I feel even more the wishes and dreams of those I left behind, the ones who want to live as Jews."[31]

EVGENY LEIN

Evgeny Lein was one of those refuseniks left behind. He was the friend in Leningrad with whom Begun visited and drank tea a few hours before his arrest at the railroad station in Moscow.[32]

Lein and his wife, Irina, had doctorates in applied mathematics and chemistry respectively. When they applied for exit visas in 1978 they were refused because of their high level of education. The Soviet government was beginning to stanch the brain drain of technical professionals to unfriendly countries. The Leins were fired from their jobs and became active participants in the scientific seminars and classes on Jewish history, culture, and traditions organized by Leningrad's refusenik community. Their apartment was often the venue for gatherings of Jews striving to revitalize Jewish learning.[33]

Gregory Kanovich and Lev Utevsky started the Jewish seminars in 1979.[34] Unlike Jewish gatherings in other cities of the Soviet Union, these seminars were not secret, and lecture schedules were openly distributed near the Leningrad Synagogue. The organizers intended that the KGB realize that the seminar participants were not covertly plotting to overthrow the Soviet government, but simply wanted to learn about their Jewish roots and emigrate to Israel.[35]

The KGB obtained a schedule of lectures for May 1981 and from it learned that the Jews would gather at Lein's apartment on Sunday, May 10 for a lecture about Israel's Independence Day. While the Leins were rearranging furniture to accommodate the students there was a loud knock on their door, but Evgeny could see plainclothesmen through the peephole and refused to open the door. Within minutes the entrance to the apartment was blocked and people trying to attend the lecture were detained. As anti-Semitic slogans were chanted, Evgeny Lein read out loud from the Soviet Constitution: "Soviet citizens are guaranteed personal immunity, immunity of dwelling place. The spreading of ethnic hatred is grounds for criminal proceedings. Spreading any hatred or hostile attitude based on religion is forbidden." The Jews dispersed and most of them went to the tiny apartment of Grisha Wasserman, a Hebrew teacher and Talmud scholar, where the lecture took place with no interference.[36]

A week later there was a lecture entitled *Shabbat* at

Wasserman's apartment. Twenty minutes after the lecture began a militia captain and eight plainclothesmen broke in and started photographing the attendees. When Lein asked the intruders for identification and their reason for breaking into a private apartment, the militia captain grabbed him. Lein and eighty-five other Jews were herded into buses and driven to a militia control point. After questioning they were let go with reprimands and Wasserman was fined 50 rubles, almost a month's salary, for illegal organization of a religious cult, but it soon became clear that Lein would be singled out for punishment as a warning to the others.[37]

One of the plainclothesmen called out to a nearby group of students, who were actually members of a KGB task force: "Here is someone who needs to be accused of resisting the militia. Two witnesses are needed. You and you go over there". When Lein protested he was driven away to prison in a standard-issue KGB black Volga car. He was interrogated for five months, with no visitors or contact with the outside world. The KGB investigator started the questioning by softly saying, "I want to help you. It is necessary for you to testify. That is, to plead guilty." Lein asked for some paper and wrote: "...PROTEST...I claim that detention was pre-planned. I demand to be freed from custody." The investigator yelled at Lein and asked, "Why are your hands trembling?" "I am worried," Lein replied as he realized that the best thing to do in this situation was to tell the truth. This was a principle recommended by Vladimir Albrecht, a dissident lawyer who had lectured to other dissidents since 1975 on how to behave during KGB interrogations.[38] Lein never met Albrecht but was impressed by the clarity and logic of his *samizdat* document.[39] Albrecht also recommended that people did not need to answer every question, and that protests that were sent abroad should also be sent to Soviet authorities, as otherwise it could be considered anti-Soviet.[40]

Lein learned that he would be tried for "resisting the authorities" by tearing the epaulet off a police officer's coat, and the maximum sentence for this crime was five years in labor camps. It was clear that the KGB was eager to prove that there was a vast conspiratorial network of Zionists generating anti-Soviet propaganda. The interrogators continually asked Lein about connections to Boris Chernobilsky, a refusenik activist in Moscow, who had just been arrested. Lein truthfully responded that he had never heard of Chernobilsky. Finally Lein was taken out of his cell to a truck for transfer to the Kresty Prison. He was delighted to see his wife and other refusenik supporters outside the jail before being dragged into the truck. Irina went to the American Consulate in Leningrad and wrote letters of protest to leading Soviet officials, sending copies to the West.[41]

Jakov Gorodezky organized over thirty participants in the seminar to testify in writing that Lein had not struck anybody, but they were not allowed to be called as witnesses in court.[42] Lein was determined to steadfastly defend his innocence and draw as much attention to his case as possible. He concluded his defense by declaring:

> "I am innocent. The circumstances of my arrest and the course of my interrogation obviously demonstrate that the prosecuting authorities adopted a biased attitude, and are preparing a reprisal against me and my family for our desire to know the history and language of the Jewish people, for our desire to leave the Soviet Union for the State of Israel. *Yesh li tikva she'ani echeye b'Yerushalayim* (I hope that I will be living in Jerusalem)."

Even though the American consul general was present at the trial and protests poured in from the West, Lein was found guilty. Although the prosecution demanded three years, the judge sentenced Lein to two years of forced labor in Siberia.[43] In Lein's view this sentence proved the value of getting support from the West. Another man who was arrested at the same time chose to keep a low profile and pled guilty. He received a four-year sentence.[44]

After a nightmarish journey, Lein arrived in Chernogorsk, near Mongolia, 3,700 miles from Leningrad. Irina was allowed to join him there in a very primitive one-room wooden hut. She brought legal books that enabled them to write protests to the authorities and to the West that resulted in a surprising reduction of his sentence. He was released and flew with Irina to a celebratory welcome with friends in Leningrad on June 6, 1982.

The only work Lein could find was as a stoker in a boiler room by day and as a mathematics tutor in the evening. The KGB and militia continued to monitor his activities.[45] Nevertheless he maintained contact with supporters in the West and was visited by members of the U.S. Congress. The Leins met with the Reagans at the American Embassy in Moscow in 1988 and also received support from Margaret Thatcher. They made aliyah in 1989 and were able to return to their pre-refusenik careers – Evgeny teaching mathematics at the Hebrew University of Jerusalem and Irina doing research in immunology at the Medical School of Hadassah University Hospital.[46]

ALEXANDER PARITSKY

In 1979 as Jews in Leningrad were organizing the Jewish history, culture and traditions seminars, Jews in Kharkov, Ukraine, were setting up their "Jewish University." During the mid-'70s as Soviet Jewish emigration grew thanks to the Jackson-Vanik Amendment, applications for exit visas soared and most applicants were allowed to emigrate, but a new environment followed the Brezhnev-Carter summit meeting of June 1979. Permissions stopped abruptly, initially in Kharkov and Odessa, and later throughout the USSR, and many Jewish families unexpectedly became refuseniks.

The Jewish University in Kharkov was started when new and old refuseniks were fired from their jobs and their children were thrown out of school. Standard courses in mathematics and sciences were supplemented by courses in Hebrew and Jewish history. Among the refuseniks there were many qualified to teach. Alexander Paritsky volunteered to give a course in Jewish history based on a textbook he received from a professor who had visited from Jerusalem.[47]

Paritsky's father had experienced anti-Semitism during Stalin's regime and served in the gulag for ten years. When he returned, Alexander, then a teenager, asked, "What does it mean to be a Jew?" His father replied, "Now that you're old enough to ask the question, you're old enough to discover the answer." His father went to a closet, pulled out an old prayer book, and as he opened the book he began to cry. "I've been in prison for ten years because I'm a Jew. I was going to teach you the *aleph-bet* but I don't even remember the letters." This experience convinced Alexander Paritsky that someday he must learn the aleph-bet and teach it to others.[48] However, attaining a doctorate in electronics engineering with expertise in acoustics and optics and a prestigious position as chief engineer on a project for the Soviet Navy were his top priorities initially.

But eventually he began to question the validity of Marxism. He read whatever dissident literature he could find and one night he and his wife, Pollina, came across a book of speeches and articles written between 1907 and 1910 by Vladimir (Ze'ev) Jabotinsky, an uncompromising militant Zionist leader from Odessa,. The book transformed Paritsky into a Zionist. He asked himself, "Why am I struggling for Russia? Why don't I think about my own people?"

He knew that with his position and access to secret technology it would be very difficult to obtain an exit visa, but he applied anyway in 1975. As he expected, his application was refused and he was fired from his position. He was told, "You will never leave the Soviet Union." Paritsky found work as an elevator repairman and used his knowledge of English to make contact with foreigners.[49] In 1976 his family was adopted by a Soviet Jewry group in England who organized a synchronized phone-in that jammed all the lines to Kharkov.[50] Visitors from Lille, France, Kharkov's sister city, also wrote to the Paritskys and expressed support for their right to emigrate in letters to the head of Kharkov OVIR.

The Paritskys sought to have a memorial established at a site near Kharkov where at least 15,000 Jews had been massacred by the Nazis. The Soviets refused to recognize it and warned Alexander against photographing and disseminating pictures of the site. KGB agents questioned him and accused him of participating in an anti-Soviet demonstration in 1978.

Just before the school year began, on August 28, 1981, Paritsky was arrested while he was using the public telephone at a post office. The KGB and police claimed he was a spy passing secret information over the phone, and charged him with anti-Soviet slander. The Kharkov police, far more harsh than those in Moscow and Leningrad, tried to beat him, Pollina and their daughters and then claimed that Paritsky had beaten them. While Paritsky was awaiting trial his fifteen-year-old daughter, Dorina, was visited at school by KGB agents who told her that unless she renounced her father, she and her younger sister, Anna, would be forcibly placed in a state orphanage.

Paritsky was found guilty and sentenced to three years of hard labor in Siberia, near the Mongolian border. He was the only political prisoner in a camp of young criminals who often beat him. His only visitor and link with the outside world was Pollina, and he spent 400 days in solitary confinement, lacking warm clothes and with nothing to eat but bread and water one day and bread and soup the next. He had several heart attacks during his ordeal in the camp, prompting Pierre Mauroy, the prime minister of France, and other Western leaders to write to Andropov asking for Paritsky's release and permission to emigrate to Israel for medical treatment.

Pollina was able to accompany her husband on the five-day train ride from the camp to Kharkov when his prison term ended in September 1984. When they reapplied for exit visas they were told that their refusal would be for life, and they were fired from their menial jobs as stokers. Dorina received permission to emigrate in 1987 and went to Israel alone that year. Alexander, Pollina and Anna remained in refusal until the following year when they received their exit visas and arrived in Israel. At age fifty,

Alexander started a new active life in Jerusalem and founded a successful electronics company, PhoneOr, which is based on a new technology, unconnected with anything he did in the USSR.[51]

YULI EDELSTEIN

By mid-1984 the KGB realized that they had failed in their attempt to totally crush all vestiges of Hebrew study and Jewish activism. Arresting and jailing activists on trumped-up charges of anti-Soviet slander weren't working so they tried a new approach – trumped-up charges of illegal drug possession and usage.[52] Tatiana Edelstein overheard a policeman in Moscow telling one of his colleagues, "You know, the Jews have a weekly drug-sniffing ceremony." Clearly the policeman was talking about the *havdalah* ritual at end of the Sabbath in which Jews bless and smell the fragrance of cloves or other spices, so she immediately rushed home, pulled the spice box off its shelf, and dumped it into the trash. Her husband, Yuli, a twenty-five-year-old activist and Hebrew teacher, had already been harassed and his Hebrew classes were often disrupted.

The following Sabbath the Edelstein apartment was raided and searched. A box of matches used for lighting the candles was confiscated. Yuli was arrested on September 4, 1984, and charged with unlawful possession of drugs. During his trial the prosecution claimed that the matchbox contained one gram of hashish. Edelstein denied the charge, and though there were inconsistencies in the testimony of the officers who searched the apartment, the judge found Edelstein guilty and sentenced him to three years in labor camps. Concurrently, another Hebrew teacher in Moscow, Alexander Kholmiansky, was convicted of "possessing a firearm" and seven other Hebrew teachers in Leningrad, Odessa, Riga and Samarkand were arrested for "malicious hooliganism," "resisting arrest," or "disseminating material defamatory to the Soviet state." In October 1984 forty-two Moscow refuseniks began a rotating hunger strike – each person fasting for three or four days – to draw world attention to the nine Hebrew teachers. A few days later they were joined by over 200 refuseniks in ten Soviet cities. They sent a cable of protest to Soviet general secretary Chernenko.[53]

Edelstein's appeal was turned down and he was sent to a labor camp in the Ulan Ude area of eastern Siberia. One of his cellmates, a man who had been convicted of drug possession for a second time, asked Edelstein about his conviction. When Edelstein told him he had got three years for being accused of possessing one gram of hashish the cellmate was amazed and replied, "I got only two years for ten kilos of hashish!" Edelstein is certain that if his wife had not gotten rid of the spice box he could have gotten twelve years for "pushing to others."[54]

Amnesty International adopted Edelstein as a prisoner of conscience in 1985 and publicized his case stating that they believed his "imprisonment stems from his non-violent exercise of the rights of freedom of expression and association." They also reported that he had been beaten by criminals in the camp.[55]

At the end of 1985 he suffered multiple fractures and a torn urethra when he slipped on an icy wooden ramp while he was making railroad ties. After having no treatment for two weeks he was flown to Novosibirsk for surgery, and then placed in a nearby labor camp's hospital. His wife and father were allowed to visit him there. Upon returning to Moscow, Tatiana launched a campaign for his early release. The president of Magen David Adom in Israel cabled his counterpart, the director of the Red Cross in Moscow, requesting that Edelstein be transferred to a major medical center in the USSR as a humanitarian gesture.[56]

Notes from Edelstein's trial that had been smuggled into Israel were read by Wayne Firestone, an aspiring law student who was spending a year at Tel Aviv University. He was appalled at the gross injustice of the case and sequestered himself for forty-eight hours writing a play called *Trial and Error* that reenacted the court proceedings. Fellow students performed it and then circulated through the audience giving out addresses of Soviet government officials and asking them to write letters of protest.

When Firestone returned to the University of Miami he organized performances of *Trial and Error* with Hillel and at other American campuses, with solicitations for support from each audience. Firestone then traveled to Russia and tape-recorded Tatiana Edelstein describing her husband's condition and appealing for help. The tape was played at subsequent performances of *Trial and Error.*[57]

Soviet Jewry organizations in the West sent letters and cables to officials in the camp and the Soviet government. The officials told Edelstein that they would release him if he admitted his guilt. He refused, declaring, "If they found a way to put me away without my cooperation, they can also find a way to release me without my cooperation."[58]

Fifteen people named Edelstone, Edelstein, Edelsteyn, Edelshtein, and Edelson in Toronto met and formed a group called Edelsteins for Edelshtein (the original spelling of his name). They sent parcels to Tatiana, got television news publicity and appealed to members of Parliament to put pressure on the Soviets for Edelstein's freedom.[59] But there was no early release; Edelstein served nearly three years until Israel's Independence Day in May 1987. Exit visas for the family came a month later.

In Israel Edelstein became chairman of Olami, a non-profit organization that offered educational programs for new immigrants, and preceded Yisrael B'Aliya, the political party that he founded with Natan Sharansky in 1996. He was elected to the Knesset that year and was appointed minister of absorption.[60]

THE LAST PRISONER OF ZION?

Like Edelstein, Alexei Magarik was a twenty-something Hebrew teacher in Moscow who was arrested on fabricated charges of drug possession. But Magarik's arrest occurred on March 14, 1986, during the supposedly more relaxed era of glasnost. His wife, Natasha Ratner, believes the KGB was really after her because of her zealous activism in the refusenik community, but didn't want to arrest the mother of an infant. Magarik, on the other hand, a cellist and amateur woodcarver, was an easy target as he traveled from Moscow to Tbilisi to visit friends. He was carrying pipes that he had handcrafted for smoking tobacco and it was easy for KGB agents to plant some hashish in his suitcase and claim that he was transporting the contraband.

Two men who were with Magarik when he packed his bag said they were willing to testify that there were no drugs in it before he left for the airport.[61] Vladimir Magarik, Alexei's father, who had been living in Israel with Vladimir's daughter since 1982, sought help from the Lishka. He couldn't believe their suggestion that if Vladimir kept a low profile, his son would get "soft" prison conditions and maybe an early release. Vladimir instead embarked on a worldwide campaign to appeal for his son's freedom. He asserted, "Alexei found his hope in Jewish culture; he did not need drugs."[62] Natasha Ratner joined Tatiana Edelstein in appealing to the Soviet Supreme Court on behalf of their husbands.[63]

On June 9, 1986, after protesting his innocence and stating that he had never used illegal drugs, Alexei Magarik was sentenced to three years in labor camps, the maximum term for possession of drugs.[64] The Soviet Jewry Education and Information Center accused the Soviet authorities of "turning Jewish activists... into scapegoats in the drugs war."[65]

A month later Magarik's appeal was denied and he was moved from Tbilisi to a labor camp in Omsk and treated as a criminal, rather than a political prisoner. Natasha was able to visit him and reported that he was beaten all over his body by cellmates and kept for two weeks in a special unit for "backward detainees." She requested that the Union of Councils for Soviet Jews undertake a campaign to protest the lack of protective clothing and equipment for prisoners who were forced to work with dangerous materials and to bring attention to the brutal and lawless administration of the Omsk prison camp.[66]

A bipartisan group of sixty-four U.S. congressmen wrote directly to Gorbachev requesting that he commute or reduce Magarik's sentence.[67] Vladimir and his daughter, Hannah, traveled across the United States by bicycle and car to publicize their campaign for Alexei's freedom.[68] Vladimir then went to Vienna and started a hunger strike during the November 1986 meetings between Soviet foreign minister Eduard Shevardnadze and US secretary of state George Shultz.[69] But the T-shirt Vladimir wore with Alexei's picture on it was considered too provocative by Austrian authorities so the Viennese arrested, detained and fined him.[70] Vladimir's next stop was Reykjavik, Iceland, with Chicago activist Sister Ann Gillen (Chapter 18), in time to protest at the Reagan-Gorbachev summit.[71]

In Moscow activists held daily demonstrations during February 1987 on behalf of Prisoners of Zion including Begun, Edelstein and Magarik. Participants were beaten and some equipment belonging to foreign correspondents was damaged.[72] In May the Tbilisi City Court cut Magarik's term in half and announced that he would be released in September 1987. Natasha and 131 other Moscow refuseniks sent a letter to Gorbachev protesting this halfway measure, and demanded Magarik's immediate release. There was no response and Magarik remained in Omsk until September, hailed by supporters as the "Last Prisoner of Zion."[73]

In a telephone conversation from Moscow after his release and four months before he and Natasha made aliyah, Magarik declared,

> I cannot be and I am not the last of the Prisoners of Zion. Even in my moment of release from jail it is known that there is at least one other, Yosef Zisels, who is still kept in confinement in the labor camp…in the sea of arrests it is very unlikely that we will know all the names, and we can never be sure of the reason behind any of the prison sentences of Jews in this country. It is certain there are Jews who are being confined and exposed to sufferings, who undoubtedly deserve to be called Prisoners of Zion, but whose names are not known to us, not known to anybody at all. Their fate is more frightening than mine, and their plight is more tragic than that of the well-known Prisoners of Zion. We knew that there was

a struggle on our behalf, that our names were known in the West, and that everything that was happening to us would be immediately reported to the free world. But those people are not known to anybody. That is why they are mocked and humiliated in every possible way, and there is no one to stand up for them. I want to say that these people need more courage to carry on. And I know that despite all kinds of pressure, despite the fact that their names are virtually unknown, they bravely deny their alleged guilt and bear their sufferings with admirable endurance. That is why, in connection with the above, I cannot be the last Prisoner of Zion. I wish that people in the West would understand this and raise their voices on behalf of those Prisoners of Zion, known to nobody, who are still tortured in the Soviet jails.[74]

sssj 1982 ad in New York Times.

CHAPTER ELEVEN

The Refusenik Community Casts its Own Safety Nets

There was no turning back. The moment a Soviet Jew submitted an application for an exit visa his or her life would change forever, without exception. The lucky ones who received permission could pack up and fly to Vienna where the Joint Distribution Committee and the Jewish Agency would assist them in their move to Israel. Once in Israel they would be housed and fed in absorption centers to prepare for their new lives as Israelis. Or, they might opt to seek refugee status in America by traveling from Vienna to Rome and receiving assistance from the Hebrew Immigrant Aid Society until they were securely settled in an American community. But for those who received refusals or were waiting for a response to their applications it could be like falling into an abyss. First their careers were shattered as they were either fired or demoted.[1] Then they were denounced as "traitors" in the newspapers, subjected to alienation from neighbors, colleagues, former friends, and even some relatives who, recalling Stalin's era, feared "guilt by association" as it became apparent that these new refuseniks or "waitniks" would be under KGB surveillance.[2]

NETWORKING AT THE SYNAGOGUE

The first task of the newly fired Jew, even if he had saved a considerable amount of money, was to find another job so that he could not be prosecuted for *parasitism*. Most often they sought help from friends who were already refuseniks and knew of employers who needed workers for low-paying jobs that had nothing to do with the military or state security.[3] These friends might be the same ones who had given the new refusenik an *instruktzia* that described in detail the daunting and complicated procedure to apply for an exit visa. The first step was to get a *vyzov*, an invitation from a close relative in Israel.[4]

How could a Soviet Jew get a vyzov if he knew no one in Israel? The procedure was to make contact with a visitor from abroad or someone who had already received permission and could convey such a request to Israel. Jews from abroad were likely to be found at the synagogues in Moscow, Leningrad and other major cities every Saturday morning. Consequently some Soviet Jews appeared at a synagogue for the first time in their lives.[5] Among them were those seeking Hebrew teachers, refuseniks striking up friendships with others in the same predicament, and friends trading news about the latest refusals, permissions, arrests and interrogations. Refuseniks who wanted support from the West would cautiously approach tourists and pass their personal contact information to them. All of this was happening in the streets in front of, but not inside, the synagogues as the synagogue elders were leery of these activities and feared reprisals from the KGB.[6]

In 1973 two activist refuseniks, Alexander Luntz and Dina Beilin, found that the Moscow synagogue and the OVIR office were excellent places to gather all possible information about applicants who received permission and those who were refused. However, the arbitrariness of refusals made analyzing the data comparable to trying to predict to the outcome of a lottery. Nevertheless, Luntz organized the publication of a semiannual report on refuseniks (with their permission) and the persecution that they had experienced.

Refuseniks from outside Moscow learned about Beilin and Luntz from BBC and Voice of America broadcasts, and provided their personal data for the lists of refuseniks and their special needs that Beilin was preparing. She passed her information on to tourists at the synagogue who would visit Vladimir Slepak and Alexander Lerner. These prominent English-speaking refuseniks could obtain support for other refuseniks from their telephone contacts abroad and from foreign correspondents in Moscow.

Beilin took responsibility for welcoming and initiating new refuseniks into the community and addressing their material needs as well as boosting their morale. A recurring problem was that of draft-age men who were called into the army when a family applied for exit visas. This could result in long-term refusal for them, so Beilin worked with physicians to find reasons, including simulated epileptic seizures, poor eyesight, urinary incontinence and psychiatric problems that would rule the draftee physically unfit for military service.[7]

Tony Barbieri, who was a correspondent based in Moscow for the *Baltimore Sun* from 1979 to 1984, often went to the synagogue and described it as "the freest place in the Soviet Union." There he and other newly arrived reporters developed mutually beneficial relationships with refuseniks who spoke English and could give advice on how to find their way around the capital city of the Soviet Union. The reporters, in turn, often conveyed materials from activists in the West to the refuseniks and publicized their plight in news stories.[8]

There were refuseniks who chose to sit home quietly, but activists like Luntz felt that those people would sit forever. He was prepared to risk arrest. At the synagogue he circulated protest letters and set up secret meetings to organize demonstrations that would last a few minutes before the KGB and militia arrived to disperse the participants and jail the ringleaders for anything from two weeks to five years.[9]

The refuseniks of Moscow celebrated Jewish holidays as a community. The first large gathering was organized by Alexander and Judith Lerner in a Moscow park.[10] Starting with Israel's Independence Day in May 1976 they would assemble in the Ovrashky Forest near Moscow during the warm months until Succot for picnics for the next twenty years. Of course there were KGB agents observing the proceedings, photographing and threatening the participants and harassing them with noisy tractors nearby. But the refuseniks were undaunted as they joyously gathered by the hundreds and shared their desire celebrate in Israel in the near future. As the refuseniks began to learn Hebrew and Jewish culture the picnics took on an Israeli appearance. Each year on *Lag B'Omer* children played with toy bows and arrows in Ovrashky just like their counterparts throughout Israel. Since 1996 former refuseniks who emigrated from all parts of the Soviet Union have been reenacting the Ovrashky picnics – of course without KGB oversight – in the Ben Shemen Forest midway between Tel Aviv and Jerusalem.[11]

SEMINARS FOR SCIENTISTS

The loose network of refuseniks helping one another worked well to satisfy material and spiritual needs, but the scientists, mathematicians and engineers among them were missing something from their lives: the ability to keep up-to-date with advances in their fields through interaction with their peers, especially those who were also in refusal. Stripped of their jobs, unable to attend professional conferences, and cut off from international journals, these refuseniks felt intellectually starved.[12] First Alexander Lerner, and two weeks later Alexander Voronel, proposed holding seminars in their own apartments for refuseniks to read papers on their latest work and discuss scientific ideas. The weekly seminars began in 1972 with about twenty participants including Mark Azbel, Irina and Victor Brailovsky, Benjamin Fain, Benjamin Levitch, and Alexander Luntz.[13]

The seminars grew in size and popularity and attracted the attention of Western scientists, who began to drop in on them when they were in Moscow for international conferences. Eventually, the Western visitors would be the featured lecturers at some of the seminars.[14] In 1973 scientists from all parts of the free world rallied in support of seven refusenik colleagues who went on their first hunger strike to protest their status. The hunger strike lasted for fifteen days and was timed to coincide with Brezhnev's visit to the United States, prompting American reporters to ask challenging questions of the visiting general secretary at every opportunity, and yielding constant publicity over the Voice of America and the BBC. An immediate result of the strike was permission for one of the seven, Anatoly Libgober, to leave for Israel. Shortly thereafter, Dan Roginsky and Alexander Voronel were allowed to emigrate.[15]

For the refusenik scientists the seminars were another way of receiving news about other refuseniks and KGB activities. Azbel estimates that 70% of the regular attendees came to every seminar regardless of the topic, just to be in contact with those whose lives were similarly affected by their refusenik status. Azbel hosted the seminars in his apartment after Voronel left for Israel, and in 1977, when Azbel himself emigrated, the seminars relocated to Brailovsky's apartment, where they continued until his arrest in 1980.[16]

Brailovsky and other seminar participants first tried to attract attention from Western scientists by inviting them to his apartment for an "International Conference on Collective Phenomena" in 1974, but an invitation they sent to scientists in England fell into the hands of KGB agents. KGB chief Yuri Andropov sent a memo to the Soviet CPSU Central Committee characterizing Brailovsky, Azbel, Luntz and Voronel as "pro-Zionist scholars and unemployed Jewish nationalists…allegedly trapped in a hopeless situation" with intentions "of provoking an anti-Soviet campaign abroad in support of their demands for free emigration from the Soviet Union" and being connected with "the plan nurtured in Zionist circles of creating in Israel an international science center." Andropov asserted that the KGB was "taking measures to thwart the provocative acts of the Zionists."[17] Indeed, Soviet authorities prevented the conference from being held and jailed Brailovsky and a dozen organizers for fifteen days. As there was no law prohibiting scientific seminars, they were arrested illegally and no formal charges were presented.[18]

In addition to his participation in the scientific seminars from 1972 until 1978, Brailovsky was one of the editors of an unofficial journal called *Jews in the USSR* that offered Russian translations of articles by Martin Buber and other Jewish authors, as well as articles that examined the problems faced by Jews in the Soviet Union. He collected material for the "Symposium on Jewish Culture," organized by Fain, to be held in December 1976, but the KGB again intervened, searched his apartment, confiscated the symposium materials, and detained him. During his interrogation he was warned, "I could arrest you immediately as we did with Sharansky...You are ill and I can assure you that you will not survive more than two years in our camps, while your sentence will be at least seven years!"

In spite of all the harassment the scientific seminars were held regularly and in 1978 a three-day International Conference on Collective Phenomena was held with scientists from America, Britain, France and Switzerland sharing ideas with their Soviet Jewish colleagues.[19] The concept of holding refusenik professional seminars spread to Leningrad, beginning in 1976, with a mathematics seminar held in the apartment of Aba and Ida Taratuta. Foreign mathematicians and scientists who were visiting in Leningrad attended. While the police didn't interfere with the seminar, the Taratutas and their guests were kept under constant surveillance.[20]

The Soviet regime got its comeuppance when Arno Penzias, an American who won the 1978 Nobel Prize in Physics for his work in radio astronomy that enabled a better understanding of the origins of the universe and the "Big Bang Theory," flew to Moscow from Stockholm and delivered his Nobel Prize acceptance speech at a refusenik seminar and, as a protest against the restrictive emigration policy of the USSR, refused to appear at the Soviet Academy of Sciences.[21]

As relations with the West soured in reaction to the Soviet invasion of Afghanistan, Soviet authorities took a harder stance against the refusenik seminars and their organizers. Brailovsky was arrested on November 13, 1980, and police prevented seminar attendees and American correspondents from entering his apartment building, claiming that "sanitary workers were disinfecting the premises for bedbugs." Brailovsky spent ten months in prison in Moscow and was then exiled for three years to Kazakhstan. His crime was defaming the Soviet system by publishing *Jews in the USSR*.[22] While he was incarcerated and exiled, the seminars were held at various times and locations under the leadership of Yakov Alpert and Alexander Ioffe, but the participants' apartments were under round-the-clock KGB surveillance.[23]

During Gorbachev's regime refuseniks held scientific seminars in Moscow more regularly. Ioffe and Yuri Chernyak led them and eventually refuseniks from outside Moscow managed to attend some sessions. In 1987 Chernyak received a Toshiba personal computer as a gift from Bill Marcus of Boston Action for Soviet Jewry.[24] Another activist from Boston, Solomon Schimmel, was able to get it through customs unchallenged. Chernyak was overjoyed, knowing that with the computer he and his group of mathematician coworkers would be able to solve certain problems that they had been working on for a very long time. Furthermore, the computer could be put to excellent use in training refuseniks for their future lives as professionals in Israel and other free countries. Over one hundred students attended classes in Chernyak's apartment that were held two days a week.[25] Within a year fourteen additional computers and printers arrived and were utilized to provide materials for the Jewish schools.[26]

THE REFUSENIKS' HOME THEATER

When entertainers applied for exit visas they were not only dismissed from their jobs; they were also barred from performing in public and their films and record albums were immediately withdrawn from circulation. Like the scientists they were eager to maintain their professional skills and arranged to perform in various apartments with other refuseniks.

Savely Kramarov, a slapstick comedian in the style of Jerry Lewis who had appeared in over forty films and a television mini-series, shocked his fans in 1979 by announcing his intention to leave Russia and live in Israel. As a refusenik he performed in a Moscow refusenik apartment along with several singers and pianist and conductor Vladimir Feltsman. Tony Barbieri was a guest at the "home theater" and immediately wrote a story for the *Baltimore Sun* about Kramarov. Thanks to the capricious nature of the Soviet system Kramarov received his exit visa a few weeks later. Kramarov eventually settled in the United States and appeared as a character actor in several films including *Moscow on the Hudson* in 1984, in which ironically he played a hot-dog vendor/KGB agent.[27] Feltsman applied for an exit visa in 1979 motivated by a desire for greater freedom of expression. He was immediately banned from performing in public and refused permission to emigrate until 1987. Upon settling in the United States he debuted at the White House and Carnegie Hall and resumed his brilliant career.[28]

THE LEGAL SEMINARS

Another series of seminars that were of life-saving value to dozens of refuseniks dealt with the intricacies of the Soviet criminal code and emigration law. Ilya Citovsky started the seminars in 1975 as meetings in various apartments under the cumbersome name of the "Moscow Judicial Humanitarian Seminar for Refuseniks." In 1979 when Citovsky emigrated he asked Mark Berenfeld, a physicist who had studied the criminal code, to take over the seminars.

Berenfeld traces his desire to leave the Soviet Union back to 1953, just before Stalin's death, when he saw a huge number of empty trains rolling into Byelorussia station in Moscow and shuddered when he learned that they were to be loaded with Jews for transport to concentration camps. Four years later he experienced anti-Semitism when he applied to enter a prestigious college and had to settle for admission to the Moscow Energy Institute. In 1977 he and his wife applied for exit visas. They were refused for security reasons even though neither of them had access to any classified information. Berenfeld soon learned that other refuseniks were in the same position so he decided to study the emigration laws and the criminal code, asserting, "It's my opinion that we must do everything legally."

Berenfeld's seminars had forty to seventy people each week and served as workshops on how to get another job after being fired, how to protest legally, how to write letters to the courts. Based on what he had learned from Vladimir Albrecht's book, he taught refuseniks how to be a witness and how to behave during interrogations. He often told his students, "If you are silent and do nothing, nothing will happen to improve your situation; however, if you start to protest, the KGB will pay attention and eventually they'll let you out." Berenfeld was finally allowed to emigrate in 1989 when British prime minister Margaret Thatcher negotiated a trade deal with Gorbachev that was conditioned on his allowing ten refusenik families to leave.[29]

While Berenfeld was studying the criminal code and holding seminars in Moscow Vladimir Kislik was doing the same thing in Kiev, where he lived as a refusenik on a pension due to radiation sickness contracted in the 1960s when he worked on nuclear reactors.[30] A refusenik since 1973, Kislik was severely beaten and forcibly prevented from traveling to meet American congressmen in Moscow in 1974 and again, in 1979, prevented from going to Moscow to attend a scientific seminar. He had also been interrogated by the KGB for signing a letter in support of Sharansky. In 1980 he was arrested and illegally imprisoned for the two weeks of the Olympic Games to keep him away from foreigners. Additionally, he was detained in a psychiatric ward when he started a hunger strike to protest, and was on trial for malicious hooliganism in 1981. He served three years in a strict-regime labor camp in Ukraine. The following year Kislik was able to move to Moscow and married Bella Gulko, a refusenik who had written letters to him and visited him while he was in the labor camp. In Moscow the couple organized a series of seminars on the legal problems of leaving the USSR.

Having been subjected to a full spectrum of injustices and having immersed himself in studying Soviet law during his precious free moments, Kislik was uniquely qualified to give advice to other refuseniks.[31] He helped Ida Nudel in 1987 when she tried to regain her residence permit to live in her Moscow apartment after her exile in Moldavia. He arranged for a court hearing to be held regarding her claims but that case became moot when she got permission to go where she really wanted to live: Israel.[32]

Although mail to him from abroad was cut off, Kislik maintained contact with a group of lawyers from Britain, Canada, France, Israel and the U.S.A., and prepared test cases of fifty refusenik families for Soviet courts. Gulko created a database of these cases, prepared numerous legal disputes against the refuseniks' former employers, and persuaded a sympathetic judge to listen to them.[33] The seminar became a member organization of the International Committee for the Protection of Human Rights and hosted a meeting of international human rights lawyers in the Kislik apartment in 1988. Staffers of the American, Dutch and French embassies in Moscow were frequent visitors. The seminar sessions were open to persecuted people of all religions and support was given to Catholics from western Ukraine and Baptists from Siberia. Kislik empathized with dissidents but often stated that he and his associates "were fighting for our right to emigrate, not to change the existing regime."[34] Gulko was also active as a legal advisor in a refusenik women's group that was initiated by long-term refusenik women in Moscow and achieved considerable press attention in the West.[35]

By the end of 1988 the Soviets had tired of the constant international pressure stemming from the judicial seminars and decided to grant Gulko and Kislik their exit visas. Gulko was already out; she had been allowed to travel to Washington with Sakharov and other human rights activists for an international conference on human rights.

REFUSENIK WOMEN'S GROUPS

In October 1977 a group of refusenik women banded together in Moscow to provide support, friendship, and advice when they could see no light at the end of the tunnel. They were primarily concerned with the psychological burden that life in refusal placed on their children. Twelve women mailed a petition to Brezhnev asking for a meeting with him to discuss their situation. The response was several days of house arrest for the twelve. They fared better three months later when they brought a petition to the directors of OVIR, and were told by Albert Ivanov that their cases would be reexamined. A committee consisting of Hanna Elinson, Batsheva Elistratova, Irene Gildengorn-Lanier, Natalia Rosenstein and Larissa Vilenskaya was formed to systematically check on the progress of the case reviews and report them to the world.

Having seen no progress at all, the committee staged its first demonstration, on International Women's Day, March 8, 1978, at the Lenin Library. Most of the women were prevented from leaving their homes by the KGB.[36] However, about ten women who got to the site with "Let My People Go" signs around their necks were arrested by the militia and interrogated for several hours. Although they were harassed, women were considered less likely to be arrested and beaten at demonstrations than men.

A rally to commemorate International Children's Day (June 1) was the group's next event and since children were involved the group wrote to the Supreme Soviet asking for protection for them.[37] According to Ida Nudel, at one demonstration near the Kremlin, bystanders shouted, "Where is Hitler to finish off this situation?"[38] Following sit-in demonstrations at the Supreme Soviet and OVIR headquarters, Rosa Ioffe and other members of the group were able to interview Boris Shumilin, the deputy minister of internal affairs, who told them that their refusals could last indefinitely.[39]

The group debated the question of participation by non-Jewish women and decided in favor of supporting Irina McClellan, a Russian Orthodox woman who had married a visiting history professor from the University of Virginia in Moscow in 1974.[40] Prof. Woodford McClellan returned to the United States when his visa expired later that year, but Irina was not allowed to emigrate, and Soviet authorities rejected her husband's requests for another visa to visit Moscow. After four years with no hope of reunification, Irina McClellan, aided by Jewish women refuseniks, tried to chain herself to the gate of the American Embassy.[41] She was finally allowed to emigrate and join her husband in 1986.[42]

In addition to protesting the group frequently met with visiting political leaders from the West, organized a Jewish kindergarten and provided food and clothing to Prisoners of Zion and formed a network of support for the prisoners' wives. Refusenik women in Leningrad, Kiev, Kharkov, Odessa and other Soviet cities organized similar groups.[43]

By 1986 two distinct groups were functioning in the Soviet Union: Jewish Women Against Refusal and Jewish Women for Emigration and Survival in Refusal. JWAR was primarily focused on aliyah while JWESR aimed to address the refuseniks' problems of social isolation, loss of professional jobs, reduced social status and financial difficulties. In addition to the International Children's Day rally both groups held a three-day hunger strike in March for International Women's Day. They marched to the Presidium of the Supreme Soviet and demanded interviews with the leaders of the Kremlin. They were told to come back in two weeks and five of the demonstrators were given permission to emigrate when the group returned two weeks later.[44]

Mara Abramovich and other members of JWESR visited sites in Kiev, Lvov, Minsk and Riga where Jews had been murdered during the Holocaust. They laid wreaths on the graves with inscriptions in Yiddish and other languages that read, "To the generation of misfortune from the generation of hope."[45]

The women of JWESR were particularly incensed in November 1987 when they read that Gorbachev had told a French audience that there were only 220 refuseniks left in the Soviet Union. They knew this was untrue and launched a data gathering project to prove that the number was actually higher. By the end of 1987 they collected lists of hundreds of refuseniks and entered data into the computer that was operating nonstop in Chernyak's apartment. The easily updatable "true lists of refuseniks" on diskettes were brought to the American Embassy every week and provided ambassador Schifter with powerful leverage in his negotiations with the Soviet Foreign Ministry. With delight, he told the Chernyaks, "They cannot lie to me anymore."[46]

JWAR, meanwhile, continued holding its demonstrations and annual hunger strikes on International Women's Day, which Inna Uspensky described as "the group's strongest instrument" for attracting attention from the press and American legislators. About one hundred women in various Soviet cities joined the three-day strike in 1987. The strikes were repeated in 1988 and 1989 with fewer participants each year for the best possible reason – many of the members had been permitted to emigrate.[47]

THE POOR RELATIVES

Unlike most JWAR members whose refusals were for state security reasons, Anna Kholmiansky was refused because her father was unwilling to sign a paper that released her from future financial obligations to him. A seemingly innocuous restriction of the Soviet Emigration Law that became effective on January 1, 1987, created this bizarre circumstance. Article 24 of the law stated that "a request to the USSR for reunification abroad with members of one's family will be considered on the basis of…certified statements of family members (including a former spouse, if there are any minor children from the common marriage) to the effect that there are no unfulfilled obligations towards them as provided by legislation of the USSR."

Anna Kholmiansky, her husband Alexander, a Hebrew teacher who had been tried and imprisoned during the same time period as Yuli Edelstein, and their baby Dora were thus prevented from reuniting with Alexander's brother in Israel.[48] Anna went on a hunger strike in October 1987 to protest the new rule. She was supported by dozens of other refuseniks who were in a similar situation. They called themselves the "Poor Relatives."[49]

Several families who realized that when the new law went into effect recalcitrant members of their own families might undermine their efforts to emigrate met in a Moscow apartment in late 1986 to form a support group. Vladimir Meshkov, whose mother-in-law refused to sign any documents, organized weekly demonstrations at OVIR and the Lenin Library to protest the new law. They also gathered to picket the workplaces of various stubborn relatives in Moscow and Leningrad. The protests were quickly broken up by the police and some of the demonstrators were jailed for fifteen days and fined 50 rubles. Meshkov recalls that vigorous protests from an official from the Dutch Embassy prevented the KGB from beating up the demonstrators.

The initial demonstrations had little effect until Reagan's visit to Moscow in 1988. Wearing yellow Magen David pins, fifty Poor Relatives and their children came to greet Reagan amid the roar of construction machinery staged by the KGB in an effort to drown out their protest. Publicizing Meshkov's case, the event received worldwide TV and newspaper coverage, prompting OVIR to give the Meshkov family permission to emigrate without the obstinate mother-in-law's signature.[50]

Other Poor Relatives were not so fortunate and were still waiting for their visas in early 1991 when the U.S. Congressional Call to Conscience Vigil pointed out that "although the number of Jews leaving has risen and the Soviets have passed their emigration legislation, the number of refuseniks and those Soviet Jews who are unable to apply to emigrate, the so-called poor relatives, remains in the hundreds." The gates finally opened for the Poor Relatives when the Soviet Union dissolved in December 1991.[51]

Many years later it is still difficult for some Poor Relatives to come to grips with their struggle. One of them who declined to be interviewed commented, "I do not think I want relive those times. They are buried deep and I wish I could say "forgotten," but no, just buried. It's too painful to talk about it...to have a problem within your family is much harder to fight than the obvious 'government evil.'"[52]

REFLECTIONS OF LIFE AS A REFUSENIK

"Life in refusal had its own bright sides," Yuri Chernyak said while being interviewed by Aba Taratuta in Boston. Chernyak asserted that "applying for a visa was the wisest step I had ever taken. My life became infinitely better, because I became a free man, I could say what I wanted to, without being afraid that I would be dismissed or demoted...This sense of freedom was such a blessing that I felt sorry for the 200 million [non-refusenik Soviet citizens]."[53]

Refusenik Scientists' Seminar, Moscow, May 1977. Left to right: Andrei Sakharov, Nahum Meiman (back to camera), Benjamin Fain, Mark Azbel, Benjamin Levich. Photo Credit: Valeri Fayerman.

Refusenik children practicing archery, a traditional Lag b'Omer activity, at a picnic in the Ovrashky Forest in 1977. In the foreground are Efraim Rosenstein (left) and David Shvartsman (right). Photo credit: Yona Shvartsman.

Part Three

The Human Rights
Connection
1968–1986

CHAPTER TWELVE

Andrei Sakharov – Champion of Human Rights

The Soviet Union was playing catch-up. On March 10, 1950, former President Harry Truman directed the U.S. Atomic Energy Commission to develop a hydrogen bomb, and four days later the Soviets responded with their decision to build their own "super" bomb.[1] The top scientists, mathematicians and engineers of the Soviet Union who were working at the "Installation," a secret nuclear weapons facility in Arzamas, about 300 miles east of Moscow, were immediately assigned to the H-bomb project. Among them was physicist Andrei Sakharov, who had joined the team two years earlier at age twenty-seven and would ultimately manage the project.[2] He may have been the only professional employee at the Installation with a prior connection to Arzamas. His great-grandfather, Ioann Sakharov, was a Russian Orthodox priest who had headed the church there from 1845 to 1864 and was noted for zealously proselytizing Catholics and Jews.[3]

AN ACT OF PHILO-SEMITISM

In early 1951 there was a scandal at the Installation. Mates Agrest, the head of the theoretical department's mathematics group, a fervently observant Jew and a friend of Sakharov, had his son circumcised there. This audacious un-Soviet act was performed by Agrest's father, an elderly bearded rabbi who looked as though he had stepped out of one of Rembrandt's paintings. When the KGB found out about the circumcision from a doctor who examined the child a few days later, Agrest's boss at the Installation summarily fired him and gave him one day to gather his family and their belongings and leave the city.

Sakharov, who had often been a guest at Agrest's cottage, felt that his friend was being treated unfairly.[4] He shook Agrest's hand sympathetically and said, "How will we manage without you?" He then added, "You and your family can move into my apartment in Moscow and use it until you find another job." Sakharov saw to it that the dismissal was due to a discovery that Agrest had relatives in Israel, rather than for an act committed by Agrest. He also helped Agrest find a suitable position at a research center in Sukhumi, Georgia.[5]

Sakharov's mentor, Igor Tamm, supported Sakharov's philo-Semitism and helped Agrest pack. Tamm once told Sakharov, "There's one foolproof way of telling if someone belongs to the Russian intelligentsia. A true member of the intelligentsia is never an anti-Semite. If he's infected with that virus, then he's something else, something terrible and dangerous."[6]

SAVIOR AND CONSCIENCE OF THE SOVIET UNION

The world's first hydrogen-based thermonuclear device was detonated by the Americans in the South Pacific on November 1, 1952. Half a world away, Stalin, impatient and paranoid, was putting extreme pressure on Lavrenty Beria, his deputy prime minister and head of the secret police. Beria visited the Installation to strike fear of failure into the hearts and minds of Sakharov and his team. They worked feverishly for long hours each day until the summer of 1953 when their thermonuclear device could be tested in Kazakhstan. A blinding flash and mushroom cloud proved the device was successful, and Sakharov was transformed into a national hero. Georgi Malenkov, Stalin's successor, personally congratulated him, and Igor Kurchatov, who headed the Soviet Union's first atomic bomb project, bowed to Sakharov and said, "It's thanks to you, the savior of Russia!"[7]

However, all this adulation and his new status as Academician Hero of Socialist Labor Sakharov, did not turn him into a bomb-loving Dr. Strangelove. He was concerned about the hazards of nuclear testing, and in 1957 he wrote an article about the effects of low-level radiation, in which he calculated that each megaton of nuclear weapons tested would lead eventually to 10,000 deaths.[8]

During the 1960s Sakharov frequently signed protests against violations of human rights and often appealed to Soviet officials on behalf of persecuted individuals. While working on projects for new weapons, he constantly urged the Soviet leadership to enter into agreements with the United States to halt the arms race. Early in 1968 he was invited to write a paper for the United Nations to mark 1968 as the "Year of Human Rights." He was exhilarated by the news from Czechoslovakia of a regime that offered "socialism with a human face" as he wrote the essay "Reflections on Progress, Peaceful Coexistence, and Intellectual Freedom."[9] Knowing that the essay would not be accepted for publication in any state-run journal, Sakharov circulated typewritten copies of the manuscript as a *samizdat* document in May 1968.[10]

A copy was smuggled out by a Dutch journalist, translated into Dutch and published in the newspaper *Het Porool* two months later and in English by *The New York Times*. The essay revealed Sakharov's concerns about the dangers of thermonuclear annihilation, ecological self-poisoning, and world hunger. He pleaded for an end to the cold war, for a convergence between the capitalist and communist systems, and for an "open society" in the Soviet Union.[11] The essay included a condemnation of anti-Semitism[12] and Sakharov's assertion that "breaking of relations with Israel [after the Six-Day War in 1967] appears a mistake, complicating a peaceful settlement in this region and complicating a necessary diplomatic recognition of Israel by the Arab governments."[13]

Sakharov's exhilaration evaporated in the summer of 1968. First he was banished from the Installation after the KGB obtained a copy of his essay, and in August he was appalled when he learned that Soviet tanks and troops had invaded Czechoslovakia and installed a Stalinist government. A third and crushing blow was the deteriorating health of his wife, Klava, who suffered from inoperable stomach cancer and died in March 1969.[14]

HUMAN RIGHTS, THE LENINGRAD
TRIALS, AND ELENA BONNER

In early 1970 General Piotr Grigorenko, a dissenter who criticized the invasion of Czechoslovakia and other Soviet blunders, was forcibly confined in a mental hospital. Valery Chalidze, the publisher of *Social Problems*, a *samizdat* journal, asked Sakharov to cosponsor a letter to the attorney-general protesting Grigorenko's incarceration. The political abuse of psychiatry greatly troubled Sakharov. He not only signed the letter; he delivered it in person and launched letter-writing campaigns on behalf of other dissenters who were confined in psychiatric institutions. Brezhnev responded to one such letter telling Sakharov that he himself might be a candidate for psychiatric attention as a person suffering from "obsessive reformist delusions."[15]

Sakharov frequently visited Chalidze and the two worked in support of dissidents who were facing trial. In November 1970 they held a press conference to announce the formation of a Human Rights Committee. The announcement was widely covered by the BBC, Voice of America, and other Western media. Later that month Sakharov met Elena Bonner at Chalidze's birthday party.[16] They saw each other again in connection with the Leningrad hijacking trial. Sakharov was shocked by the severity of the sentences (see Chapter 8) and decided to protest to former Soviet President Podgorny. At about the same time in the United States, Angela Davis, a Communist, was indicted for complicity in an armed attempt to free several prisoners during their trial. Sakharov decided to write to Nixon and Podgorny requesting clemency for Davis and the Leningrad defendants. Bonner, whom he called Lyusya, worked with him on the letter to Nixon that was sent via a foreign correspondent. Nixon replied that Sakharov would be welcome at the trial of Angela Davis if he could travel to the United States.[17]

Bonner went to Leningrad in May 1971 for the trial of Butman and others involved in the hijack plot. She was not allowed to enter the courtroom, so she collected accounts of each day's proceedings from the defendants' relatives and then telephoned the information to foreign reporters, human rights activists and Sakharov in Moscow. For the next year and a half Bonner and Sakharov traveled together to cultural events, for camping trips, visits to friends, and events in support of dissidents. On January 7, 1972, they registered their marriage in Moscow.[18]

Later that year the Olympic Games in Munich were marred by the murder of eleven Israeli athletes by Arab terrorists. Thirty protesters outside the Lebanese Embassy in Moscow were detained by the police. Sakharov was one of them.[19]

SUPPORT FOR FREE EMIGRATION

In his memoirs Sakharov pointed out that "of those who came to me for help in the 1970s, more than half were seeking to emigrate." He felt that the right to choose one's country of residence was important, and agreed with senator Henry Jackson, who called this right the "first among equals."[20]

Sakharov wrote to the Supreme Soviet in 1971 urging the adoption of legislation that would be in accord with the Universal Declaration of Human Rights with regard to emigration. In his letter he said, "The freedom to emigrate, which only a small number of people would in fact use, is an essential condition of spiritual freedom. A free country cannot resemble a cage, even if it is gilded and supplied with material things."

While he often wrote such letters to Soviet legislators,

Sakharov rarely sent appeals to foreign governments. One exception was the open letter he wrote to the United States Congress on September 14, 1973, in support of the Jackson-Vanik Amendment.[21] The proposed amendment to a forthcoming foreign trade bill would link improved trade conditions with the USSR to unrestricted emigration. Sakharov asserted that passage of the amendment was an indispensable first step to assuring détente and warned that failure to pass it would be "tantamount to total capitulation of democratic principles in the face of blackmail, deceit and violence." Within months of sending the letter, Sakharov was vilified by the Soviet press and subjected to denunciation as a "traitor" and an "enemy of détente" from nearly every quarter of Soviet society. There were threats of death to his and Bonner's children and grandchildren.[22]

THE NOBEL PEACE PRIZE

On October 9, 1975, Sakharov went to have tea at the apartment of a Jewish friend, Yuri Tuvim, who had just gotten an exit visa. Just as the kettle was put on the stove, dissidents and foreign journalists arrived with the news that Sakharov had been awarded the Nobel Peace Prize, the first Russian to receive it. They videotaped his impromptu comments and broadcast them over European television:

> This is a great honor not just for me but for the whole human rights movement. I feel I share this honor with our prisoners of conscience – they have sacrificed their most precious possession, their liberty, in defending others by open and non-violent means. I hope for an improvement in the lot of political prisoners in the USSR and for a worldwide political amnesty.[23]

That day two activists from the Bay Area Council for Soviet Jews (in San Francisco), Selma Light and Gina Waldman, were in

London getting ready to check in for a flight to Moscow. Waldman purchased a copy of *The Times* and was astonished to read a
front-page story about Sakharov winning the Nobel Peace Prize.
She immediately folded the front page into the middle of the paper and packed it into her suitcase.

The newspaper was overlooked by the customs agent in Moscow who inspected Waldman's suitcase. She showed it to the first
refuseniks that she and Light visited that day, Vladimir Slepak
and Alexander Lerner, and then took it to Sakharov. He told Light
and Waldman that he had already learned about the award from
some foreign correspondents, but Waldman recalls that he was
"like a little kid with a new toy" when he saw the story in print. He
said he was sure that Soviet authorities would never allow him
to go to Oslo to accept the Nobel Peace Prize, and then added, "I
would like to send a letter to my wife, who is now in Italy for eye
surgery. Do you think you could mail it when you leave the Soviet Union?" Waldman replied, "I won't mail the letter; I'll take
it to her personally because we're going to Italy." Sakharov was
delighted and meticulously wrote and rewrote the letter which,
as Waldman learned later, contained Sakharov's Nobel Prize acceptance speech. He also gave Waldman a list of prisoners, their
photographs and information about what they needed from supporters in the West.[24]

Sakharov's prediction that he would not be permitted to
travel to Oslo for the award ceremony was based on the precedent
set in 1970 when Alexander Sozhenitsyn, the author of *One Day
in the Life of Ivan Denisovich*, a novel critical of the Soviet regime,
was barred from going to Stockholm to accept the Nobel Prize
for literature. Sakharov and Solzhenitsyn had great respect for
each other but differed in their attitudes about free emigration.
Sakharov, of course, supported the right of everyone to live in the
country of their choice and was very supportive of refuseniks and
other minorities, while Solzhenitsyn was a proponent of Russian
nationalism and had no use for those who wanted to emigrate.[25]

Indeed, Sakharov was not permitted to travel to Oslo, so Elena Bonner went there to receive the award on his behalf. The Nobel Committee's citation stated that "Uncompromisingly and with unflagging strength, Sakharov has fought against the abuse of power and all forms of violation of human dignity, and he has fought no less courageously for the idea of government based on the rule of law." On the day of the award ceremony Sakharov was attending the trial of Sergei Kovalev, a human rights activist in Vilnius.[26]

THE HELSINKI WATCH GROUP

While the u.s. Congress was debating the Jackson-Vanik Amendment – it passed and was signed by President Gerald Ford on January 3, 1975 – negotiators of the Conference on Security and Cooperation in Europe were hammering out a document that became known as the Helsinki Final Act. For the Soviets this document was an affirmation of the territorial status quo in Europe. In exchange the West expected Soviet compliance with provisions for the "free movement of people and ideas and for the protection of human rights and fundamental freedoms."[27]

By publishing the text of the Final Act, the Soviet Union fulfilled its first obligation and unwittingly enabled dissidents like to Sakharov to become familiar with the human rights commitments for which their government could be held accountable.[28] After studying the document Yuri Orlov, a physicist, Anatoly Shcharansky (now Natan Sharansky) and other human rights activists approached Sakharov with the idea of forming a group devoted to monitoring Soviet observance of the human rights aspects of the Helsinki Accords. The first group started with a press conference called by Sakharov in Moscow, and other groups soon sprang up in Armenia, Georgia, Lithuania and Ukraine.[29]

A few days after Carter's inauguration in January 1977, he received a letter from Sakharov that was hand-carried by Martin Garbus, an American civil rights attorney who had visited

Moscow to aid refuseniks.[30] The letter urged Carter to "defend those who suffer because of their non-violent struggle for an open society, for justice, and for other people whose rights are violated." Sakharov was elated to be invited to the American Embassy to receive Carter's reply, which affirmed, "Human rights is a central concern of my administration...We shall use our good offices to seek the release of prisoners of conscience." Sakharov followed up with another letter to Carter informing him that four Helsinki Watch Group members had been arrested. Brezhnev denounced the exchange of letters as "outright attempts by American official agencies to interfere in the internal affairs of the Soviet Union." American journalists and op-ed writers quickly argued on both sides of the issue.[31]

Representatives of the CSCE nations had their first follow-up meeting in Belgrade in October 1977. Those from the West received a challenging message from Sakharov. He asked, "Is the West prepared to defend these noble and vitally important principles?" and warned that "failure to support freedom of conscience in an open society would lead to surrender to totalitarianism and the loss of all precious freedom."

Ambassador Arthur Goldberg, who led the U.S. delegation in Belgrade, stated that the American position would be a focus on implementation of Helsinki's provisions. He also announced that there would be public broadcasts of the record of the Belgrade meetings over the Voice of America and Radio Free Europe/Radio Liberty. These statements indicated that the United States was aligned with Sakharov, rather than with those who advocated "quiet diplomacy" out of fear that raising human rights issues would make life worse for Soviet dissidents and political prisoners.[32]

The KGB did try to quash the dissidents by destroying the Helsinki Watch Groups. In 1978 there were trials in Moscow and Tbilisi, Georgia. Yuri Orlov was sentenced to seven years in a labor camp plus five years of internal exile. Sakharov was not allowed to enter the courtroom when the verdict was read and, during a fight between Orlov's friends and KGB agents, Sakharov slapped a policeman's face.[33]

LIFE IN EXILE

The KGB was fed up with the anti-Soviet campaigns that Sakharov and Bonner were inspiring in the West. Its chief, Yuri Andropov, suggested to his Politburo colleagues that they be exiled to Gorky (now Nizhny Novgorod), the third largest city in the Soviet Union, but closed to foreigners.[34] In January 1980, after criticizing the Soviet invasion of Afghanistan, and as part of a general crackdown on dissidents, Sakharov and Bonner were exiled there.[35] They were prohibited from leaving the city and from meeting, corresponding or having telephone conversations with foreigners, including their children and grandchildren who had emigrated to the United States.

Sakharov struggled to write his memoirs in Gorky, but KGB agents stole the thousand-page manuscript three times and each time he rewrote his book from memory.[36] He was able to write letters and appeals and got them smuggled out to the West. In one article he stated that "everything is as it was under Stalin," and advocated a total boycott of that summer's Moscow Olympics.[37]

After nearly four years of isolation in Gorky, Bonner suffered several heart attacks but was denied medical care. Arguing that she could not receive any "effective treatment in the USSR while she is subject to an organized campaign of persecution and KGB interference," Sakharov announced that he was "beginning a hunger strike with the demand that Elena Bonner be allowed to travel abroad for medical treatment and for a meeting with her mother, children and grandchildren". Sakharov vowed that the hunger strike would be "of indefinite duration" and end "only when my wife receives permission to go abroad." [38]

In May 1984 Sakharov was forcibly hospitalized, tied to his bed and given both intravenous feeding and an injection that caused him to pass out and develop cerebral stroke symptoms.

After five days he was force fed through a tube in his nose for nine days and finally given the choice of swallowing food by mouth or suffocating. He reluctantly chose to swallow and thus ended his hunger strike. After 123 days in the hospital, he was discharged and went home to learn that Bonner had been convicted of slandering the Soviet state and sentenced to five years in exile to a place not indicated.[39]

Reagan called ambassador Dobrynin to ask that Bonner be allowed to come to America for medical treatment. The reply that came from foreign minister Gromyko was that "the lady and her accomplices were deliberately trying to dramatize the situation to discredit the Soviet Union." A year later, with Mikhail Gorbachev as general secretary, after much negotiation and Sakharov's third hunger strike, the decision was reversed. Sakharov, however, would not be allowed to accompany her, because of his knowledge of nuclear weapons secrets.[40]

Bonner flew from Moscow on December 2, 1985, and returned to Gorky seven months later. She had a successful sextuple bypass operation in Boston, many family visits, and meetings throughout the United States with Soviet Jewry and human rights activists.[41]

In December 1986 Bonner and Sakharov experienced the relief of life returning to normalcy. A telephone was installed in their Gorky apartment, the police guards surrounding the building were removed, and Gorbachev personally called Sakharov to tell him that his exile was over and Bonner had been pardoned. Two hundred correspondents greeted the happy couple when their train arrived in Moscow.[42]

LIFE UNDER GLASNOST

Back in Moscow, Sakharov was no longer prohibited from meeting foreigners, so congressional visitors and other prominent Americans beat a path to his door.[43] Two years later he was allowed to travel abroad, and flew to the United States for visits in Boston with his children and grandchildren, and meetings in Washington with Reagan and Edward Teller, the father of America's H-Bomb, and in California with activists who had supported him during the dark years in Gorky.[44]

In April 1989 Sakharov was elected to the new parliament, the Congress of People's Deputies. That month demonstrators in Tbilisi were demanding greater autonomy from Moscow. Nineteen of them were killed and many injured as military forces attacked them with poison gas and sharpened trenching shovels. Sakharov and Bonner flew to Tbilisi to assess the situation and called ambassador Jack Matlock, asking for information about the gas and its antidote. Matlock immediately got the answers they needed from Washington.[45] Bonner and Sakharov then supervised the treatment in several Tbilisi hospitals with help from Bonner's contacts in *Medecins sans Frontières* (Doctors without Borders).[46]

The massacre in Tbilisi served as a wake-up call for a new Soviet constitution, one that would protect freedom of speech and assembly, as well as place the KGB under civilian control. Gorbachev knew that the commission that would draft the new constitution needed Sakharov's participation to give it credibility. Sakharov proposed a full range of sweeping reforms including curbs on the power of the Communist Party and the granting of equal rights to all minorities.[47] Gorbachev was disdainful of Sakharov's proposals and the two sparred verbally in Congress. Sakharov was discouraged by Gorbachev's "half-measures" of reform and the debates left him drained and worn out.[48]

On December 14, 1989, Sakharov suffered a sudden massive heart attack. Bonner found him dead in their apartment. The day before he died, he finished the epilogue to his memoirs with a dedication reading, "This book is devoted to my dear and lovely Lyusya. Life goes on. We are together."[49]

At Sakharov's state funeral a reporter asked Gorbachev a question about Sakharov's Nobel Peace Prize in 1975, an event that the Brezhnev regime resented as a gift to a traitor. Gorbachev replied, "It is clear now that he deserved it."[50]

CHAPTER THIRTEEN

The Helsinki Watch Groups

When the Conference on Security and Cooperation in Europe held its final session in Helsinki, Finland, from July 30 to August 1, 1975, its participants constituted the most representative meeting of the heads of European states since the Congress of Vienna in 1815.[1] After twenty-two months of negotiations involving 375 diplomats from thirty-five nations, including the United States, Canada and the Soviet Union, agreement was reached on what would be called the Helsinki Final Act or Helsinki Accords.[2]

THE PATH TO HELSINKI

The idea of an all-European conference to achieve collective security was first proposed in 1954 by Soviet foreign minister V.M. Molotov. His aim was to obtain formal recognition that the borders of the Soviet Union must include all the territory annexed after World War II. Over the following two decades the continuing arms build-up by NATO and Warsaw Pact nations led to fear of nuclear war. It became clear to leaders on both sides of the Iron Curtain that diplomatic solutions could avert armed conflict and might even lead to greater cooperation in trade, technology, art and culture.[3]

In 1969 NATO responded to a Warsaw Pact proposal for a conference on European security by stating that such a conference would have to address the subject of free movement of people, information and ideas. The right of a person to leave any country, including his own, and to return to his country, is a key element of the Universal Declaration of Human Rights that was adopted by the United Nations in 1948. NATO leaders, especially those from Western Europe, felt that in exchange for guarantees of Soviet borders the Soviet government would have to grant basic human rights to the people who lived within those borders.[4] U.S. Secretary of State Henry Kissinger was opposed to using human rights as a lever for changing Soviet policies.[5] He did support "protecting human rights and fundamental freedoms" for the purpose of inhibiting, by means of international agreement, Soviet repression of popular protests such as their invasions of Hungary in 1956 and Czechoslovakia in 1968.[6] Kissinger looked at the Helsinki process as little more than "damage control" to prevent Western Europe from dealing with Moscow in the absence of American involvement.

THREE BASKETS

The Final Act that, signed by the leaders of the 35 nations on August 1, 1975, consisted of three sections known as "baskets." Basket I dealt with security issues and Basket II focused on scientific, technological and trade issues including migrant labor and the promotion of tourism. The aspirations of the Soviet leaders were satisfied by these two baskets. Basket III was devoted to cooperation in humanitarian fields including freer movement of people and the reunification of families.[7]

Within a few weeks of the signing of the Final Act and the publication of its text within the USSR, Soviet Jews began citing the Helsinki Final Act and its provision for family reunification on their applications for exit visas.[8] The Kremlin was not impressed. According to ambassador Dobrynin, "The Politburo's acceptance of the Helsinki humanitarian principles implied some noncompliance."[9] In an unusual meeting with Moscow refuseniks, Colonel Obidin, the chairman of the Visa Department, stated that family reunification would be limited to next-of-kin.[10] Nevertheless, the Helsinki Final Act would ultimately turn out to be what British activist Doreen Gainsford called, "A gift from God. It was the catalyst."[11]

THE GENTLEWOMAN FROM NEW JERSEY

She had a husky voice and smoked a pipe, unusual for a patrician woman named Millicent Fenwick, who served as a Republican member of Congress. Shortly after the signing of the Final Act she flew to Russia with a congressional fact-finding delegation. Refuseniks and dissidents came to the hotels in Moscow and Leningrad where the Americans were staying. Fenwick asked, "How do you dare to come see us here?" and they replied, "Don't you understand? That's our only hope. We've seen you and the KGB now knows that you have seen us." Fenwick would later relate that she felt like "being on a transatlantic steamer in a terrible storm, and seeing people go by in rafts, and we're trying to pick them up, but can't. But at least we've got our searchlights on them."[12]

At the suggestion of *New York Times* reporter Christopher Wren, Fenwick went to the apartment of Valentin Turchin, who headed Moscow's chapter of Amnesty International.[13] Also present were Yuri Orlov, a co-founder of Amnesty International, and Benjamin Levich, a refusenik. They talked about the Helsinki Final Act and the possibility of the West using the agreement to pressure the Soviets to uphold their human rights obligations and monitor how well they were being honored.[14]

The congressional delegation met with general secretary Brezhnev in Yalta on the last day of the trip. When Fenwick asked him to look into some of the humanitarian cases she had encountered he responded that she was obsessed.[15]

Fenwick took her obsession directly to the halls of Congress and introduced a bill to create a bipartisan commission on security and cooperation in Europe that would monitor the Helsinki Accords. Kissinger opposed it a "dangerous precedent" because it would get Congress involved in carrying out foreign policy.[16] The bill passed the House after Jerry Goodman, the executive director of the National Conference on Soviet Jewry, testified on harassment of refuseniks and other Soviet violations.[17] Senator Clifford Case, (R-NJ) drove the bill through the Senate to unanimous approval. President Ford signed it on June 3, 1976.

YURI ORLOV: FROM MOSCOW TO YEREVAN AND BACK TO MOSCOW

While Fenwick and Case were lining up support for their bill in the U.S. Congress, Yuri Orlov was considering the formation of a group in Moscow that would monitor Soviet adherence to its human rights obligations.

Orlov was born to a peasant family in 1924 and moved with them to Moscow as a child. His first book was the New Testament that his grandmother haltingly read to him, oblivious to Stalin's anti-religious decrees. He recalls first becoming disillusioned with Communism in 1946 while he served in the Soviet Army. However, he did not admit to vacillating in carrying out the Party line when he applied for admission to the prestigious Physico-Technical Department of Moscow State University and was admitted to study under Prof. Lev Landau. In 1951 the department was reorganized to support Stalin's anti-Semitic paranoia, and Orlov was distressed to see his Jewish friends kicked out and sent to provincial and minor institutes with no access to "secret" work. Fear and distrust precluded any discussion of the situation.[18]

Five years later, after Khrushchev denounced Stalin at the Twentieth Party Congress, Orlov went further by asserting, "In order for what has happened not to happen again, we must switch to democracy on a foundation of socialism!" Members of the Party bureau at the physics research institute where he worked were stunned. Orlov, along with three like-minded colleagues, was fired and expelled from the Party. *Pravda* denounced them as Mensheviks in an editorial.[19] Calling it the "worst mistake of his life," Orlov took a position in Armenia at the Yerevan Physics Institute, leaving his wife, Galya, and two children in Moscow.[20] He defended his thesis there, became chief of a laboratory and divorced Galya.[21] In 1972 he was able to return to Moscow and looked forward to joining dissidents including Andrei Sakharov and Elena Bonner. He married Irina Valitova and they moved into an apartment in the "dissidents' quarter" close to his friends Valentin Turchin, Alexander Ginzburg, and several families of refuseniks.[22] Orlov had a short-lived job at a physics institute and then began tutoring high-school students.

In October 1973 Orlov, Turchin and Andrei Tverdokhlebov organized the Soviet Amnesty International Group. About thirty scientists and writers from Moscow, Leningrad, Kiev and Tbilisi were determined to demonstrate a commitment to pluralism and non-violent promotion of ideas in defense of human rights. The group did not focus on Soviet political prisoners but wrote letters on behalf of prisoners in South Vietnam, Indonesia, Poland and Yugoslavia.[23]

Orlov had much in common with unemployed refuseniks. He attended the physics seminars that were held in their apartments, and they attended those he hosted every two weeks. Through them he met refusenik Anatoly Shcharansky (now Natan Sharansky) who taught English to other refuseniks and dissidents to avoid being charged with parasitism. Orlov enjoyed the opportunity to improve his English and have stimulating conversations on human rights issues.[24]

IT'S UP TO US TO MONITOR THE HELSINKI FINAL ACT

In March 1976 Shcharansky presented a radical idea to Orlov and Andrei Amalrik, who had served five years in prison for writing the provocative essay in 1969, "Will the Soviet Union Survive until 1984?" Shcharansky proposed that Soviet intelligentsia invite their Western counterparts to hold seminars on human rights issues. Soviet activists would then organize similar events, including international seminars that would make compliance with the Helsinki Final Act a public issue.

Orlov decided to go one step further. He felt that "if we wanted compliance with the Final Act, it was up to us to monitor it. Nobody would do it for us." He determined that a group comprised of the leading dissidents needed to be formed in Moscow for this purpose.[25] After discussions with veterans of the human rights movement Ludmilla Alexeyeva, Larisa Bogoraz, Alexander Ginzburg, Vitaly Rubin and Anatoly Shcharansky, Orlov wrote a declaration stating that "The Public Group to Support Compliance with the Helsinki Accords in the USSR" (later shortened to "Helsinki Watch Group") would send expert documents on Soviet violations to the heads of states that had signed the Helsinki Accords. Other human rights activists including Elena Bonner soon joined. Sakharov didn't become a member but expressed his support and allowed Orlov to use his apartment for a press conference to announce the group's founding on May 12, 1976.[26]

The next step for the group was to dispatch documents to Western governments; they could not expect the Soviet postal service to deliver them. An American diplomat told Orlov that "although we cannot accept documents from your group officially, you can give them to U.S. citizens who are visiting and are willing to bring them to our embassy and we will then distribute copies to the British and Canadian embassies."[27]

Helsinki Watch Groups were soon initiated in the non-Russian republics of Ukraine, Lithuania and Armenia, and also in East European satellites Czechoslovakia, Poland and Romania. Linked to the Helsinki group in Moscow was a "Working Commission to Investigate the Use of Psychiatry for Political Purposes."[28] Documents were soon arriving in the West about abuses in Soviet psychiatric hospitals, labor camps and prisons. The Helsinki Watch Groups were active in reporting on brutal violations of the human rights of Jews, Pentecostals, Catholics and Crimean Tatars.[29] Activists in the Soviet Union learned about prison regulations from the Helsinki Watch Groups. For example, Shcharansky knew when his rights were being violated in prison and could demand warmer clothes during the winter.[30]

INTERNATIONAL FOLLOW-UP

A key element of the Helsinki Final Act was the provision for periodic conferences to review compliance with the obligations that the signatory nations agreed to. The United States and many Western European countries used these follow-up conferences to put pressure on the Communist countries to live up to their human rights commitments.[31]

The first of these conferences opened in Belgrade in October 1977. The Soviets apparently expected criticism of their human rights performance, especially with regard to Jewish emigration, so they increased the number of exit visas issued by 25 percent to about 1,500 a month during the latter half of 1977.[32] Ambassador Arthur Goldberg, who had been identified with human rights causes when he served on the U.S. Supreme Court, led the American delegation, and brought up specific cases including Shcharansky, Orlov and Ginzburg. The latter two had been arrested and imprisoned for their monitoring activities and in an emergency phone call reported by *The Times* (London), Irina Orlov appealed to the West to speak out in Belgrade for them and for other imprisoned Helsinki Watch Group members.[33]

KGB REPRISALS

When Orlov announced the formation of the Helsinki Watch Group he knew that the KGB was on his tail and that he could be arrested at any time. He also thought that luck might be on his side and that, as in 1956, he would not be imprisoned.[34] Less than a year after the Helsinki Watch Group announcement his luck ran out. On February 3, 1977, Ginzburg was arrested and Orlov held a press conference in Alexeyeva's apartment a few days later. After the American and English correspondents left, three black Volgas filled with KGB agents rolled up to the apartment building's entrance. Eight agents entered the apartment, arrested Orlov and took him for interrogation to Lefortovo Prison.[35]

British playwright Tom Stoppard recalls visiting Irina Orlov three days after her husband's arrest. He was in Moscow to gather information for a TV play to promote 1977 as Amnesty International's "Prisoner of Conscience Year." She told him that eight KGB men searched their flat and when she tried to get help – a Soviet citizen is entitled to two witnesses during a search – she had her arm twisted behind her back.[36]

For fifteen months Orlov was held incommunicado and interrogated about his case and other Helsinki Watch Group cases before his trial opened. Reminiscent of the Leningrad Trials of 1970 and 1971, the courtroom was packed with party hacks and only a handful of Orlov's closest relatives. After four days in which he could not call witnesses or review the evidence, he was sentenced to seven years in a strict-regime labor camp followed by five years of internal exile.[37] In September 1980 he was sentenced to six months of solitary confinement for demanding improvements in camp conditions.[38]

With Orlov and Ginzburg, and later, Shcharansky, imprisoned, the KGB used another approach to crush the Helsinki Watch Groups – forced emigration. Soviet authorities advised several members to apply for emigration and they were quickly granted exit visas. Rubin went to Israel and his non-Jewish friend, Amalrik, was ordered by the KGB to go to the Netherlands Embassy to request an invitation from Israel.[39] Vladimir Slepak replaced Rubin as the leading dissident-refusenik member of the Helsinki Watch Group.[40]

Alexeyeva and her husband, Nikolai Williams, flew to Vienna and then to London. After a series of meetings in the House of Commons she met John Macdonald, a Liberal Party activist attorney, who told her that he wanted to work for Orlov's release and that he viewed the injustice prevailing in the Soviet Union as akin to the fascism under Hitler that Chamberlain had been willing to accommodate. When fascism rears its head, Macdonald said, "it must be fought by every free man in every nation." In June 1977, a year ahead of Orlov's actual trial in Moscow, Macdonald staged a mock tribunal in London to galvanize public opinion in support of Orlov via newspapers and television.[41] Macdonald did what a sincere defense attorney would do in a free country, including sending an appeal to Moscow after Orlov's guilty verdict. For expressing concern over the trial, the Soviet press agency, *Tass*, accused the British Foreign Office of violating the Helsinki Accords.[42]

The KGB didn't limit its vengeance to leaders of the Moscow Helsinki Watch Group. Most members of the Ukrainian group were imprisoned or exiled. In 1978 Victoras Piatkus, a devout Catholic and leader of the Lithuanian Helsinki Group, was put on trial and sentenced to ten years in prison plus five years of internal exile. As a third-time offender, or "recidivist," he was put on "special regime," the most severe punishment. Piatkus became Shcharansky's cellmate in Chistopol Prison. It appeared that their captors felt that they were incorrigible anti-Soviet troublemakers who would unduly influence other prisoners if they had cellmates who were not Helsinki Watch Group activists.[43]

In 1980, the first year of his exile in Gorky, Sakharov wrote an essay for the US Helsinki Watch Committee that was published by the *Boston Globe*. In it he stated that more than forty Helsinki Watch Group members were imprisoned and many others who were not formal members of the Watch Groups but worked to promote the exchange of information and defense of human rights had been arrested.[44]

The next two years were bleak for both Soviet Jewish emigration (exit visas plummeted to 14% of the 1978–1979 level) and for the Helsinki Watch Groups. A KGB official openly said, "Previously we brought people to trial only for their actions. Now we will try them for preparing to act and assisting others." In September 1981 another KGB agent told a dissident that by the following summer there would be no democrats or Jewish nationalists left in Moscow."[45] Indeed, by the middle of 1982 the Moscow group had only three elderly members and the Voice of America reported that they had decided to disband because they could no longer endure the constant police and KGB pressure. Concurrently the International Helsinki Federation for Human Rights was formed to link the committees in North America and Western Europe to defend the rights of the beleaguered in the Soviet Union and Eastern Europe.[46]

BREAKTHROUGHS

There was high expectation in the dissident, human rights and Soviet Jewry communities that the second Helsinki follow-up meeting scheduled to convene in Madrid in November 1980 would bring more attention to their favorite causes. Because so many supporters of prisoners of conscience arrived in the Spanish capital, *Le Monde* called Madrid the "city of dissidence." At the opening, however, it did not appear that human rights would take center stage. There was tension over the Soviet conquest of Afghanistan and the American support for Moslem insurgents. The build-up of missiles by NATO and the Warsaw Pact gave a sense of urgency to arms control issues. Within the United States the Helsinki Commission chairman, Dante Fascell, was feuding with the State Department over policy and strategy. During the first few days of the conference there was so much wrangling over the agenda and procedures that no one could predict that anything significant would come out of the conference.

Ambassador Max Kampelman, heading the U.S. delegation, distinguished himself by bringing up human rights in both formal and private meetings. During the first month of the meeting the cases of sixty-five people, many of them Helsinki Watch Group members, were presented. This was a significant increase over the seven prisoners named by Ambassador Goldberg during the 1977 Belgrade meeting. Furthermore the U.S. was now joined by eight Western European nations in citing specific cases as well as expressing dismay about the sharp reduction in Soviet Jewish emigration.

When the meeting closed on September 9, 1983, there was an agreement to hold an "Experts Meeting on Human Rights and Fundamental Freedoms" in Ottawa in May 1985. Secretary of state George Shultz reaffirmed America's commitment to the Helsinki process, saying that "lasting security or cooperation cannot be achieved so long as one government is afraid of its own people and its next-door neighbors." The Ottawa meeting was the first one solely devoted to human rights, but it did not result in a concluding document.[47]

Shultz met with Soviet foreign minister Eduard Shevardnadze in September 1986 in preparation for the Reagan-Gorbachev summit meeting that would take place the following month in Reykjavik, Iceland. A contentious issue that had to be resolved immediately was the "Zakharov-Daniloff Affair". Gennady Zakharov was a Soviet citizen who was working for the UN Secretariat in New York. He was arrested by the FBI when he gave money to a double agent for a package of classified material. A week after his arrest the KGB arrested Nicholas Daniloff, an American journalist in Moscow, on charges of espionage.

CIA director William Casey attested to Reagan that Daniloff had never been employed by the CIA. Reagan then sent a message directly to Gorbachev to assure him of Daniloff's innocence. When Gorbachev refused to release Daniloff, Reagan was furious and was prepared to expel dozens of Soviet members of the Soviet UN mission. Reagan and the State Department were adamant that simply trading Zakharov (a spy) for Daniloff (a hostage) would be unacceptable. What Shultz and Shevardnadze worked out was a deal to trade Zakharov for Daniloff plus Yuri Orlov.[48]

Orlov was serving the internal exile phase of his sentence near Yakutsk in Siberia, over 4,000 miles from Moscow, when two men came to his house, forced open his locked door and told him that he had an hour to pack. Orlov expected the worst and prepared to be a prisoner again. He and his KGB guards were put on a plane for Moscow, where he was questioned for four days about people who had helped him in camp and in exile. Orlov refused to answer them. Finally two KGB officials arrived and informed him that he was being deprived of his Soviet citizenship and would be sent to the U.S. with his wife. A few days after his arrival in New York, Orlov met Reagan and Shultz and discussed what could be done to help Sakharov.[49]

Several weeks later Orlov met in New York with Bob Bernstein and Jeri Laber of the International Helsinki Federation and offered to campaign for his friend Anatoly Marchenko, who was on a hunger strike in Chistopol Prison, and for Nelson Mandela, who was imprisoned on Robben Island in South Africa.[50] Orlov has often said, "When I see people suffering I feel for them."[51]

Yuri Orlov at Cornell in 2005 after receiving the first Sakharov Prize for human rights. Photo credit: Robert Barker/University Photography

CHAPTER FOURTEEN

Natan Sharansky – Prisoner of Zion, Spokesman for Democracy

O n the day of Stalin's funeral, Boris Shcharansky, a loyal party member and journalist in Donetsk, Ukraine[1], took his sons, Leonid, 7, and Anatoly, 5, to a safe spot in their communal apartment where they could not be overheard, and told them, "This is a great day that you should always remember!"[2] He explained that Stalin, who loved to be called "Our Leader and Teacher," was really a terrible butcher who killed millions of people and was planning to persecute all the Jews. Shcharansky, of course, warned his sons not to mention to anyone what they just heard and to behave in school like all the other children. So Leonid and Anatoly went to their classes, cried on cue, and sang the obligatory praises to the dead man who they now knew had been an evil tyrant.[3]

ESCAPE FROM DOUBLETHINK

What young Anatoly learned from this experience was that grown-ups in the Soviet Union lived in a world of doublethink.[4] He excelled in school and scored well enough on exams to overcome anti-Semitic discrimination, and gained admission to the Moscow

Institute of Physics and Technology, followed by a good position as a computer specialist at the Institute for Oil and Gas.[5] But he detested the constant need to keep silent and avoid expressing what he knew to be true, but would not sit well with the authorities. As an assimilated student he became curious about what it meant to be Jewish. Could there be anything positive about it? In 1966 he went with a friend to the main synagogue in Moscow on Simchat Torah, knowing that large groups of Jews would be singing and dancing in the street, but they were uncomfortable not knowing the songs and dances, and were alarmed by flashes from KGB cameras.[6]

The following year Israel's victory in the Six-Day War convinced Shcharansky that assimilation was not the answer; personal freedom and escape from doublethink could come only from reclaiming his Jewish roots.[7] Then, in 1968, appalled at the Soviet invasion of Czechoslovakia and after reading Sakharov's essay "Reflections on Progress, Peaceful Coexistence, and Intellectual Freedom," he felt ashamed to be a Soviet citizen.[8]

Like others in Moscow who were seriously thinking about Zionism, he began asking foreign tourists for books about Israel and Judaism. *Exodus* by Leon Uris was a favorite, reproduced and circulated in *samizdat*, as was the Hebrew primer *Elef Milim*, ("1000 Words"). In 1972 Shcharansky, galvanized by the courage of the activists who had been tried in Leningrad, determined that aliyah would be his path to freedom from doublethink and he asked for a *vysov*.

LIFE AND LOVE AS A REFUSENIK

Shcharansky applied for an exit visa in early 1973 and resigned from *Komsomol* (the Communist Youth Organization). He confidently defended his action and Israel's policies at an angry meeting of his colleagues at the Oil and Gas Institute. He was able to keep his job there until March 1975, but the focus of his life was the refusenik community. He lived for the Saturday morning gatherings outside the synagogue and Sunday seminars in Alexander

Lerner's apartment.[9] He also joined a small group of activists who organized brief demonstrations, risking arrest and jail time for a few minutes of holding a "Let Us Go to Israel" placard that might attract the attention of a Western journalist.[10]

When a tall young man named Misha Steiglits showed up at the synagogue, Shcharansky helped him join demonstrations and at one of them Misha was arrested and detained. A week later on the Saturday when the Yom Kippur War broke out in Israel, Misha's sister, Nataliya, came to the synagogue looking for him. When Shcharansky saw her it was love at first sight. He told her, "Don't worry about your brother. It's nothing. I was just released myself after fifteen days in jail." They talked of aliyah, studying Hebrew, and how Misha and Nataliya had rebelled and run away from their staunchly Communist parents. They were strongly attracted to each other even though Nataliya was much taller than the pudgy, balding Anatoly.[11] The following Passover, at the apartment of refusenik friends, they attended a Seder together for the first time in their lives, and fervently wished that "Next year in Jerusalem" would become true for them as a married couple. They looked forward to joining Misha, who had emigrated to Israel soon after his release from jail.

In June 1974, when Nixon visited the Soviet Union, Shcharansky and the "usual suspects" among the activist refuseniks were rounded up and incarcerated to prevent any embarrassing demonstrations. Meanwhile Nataliya was summoned to OVIR and given a visa to Israel, with one special restriction – it would expire in two weeks – and warned that if she failed to use it, she would never get another. Estimating that the activists would be freed by July 3 or 4, and knowing that she had to leave for Israel by the fifth, she scheduled a wedding for the fourth. She found an elder of the synagogue who was sympathetic and agreed to perform the wedding under a *chuppah*.[12] It took a while for a minyan to assemble as some of the guests had also just gotten released from jail.[13] The wedding was joyous, but the newlyweds had less than twenty-four hours together before they embraced at the airport, and as Nataliya entered the departure area Anatoly could just wave and say, "See you soon in Jerusalem."

TWO SIDES OF THE SAME COIN

When she arrived in Israel Nataliya changed her name to Avital. Shcharansky expected to be permitted to reunite with her in a just few months and stepped up his activism in hopes that he would be viewed as such a troublemaker that the authorities would simply want to throw him out of Russia.[14] But all he got from them was continuous KGB surveillance due to his involvement with dissident Andrei Sakharov in addition to his role as spokesman for the activist refuseniks. Shcharansky and the KGB were in a constant cat-and-mouse game that sometimes turned into a chutzpah contest.[15] Whenever a KGB agent followed him into a taxicab Shcharansky would naturally insist that the agent pay half the fare.[16]

Shcharansky first met Sakharov outside a courthouse in 1973. Over the next two years they had serious discussions, and Shcharansky introduced some of his acquaintances from the Western press corps in Moscow to Sakharov, whom he has always fondly described as "my rabbi" or moral mentor.[17] When Alexander Goldfarb, who had been an English translator for Sakharov and a spokesman for the refusenik community, was permitted to emigrate, Shcharansky succeeded him in both roles. Concurrently Shcharansky's employment at the Oil and Gas Institute ceased. In order to support himself and avoid charges of parasitism, he gave private English lessons and tutored students in math and physics.[18]

Shcharansky regarded linkage of the refusenik and human rights movements as two sides of the same coin. He asserted: "I want to speak the truth. My Zionist and democratic activities are inseparable."[19] His stance was applauded by a number of leading refuseniks including Dina Beilin, Alexander Lerner, Alexander Luntz, Ida Nudel, Vitaly Rubin and Vladimir Slepak, who were concerned with humanitarian problems that violated the Helsinki

Accords, including abuses of prisoners, illegal searches, and confiscation of Hebrew books.[20] The Lishka disapproved of this group because they were involved in public demonstrations and had adopted the imprisoned Leningrad hijackers. On the other hand, there were other refuseniks who favored working only for aliyah and abhorred involvement in Russia's internal problems. Their position had the blessings of the Lishka.

Shcharansky disagreed with the Lishka on two other contentious issues. One was the right of Soviet Jews to emigrate to countries other than Israel. The Lishka was adamant about Israel being the only destination for Soviet Jews, whereas Shcharansky felt that what really mattered was opening the doors of the Soviet Union. The other dispute was over whether to encourage the study of Jewish culture in the USSR. The Lishka initially feared that it was anti-Zionist to strengthen Jewish life in the Soviet Union, but Shcharansky, like the leaders of the *Tarbut* (culture) movement felt that knowledge of Jewish culture would be a significant asset for Zionism.[21] The wrangling between the Lishka and Shcharansky could be viewed as a replay of the debates between the followers of the conservative Shammai and those of the liberal Hillel that took place in Roman-occupied Palestine two millennia ago in a similarly oppressive environment.

The issue of linking the human rights and aliyah movements was by far the most serious controversy between the Lishka and Shcharansky. The Lishka regarded Shcharansky as a betrayer of the Soviet Jewish struggle when he became one of the founders of the Helsinki Watch Group, and warned Avital that if her husband were to be arrested they would do nothing to help him. Shcharansky's supporters were similarly threatened.[22] Dina Beilin recalls a visit from an American tourist who claimed to have been sent by Nechemia Levanon and told her, "If you defend Shcharansky you will never get permission to emigrate to Israel." It was an empty threat; Beilin continued to work closely on behalf of Shcharansky and was permitted to emigrate in 1978.[23]

THE FINAL ARREST

On the 24th anniversary of Stalin's death, March 5, 1977, *Izvestia* published an article by a refusenik named Sanya Lipavsky who had befriended Shcharansky and other activists. He had briefly shared an apartment with Shcharansky. In the article Lipavsky announced that he was withdrawing his application for an exit visa and claimed to be an informer for the CIA. He listed Mark Azbel, Alexander Lerner, Anatoly Shcharansky and Vladimir Slepak as traitors who were in contact with him and had passed secret information to foreign agents for the CIA.[24] That evening the KGB conducted searches of the apartments of Beilin, Lerner, Slepak and others. Lerner was told, "Today is the anniversary of Stalin's death. You are happy to celebrate this day but tomorrow you will not be so happy."[25] For the next ten days Shcharansky was tailed by four to eight KGB agents at all times. Sakharov offered his dacha as a safe house, but Shcharansky felt he had to continue his activity and declined the invitation.[26]

Shcharansky met with Lerner, Slepak, Beilin and Ida Nudel to work out a common defense as they realized they were all in danger even though none of them had anything to do with the CIA. They agreed to refuse to cooperate with any investigation that would incriminate the others.[27] Shcharansky was considered to be the most likely KGB target because he was the youngest, most active with foreign correspondents, and was involved with the Helsinki Watch Group.[28]

March 15 started out as a normal day for Shcharansky. He was attending a Hebrew class given by Vladimir Shakhnovsky in Slepak's apartment when reporters Hal Piper of the *Baltimore Sun* and David Satter of the London *Financial Times* showed up.[29] They had just learned that Mikhail Shtern, a refusenik endocrinologist in Vinnitsa, Ukraine, who had been in prison for three years on false charges of bribery, had been unexpectedly released. To celebrate Slepak poured some Armenian brandy for everyone. Prophetically, Shcharansky remarked, "They may let some Jews out and then frighten others with a new trial." As he escorted the reporters down in the elevator and to the street, Shcharansky was grabbed by the ever-present KGB men and dragged into a car headed for Lefortovo prison.[30] News of the arrest spread quickly and on the following Shabbat the street near the Moscow synagogue was deserted. Jews were terrified, fearing that the terror of Stalin's era had returned.[31]

Shcharansky was charged with two counts of high treason. One was for aiding capitalist countries against the Soviet Union by holding press conferences, meetings encouraging Americans to support the Jackson-Vanik Amendment, and working with the Helsinki Watch Group. The other was for passing state secrets to the West, based on lists of refuseniks that had been given to over 300 foreign reporters and tourists. Conviction on either count could result in death by firing squad.[32]

At a press conference on June 13, 1977, Carter stated: "I have inquired deeply within the State Department and within the CIA, as to whether or not Mr. Shcharansky has ever had any known relationship in a subversive way, or otherwise, with the CIA. The answer is no. We have double-checked this, and I have been hesitant to make that public announcement, but now I am completely convinced." Carter's statement was unprecedented and an exception to CIA policy of never affirming or denying alleged association with the agency.[33] As William Korey wrote in the *American Jewish Year Book* for 1980, "Shcharansky's arrest was perceived by the U.S. government as a direct challenge to the Helsinki Final Act and, therefore, a thrust at détente itself."[34] Later that summer when Soviet foreign minister Gromyko visited the White House, Carter brought up Shcharansky's case. Gromyko amazed the president and ambassador Dobrynin by indicating that he had never heard of Shcharansky. Dobrynin later learned that Gromyko had instructed his subordinates in Moscow to avoid bothering him with the "absurd" matters of dissidents and refuseniks.[35]

Meanwhile Shcharansky remained incarcerated, isolated and interrogated in Lefortovo for sixteen months. He was allowed no mail and no visits and, despite repeated requests to the KGB, his mother, Ida Milgrom, was not permitted to learn of his condition.[36] Avital had no word from him for that entire time.[37] For sharpening his toothbrush so that it could be used to cut sausages, he was placed in a punishment cell for ten days with diminished rations. The cell was extremely cold in violation of prison conditions, and he was convinced the real reason for the punishment was to psychologically weaken him and terrorize him into a confession. He refused to do so and survived by dreaming of reuniting with Avital. He was certain that she must be working with supporters in the West in a campaign to win his release.[38] Shcharansky also infuriated prison guards but satisfied himself by frequently repeating his vocabulary of 2,000 Hebrew words and singing a song based on a quote of the eighteenth century Chassidic Rabbi Nachman of Bratslav, "The entire world is a narrow bridge; but the main thing is not to fear at all."[39]

TRIAL AND PUNISHMENT

KGB Chief Andropov addressed the Politburo on June 22, 1978, regarding the Shcharansky case. Minutes of the meeting that had been classified "Top Secret" but made public after the breakup of the Soviet Union revealed that Andropov recommended a trial beginning on the July 10 with a small, "properly prepared" audience, and that "it is not in our interest to allow any correspondents at the trial." The minutes indicate that everyone agreed to exclude reporters. Andropov then continued, "What will be Shcharansky's sentence? Everything will depend on how he behaves himself. For example, the intention was to give Orlov three years in accordance with the articles of the Criminal Code, but he behaved so indecently at the trial that the court was obliged to sentence him to seven years with subsequent exile for five years. Of course, Shcharansky will not receive the death penalty, but the court will give him a severe sentence, say, for example, fifteen years."[40]

Seventeen investigators worked on the case and over 200 refuseniks, political prisoners, and associates of Shcharansky from his life before refusal were questioned. Only a few collaborators signed statements that were dictated by KGB agents. Most of the 200 courageously resisted threats of arrest and refused to sign any false accusations.[41]

The trial did open on July 10, 1978, and Shcharansky's brother, Leonid, was the only friend or relative of the defendant who was allowed to attend. Leonid managed to write notes of the proceedings on the palm of his hand and read them to foreign reporters.[42] Rejecting the court-appointed lawyer and choosing to defend himself, Anatoly Shcharansky listened to the indictment and declared, "I do not plead guilty. I consider all the charges brought against me to be absurd."

Sanya Lipavsky was called as a witness and reiterated his accusations of anti-Soviet activities that had been published in *Izvestia*,[43] David Shipler, in Israel several years after completing his assignment for the *New York Times*, met the prosecutor in the Shcharansky case and learned that Lipavsky had been a KGB informer since the 1960s, had infiltrated the refusenik community, and completely fabricated the evidence that he presented in testimony against Shcharansky.[44] A key part of that evidence was a list of about 1,300 refuseniks. This list was allegedly discovered a month after Shcharansky's arrest by a janitor in a trash can outside the apartment of Robert Toth, a *Los Angeles Times* reporter and acquaintance of the defendant, who was called a CIA contact by the prosecution. There was no proof that Shcharansky prepared the list, and testimony showed that it was actually typed by a Mrs. Zapylaeva, who was employed by Lipavsky. Nevertheless, the trial went as planned by the Politburo and on July 14 Shcharansky was allowed to make his closing statement before sentencing:

> Five years ago I applied to emigrate to Israel. Today I am further from that dream than ever before. It would seem that I would regret what has happened, but it is not so. I am happy. I am happy that I have lived honestly, at peace with my conscience, staying true to my soul even under the threat of death. I am happy that I have met and worked with such

honest and brave people as Sakharov, Orlov, and Ginzburg, the carriers of traditions of the Russian intelligentsia. I am happy that I have witnessed the revival of the Jewish people in the USSR. I hope that the absurd accusation leveled against me and the entire Jewish emigration movement will not hinder the liberation of my people. My friends and those very close to me know how much I would like to have traded my role of an activist in the emigration movement for a quiet life in Israel. For over two thousand years my people have been in the Diaspora, but wherever they were, they repeated, 'Next year in Jerusalem!' This minute, as I am further than ever from my people, from my Avital, and I as face many difficult years of imprisonment, I say to my people, to my Avital, 'Next year in Jerusalem.' As for this court, which must merely confirm the sentence that has already been passed, to this court I have nothing to say.[45]

The verdict was guilty of treason and anti-Soviet propaganda, and Shcharansky was sentenced to three years in prison, followed by ten years in labor camps. Leonid cried out, "Tolya! The whole world is with you!"[46] Outside the courtroom, Ida Milgrom screamed at the guards taking her son by van from the court back to Lefortovo Prison, "Shame on you! Shame on you! Why wouldn't you let me see him?" Andrei Sakharov was there comforting her and shouting, "You are not human! Fascists! Fascists!"[47]

Shcharansky's mother was allowed to visit with him briefly in Lefortovo four days after the trial. The next day he was on a train with other prisoners, headed for Vladimir Prison.[48] He remained there for a few weeks until all the political prisoners were transferred to the more remote Chistopol Prison, 330 miles east of Moscow. Without explanation the authorities canceled a scheduled visit from his mother and mail from well-wishers was never delivered to him. It appeared that the Interior Ministry was determined to isolate Shcharansky from the outside world in an effort to break his spirit, something they could not do while he was being interrogated prior to the trial. He assiduously refused to talk with KGB officers and argued that there was no law requiring a prisoner to communicate with the KGB.[49]

In accordance with his sentence, Shcharansky was transferred from Chistopol Prison to a camp in the Perm region of the Ural Mountains on March 15, 1980, for the next ten years. Theoretically he could have visits from his mother and brother and learn what was being done in the West in his behalf. He had been told by a fellow inmate that compared with prison, camp was "like being free. There's fresh air, you see other people, and you can walk around without a guard."[50] But for Shcharansky, camp meant years of ordeal punctuated by 405 days of confinement in punishment cells, solitary confinement, hospital treatment and hunger strikes.[51]

THE ARMY OF STUDENTS AND HOUSEWIVES

Two decades after his ordeal Shcharansky (now as an Israeli, Natan Sharansky) told many audiences how during his pre-trial preparation in Lefortovo he had the right to see the evidence that would be presented against him. One item was a film that showed Avital leading a demonstration. It gave him hope and he asked to see the film again and again. After three or four showings the KGB officer became angry and yelled, "They can't help you. They're just students and housewives and can't help you. We're the KGB." During a lecture at Stanford University in 2004, Sharansky spotted Morey Schapira in the audience. Because Schapira had been the president of the Union of Councils for Soviet Jews while Sharansky was in the gulag, Sharansky immediately introduced him as a "Five-Star General in the Army of Students and Housewives."[52]

But surely the Supreme Commander-in-Chief of this international army was none other than Sharansky's wife, Avital, who started campaigning in his behalf well before his 1977 arrest. She and her brother Misha first traveled to North America and spoke at rallies and meetings of Soviet Jewry groups in late 1975. Knowing that her best sources of international support would come from the English-speaking world she studied English, and after a year she was effectively communicating with Americans, Britons and Canadians. She also studied Judaism and became more religiously observant.[53]

Avital went directly to her mentor, Rav Tzvi Yehuda Kook, the octogenarian head of the Mercaz HaRav Yeshiva in Jerusalem, as soon as she learned the alarming news that her husband had been accused of treason in Lipavsky's *Izvestia* article.[54] It was 2 A.M. but Rav Kook understood the gravity of the situation immediately. He called all the young men of the yeshiva and screamed, "The Jews of Russia are in danger! We need to tell the whole world!" A few days later Avital was traveling to Geneva and America to publicize her husband's situation.[55]

Women in England led by Rochelle Duke and Doreen Gainsford launched a "Free Sharansky" campaign with a letter signed by 143 members of Parliament appealing to the United Nations to "take every possible action to ensure that the Soviet Union frees Anatoly Shcharansky and ceases its anti-Semitic policies."[56]

Two distinguished law professors, Irwin Cotler of McGill University in Montreal, who would later serve as Canada's minister of justice, and Alan Dershowitz of Harvard, traveled to Israel upon learning of Sharansky's arrest. They wanted to offer support to Avital and to interview Soviet Jews who had recently moved to Israel and possibly had relevant information. Avital and Ida Milgrom asked Cotler and Dershowitz to represent Shcharansky but the Soviet authorities would allow only a Soviet court-approved attorney.[57] Dershowitz's application for a visa to enter the USSR was rejected. Nevertheless, Cotler and Dershowitz represented Shcharansky in the West and met frequently with Avital in Israel, New York, Washington, London, Paris, and Madrid. But the Lishka was strongly opposed to their efforts and urged them to "drop the Shcharansky case" because they felt that Shcharansky was a human rights activist, and therefore not a true Prisoner of Zion. Cotler and Dershowitz responded that they would continue their efforts even without any assistance from the Israeli government.[58]

Irene Manekofsky, the president of UCSJ at the time of Shcharansky's arrest, was summoned to the Israeli Embassy in Washington and told to desist from supporting the human rights activist. Manekofsky had been instrumental in arranging meetings for Avital with Carter administration officials and members of Congress, and openly rebuked the Lishka for downplaying the Shcharansky case and influencing American Jewish establishment organizations to do likewise.[59]

While some American Jewish groups followed the Israeli government's orders and focused on other Prisoners of Zion such as Yosef Begun and Ida Nudel, the UCSJ and other grassroots activist groups including the Student Struggle for Soviet Jews campaigned vigorously for Shcharansky.[60] Glenn Richter recalls that "the SSSJ carried on campaigns for hundreds of refuseniks and prisoners, but Sharansky's was the most important."[61] They were joined in their efforts by a variety of ad-hoc groups and human rights organizations. Joan Baez was introduced to Avital by mutual friends in Amnesty International. When she sang at rallies for Shcharansky in California some people were surprised because she was considered a "leftist," but she recalls that it wasn't a matter of politics. Baez expressed a "strong empathy with anybody who is willing to sacrifice personal freedoms" and felt that Shcharansky was being unjustly punished.[62]

Avital augmented her army of students and housewives with an impressive array of political leaders throughout the free world. After working day and night for six weeks after Shcharansky's sentencing, Irwin Cotler produced an appeal that charged the court with violations of Soviet law. His 800-page legal brief called "The Shcharansky Case" was served by a bailiff to the Soviet ambassador in Ottawa. Although the Soviet leadership had no interest in reading the document, its production was well publicized in the West.[63] Canadian prime minister Pierre Trudeau assured Avital and Cotler that the Shcharansky case would "remain on the agenda for discussions we hold with the Soviet government on human rights matters." Regarding Shcharansky's treatment in prison,

Trudeau stated, "I can only deplore such inhumane treatment of a prisoner and hope that the Soviet government will release him to come to Canada. Our offer to receive him remains open."[64]

In Washington Congressman Robert Drinan (D-MA), a Jesuit priest with a well-known passion for human rights, organized an international committee for the release of Anatoly Shcharansky. In March 1979 Avital, in Washington, marked the second anniversary of her husband's arrest by taking her case to members of the U.S. Congress.[65] Drinan was her host, and the usually blasé Washington press corps gave maximum coverage to Avital's tragic story and the idea of a congressman in a Roman collar supporting a Jew incarcerated in Russia.[66] The publicity led to formation of protest groups such as Scientists for Orlov and Shcharansky, 2,400 of whom pledged to withhold cooperation with the Soviet Union until Orlov and Shcharansky were released. American Jews continued to call the Kremlin accountable for justice in Shcharansky's case; their protest would not let up even after Soviet Jewish emigration had reached a high of 50,000 for the year 1979.[67]

The outcry was led by Rabbi Avi Weiss in New York, who served as chairman of the SSSJ, had a close working relationship with Avital, and frequently traveled with her to raise funds.[68] In 1982 when word arrived in the West that Shcharansky was on a hunger strike in prison, Weiss parked himself in front of the Soviet UN Mission and announced that, in solidarity with Shcharansky, he would eat no food for a week.[69]

KEEPING THE FAITH IN PRISON

Two weeks after his conviction and arrival in Vladimir Prison, Shcharansky was thrilled to learn that two other Prisoners of Zion, Yosef Mendelevich and Hillel Butman, from the Leningrad Trials of 1970 and 1971, were also in Vladimir. He learned that he could communicate with them through the cooperation of fellow prisoners in adjacent cells. One method involved removing the water from a toilet bowl, sticking one's head inside it and whispering while making sure not to be seen or heard by any prison guards.[70] The toilet telephone network was employed the day a copy of *Pravda* with headlines that condemned Reagan for calling the Soviet Union an "evil empire" found its way into the prison. The prisoners were overjoyed to learn the news that America finally had a president who would call a spade a spade.[71]

Although they weren't Jewish, some of Shcharansky's fellow prisoners in Perm 35, the forced labor camp to which he had been transferred after three years in prison, helped him celebrate Chanukah. He had explained to them that it was a holiday to commemorate freedom to practice one's own culture even while living in a tyrannical regime. They built a wooden menorah for him and found some candles which Shcharansky lit for them each evening. The guards didn't interfere until the sixth night, when they confiscated the menorah and candles, which they deemed "state materials." Shcharansky declared a hunger strike in protest. Two days later he was summoned to the office of Major Osin, the head of Perm 35. Osin wanted Shcharansky to end his hunger strike but didn't want the entire camp to know that he was returning the confiscated materials. Shcharansky gave him a way out, saying, "It's very important to me to celebrate the last night of Chanukah. Why not let me do it here and now with you? You'll give me back the menorah, I'll light the candles and say the prayer, and if it all goes well I'll end the hunger strike." Osin agreed and cut a large candle into eight pieces. Following Shcharansky's instructions, Osin donned his major's hat, and at the end of Shcharansky's prayer said, "Amen." An elated Shcharansky returned to his cell and later told his fellow prisoners abouts Osin's "conversion."[72]

Another one of Shcharansky's strikes was precipitated by the seizure of his tiny psalm book, a gift from Avital that was originally confiscated with other belongings when he was arrested. In 1980 it was unexpectedly returned to him and he was greatly comforted by the words of King David and the opportunity to continue studying Hebrew. Psalm 23 had particular meaning. "When I walk through the valley of death I will fear no evil because you are with me" became his mantra.[73]

But two months after his Chanukah celebration the prison authorities decided to confiscate his "religious literature." They also took away a Bible belonging to his Christian friend Vladimir Poresh. Shcharansky declared a work strike and was put in a punishment cell. Poresh went on a hunger strike for seventy days but didn't get his Bible back. Every fifteen days Shcharansky was allowed out of the punishment cell for one hour. After 100 days he was transferred to the prison hospital for three weeks and then back to the punishment cell. After a total of 186 days in the punishment cell, he was sentenced to three years in prison and transferred back to Chistopol, in November 1981. However, the authorities agreed to his request and returned his psalm book.[74]

FREEDOM

Still in prison in early 1986, Shcharansky had outlived Brezhnev, Andropov, and Chernenko, who had kept him in the gulag. Their successor, Gorbachev, may have felt he would be in a better position to negotiate with the West on disarmament and other issues if he first made the gesture of releasing Shcharansky.[75] He authorized veteran spy trader and prominent East German lawyer Wolfgang Vogel to negotiate the exchange of Shcharansky for Communist agents held in the West.[76] At a meeting at an Austrian ski resort in January 1986, Vogel and his West German counterpart, Ludwig Rehlinger, and U.S. Ambassador to East Germany Frank Meehan came up with an agreement to trade Shcharansky and three captured Western agents for two Czech spies arrested in the United States and three Communist agents jailed in West Germany.

The exchanges took place on the snow-covered Glieneke Bridge connecting Potsdam, East Germany, with West Berlin on February 11, 1986. Shcharansky, escorted by Meehan from Potsdam, was allowed to cross well in advance of the others so that he would not look like a spy to the world watching with rapt attention on television. Although the prison authorities were aware of Shcharansky's impending release and tried to fatten him up for the event, it was obvious that his clothes were still too big.[77] Rabbi Avi Weiss once asked Shcharansky what he was thinking about when he crossed the bridge to the free world, and the former Prisoner of Zion replied, "Oh God, please don't let my pants fall down!"[78]

A limousine brought Shcharansky to Tempelhof Airport for the short flight to Frankfurt and his long-awaited reunion with Avital. After a long embrace his first words to her were, "Sorry I'm late." Twelve years of forced separation had not diminished his knack for expressing himself in humorous one-liners.[79]

The Israeli Ambassador to West Germany Yitzhak Ben-Ari gave him a passport with his new name, Natan Sharansky. Within an hour the happy couple boarded a jet headed home to Israel.[80]

A NEW LIFE IN ISRAEL

When Ambassador Ben-Ari gave Sharansky his new passport he commented, "When you were imprisoned the whole Jewish world stood behind you, but now that you are free you may face a difficult time as various groups will try to pull you to their side." Sharansky replied that he thought he could handle that.[81] Their exchange proved prophetic.

Once the homecoming celebrations with religious and political leaders, and the reunions with former refusenik activists, were over, Sharansky traveled to a meeting of worldwide Soviet Jewry leaders in Paris. He asked them to speak out in support of Andrei Sakharov, who was still exiled in Gorky, and was regarded by Sharansky as a Righteous Gentile. However, the establishment leaders, heeding the Lishka's sentiments, continued to be fearful of meddling in Soviet internal affairs and did nothing.[82]

In May 1986 Sharansky triumphantly toured America expressing gratitude to his supporters and urging them to keep fighting for the release of all the Prisoners of Zion and for free emigration from the Soviet Union. He suggested that when Gorbachev came to the United States for a summit meeting there should be a massive demonstration of American Jews, perhaps 400,000, to remind Gorbachev that there were 400,000 Soviet Jews who wanted to emigrate. When the Jewish establishment questioned whether they could muster so many for a demonstration Sharansky took his proposal to the grassroots. He and Avital visited thirty American Jewish communities from August through October. The response was overwhelming, forcing the establishment to rethink its skepticism and start organizing for the largest demonstration in the u.s. capital since Martin Luther King's March on Washington in 1963. The Sharanskys were cheered by a crowd of 250,000 who gathered in the capital on December 6, 1987, two days before the Gorbachev-Reagan summit meeting.[83]

In 1988 Sharansky was elected president of the Zionist Forum, an umbrella organization of former refuseniks dedicated to helping new immigrants and educating the public about absorption. The following year he revisited the United States and received the Medal of Freedom from Reagan. After the Oslo Accords were signed by Israeli and Palestinian leaders in 1993 Sharansky organized Peace Watch, a non-partisan, independent group whose purpose was to monitor compliance with the agreements.

Sharansky entered Israeli politics in 1995 by founding his own political party, Yisrael B'Aliyah, which can be translated as both "Israel on the rise" and "Israel for immigration". The party promoted increased funding for absorption of Soviet Jews into Israeli society. In the 1996 elections the party won seven Knesset seats and joined the coalition with Likud, enabling Sharansky to become minister of industry and trade. He held this post until 1999 when he was appointed interior minister. He also served as minister of construction and housing, minister of Jerusalem affairs and deputy prime minister under Ariel Sharon. Because of his disagreement with Sharon's disengagement plan he resigned from the government in 2005 and became a Distinguished Fellow at the Shalem Center, a think tank in Jerusalem.[84] Sharansky was elected to the Knesset in 2006 as a member of the Likud Party but resigned after seven months to rejoin the Shalem Center and head its new Institute for Strategic Studies. It is believed he left politics for academia because he was frustrated by his inability to convince Israelis to accept his ideas. Some former refusenks in Israel resented Sharansky basking in glory and government perks while they were struggling to make ends meet on meager pensions.[85]

One former refusenik, Yuli Nudelman, published a book in 1999 entitled *Sharansky Unmasked*, which charged that Sharansky's heroism was a myth created by the KGB and Sharansky's family.[86] Sharansky sued Nudelman for libel and the Jerusalem District Court, finding that Nudelman's claims were preposterous, awarded Sharansky NIS 900,000 (approximately U.S. $200,000).[87]

Sharansky continues to be an influential hero in America. In 2004 he visited dozens of American college campuses to bolster the morale of Jewish students who are trying to support Israel in the shadow of anti-Semitic faculty members and pro-Palestinian groups. That same year he co-authored *The Case for Democracy: The Power of Freedom to Overcome Tyranny and Terror* with Ron Dermer. Its premise that freedom is the right to dissent without fear of punishment resonated with President George W. Bush, who told reporters and staffers to read it if they wanted to understand the administration's agenda for the Middle East.[88]

On December 15, 2006, Bush presented the U.S. Presidential Medal of Freedom to Sharansky, saying, "Today the Soviet Union is history, but the world still knows the name Sharansky. As a free man, he's become a political leader in Israel, winning four elections to the Knesset and serving more than eight years in the Cabinet. He remains, above all, an eloquent champion for liberty and democracy. Natan reminds us that every soul carries the desire to live in freedom, and that freedom has a unique power to lift up nations, transform regions and secure a future for peace. Natan Sharansky is a witness to that power, and his testimony brings hope to those who still live under oppression."[89]

Alexander Lerner painted "The Last Seminar" depicting a gathering of prominent refuseniks in his Moscow apartment prior to the betrayal and final arrest of Sharansky. Clockwise from the far left: Sanya Lipavsky with his arm around Sharansky pretending to reassure him, Isaac Goldstein (pointing), Dina Beilin, Vladimir Slepak (standing with folded arms), Yuli Kosharovsky, Eitan Finkelstein, Ida Nudel, Lev Ovsicher (standing), Vitaly Rubin, Yosef Begun, Vladimir Lerner, Alexander Lerner. Reproduced courtesy of Sofia and Vladimir Lerner.

Natan Sharansky in San Francisco prior to a demonstration at the Soviet Consulate in 1987, with the author and his wife, reading about refusenik Alex Ioffe. Photo credit: John Rothmann.

Part Four

Support Groups in
the Free World
1967–2007

CHAPTER FIFTEEN

Two Conferences on Soviet Jewry

*I*n the wake of the harsh sentences of the Leningrad trial at the end of 1970, twenty-seven American Jewish organizations agreed to form the National Conference on Soviet Jewry. These national organizations represented the Conservative, Orthodox, and Reform movements as well as Zionist and community relations groups. They had determined that a well-funded, professionally managed organization was needed to speak for Soviet Jews and achieve the single goal of enabling them to be reunited with their relatives and the Jewish people in Israel.[1] Also in 1971 the Greater New York Conference on Soviet Jewry (GNYCSJ) replaced the New York Conference on Soviet Jewry, received funding, opened an office and launched a campaign that truly represented the world's largest metropolitan Jewish population.[2]

THE EVOLUTION OF THE AJCSJ INTO THE NCSJ

Since 1964 the major national American Jewish organizations had entrusted the problem of Soviet Jewry to the American Jewish Conference on Soviet Jewry, an ad-hoc association with representatives from major Jewish groups, but lacking adequate finances, permanent staff and offices. Initially it had a steering committee with a rotating CEO and chairman.[3] Its first chairman was George Maislen, the president of the United Synagogue of America.[4] In 1965 the National Jewish Community Relations Advisory Council assigned Albert Chernin of its staff to coordinate day-to-day operations of the AJCSJ.[5] He was succeeded by Abraham Bayer in 1968, when Chernin became executive director of the Philadelphia JCRC.[6] By 1970 demands for decisive action were heard from student groups like SSSJ, and as Bayer recalled, "the shrillness of their voices increased tremendously. It was beginning to grate on the ears of the adult Jewish establishment."[7]

The Leningrad Trial was a turning point for AJCSJ leaders; they decided to raise an emergency fund of $100,000 to be provided by local federations that would enable the launching of new programs that were beyond the capabilities of the NJCRAC budget. The Lishka also pressured Jewish leaders to reconstitute the AJCSJ as a more effective organization with its own staff and office. During the summer of 1971 it changed its name to the National Conference on Soviet Jewry, with Richard Maass of the American Jewish Committee as its chairman.[8]

JERRY GOODMAN

The American Jewish Committee gave Jerry Goodman, its director of European Affairs, a two-year leave of absence to become executive director of the NCSJ in 1971. That leave lasted for the next seventeen years.

Goodman's interest in Soviet Jewry stemmed from a visit, as a political science student, in 1961 to his uncle, a Holocaust survivor who lived in Riga and was one of the Jews who voluntarily cleaned the mass graves and set up an unauthorized monument at Rumbula (Chapter 7) After college Goodman was employed by the American Jewish Committee and became the person dealing with Soviet Jewry.[9] In 1965, together with Rabbi Richard Hirsch of the Religious Action Center of Reform Judaism, he helped organize the week-long Eternal Light Vigil in Washington that drew 6000 participants. This event was a departure from the establishment's opposition to picketing and mass demonstrations.[10]

At NCSJ Goodman embarked on an education and information campaign to inform Americans about the plight of Soviet Jewry. The first issue of the NCSJ's *Newsletter on Jews in the Soviet Union* was published in October 1971. Other publications, including monographs on refuseniks and prisoners of conscience, and *Outlook*, in newspaper format, followed and were published on a regular basis to keep NCSJ supporters aware of the problems faced by Jews in the USSR.[11] By the end of its first year of operation there was a budgetary shortfall of $100,000.[12] However, Goodman put the NCSJ on a sound financial footing by raising money through a network of Jewish federations and individual donors to augment the dues assessed from its member organizations.

Goodman dealt with the Lishka's representatives in New York, Los Angeles and Washington. He recalls that the NCSJ didn't always agree with the Israelis on tactical issues, but the relationship was collegial rather than confrontational. Furthermore, the Lishka was a primary source of information about was going on in the Soviet Union.[13]

Over the objections of a few NCSJ organizational members, Goodman opened an office in Washington to be close to Congress and the White House.[14] Through that office the NCSJ effectively spoke with one voice for thirty-four member organizations, and through NJCRAC and the Council of Jewish Federations (CJF), for over 200 Jewish communities in the United States.[15]

TWO NCSJ ACCOMPLISHMENTS

In Washington the NCSJ fought for passage of the Jackson-Vanik Amendment to the 1975 Trade Act, and promoted the creation of the Commission on Security and Cooperation in Europe.

The NCSJ viewed the promulgation of the Soviet education tax in 1972 as an onerous method of restricting emigration. Goodman described it as a ransom rather than a tax, and set up meetings with senators Jackson, Javits and Ribicoff (D-CT). The NCSJ, with encouragement from the Lishka, strongly supported the passage of the Jackson-Vanik Amendment as it was debated in Congress.[16] Even during the Yom Kippur War of 1973, when Kissinger tried to put pressure on the Jewish community by saying that support for the Jackson-Vanik Amendment could hurt Israel, a Lishka representative told Goodman, "You do what you have to do for Soviet Jews. Let Israel take care of itself."[17]

In June 1973, when Brezhnev visited Nixon in Washington, the NCSJ organized a huge demonstration on behalf of Soviet Jewry. However to satisfy some in the organization who opposed protest rallies it was called the "National Freedom Assembly". There was also some hesitation about allowing Senator Jackson to speak at the event because a few NCSJ leaders were fearful of antagonizing Nixon, Brezhnev's host.[18] The demonstration was very successful and its parade was led by a group of academics in gowns and mortar boards each carrying the name of a refusenik scientist or academic. Several hundred Jewish Defense League marchers tried to upstage the parade but were outmaneuvered by Jack Cohen who led the academics into an alternate route.[19]

Concerned by the declining emigration rate following the passage of the Jackson-Vanik Amendment, the NCSJ enthusiastically supported Congresswoman Millicent Fenwick's (Chapter 13) bill to create a U.S. commission that would monitor implementation of the human rights aspects of the Helsinki Final Act.[20] Congressman Dante Fascell (D-FL), who chaired the House International Affairs Committee, was moved by testimony on the drop in Soviet Jewish emigration and the harassment of refuseniks presented by Goodman and NCSJ Washington office director, Jon Rotenberg, to drive the bill to passage. As in the case of the Jackson-Vanik Amendment, secretary of state Kissinger was a formidable opponent. However, Fenwick's bill passed with overwhelming congressional support and was signed by former President Gerald Ford on June 3, 1976.

Fascell became the first chairman of the Commission on

Security and Cooperation in Europe (CSCE), often referred to as the Helsinki Commission. Meg Donovan of the NCSJ staff joined the commission and helped document data on a rapidly growing list of emigration violations. The CSCE was a unique creation in the American foreign policy establishment since it included representatives from Congress and the White House. It was extremely effective in holding Soviet feet to the fire on human rights issues.[21] Congressman Steny Hoyer (D-MD) succeeded Fascell as commission chairman, and served in that role for ten years, frequently visiting refuseniks and dissidents in the Soviet Union. He recalls how the CSCE could be more confrontational and assertive than the State Department which was constrained by norms of international diplomacy. The CSCE often followed up on requests for help from American relatives of refuseniks or from non-governmental organizations like the NCSJ requesting support for specific cases. Hoyer met with the official in charge of approving visas in Moscow and interceded on behalf of refuseniks whose security refusals had been ruled illegal by a Soviet court but had not received their exit visas from OVIR.[22] Reflecting on his years of advocacy for Soviet Jews, Hoyer stated that "those of us who are non-Jewish need to know, as Martin Luther King said, 'if there is one of us in prison, if there is one of us without our rights, if there is one of us at risk, then we are all at risk.'"[23]

MORRIS ABRAM

Like Steny Hoyer, Morris Abram, who helped found the NCSJ and became its chairman in 1982, entered the Soviet Jewry movement with a background of achievement in civil rights. A native of Georgia and the son of a Romanian immigrant, Abram served on the prosecution staff at the Nuremberg war-crimes trials. His fourteen-year effort as a lawyer in Atlanta resulted in establishment of the "one man, one vote" principle of American constitutional law.[24]

In 1963 he became president of the American Jewish Committee, and with its board, pledged to "arouse mankind to the plight of nearly three million [Soviet] Jews…who are threatened with the destruction of their cultural and religious identity." In his role as u.s. representative to the u.n. Commission on Human Rights, Abram exposed a viciously anti-Semitic book, *Judaism without Embellishment*, published by Trofim Kichko, a Ukrainian professor, in 1963. Abram's disclosure elicited a response from *Pravda*. The official Soviet newspaper blended denial of anti-Semitism in the ussr with a mild repudiation of the book.[25]

As chairman of the ncsj, Abram was a strong advocate for the Israeli position on Israel as the primary destination for Soviet Jews seeking to emigrate. His close friendship with Nechemia Levanon helped cement the bond between the Lishka and the ncsj. Abram also had a close relationship with secretary of state George Shultz and frequently gave Shultz lists of refuseniks prepared by the ncsj based on information from the Lishka and smuggled out of the Soviet Union. These lists were presented by Shultz to the Soviet leaders, and in the late 1980s resulted in exit visas for many of the refuseniks who were lucky enough to be on the lists.[26]

THE WASHINGTON RALLY

Abram, in his dual role as chairman of the ncsj and of the Conference of Presidents of Major American Jewish Organizations, told Sharansky in 1986 that expecting and publicizing in advance that 400,000 American Jews to show up at a rally in Washington was unrealistic. Sharansky was proposing that number as way of reminding Gorbachev that 400,000 Soviet Jews wanted to emigrate.[27] Abram and Goodman opposed committing to any fixed number because if fewer people showed up it would be interpreted as a sign of weakness. But they were eager to have an impressive rally in December 1987 on the eve of Gorbachev's meeting with Reagan in Washington. As soon as the summit meeting was announced, planning for a massive rally went full speed ahead.[28]

The planners had no more than forty days' notice to arrange an event. The ncsj asked David Harris, who was director of governmental and international affairs for the American Jewish

Committee in Washington, to be the principal organizer. He had a long resumé of familiarity with Soviet Jewry; his mother was from Moscow, he had experienced detention by the KGB in 1974 when he met Jews during his time on an exchange program as an English teacher in Russia, and he had participated in the Moscow International Book Fair in 1981. More importantly, he had also directed the NCSJ's Washington office.[29]

The big question was whether enough people would come to Washington in December to make an impression on the Soviet leader. Up this point the largest Soviet Jewry rally in the nation's capital had drawn 10,000 people.[30] Nevertheless Harris and his organization, joined by the SSSJ and UCSJ, worked tirelessly and appealed to "Jews and Christians, Democrats and Republicans, blacks and whites, public officials and private citizens" to gather in a mass mobilization on Sunday, December 6, 1987 to "remind the Soviet leaders that, for Americans, peace and human rights are indivisible." He advised readers of the *Washington Jewish Week* that the world would be watching as "thousands of journalists from around the globe descend on Washington for the summit. But nowhere will the reports be more closely watched than in the Soviet Union...The Kremlin wishes our movement would fizzle and die. On the other hand Soviet Jews will be eagerly awaiting reports of the rally, for they rightly believe that such public manifestations represent their lifeline."

The response on "Freedom Sunday" exceeded all expectations. Despite freezing temperatures there were 250,000 participants from all over the United States, Canada, and other nations of the free world, assembled on the Ellipse south of the White House. It was the largest Jewish demonstration ever held in the United States and David Harris called it an event that showed what American Jews can do when we choose to act in unison."[31]

Dignitaries including Vice President George H.W. Bush, House Speaker Jim Wright, and Nobel laureate Elie Wiesel, joined numerous former Prisoners of Zion in demanding freedom for Soviet Jewry.[32] Abram read a statement of assurance from Reagan saying that refuseniks would be the "unseen guests" at his side during the talks with Gorbachev.[33] And when Gorbachev finally arrived at the White House, Reagan asked him, "Have you heard about the rally on the mall last Sunday?"[34] Refuseniks heard about the success of the event, and Evgeny Lein described that day as "a milestone in the history of the struggle for free emigration of Soviet Jews."[35]

MISSION ACCOMPLISHED

During the year that followed the rally nearly 20,000 Jews received permission to emigrate, all of the Prisoners of Zion were out of prison and restrictions on studying Judaism and Jewish culture were lifted. As Myrna Shinbaum of the NCSJ wrote, "... NCSJ achieved the goals it set out to achieve precisely because of its makeup. It was the support of the national agencies that proved to be its strength."[36]

However, rather than basking in the glory of forcing a superpower to change its behavior, the NCSJ continued to pursue assurance that the Soviet Union would continue to adhere to its human rights commitments. In March 1988 Abram wrote to ambassador Warren Zimmermann, head of the U.S. delegation to the CSCE conference in Vienna asking the U.S. delegation to seek guarantees of "significant performance" on human rights from the Soviets. Zimmermann responded: "For us, performance is more important than additional texts, because the Soviets and their allies in the past have ignored textual commitments when it suited them to do so."[37] A year later Abram was leading the U.S. delegation at the CSCE Meeting on the Human Dimension in Paris, and stated that "the principal goal of the U.S. delegation...will be to engage in a thorough and open review of how human rights commitments are being implemented by the signatory states."[38]

In an effort to demonstrate Soviet willingness to live up to its human rights commitments, deputy foreign minister Anatoly Adamishin paid an unprecedented visit to the NCSJ office on July 26, 1989, and over a three-hour luncheon discussed all of the existing emigration issues in a serious businesslike manner.[39] Four months later at the NCSJ annual meeting in Washington, a surprise guest, Yuri Reshetov of the Soviet Foreign Ministry, assured the delegates that their aspirations for free emigration and Jewish culture in the USSR were being fulfilled.[40]

Shoshana Cardin succeeded Abram as NCSJ chair in 1988. She had been active in the Baltimore Jewish community where she participated in some of the early rallies for Soviet Jewry. She later served as president of the Council of Jewish Federations.

As Jews in the Soviet Union were finally becoming free to leave or to stay and learn about their Jewish heritage, anti-Semitism became the dominant concern.[41] Thanks to leadership from American ambassador Max Kampelman and assistance from Cardin, the concluding document of the CSCE meeting in Copenhagen in 1990 included a condemnation of anti-Semitism. Cardin met with Gorbachev and urged him to denounce anti-Semitism.[42] He was not eager to give the issue a high priority and commented, "It would be a mistake to single out one problem when we have so many here." Nevertheless, he was aware of the concerns of American Jewry and took the unprecedented step of sending Alexander Yakovlev, a Politburo member and confidant, to represent him at the ceremonies commemorating the fiftieth anniversary of the massacres at Babi Yar on October 6, 1991.[43]

Cardin also met with Israel's prime minister Yitzhak Shamir, and in anticipation of the waves of immigrants landing in Tel Aviv, prevailed upon him to accelerate the construction of housing to accommodate the new arrivals. He was rather nonchalant initially, expecting that it would take at least ten years for a million Jews to arrive.[44] Over the next few years a massive fund-raising campaign called "Operation Exodus" would provide Israel the financial resources needed to absorb a million Jews in half that time.

THE GNYCSJ – A LOCAL ORGANIZATION
WITH INTERNATIONAL CLOUT

Concurrent with the establishment of the NCSJ, the GNYCSJ

received a $100,000 loan from New York's Federation of Jewish Philanthropies and was able to open an office in New York City. Its executive director was Malcolm Hoenlein, who had been employed by the JCRC in Philadelphia as the staff member in charge of international affairs and its Council on Soviet Jewry for two years. He moved to New York to head what would become the Greater New York Conference on Soviet Jewry. During the summer of 1971 Hoenlein and his wife traveled to the Soviet Union, and in Kishinev they tried to observe the trial of several Jews. The authorities detained the Hoenleins and postponed the trial of the Soviet Jews. Upon returning to New York Hoenlein opened the GNYCSJ office and hired two assistants, Margie Davis and Zeesy Schnur. Davis became the GNYCSJ director in 1976 when Hoenlein moved on to head the New York JCRC.[45] Schnur served as GNYCSJ executive director from 1980 to 1992 when the organization merged into the JCRC.[46]

Although the GNYCSJ was affiliated with the NCSJ, it was quite willing to hold demonstrations and rallies, and tried to bridge the gap between the activists and the establishment and harnessed the energies of both camps.[47] Its first major event, the Freedom Lights for Soviet Jewry, held jointly with the SSSJ on December 13, 1971, sold out all 20,000 seats in Madison Square Garden and featured Gerald Ford as one of the speakers.[48] The rally was originally conceived by grassroots activists Azriel and Ahuva Genack, who planned it in their kitchen and borrowed money to rent Madison Square Garden.[49] Ultimately the GNYCSJ and NCSJ teamed up with the SSSJ activists and signed on as co-sponsors.[50]

While the GNYCSJ and SSSJ generally worked well together, there were some disagreements and competitiveness when the students proposed to take their civil disobedience a step beyond what adults felt was appropriate behavior. The GNYCSJ also had a very creative staff and developed original and creative materials for promoting the movement that were circulated globally.[51]

In 1973 when Brezhnev came to speak at the United Nations,

a huge banner reading "Soviet Jewry Freedom Island" was unfurled and hung on a small island in the East River facing the U.N.
headquarters. The island had been deeded to the GNYCSJ by an act
of New York state legislature. A boat hired by the GNYCSJ brought
150 reporters, two New York borough presidents and other public
officials to the island.[52]

The first Solidarity Sunday demonstration in 1972 was organized by GNYCSJ and NCSJ in spite of skepticism from some establishment leaders. They later recognized the value of the event
and endorsed participation by members of their participation
as these rallies were repeated annually by the GNYCSJ until free
emigration of Soviet Jews was achieved.[53] Massive crowds were
attracted, along with substantial press coverage, as politicians, especially candidates for high office, eagerly requested permission
from the GNYCSJ to speak at the rallies.[54] During the 1980s over
100,000 participants would march on Fifth Avenue and on to Dag
Hammarskjold Plaza at the United Nations each year.[55]

One of the most dramatic Solidarity Sundays occurred in
1979 when Mark Dymshitz and Edward Kuznetsov were in New
York immediately after being released from the Gulag in a prisoner
swap. They appeared at the rally two days later and were cheered
by a tumultuous crowd as Kuznetsov, almost choking with emotion, declared, "Your devotion and energy not only shortened my
prison term by two thousand and forty unbearable days, but also
saved my life!" After the rally the two former prisoners flew to
Israel and reunions with their families.[56]

With more advanced notice in 1986, a crowd of 300,000
squeezed into Dag Hammarskjold Plaza and enthusiastically welcomed Natan Sharansky, who expressed his appreciation: "Every
year from this place my wife, Avital, spoke to you, trying to convince you that your efforts were not in vain. The fact that I am
speaking to you today is the best proof that she was right." Holding up the little psalm book that had been so dear to him during
his years of incarceration, he continued, "The KGB, my interrogators and my prison guards tried to convince me that I was alone,

powerless in their hands. I knew I was never alone. I knew that my wife, my people and all of you were with me. All the resources of a superpower cannot isolate a man who hears the voice of freedom. It was a voice I heard from the very chamber of my soul."[57]

As emigration rates of Soviet Jews increased senator Daniel Patrick Moynihan (D-NY) suggested that the Solidarity Sunday be set aside as a reciprocal gesture. The GNYCSJ agreed and canceled the marches in 1989 and 1990. They resumed in 1991 to protest the rising tide of Russian anti-Semitism.[58]

In addition to campaigning for free emigration, the GNYCSJ created a "Commission on Soviet Jewry Life" to nurture the refusenik Tarbut (culture) movement by encouraging Jewish identity and Judaic knowledge among Soviet Jews. Dr. Norman Lamm of Yeshiva University spearheaded these efforts.[59] Rabbi Haskel Lookstein, who was chairman of the GNYCSJ from 1987 to 1991, traveled to Russia several times, sponsored by the Ezra Fund of the Rabbinical Council of America, to promote the study of Judaism there. On his first trip in 1972 he assessed who in the synagogues of Leningrad, Kiev and Moscow were KGB collaborators and who, like Zeev Shachnovsky, were leaders of the underground Hebrew schools. In 1975, as well as officiating at the wedding of Yuli and Inna Kosharovsky (Chapter 9), Rabbi Lookstein met with leading refuseniks and provided them with tapes of Jewish rituals. He found that while there was considerable study of Hebrew there was an appalling ignorance of religion.[60] His 1975 trip report relayed the feelings expressed by Eliyahu Essas and Vladimir Prestin that spreading Tarbut would go hand-in-hand with an increasing desire for Jews to go to Israel.[61]

Back in New York, students at Ramaz High School, under Lookstein's direction, organized a daily morning minyan, hunger strikes and rallies at the Soviet Mission to support Sharansky and other refuseniks. Lookstein often said, "An hour or two spent at a rally to help Jews is worth ten to twenty hours in the classroom."[62]

*Sharansky applauded at 1986 meeting of the Conference of Presidents.
Left to right: Morey Schapira, UCSJ President; Natan Sharansky;
Ken Bialkin, Conference of Presidents Chairman; Yehuda Hellman,
Conference of Presidents Executive Director; Morris Abram, NCSJ
Chairman. Photo credit: UCSJ Archives/Alexander Archer.*

Rabbi Haskel Lookstein in his office in 2005. His book, Were We Our
Brothers' Keepers?, *expresses the moral imperative that motivated
the Soviet Jewry movement. Photo credit: Philip Spiegel.*

CHAPTER SIXTEEN

Grassroots Activism in California

"Tell them [in America] we cannot hold out much longer here. Tell them we need help desperately – it is terrible, it is terrible."[1] This was the plea of an elderly Jew in Kiev, spoken between sobs to David Weiss, a visitor from California, and repeated by Weiss to a spellbound audience at Temple Sherith Israel in San Francisco during the summer of 1967. When Weiss concluded his lecture, four members of the congregation, Rabbi Morris Hershman, Sidney Kluger, Hal Light and Ed Tamler, agreed that they had to do something; within a week the Bay Area Council on Soviet Jewry was founded.[2]

DAVID WEISS

As soon as he opened the invitation David Weiss knew he was facing an ethical dilemma. Weiss was a professor of immunology at the University of California, Berkeley, and he was being invited by the Soviet Academy of Medical Science to the 1965 meeting on immunology against cancer that would take place in Sukhumi, a Black Sea resort. This was a new field that Weiss was engaged in, and he was professionally very eager to be one of fifty scientists, including twenty-five from the USSR, to participate in the meeting. But Weiss was an observant Jew who had fled Nazi-controlled Austria as a child and was loath to ever set foot again in an anti-Semitic country.[3] He called his close friend Rabbi Abraham Joshua Heschel and proposed making a public rejection of the invitation. "Absolutely not!" was Heschel's reply, urging Weiss to "go and see yourself [about anti-Semitism] and what can be done for Soviet Jews."

Heschel contacted the Israeli Consulate in New York, and Israel's ambassador to the u.s. and u.n., Avraham Harman, visited Weiss in Berkeley and persuaded him to accept the invitation. Meir Rosenne (who would later brief Elie Wiesel for his Soviet journey) was dispatched to Berkeley to brief Weiss on how to make contact with Jews during his free time. After the meeting in Sukhumi, Weiss, as an invited guest, had a car and a guide at his disposal six hours a day for the next two weeks to show him the sights of Kiev and Moscow. Mostly he just wanted to visit synagogues and to sit on a park bench with his El Al Israel Airlines bag and a Hebrew newspaper.[4] He had conversations, usually in Yiddish, with more than 150 Jews, and was shocked by the "strong palpable fear" of those he met. He became convinced that the anti-Semitism was real, and not a figment of Cold War propaganda.[5]

Returning home, Weiss reported his findings to Nechemia Levanon and Yoram Dinstein at the Israeli Consulate in New York. He also met with Moshe Decter and Lou Rosenblum, and founded the Professional and Academic Committee for Soviet Jewry. Over the next two years, until he and his family made aliyah, he spoke to various groups in twenty-five states, including the aforementioned event at Sherith Israel. From his new home in Jerusalem Weiss continued to give advice and support to Hal Light and the leaders of the fledgling Bay Area Council on Soviet Jewry.[6]

HAL LIGHT

When Hal Light wrote up a set of objectives for the BACSJ in 1967 he was no stranger to social action. He and his wife, Selma, had organized a group called "Parents Mississippi" to support young people, like their son, Bill, who were in Mississippi working in the civil rights movement. Although Hal hadn't been politically active until 1964, he sold his soda dispensing equipment business and devoted his time and energy to raising funds and testifying before Congressional committees on civil rights legislation.[7]

After the meeting at Sherith Israel, Light decided to work full-time on programs that would do more for Soviet Jews than the relatively few and ineffectual statements from the local Jewish establishment.[8] The first BACSJ event was an all-day rally on October 22, 1967, attended by 700 people who listened to public officials and clergy of various faiths and signed petitions to the U.S. government.

David Weiss introduced Light to Lou Rosenblum, who provided copies of the constitution of the Cleveland Council on Soviet Anti-Semitism, as well as advice on applying for tax-exempt status. Jacob Birnbaum also corresponded with Light, sharing his experience of starting a grassroots activist organization for Soviet Jewry.[9] Light reached out to the establishment, telling Abe Bayer of the National Jewish Community Relations Advisory Council that "a lot of people out there are getting excited…they're growing more worried about the Jews of the Soviet Union." He urged Bayer to "make use of a most important public that wants to be involved."[10]

In 1968 Hal and Selma Light traveled to the Soviet Union to see for themselves what their brethren were going through. They saw the fear that Elie Wiesel had described in *The Jews of Silence*, and were deeply moved by a man on the street who would say only two words to them, "*nicht vergessen*", "do not forget [us]". The trip intensified Light's passion to save Soviet Jews, and he was delighted to recruit volunteers and brief people who wanted to travel to the USSR.[11]

One individual who called Light prior to embarking on a trip to Russia and Eastern Europe in 1969 was John Rothmann, a Whittier College student who had worked for former President Richard Nixon. Rothmann recalls the trip as "a defining moment in my life." He visited with Rabbi Levin in the Moscow synagogue and asked, "Is it good for Jews here?" Levin said "Yes" but nodded negatively. When Rothmann asked if Russian Jews wanted to go to Israel, Levin said "No!" but nodded affirmatively. Rothmann and his group went to Kiev, and there, following Light's instructions, took a bus to the site of Babi Yar. An old man saying *Kaddish* told Rothmann, "This is a terrible place. My first wife and children were killed here. There's no future for Jews in this land. Our only hope is to leave this place and go to Israel." And then he pointed to the ravine where 33,000 Jews were murdered in two days and said, "If they were alive, they would want to go to Israel too!"

Upon returning to California Rothmann called Light and said, "I'll do anything you want me to do!" They first did a series of interviews, and stories of their trips were published in the San Francisco *Examiner* and the Northern California *Jewish Bulletin*.[12] Light organized a rally in San Francisco that drew 5,000 people and received national attention.[13] The audience was riveted by the twenty-year-old Rothmann's vivid and compelling account of his experience in the Soviet Union.

The next major BACSJ gathering was a candlelight vigil in San Francisco's Union Square in December on behalf of the eighteen Georgian Jewish families who had sent their appeal for permission to emigrate to prime minister Golda Meir and to the United Nations Human Rights Commission.[14] Christmas cards were sent to Soviet ambassador Dobrynin with stickers that read, "Please let the 18 Georgian Jewish families leave." Light personally got involved in letter writing. Using the pseudonym Gershon Lazar, he pretended to be related to the Lazar family of Vilnius and received letters from them until they emigrated in 1973.[15] These activities, as well as the mailing of Rosh Hashanah cards to Soviet synagogues, were frowned upon by the American Jewish establishment until the Israelis reversed their position and endorsed the plea of the 18 Georgian Jewish families.

While the cautious attitude of both the Jewish establishment in America and the Israeli government were frustrating to Light, he regarded the violent behavior of the Jewish Defense League as even more objectionable.[16] After Rabbi Meir Kahane, the chairman and founder of JDL, approved the bombing of the New York offices of Aeroflot and Intourist in 1970 but denied responsibility for the acts, Light expressed his position in an editorial titled, "Confrontation? Yes! Violence? No!!!" that appeared in *Exodus,* a newsletter published by the Soviet Jewry Action Group.[17]

SJAG was a group of young adults in the San Francisco Bay Area who organized in late 1969 and created projects of non-violent civil disobedience to draw attention to the plight of Soviet Jewry. One of their most memorable actions was painting "LET THE JEWS OUT!" on a Soviet freighter that was docked in San Francisco.[18] The next morning Hal Light and activists from the BACSJ and SJAG holding picket signs that read "Free Boris Kochubievsky Now" and "Let Them Live as Jews or Leave as Jews" confronted the ship's captain, but he told them, "I don't want to discuss any political question."

There was soon an opportunity for the BACSJ to greet another Russian visitor to San Francisco – Soviet U.N. ambassador Jacob Malik. He was scheduled to address the 25th anniversary session of the United Nations at the War Memorial Opera House where the UN had been founded. It was just ten days after the Leningrad hijacking and the massive arrests of Jewish activists throughout the USSR.[19] The BACSJ was fearful that the would-be hijackers would be executed and that the Soviet regime was reverting to Stalinist tactics. Bob Hirsch, one of the founding members of BACSJ, dressed as Stalin and paraded in front of the Opera House while other BACSJ held placards that read "STALIN IS ALIVE." A photo of the spectacle appeared in Paris edition of the *Herald Tribune.*[20]

The Leningrad hijacking episode convinced Lillian Foreman, a housewife and former bookkeeper, to ask Hal Light how she could become an active BACSJ volunteer.[21] In the pre-computer 1970s she created and maintained a card index of every known refusenik and prisoner. The data proved extremely valuable in disseminating refusenik profiles for use in letter writing campaigns and in the briefings of thousands of tourists who went to visit the refuseniks in the Soviet Union. Foreman herself traveled to the Soviet Union five times. Her first trip was with Lillian Hoffman, who had founded an activist group in Denver. The two Lillians were known to be activists by the Soviet Consulate in San Francisco, so they went to England to obtain their entry visas. In Moscow they met with Ida Nudel, and brought back important information to add to the database. Data on refuseniks were shared with other Soviet Jewry support groups in America and Europe, especially those affiliated with the Union of Councils for Soviet Jews.[22]

The founding and growth of the UCSJ was largely a product of Hal Light's zeal, vision, charisma and organizational acumen. Light succeeded Rosenblum as president of the UCSJ. During its annual meeting in Washington, on September 10, 1974, he suffered a fatal heart attack. Fellow BACSJ founder Ed Tamler eulogized Light, comparing him to Moses as one who cared and acted for his suffering people: "Like Moses, he looked this way and that way for help for Soviet Jewry and found there was no recourse in the establishment, and so he set out to solve the problem himself."[23] Former President Gerald Ford, in a letter to Selma Light, wrote "His death is a great loss to all those who work in the cause of human rights."[24]

THE SOUTHERN CALIFORNIA
COUNCIL FOR SOVIET JEWS

Hal Light was succeeded as UCSJ resident by Si Frumkin of Los Angeles. Frumkin was born in Lithuania and liberated by the American army at age fourteen from Dachau, where his father had perished. He considered returning to Lithuania, but heard rumors that the Soviets were accusing Jews who had survived the Holocaust of being Nazi collaborators. He regards his decision not to return as the best he ever made. Frumkin reunited with his mother in Italy, attended schools in Switzerland and England, immigrated to America, and earned a B.A. from New York University.

He joined his stepfather's drapery business in Los Angeles, and had no connection with Soviet Jews until he attended a lecture in early 1969 at the Jewish Federation Commission on Soviet Jewry. Hearing about official anti-Semitism in the Soviet Union motivated Frumkin to offer his services as one who read and spoke Russian, but he got no response. Six months and several phone calls later he went to a meeting of the commission and listened to the members talk about symbolic gestures on behalf of Soviet Jewry like an empty chair at the Passover Seder table and an under-publicized Simchat Torah rally. Frumkin and one young member of the commission, Zev Yaroslavsky, wanted Soviet Jewry to be more than a twice-a-year event.[25]

Yaroslavsky, a UCLA sophomore whose parents had emigrated from Ukraine, flew to Moscow to visit his aunts and cousins in 1968.[26] His Aunt Rosa took him to see the sights and on a walk through Red Square, he asked her, "How is it for Jews in Russia?" Her reply, "Shhh, the walls have ears," rang in his ears and aroused him to start giving speeches at synagogues and form the California Students for Soviet Jews when he returned home. The following summer Yaroslavsky and his friends from CSSJ picketed a track team from the Soviet Union who were at the Los Angeles Coliseum to compete against an American team. They made signs with the usual "Let My People Go" and "Let the Jews Go" slogans, as well as one that read "Wouldn't it be nice if Jews could sprint to Israel?" Ignoring Jewish establishment leaders who warned them not to antagonize the Russians, Yaroslavsky called the local press. Reporters from several radio stations, TV channels, and newspapers arrived to cover the first demonstration to confront a Soviet delegation in Southern California. Yaroslavsky realized that such demonstrations could have a morale-building effect on Soviet Jews who could learn about them from telephone calls, tourists, and broadcasts of the Voice of America and Radio

Free Europe. He was also fond of saying, "One Jew talking to another Jew won't get a Soviet Jew out of Russia; we have got to talk to real world opinion makers and elected officials who can put this issue on the radar screen."[27]

Yaroslavsky and Frumkin enlisted the support of George Putnam, an influential and conservative TV newscaster in Los Angeles. Frumkin phoned Putnam's office claiming to be a professor whose student, Zev Yaroslavsky, had just returned from the USSR with an interesting story to tell. Putnam invited them to dinner and was extremely sympathetic about "those poor Soviet Jews." Putnam proposed a candlelight march of thousands of people in downtown Los Angeles on the first night of Chanukah, but Frumkin and Yaroslavsky doubted whether more than 200 would show up. Every night for two weeks Putnam's booming voice reminded his audience to "Carry a candle with me for the old folks of Russia. They must be free..." Ten thousand people, including mayor Sam Yorty and several congressmen, carried candles and signed petitions urging the Soviet government to "Let the Jews go." The petitions were sent to Hal Light, who brought them to the Soviet Embassy.

Light was impressed with what Frumkin and Yaroslavsky were doing and encouraged them to get organized with tax-exempt status as the Southern California Council for Soviet Jews. There was a hard core of twenty active people and a mailing list of about 1,500. Funds were generated by the sale of greeting cards for mailing to refuseniks, as well as bumper stickers and pins. One slogan on the pins, "Russia is not healthy for Jews and other living things," elicited the threat of a lawsuit from Mothers for Peace, the group who claimed to have patented the slogan, "War is not healthy for children and other living things."

As one of the first projects of the SCCSJ and UCSJ, supportive Americans mailed Passover greeting cards to Soviet Jews who had previously indicated a willingness to receive communications from the West and were on UCSJ lists. Many of the recipients responded with letters of appreciation and the Americans felt a great deal of satisfaction in achieving person-to-person contact with

Soviet Jews. But the National Conference of Soviet Jews castigated the UCSJ for sending the cards, saying, "If you make phone calls or send letters the Soviet authorities will know and will probably harass the Soviet Jews who receive them." This stemmed from the Israeli policy that also advocated prevention of emigrants from the Soviet Union from speaking before American audiences under any circumstances because "if they say anything critical about the Soviet Union, the small numbers of emigrants that we have today will be reduced to zero".

The Israeli policy of non-communication with Soviet Jews was very troubling to Frumkin, Light and Lou Rosenblum from Cleveland. They were not sure who was right and they certainly didn't want to put jeopardize anyone so they decided to leave it up to the activists among the Soviet Jews. Frumkin made several phone calls to them in Russian, and without exception they responded, "Please keep it up. We're not afraid."[28]

In March 1972 Yaroslavsky had a dramatic telephone conversation with Vladimir Slepak in Moscow that was heard by a crowd of CSSA members. Slepak reported that nine Jews and ten non-Jews had begun a hunger strike in the Potma labor camp over denial of visitation rights. Yaroslavsky taped the conversation for replay on the CSSA Soviet Jewry Hotline.[29]

JCRC SUPPORT – POSITIVE IN THE NORTH, NEGATIVE IN THE SOUTH

While most of the established Jewish organizations in San Francisco were indifferent to the BACSJ and Light's brand of activism, the Jewish Community Relations Council under Earl Raab, its executive director since 1951, was an exception. Raab had close ties to the Jewish Labor Committee and from them heard about Stalin's excesses including the murder of Jewish poets and the Doctors' Plot. To protest these crimes Raab organized rallies and radio programs on behalf of Soviet Jewry during the 1950s. Even though there was no chance that his efforts would influence the Kremlin, Raab felt that there was a need to keep alive an understanding of what was happening to the Jews of Russia. He and his wife visited the USSR in January 1967 as part of a fact-finding tour organized by NJCRAC director Al Chernin. Speaking Yiddish to attract Jews, they handed out mementos from Israel. At the synagogue in Moscow a few brave Russian Jews urged the Raabs to tell Americans about their situation.[30]

A few months after the Raabs returned to California, the BACSJ was formed. Raab and the San Francisco JCRC were much more sympathetic to it than the establishment-oriented NJCRAC would have liked. JCRCs in most other American cities followed NJCRAC directions and were generally ambivalent, indifferent, and sometimes hostile toward grassroots activists for Soviet Jewry.[31] Rabbi Doug Kahn, who joined the San Francisco JCRC staff in 1982 and became its executive director, and like John Rothmann had grown up in the activism of the BACSJ, recalls how Raab had a "very enlightened view" about the issue of Soviet Jewry.[32]

The SCCSJ did not fare so well with its JCRC. The Jewish Federation was frustrated with the SCCSJ and not only would not fund any of its activities, but allowed the executive director of the JCRC to visit college campuses and falsely allege that Frumkin was keeping the proceeds of greeting card sales for himself.[33]

THE STRUGGLE FOR PUBLIC AWARENESS

Although there was JCRC support for the BACSJ, Light frequently lamented the lack of coverage of the issue in the local Jewish press.[34] The pages of the weekly Northern California *Jewish Bulletin* did not mention Soviet Jewry until the mid-Seventies when Norm Schlossberg, an insurance salesman, told Selma Light that his firm would pay for informational advertising for the BACSJ in that paper. Schlossberg was motivated to make this offer after he had attended two lectures in one week. The first dealt with endangered dolphins and attracted an overflow crowd of at least 200, while only twenty people showed up for a talk on Soviet Jewry. Schlossberg was flabbergasted that saving dolphins appeared to be ten times as popular as saving people.[35]

The BACSJ needed more than advertising to put the issue in front of the public; they had to come up with creative events that would force the local press and media to take notice. In November 1972 fifty BACSJ protesters gathered in front of the I. Magnin department store in San Francisco with signs that read: "We won't buy where RUSSIAN FURS are sold until RUSSIAN JEWS ARE FREE." They were photographed burning their I. Magnin credit cards, and had an argument with a store executive that was quoted in the San Francisco *Chronicle*.[36] The newspaper coverage also had a disconcerting effect on the BACSJ – an audit by the Internal Revenue Service that could jeopardize its tax status, something that happened frequently during Nixon's presidency to organizations and individuals who were deemed antagonistic to administration policies. In this case, the BACSJ was regarded as opposed to détente. The IRS called the store protest a boycott and did a thorough search of the BACSJ office. Lawyers representing the BACSJ convinced the IRS that the protest was no more than a one-time publicity-seeking gimmick.[37]

Other publicity-generating events were concocted whenever Soviet cultural and sports groups were visiting the city. Typically a BACSJ group would unfurl a massive "Let My People Go" banner at a sports event. Before performances of the Bolshoi or Kirov ballets BACSJ activists dressed up as ushers and handed out what appeared to be programs but actually contained a summary of the Soviet Jewry situation, a list of long-term refuseniks, and a postcard that could be sent to the Soviet president.[38]

Over the next few years Frumkin and Yaroslavsky seized every opportunity to generate publicity for Soviet Jews from balloons with slogans over San Clemente when Brezhnev visited Nixon, to having a helicopter fly over the Super Bowl, to painting "Let Jews Go" on a Soviet freighter that was docked in Long Beach harbor.[39] The last of these stunts was accomplished by Yaroslavsky spray painting from a motorboat while two other SCCSJ activists held onto toilet plungers that were suctioned to the freighter.[40] Yaroslavsky recalls how every official "Soviet visitor and cultural group had to reconcile how they would deal with our protests; we were waging a non-violent guerrilla war."[41]

Yaroslavsky was elected to the Los Angeles City Council in 1975. He attributed his victory to votes from the Jewish community and others who knew about his work as a Soviet Jewry activist. In 1994, when he was elected to the Los Angeles County Board of Supervisors, he invoked his anti-Soviet background by vowing to tear down the country's "Berlin Wall" of isolation from the taxpaying public.[42]

After Frumkin retired from the drapery business he began devoting much of his time to serving the needs of Russian-speaking émigrés in Los Angeles and publishing a newsletter called *Graffiti for Intellectuals*.[43]

THE FORBIDDEN FORTRESS ON GREEN STREET

The Soviet government inadvertently gave the BACSJ a valuable gift by purchasing and using the building at 2790 Green Street as its consulate to match the U.S. Consulate in Leningrad. Washington had the Soviet Embassy and New York had the Soviet U.N. Mission, but San Francisco was the only U.S. city with a Soviet Consulate. The activists no longer had to wait for visiting delegations to make news; they now had a high-profile venue for demonstrations.[44] Starting in 1977 thousands of Soviet Jewry supporters gathered on Green Street for Simchat Torah rallies and street fairs organized by the BACSJ and JCRC every fall for a dozen years.[45]

A highlight of the rally in 1982 was the appearance of incumbent Democratic congressman Phil Burton and his opponent, Republican Milton Marks. They didn't want to be near each other but John Rothmann, then BACSJ president, raised their hands over his head and said, "There's one thing that Burton and Marks agree on and that's Soviet Jewry!" The crowd roared its approval as Rothmann continued, "This is not a partisan issue. This is not Republican or Democrat. This is an issue that affects everyone who believes in freedom!"[46]

That year Ed Tamler's wife, Rose, came up with the idea of

letting Soviet Consulate employees and passersby know that the issue of Soviet Jewry was not just a once-a- year event, and that the BACSJ was in solidarity with Prisoner of Zion Natan Sharansky, who was on a hunger strike. She organized and coordinated a daily vigil at noon in front of the consulate involving volunteers from various synagogues and organizations who carried placards. The vigils continued until 1989.[47]

The consulate, protected by a federal law prohibiting intimidation, harassment or threats against consular officials within one hundred feet of their workplace, was a magnet for civil disobedience.[48] On several occasions local rabbis and activists chained themselves to the consulate gates and were arrested by the San Francisco Police. In 1986 BACSJ board member Reuben Haller, clad in prison stripes, and accompanied by placard-waving supporters, went on a hunger strike in front of the consulate to protest the twenty years of refusal suffered by the Bogomolny family.[49] All of these rallies and demonstrations were coordinated with the San Francisco Police Force by board member Greg Smith, who had been a police officer in Los Angeles. In 1979 Smith, a Roman Catholic, moved to San Francisco and became the building manager of the Menorah Park senior housing complex where over one-third of the residents were Russian Jews. His heart went out to those who had been waiting for years to be reunited with their refusenik family members.[50]

In February 1987, nearly a year after his release from the gulag, Sharansky was the guest of honor at a special rally in front of the consulate. An energetic crowd of 10,000 chanted "Let My People Go" and sang "I am Leaving Mother Russia" and "*Am Yisrael Chai*".[51] Sharansky thanked his cheering supporters and said that he was in San Francisco because "Avital told me the people of this city were the spearhead of the effort to release me."[52]

The progress of glasnost could be measured by the behavior of Soviet consular officials at each Simchat Torah rally. As in prior years, the rally of 1986 ended with a BACSJ/JCRC delegation bearing petitions, walking to the front door of the consulate, ringing the doorbell, hearing no response, and leaving the petitions at the doorstep. In 1987, the three-person delegation was amazed when the doorbell was answered and they were invited inside. The Soviet consul then scolded them for their noisy anti-Soviet conduct. The following year the delegation was again invited in and the Soviet consul told them, "We know your rally is not anti-Soviet, but rather pro-Soviet Jews. We will convey your concerns to our government." A planned rally in 1989 was canceled because of recent earthquake damage nearby.[53]

Ten years later the once-forbidden fortress became the venue of a "Celebration of Freedom," as over 100 former BACSJ activists and former refuseniks were invited by Russian consul general Yuri Popov to enjoy hors d'oeuvres and drinks with his staff.[54]

GINA WALDMAN

Gina Waldman was one of the few BACSJ activists who had actually been inside the consulate prior to 1999. Two decades earlier, as BACSJ executive director, she had devised a publicity stunt to crash a formal party celebrating a Soviet holiday. Dressed in an elegant gown and stepping out of a taxi, she pointed at the phalanx of BACSJ protesters and yelled to a security guard, "Can't you get rid of these terrible people?" She handed him a BACSJ protest brochure in lieu of an official invitation and calmly walked inside. She proceeded to the women's bathroom and wrote "Free Anatoly Sharansky" in red lipstick on the mirror. Spotting Herb Caen of the San Francisco *Chronicle*, she invited him to see her handiwork and have something juicy to report in his next column.

Gina Waldman was Gina Bublil, a young refugee from Libya, when she first arrived in San Francisco. She and her family had fled to Italy when anti-Semitic mobs were rampaging in Tripoli in the wake of Israel's Six-Day War victory. A college friend invited Gina to San Francisco in 1969 and helped her find a job in an international bank. One day Gina saw "Let My People Go" banners and people chanting, "Pou Pou Pompidou" in front of the St. Francis Hotel. She inquired what that was all about and learned that the BACSJ was protesting the visit of former French President Georges Pompidou, who had just signed a trade deal with the Soviet Union. She was fascinated to learn that in America people are free to speak out about what they stand for.[55]

Gina soon started speaking in public herself, telling an audience at the Jewish Community Center how her family got out of Libya. Bob Hirsch recalls being in that audience with his wife, Doris, who was the BACSJ executive secretary. Doris remarked to Hal and Selma Light, "There's a girl who could really be an asset to our organization."[56] Light offered Gina a job that paid less than what she was earning at the bank, but the excitement of working for a Jewish cause was irresistible. She quickly learned about the needs of Soviet Jewry and the oppressive regime in which they lived, and also became trained by Hal Light in his assertive methods.

When announcements heralded the visit of a Soviet cultural group Gina would investigate where they would be staying so BACSJ activists could greet them with informational picketing. She called several hotels claiming to be employed by a florist who had to deliver a bouquet to the visiting prima ballerina. An affirmative response directed the BACSJ team to the correct hotel where they handed copies of *The Gulag Archipelago* by Alexander Solzhenitsyn – it was banned in Russia – to members of the Kirov Ballet.

Gina was also looking out for international scientific conferences that might include attendees from the Soviet Union. Realizing that just telling people that Jewish scientists were being persecuted in Russia would not be very effective, she would focus on an individual case. In 1974 BACSJ staffers came to a conference with handouts and petitions on behalf of Alexander Goldfarb, a molecular biologist and refusenik who was Sharansky's predecessor as English translator for Andrei Sakharov. Many of the conference attendees signed the petition urging the Soviet government to allow Goldfarb to emigrate, and when Russians presented their papers and expected to be questioned on their technical content, what they heard instead was: "Could you please tell us why your government refuses to allow Alexander Goldfarb to emigrate?" Upon returning to Moscow the delegates were debriefed by the KGB and described how embarrassed they were facing the San Francisco audience.[57] Within a month Goldfarb received permission to leave Russia and gave credit to Western scientists for influencing the Soviet government.[58]

When Gina married she was able to get a visa in her married name of Gina Waldman to enter the Soviet Union by applying at the Soviet Embassy in London. She was too well known as the ringleader of sit-in demonstrations and noisy rallies to ever get a visa at the consulate in San Francisco under her maiden name. As described in Chapter 12, she traveled to Russia with Selma Light and had a dramatic meeting with Andrei Sakharov in 1975.[59] She also viewed art by the "Aleph" group of twelve Russian Jewish artists that was on display without government approval in the one-room Leningrad apartment of refusenik artist Evgeny Abezgauz. The Soviet government was treating avant-garde art with the same contempt that was shown to political dissidents and refuseniks.[60] Abezgauz made slides and negatives of the Aleph group's art and had them smuggled them out of Russia to the BACSJ. From the slides and negatives Waldman organized a documentary exhibit of forty paintings called "Twelve from the Underground."[61] The art show opened in San Francisco in August 1976 and toured forty-one cities in North America.[62]

A year later the BACSJ launched a massive rally after Anatoly Shcharansky was arrested and charged with treason. Avital was overwhelmed by the support and upon her return to San Francisco in 1979 she went with Waldman to the Soviet Consulate. The two women asked consular officials to send a letter to Anatoly, who was in Chistopol Prison, but they would not accept it.[63] Avital Sharansky and Gina Waldman refused to leave, even at 5 P.M. as the office was closing, so in front of TV cameras they were arrested.[64]

In the early 1980s, referred to as the "the bleak years" for Soviet Jewry by Dutch ambassador Petrus Buwalda, it became clear that the Soviet government was being more repressive than ever.[65] The BACSJ was fortunate to grow with new volunteers nurtured by Waldman to meet the challenges. Morey Schapira, who had been an activist in Cleveland and Boston while attending college and graduate school, moved to the Bay Area and immediately plunged into BACSJ activities, and served as president of the council from 1980 to1982.[66] Eva Seligman-Kennard, who had retired from a nursing career, was looking for a Jewish cause to support and chose to work four days a week at the BACSJ because volunteers there were "involved with their souls."[67]

DAVID WAKSBERG

At age twenty-four in 1981 David Waksberg had the perfect background to fill a job opening as assistant director of the BACSJ. He had participated in SSSJ rallies as a high-school student, served as Soviet Jewry chairman for the United Synagogue Youth of Connecticut, had a B.A. from Brandeis, and had been arrested in South Africa for violating the apartheid laws. A few weeks after he was hired, Gina Waldman went on a two-month vacation to Italy, leaving Waksberg in charge. Soon the West learned that Victor Brailovsky, a refusenik scientist in Moscow, had been sentenced to five years' exile. Waksberg quickly organized a protest vigil outside the Soviet Consulate.

At the end of 1981 Gina Waldman was pregnant and decided to retire. She told the Board that "David can handle it" and encouraged them to promote him to executive director. In his new role he worked on getting more community awareness of BACSJ objectives and more support from mainstream Jewish organizations.

He also embarked on a visit to the Soviet Union with a gentile friend from college who had relatives in Belarus. During his visit with Alexander Lerner, Waksberg proposed organizing an international tribunal to investigate the crimes against Shcharansky. Lerner heartily endorsed the project and suggested that Avital be invited. Upon returning home Waksberg called Avital and she replied, "If Dr. Lerner says I should come, I'll come."[68] Attorneys

Irwin Cotler and Alan Dershowitz agreed to represent Shcharansky. California Supreme Court Justices Stanley Mosk and Frank Newman, and municipal court judge Lillian Sing offered to serve on a three-judge panel. As expected, the Soviet Consulate refused to participate but Soviet émigré lawyer Boris Gorbis volunteered to represent the USSR. Sister Ann Gillen and Congressman Tom Lantos were among the witnesses for Shcharansky. The well-publicized tribunal took place on January 23, 1983, at Fort Mason, a former military base that had been turned into a public cultural center in San Francisco, and drew national attention as it found the Soviet Union guilty as charged of the illegal detention and imprisonment of Anatoly Shcharansky.[69]

Cultural genocide in the Soviet Union became the next major issue for the BACSJ as Hebrew teachers were being arrested and imprisoned. A symposium on cultural genocide was held in 1984 with "Let My People Know" as its slogan. Campaigns were launched appealing for the release of Prisoners of Zion Yuli Edelstein and Leonid Volvovsky.

With emigration reduced to trickle during the early 1980s many refuseniks joined the *Tarbut* movement to study Jewish culture, saying, "If we can't get out, let's make a Jewish life for ourselves here." The BACSJ acknowledged their desire to learn by including Jewish books and tapes, along with medicine and material goods, such as jeans, that could be sold, in the list of direct aid items for travelers to Soviet Union to deliver to refuseniks. In addition to direct support, the BACSJ worked for political advocacy, encouraging members of Congress to adopt specific refuseniks and speak out for them in Washington, and promoted public awareness, seeking press and media coverage of the Soviet Jewry issue. Andrei Sakharov was vocal on this last point, saying: "Our only hope is to spotlight public attention. It's our pen against the Soviet sword."[70]

During the early 1980s when fewer Americans were traveling to the USSR, Waksberg arranged for Jewish books for refuseniks to be brought across the border in diplomatic pouches. Daniel

Grossman, a San Francisco native, served as consul in the U.S. Consulate in Leningrad from March 1985 until October 1986, with a portfolio that included human rights. In addition to conveying documents and information between refuseniks and the BACSJ, he met frequently with refuseniks, and attended and reported on the trial of Vladimir Lifshitz, a Hebrew teacher charged with anti-Soviet activity.[71]

After two years of Gorbachev's regime emigration rates began to rise, but not for those who were refused because they possessed state secrets. American officials negotiating with the Soviets were put off whenever the Soviets claimed that since all nations had the right to protect their state secrets, the Soviets would not consider any cases of refusals for state secrecy reasons. Under Waksberg's direction, Marshall Platt, the public affairs director of BACSJ, found that only totalitarian governments placed blanket restrictions on the freedom of movement of those possessing state secrets. In the United States a person with a high security clearance may travel abroad but must advise the security agency of the intended destination and appear for a debriefing upon returning. Platt published his findings and distributed them to other councils and Jewish agencies. Copies were brought to the USSR and given to refuseniks for use with their lawyers. Roald Zelichenok, a newly released Prisoner of Zion, had received a copy and was overwhelmed to meet the author when Platt visited the Soviet Union in 1987. He told his visitor, "I can't explain to you the value of what you have done."[72]

The Gorbachev era brought forth in the West an upsurge in expectations of renewing détente. The BACSJ and San Francisco JCRC agreed upon a policy statement entitled "Guidelines for Measured Responses" that read:

"We endorse the concept of responses linked to Soviet behavior toward Soviet Jews. Increased Soviet persecution, harassment and imprisonment have been and will be met by increased activity on behalf of Soviet Jewry. By the same token, tangible progress would be cause for measured responses from the Jewish community. Responses should be undertaken only when there is a consensus of the organized Jewish community, including Soviet Jewry activists, on a particular issue."[73]

During her last year as mayor of San Francisco, Dianne Feinstein was eager to sign a sister city agreement with the city of Leningrad. She was supported by various "Peace and Friendship" groups who claimed to be humanitarian and liberal, but were actually antipathetic toward Soviet Jews. The BACSJ and JCRC urged her to obtain from the Soviets an agreement that all refuseniks and Prisoners of Zion would be released before giving them the prestige of a sister city relationship. The sister city proposal died when her successor, Art Agnos, took office in 1988 and supported the Soviet Jewry activists.[74]

In Seattle, which had had a sister city relationship with Tashkent since 1973, Judy Balint, who founded Seattle Action for Soviet Jewry in 1974 led demonstrations and got press coverage whenever the mayor of Tashkent and various cultural delegations came to visit Seattle. Balint became a member of the Seattle-Tashkent Sister City Association, but was told "You're going to destroy the relationship" each time she brought up human rights issues. Balint argued, "What's the point of having a relationship if you can't talk about problems?" As in San Francisco, the "Peace and Friendship" people of Seattle were unwilling to hear about Soviet human rights abuses.[75]

The Jewish Community Federation was supporting the BACSJ in the late 1980s with funding – in earlier years their contributions had been minimal – and initiated visits of their leaders to refuseniks in the Soviet Union. Sheldon Wolfe, a San Francisco attorney, spent ten days in Russia in 1987 with a JCF tour group and videotaped interviews with refuseniks. They were initially fearful of being filmed but their concerns were alleviated when Wolfe assured them that the videotape would be sent by diplomatic pouch to Congressman Tom Lantos. Wolfe joined the BACSJ board soon after returning from Russia and became its president in 1989.[76]

BACSJ sponsored Rabbi Shlomo Carlebach's (Chapter 6)

unprecedented and highly successful tour through Russia, Ukraine and Lithuania in September 1989, bringing Jewish folk music to over 60,000 Jews, many of whom enthusiastically danced in the aisles at each venue.[77]

David Waksberg was able to lead a delegation of JCF leaders to Moscow in 1988 for serious meetings with prominent refuseniks on the controversial issue of aliyah only versus open emigration. He returned annually for the next four years. In 1990 he helped open the Moscow Bureau on Human Rights that served Soviet Jews who had problems or questions regarding emigration.[78] An attempt by a few bureau employees to convert it into a private emigration office was quashed by Greg Smith spending a month in Moscow working with Leonid Stonov to gain control of the bureau.[79]

POST-SOVIET ACTIVITIES

After the collapse of the Soviet Union a human rights bureau was opened in St. Petersburg and named the Harold Light Emigration and Aliyah Center. Selma and her son Bill were present at the dedication in 1992. In addition to helping Jews emigrate, the Light Center works to promote civil society for all in Russia by supporting people who have experienced anti-Semitism and other forms of discrimination.[80] Working with a council of Jewish leaders in St. Petersburg, the BACSJ in a non-paternalistic manner funded projects to offer Hebrew language classes and create a newspaper, nursery school, university, and charity for the Jewish community. An apartment in St. Petersburg was purchased and became the first home of its JCC. As the scope of these projects grew they were taken over by the Joint Distribution Committee.

In 1994 the BACSJ changed its name and mission to the Bay Area Council for Jewish Rescue and Renewal and David Waksberg resigned as executive director to become director of the UCSJ's Center for Jewish Renewal.[81] In 2007 he became executive director of the Bureau of Jewish Education in San Francisco.

Gina Waldman presents a refusenik painting to Senator Alan Cranston. Selma Light is at right. Photo credit: BACSJ Archives

"What do we want for Soviet Jews? FREEDOM! When do we want it? NOW," was the chant heard outside the Soviet Consulate in San Francisco at every Simchat Torah rally. Photo credit: BACSJ Archives.

CHAPTER SEVENTEEN

The Union of Councils
for Soviet Jews

During the 1970s the grassroots activists who formed councils that aligned themselves with the Union of Councils for Soviet Jews were derided and marginalized by the national Jewish establishment, who feared that the antics of these unprofessional upstarts would embarrass the local Jewish communities and endanger the Jews of Russia. The UCSJ activists, however, were undaunted and took their cues from their partners in courage: the refuseniks. They may have been amateurs at first, but in their zeal to save Soviet Jews, they worked day and night, soon mastering the arts of organization-building, fund-raising, influencing political leaders, and publicizing their campaigns through the media. For over two decades they challenged a totalitarian superpower – one refusenik and one prisoner at a time.

A TURBULENT BEGINNING

In early 1970 Lou Rosenblum, chairman of the Cleveland Council on Soviet Anti-Semitism (CCSA) had won the support of grassroots activists in California, Florida and Washington D.C. to organize an effective umbrella group that would generate and support sustained community action on behalf of Soviet Jewry more effectively than the American Jewish Conference on Soviet Jewry (AJCSJ, a group of representatives from various Jewish establishment organizations that was originally drawn together in 1964 but had no budget, full-time staff or action plan). They had no idea that an unfair trial in Leningrad at the end of the year would lead to the reconfiguration of the much more effective National Conference on Soviet Jewry (NCSJ).[1]

Yoram Dinstein, a member of the Israeli Diplomatic Service based in New York, was opposed to Rosenblum's proposed new organization and made his feelings known in no uncertain terms, threatening to "destroy" everyone connected with it.[2] Despite the death threat, the new group, called the Union of Councils for Soviet Jews (UCSJ), was founded with five councils (Cleveland, San Francisco Bay Area, Southern California, South Florida and Washington) plus the California Students for Soviet Jews, in March 1970 with Rosenblum as president. The UCSJ grew to 16 councils by September 1971, when it held its first national convention in Philadelphia, attended by twenty-five activists.

Less than two months after the UCSJ was launched Rosenblum wrote a letter to Yitzhak Rabin, then Israel's ambassador to the United States, complaining about Dinstein's bullying tactics. In addition to relating his own experience, Rosenblum was acting on behalf of Yaroslavsky, who had just been fired from his part-time job on the staff of Los Angeles Jewish Federation because Dinstein objected to Yaroslavsky's involvement with the California Students for Soviet Jewry.[3] Rabin's response was to have a meeting set up for Rosenblum in Washington with Nechemia Levanon, Dinstein's boss in the Israeli Lishkat HaKesher, the liaison office that handled Soviet Jewry issues.

Although Levanon was more diplomatic than Dinstein, there was no reconciliation, and Rosenblum's request for a list of Soviet Jews who had applied for exit visas was never acted upon. In earlier years the CCSA had received valuable information from the

Lishkat HaKesher including lists of potential donors and instructions for Soviet Union-bound tourists.[4]

In 1971 the CCSA launched a project, coordinated with the UCSJ, on behalf of Prisoners of Conscience in the Soviet Union. Rosenblum edited *Potma, Repression of Jews in the Soviet Union*, a compilation of descriptions of attempts by the Soviet government to repress Jewish national feelings, trials held, the sentences meted out, the fate of prisoners in the labor camps, and a list of Jewish prisoners and their vital data. A People-to-People campaign involved letters and food parcels to the prisoners as well as letters and financial help to their families and appeals to international organizations.[5] This project ran afoul of the United Jewish Appeal guidelines concerning "the proliferation of campaigns for Israel and overseas needs which require careful scrutiny and the highest degree of coordination…" The Committee on Control and Authorization of Campaigns announced that the needs of Soviet Jewry were being provided for by the United Jewish Appeal and the Jewish Welfare Federations and all should channel aid only through the United Jewish Appeal. Furthermore, they said that the Joint Distribution Committee was dispatching packages from Geneva to the Soviet Union and every Jew in need was being taken care of. Rosenblum disputed this statement and claimed that parcels from the JDC were often failing to reach their destinations. Attempts to reconcile UCSJ and establishment positions resulted in a standoff. Finally in February 1972 Levanon said: "Let them send packages, money, whatever, as long as there is no separate fund-raising."[6]

A DARING TRIP TO THE SOVIET UNION

UCSJ board members Lou Rosenblum, Si Frumkin and Zev Yaroslavsky along with Bob Wolf from Miami, traveled to Moscow and Leningrad in 1974 to meet with activists. For Frumkin it was exceptionally risky because his passport showed his birthplace as Lithuania. Fortunately, they arrived on May Day, a national holiday, so the scrutiny of incoming travelers was somewhat relaxed.

The UCSJ quartet had a fair amount of unsupervised time to visit refuseniks.[7] In addition to seeing and filming ballet stars Valery and Galina Panov in Leningrad, they met with a convention of refusenik leaders in Alexander Luntz's Moscow apartment.

They had a 16mm camera and filmed an exercise routine by the Panovs, regarded at the time as the world's greatest dancers. The famous duo had been fired by the Kirov Ballet in Leningrad after they had applied for exit visas to Israel. Barred from using their studio at the Kirov Theater, the Panovs set up a ballet practice area in their apartment. They had requested permission to emigrate largely because of their frustration with Soviet authorities who interfered with Valery's creativity as a choreographer. The official reason they were denied permission to emigrate was because Galina's mother, who was not Jewish, would not give her consent to the application for exit visas. Valery was arrested and imprisoned on charges of hooliganism.[8] He was not released until a group of prominent Americans led by Leonard Bernstein, Arthur Miller and Isaac Stern threatened to lead a protest rally and boycott of the forthcoming Kirov Kiryat Malachi Ballet performances in New York.[9]

Although he was no longer in prison Valery Panov had no income and was continually harassed by the KGB, who also suggested to Galina that she could save her career by abandoning her husband. Valery told his American visitors of a chilling encounter with the KGB. As he was waiting on a subway platform, a couple of KGB men came up from behind, pinning him between them, and cautioned him that it would be wise to withdraw his application to emigrate. Then, as a train approached the station, they propelled him forward toward the rails. He thought he was about to become a "suicide." Fortunately, it was just a warning but it left him quite shaken.

When the four activists returned home they used their film to support demonstrations and a petition appeal for the Panovs. The international pressure worked and the Panovs were given permission to leave for Israel later that year.[10]

THE SOUTH FLORIDA CONFERENCE ON SOVIET JEWRY

Bob Wolf, a Miami dentist, was an organizer and first chairman of the South Florida Conference on Soviet Jewry (SFCSJ) when he joined Rosenblum, Frumkin and Yaroslavsky on their 1974 trip to Russia. He and his wife, Myriam, became involved in the Soviet Jewry movement after attending an inspiring talk in 1971 given by Avraham Shifrin, a former Prisoner of Zion who had recently arrived in Israel.[11] Shifrin had lost a leg during the ten years he served in slave labor camps in the Gulag for expressing his Zionist ideals.[12]

Adele and Joel Sandberg were also at the talk. They had met Soviet émigrés in their ulpan classes while spending a year in Israel. Upon their return to America, Adele volunteered to be a contact person from her synagogue in Miami to the SFCSJ, a group that was started by Yosef Yanich, a director of the American Jewish Congress who had contacted Soviet Jews on a visit to Russia in the late 1960s.[13] Yanich also consulted with Moshe Decter, Jacob Birnbaum and Lou Rosenblum on the Soviet Jewry issue in New York in 1968.[14] Yanich's description of the plight of Soviet Jews resonated with Myriam Wolf because she had experienced anti-Semitism and emigration difficulties when she left her native Egypt in 1955.[15]

The Sandbergs were motivated by concern about the Holocaust and the very recent Leningrad Trials. They could not stand by and do nothing to help Soviet Jews. Eager to get an activist organization going in Miami, they worked with the Wolfs and contacted Rosenblum, who encouraged them to become associated with the UCSJ, and showed them how to make telephone calls to Jews in the Soviet Union.

Adele Sandberg launched and coordinated an "Adopt-A-Family" project for SFCSJ in 1972, and taken over in 1977 by Judith Matz.[16] It was similar to a program initiated by the Minnesota/Dakotas Action Committee for Soviet Jewry. Over 300 refusenik families were adopted by synagogues, organizations and individuals in the SFCSJ who contributed financial aid as well as writing letters and making phone calls to them.[17] Starting with their own son, Eric, the Wolfs instituted a custom of having rabbis present "Prisoner of Conscience" Magen David medallions to each bar or bat mitzvah in their synagogues and telling the story of the prisoners whose names appeared on them. Other UCSJ councils soon emulated this program.[18]

In 1973 billboards donated by Donnelly Advertising bore the message, "Soviet Jews…Let Them Live or Let Them Leave," and the SFCSJ phone number.[19] Even greater visibility for the message came two years later at Cape Canaveral during the launch of the Apollo-Soyuz joint space mission. The SFCSJ rented a balloon that was as tall as six-story building and affixed to it a bilingual sign reading, "Launch Soviet Jews to Freedom"[20].

In 1975 the SFCSJ initiated an international hunger strike to draw attention to the Slepaks (Chapter 9) who had begun a protest hunger strike in Moscow on the fifth anniversary of their refusal. It was the first organized hunger strike in the West in support of Soviet Jews.[21]

A major contribution of the SFCSJ was a series of books on the refuseniks. It began when Tina and Morton Freiman returned from the Soviet Union and told of meeting young refuseniks whose parents were in Israel. These young men, who had been refused permission to emigrate for security reasons or due to the unpredictable nature of the Soviet bureaucracy, said they felt like orphans. SFCSJ members wrote to them asking for letters from other refuseniks with parents in Israel. Thirty-five detailed letters were received, and additional case histories of separated families were collected by tourists and in response to advertisements placed by SFCSJ in Israeli newspapers. Margery Sanford edited the information into the first edition of *Orphans of the Exodus* and described it as a "chronicle of human suffering."[22] The book was considered a valuable document in Brussels at the Second World Conference of Jewish Communities on Soviet Jewry in 1976. Copies were sent to former President Gerald Ford, the State

Department and members of the Senate and House Foreign Relations Committees.[23]

Congressman Joshua Eilberg (D-PA) read it and was inspired to read a case history into the *Congressional Record*. Together with Rep. Elizabeth Holtzman (D-NY), he sponsored a Congressional Vigil in which various members of the House read case histories into the *Congressional Record* on a weekly basis. One year after the vigil was initiated 25% of the separated families had received permission to emigrate.[24]

Sanford and her SFCSJ documentation committee produced two volumes, *Separated Soviet Families* in 1976, and *Helsinki – Promise or Betrayal?* in 1977, and an annual volume for each of the next eleven years. The books eventually became well established in the Soviet Jewry movement and had introductions written by prominent activists including Martin Gilbert in 1984, Alan Dershowitz in 1985, Elie Wiesel in 1986 and Natan Sharansky in 1987. Each of the subsequent volumes had the photo of a featured refusenik family on its cover. Deciding who to put on the cover was a heart-rending decision because whoever was on the cover was likely to get permission to emigrate soon after the book appeared. The editors often selected refuseniks who were in jeopardy or resided in remote areas of the USSR, and were not well publicized and thus had less protection than better-known refuseniks.[25]

The SFCSJ joined the Greater Miami Jewish Federation in 1975 with a special agreement allowing them to maintain their autonomy and their relationship with the UCSJ.[26] While the initial volume of the refusenik series of books was published with funding from the NCSJ, the SFCSJ chose to go it alone after the NCSJ tried to take credit and control of the program.[27] By 1980 when Hinda Cantor became the chairwoman, the SFCSJ was aligned solely with the UCSJ.[28] During the early '80s, as increasing numbers of Hebrew teachers and refusenik activists were imprisoned in the USSR, the UCSJ compiled a list of imprisoned academics. The list indicated their disciplines and Cantor initiated a program of finding colleagues in Florida to adopt them. Wayne Firestone, who had campaigned for Yuli Edelstein (Chapter 10), visited professors at the University of Miami and enlisted them, and fellow students, in the twinning program. Cuban students who had strong anti-Soviet feelings were especially receptive to the program in support of oppressed Soviet Jews.[29]

When the Soviet Union collapsed Cantor spearheaded formation of the Yad l'Yad program of Florida Action for Jews in the former Soviet Union (as the organization renamed itself) and became a UCSJ vice president while her husband, Howard, served as UCSJ's Treasurer.[30]

THE GREATER PHILADELPHIA
COUNCIL FOR SOVIET JEWS

Like their colleagues in Florida, Soviet Jewry activists in Philadelphia endeavored to maintain good relations with both the UCSJ and the NCSJ. The Philadelphia Jewish Community Relations Council (JCRC) held a conference in December 1962 to educate the public about the plight of Soviet Jews, resulting in a resolution passed unanimously by the Philadelphia City Council condemning Soviet anti-Semitism.[31] In March 1965, the Philadelphia JCRC became the first communal agency in the United States to picket the Soviet Embassy.[32] Over 1,000 Jews and non-Jews from forty organizations participated. Linking the Soviet Jewry and civil rights struggles that month, the JCRC held a rally in Philadelphia's Independence Square and unfurled a banner that read, "Selma or Moscow: Human Liberty is Indivisible. End Soviet Anti-Semitism."[33]

Malcolm Hoenlein, then a University of Pennsylvania graduate student, brought Student Struggle for Soviet Jewry materials from Jacob Birnbaum in New York for distribution on college campuses in Philadelphia. He organized Soviet Jewry demonstrations and joined the JCRC staff, in charge of international affairs and the Council on Soviet Jewry. He also led annual Simchat Torah rallies at the Philadelphia Art Museum.[34] In 1971 the

JCRC created the "Committee of 1000" to focus on Soviet Jewry matters. [35]

Aside from these activities there was little organized grassroots support for Soviet Jewry until Len Shuster returned from U.S. Army service in Germany, where he had learned about the plight of Soviet Jews and become obsessed with the idea of doing something to aid them. Len and his wife, Toby, traveled to Russia in 1971 and visited with Ruta Alexandrovich (Chapter 7) and the Slepaks (Chapter 9). The Shusters were interrogated by the KGB and expelled to England, where they met other Soviet Jewry activists. [36] After returning to Philadelphia Len Shuster organized demonstrations and, as Andrew Harrison relates, "made the Soviet Jewry issue the driving point in his life until his untimely death in 1985." He was instrumental in organizing the Greater Philadelphia Council for Soviet Jews, which, after consultation with Rosenblum and Frumkin, became aligned with the UCSJ. [37]

Enid and Stuart Wurtman, friends of the Shusters, traveled to Russia in 1973 and returned to the Soviet Union in July 1974 bringing with them Connie and Joe Smukler, who were involved in the JCRC leadership. Their first eight-day visit transformed their lives dramatically as they identified with, and were inspired by, the refuseniks they met. Shortly after their return home, Enid contacted Glenn Richter and became SSSJ coordinator in Philadelphia, while Stuart became active in the UCSJ. The Smuklers remained committed to the JCRC and NCSJ. [38] However, they all felt it was senseless to have two Soviet Jewry organizations in Philadelphia. A meeting was held in Wurtman's sukkah in October 1974 and the Soviet Jewry Council was created out of the merger of the Committee of 1000 and the Greater Philadelphia Council for Soviet Jews, with an agreement that the new organization would pay dues to both the NCSJ and UCSJ and share information with each. Their first major fund-raising event was a ballet performance by newly released former refuseniks Galina and Valery Panov. [39]

In 1975 Stuart Wurtman succeeded Si Frumkin as UCSJ president and continued in that role, running the organization from home, until 1977. During this period the Helsinki Accords were signed and large numbers of Soviet Jews were choosing to go to America rather than Israel. Wurtman sent a memo to UCSJ councils expressing concern that Soviet government might be able to say that "they have been deceived by Soviet Jews who apply to go to Israel, but when they reach Vienna they indicate that their real destination is another Western country." He suggested providing Soviet Jews with information about Israel and Judaism. In the same memo he proposed a project to test Soviet compliance with the Helsinki Final Act. It was called RTI – Right to Identity, and it involved supplying Jewish books and materials to Soviet Jews in order to enable them to regain their cultural heritage.[40]

After Wurtman's term as UCSJ president expired, the Wurtmans practiced what they had preached and made aliyah. From Jerusalem Enid continued her activism for Soviet Jewry by starting a volunteer group, working at the Israel Public Council for Soviet Jewry, and writing a bi-monthly column in *The Jerusalem Post* on news about refuseniks and Prisoners of Zion.[41] In 1994 it became apparent that many elderly former refuseniks and Prisoners of Zion in Israel were unemployed and struggling to make ends meet on very meager pensions. The Wurtmans and former refusenik Inna Uspensky responded to these needs by launching a campaign that raised over $400,000 over six years.[42] It was later named the Ida Milgrom Fund in honor of Natan Sharansky's mother.[43]

THE WASHINGTON COMMITTEE FOR SOVIET JEWRY

Irene Manekofsky followed Stuart Wurtman as UCSJ president. She had served as president of the Washington Committee for Soviet Jewry since 1973 and, in that role, she was instrumental in pushing for passage of the Jackson-Vanik Amendment, the initiation of the Congressional Call to Conscience Vigil, and the establishment of the Commission on Security and Cooperation in Europe (the Helsinki Commission).[44] Avital Sharansky was a close friend and stayed at Manekofsky's home when she visited Washington.[45]

The Washington Committee for Soviet Jewry was founded in 1968 with a project of sending Rosh Hashanah cards to synagogues in the Soviet Union.[46] Moshe Brodetzky was its president from 1968 to 1973.[47]

The Soviet Embassy was an obvious magnet for local protest rallies, but violating the District of Columbia law that prohibited demonstrations within 500 feet of an embassy resulted in arrests of those who participated in the 1969 demonstration for the imprisoned Boris Kochubievsky. The International Union of Electrical Workers provided a solution. Their headquarters was located directly across the street from the Soviet Embassy and they had no objection to quiet gatherings in front of their building. After the harsh sentences were meted out to the defendants in the 1970 Leningrad Trial, the Washington Committee instituted a program of daily silent vigils during the noon hour.[48]

The vigils continued with numbers of participants ranging from handfuls to hundreds, from various groups and synagogues, and churches on Jewish holidays. The Washington Committee produced and distributed flyers to inform passersby about the purpose of the vigil. Avital Sharansky and other relatives of refuseniks and prisoners often came to the vigils to publicize their separated family situations. Joan Dodek, who served as president of the committee from 1979 to 1989, recalls that it was "exhilarating to be standing there for people who couldn't stand and speak for themselves."

Dodek's involvement had started the previous year when she and her husband planned to join a tour of Russia sponsored by the Washington Hebrew Congregation. Manekofsky invited the tour participants to her home and offered to make the trip "more exciting than you can possibly imagine." They were briefed on the plight of refuseniks, given names and phone numbers, and various items to bring them. Her parting words of reassurance: "We've never lost a tourist."[49]

Ruth Newman, who had been active in the Washington Committee since 1970, became executive director in 1979, and also briefed tourists although she had never been to the Soviet Union. She became an expert in mailing letters to the Soviet Union and testified on problems with the Soviet postal system. All of the UCSJ councils benefited from the instruction book she wrote on the subject.

Another innovation that Newman brought to the UCSJ was the Bar and Bat Mitzvah Twinning Program. On August 11, 1979, her son Lenny celebrated his bar mitzvah and announced that he was saying the blessings on behalf of a Moscow refusenik of his age who was not permitted to learn Hebrew and practice Judaism. The UCSJ coordinated the program nationwide and received $18 for each certificate that showed the names and cities of the bar/bar mitzvah "twins".[50]

One didn't have to be Jewish to experience the profound impact of the twinning program. Terence Flynn of Novato, California, attended a friend's bat mitzvah in 1983, and moved by hearing about Naomi Shapiro, the twin in Leningrad, went to Russia with his daughter, Becky, and met the Shapiro family.[51] They were warmly welcomed by the Shapiros[52] and other refuseniks, and upon returning, Flynn spoke at a local synagogue and was invited to join the board of the Bay Area Council for Soviet Jews. He became obsessed with the Soviet Jewry movement and revisited Russia annually, bringing medicine, clothing, and a Jewish encyclopedia to refuseniks. Flynn continued to serve on the BACSJ Board for over twenty years and has been one of its most effective fund-raisers.[53]

CIVIL DISOBEDIENCE IN WASHINGTON

In 1985 Rabbi David Oler, the chairman of the UCSJ Rabbinical Committee met with UCSJ president Morey Schapira and executive director Mark Epstein. They had learned that anti-apartheid protesters who violated the 500-foot law in front of the South African Embassy were not prosecuted, and thought that it would be safe to stage a protest right at the gates of Soviet Embassy. They believed that the repressive situation in the Soviet Union warranted the same kind of civil disobedience that Martin Luther King had inspired.[54]

On May 1, 1985, Oler and twenty-four other members of the Washington Board of Rabbis, wearing prayer shawls, carrying six Torah scrolls, and sounding shofars, stood less than 500 feet from the Soviet Embassy. They were joined by John Steinbruck, a Lutheran pastor, and declared that they were protesting the brutal treatment of Hebrew teachers in the Soviet Union. But unlike the anti-apartheid protesters, the rabbis were arrested and prosecuted. The judge refused to dismiss the charges and found them all guilty. Their sentence was a $50 fine, a fifteen-day suspended jail term and probation for six months, which meant that the jail term would be imposed if they returned to the scene of the crime.

Oler and four other rabbis rejected the restrictive terms of probation and were jailed for fifteen days at the Petersburg (Virginia) Correctional Institution. After his release Oler went directly back to protest at the Soviet Embassy. In an op-ed piece for the *Washington Post* he stated, "We cannot and will not remain silent while the Kremlin continues a 'final solution' for Soviet Jews."[55] On a regular basis several hundred clergymen – including Christians on Yom Kippur – protested by chaining themselves to gates of the Soviet Embassy and were arrested. The UCSJ initiated a strong legal defense and received pro-bono support from Henry Asbill, a brilliant trial lawyer and former Washington D.C. public defender. He successfully argued that the rabbis had been subjected to selective prosecution, and a mounted a "necessity defense" because lives were at risk.[56]

The publicity generated by the case and the ongoing protests at the Soviet Embassy helped sway American public opinion to greater support for the Soviet Jewry movement and contributed to the massive success of the demonstration in Washington on December 6, 1987.

In 1988 the 500-foot law – it had been enacted in 1938 at the behest of Nazi Germany to insulate its embassy from protests – was overturned by the courts as an unconstitutional infringement on freedom of speech. From then on protests at the gates of the Soviet Embassy were legal.[57] The daily vigils ended on January 28, 1991, when a ceremony was held announcing their suspension because emigration had improved, and Soviet Jewry concerns could be presented directly to an official inside the Soviet Embassy.[58]

BOSTON – ACTION FOR SOVIET JEWRY

Bob Gordon, a Boston entrepreneur, was elected president of the UCSJ in 1978. Gordon had been a founder and co-president of Action for Soviet Jewry (ASJ). He learned about Soviet anti-Semitism from former Soviet Jews who had emigrated to Israel and from Yuri Glazov, an émigré from Moscow. Glazov asked for help for his refusenik and dissident friends (including Andrei Sakharov).

Gordon became eager to get more resources for the Soviet Jewry Committee of Boston's JCRC.[59] Frustrated by promises to provide funding for programming that failed to materialize, Gordon, together with Morey Schapira, founded Action for Soviet Jewry in 1973. The new organization immediately associated itself with the UCSJ and announced its intentions in a full-page ad in the *Jewish Advocate* that Schapira likened to the Declaration of Independence. The ad rankled the established Jewish organizations of Boston and kept Action for Soviet Jewry without support from the mainstream.[60] Earlier that year the UCSJ had launched a boycott of Pepsi-Cola to protest Pepsi's trade deals with the Soviet Union, and a student group in Boston staged a Pepsi dumping party in Boston Harbor that mimicked the original Boston Tea Party.[61]

Gordon traveled to Moscow, Kiev and Leningrad in July 1975, and was able to visit Glazov's friends and other refuseniks. He brought back detailed information on trials, visa applications, financial donations, seminars, etc. and presented his policy recommendations to the UCSJ.[62]

Like his predecessors, when he became president Gordon moved the base of UCSJ operations close to his home in an expanded office of ASJ, and hired a director, Davida Manon (Irene Manekofsky's daughter-in-law). But he realized that a presence in the nation's capital was essential so he rented an office in Washington. Gordon also initiated a program of fund-raising for UCSJ by direct mail solicitations to Jewish lists, a significant improvement over previous, less effective approaches.

One of the UCSJ's staunchest allies in Congress was Father Robert F. Drinan, a Jesuit priest who represented a Boston district.[63] In 1980 the UCSJ set up the Robert F. Drinan Human Rights Information Center in Madrid during the Helsinki Accord review meetings. The center coordinated activities of refusenik advocates including Avital Sharansky and facilitated meetings for delegates with the international press.[64]

Senator Edward Kennedy was an influential supporter of the UCSJ and Boston Action in its campaign on behalf of refuseniks Boris and Natalya Katz. Their infant daughter, Jessica, had been dubbed the "littlest refusenik" by the press because she had lactose intolerance and was not growing. For a year Boston Action sent tourists to Moscow with suitcases full of a special formula that would enable Jessica to survive. Finally in 1978 Kennedy interceded with Brezhnev and the Katz family was given permission to emigrate.[65]

Gordon recalls that he spent half of his time tending to UCSJ matters during his presidency. While it didn't hurt his business (he was CEO of a chain of convenience stores) it took its toll on his family life, and, as in Si Frumkin's case several years earlier, was a major factor leading to his divorce. Both have since happily remarried.[66]

While Gordon was UCSJ president, ASJ was led by Bailey Barron and Judy Patkin, two housewives who had been to Moscow and Leningrad in 1979. Upon returning they spoke enthusiastically at synagogues and briefed other travelers.[67]

THE LONG ISLAND COMMITTEE FOR SOVIET JEWRY

Lynn Singer, one of the founders of the Long Island Committee for Soviet Jewry and for many years its executive director, became the UCSJ's seventh president in 1980. She had been awakened to the plight of Soviet Jewry by the Leningrad arrests and trials of 1970, and on the last night of Chanukah that year she led a protest march, after having invited every elected official and clergyman on the North Shore of Long Island.[68] Other demonstrations followed, including an event in which an unused military airplane hangar was decorated with barbed wire to resemble a Soviet prison and young people dressed as guards and prisoners served black bread to over 5,000 people.[69]

A program called "Adopt-A-Prisoner" was initiated by the LICSJ in 1972 to pair members of Congress with prisoners of conscience in the Gulag. The congressmen wrote letters to the prisoners and to Soviet authorities urging their release. During the first ten years of the program more than half the prisoners adopted through the LICSJ were released.[70]

Singer's first of seven trips to Soviet Union was in 1975 and her meeting with Aba Taratuta led to a schedule of weekly telephone calls to him. When the telephone in his apartment was disconnected he would go to a post office to receive Singer's calls and provide up-to-date information for the UCSJ.

Singer and the LICSJ arranged for the dedication of the "Anatoly Shcharansky Freedom Grove" on the grounds of the Nassau County Supreme Court Building in Mineola. This was the venue for numerous demonstrations of activists fasting for a day during times when Sharansky was on a hunger strike.[71] It was also the site of a ceremony commemorating the first anniversary of Ida Nudel's arrest and imprisonment. When Sharansky was free and able to visit the United States, he visited the grove and thanked the students and housewives who had assembled there for all their support during his struggle.

The Soviet delegation to the United Nations rented a country estate in Glen Cove on Long Island and LICSJ events, including an annual vigil on *Tisha B'Av* (a fast day recalling the destruction of the First and Second Temples), were often staged in front of its gates.[72] The opening of the 1980 Olympics in Moscow coincided with the third anniversary of the Shcharansky trial, the third year in exile for Ida Nudel and Vladimir Slepak, and the eleventh year of imprisonment for Yuri Fedorov, Yosef Mendelevich and Alexsey Murzhenko, as well as the week of Tisha B'Av. An all-night demonstration called "The Olympic Village in Exile" was staged opposite the Soviet compound to call attention to these anniversaries, and to protest forced relocation of refuseniks from Moscow, Leningrad and Kiev during the Olympics.[73]

Singer and the LICSJ were always concerned about the prisoners of conscience, and in 1979 compiled a book of their case histories called *Life Behind the Gates of Hell*. A copy was presented to Israeli prime minister Menachem Begin when a UCSJ delegation met in Jerusalem.

The LICSJ was extremely successful in dealing with elected officials and in fund-raising. Through the 1980s an annual dinner was held that attracted upwards of a thousand guests and raised several hundred thousand dollars each year for resettlement of Soviet Jews in Israel and for material aid to refuseniks.[74]

When Singer passed away on November 30, 2005, she was eulogized on a memorial website signed by over 100 former refuseniks as "our Yiddishe Mama...the quintessential activist of the grassroots movement."[75]

CHICAGO ACTION FOR SOVIET JEWRY

Morey Schapira (Chapter 14) followed Lynn Singer as UCSJ president, and in 1986 was succeeded by Pamela Cohen, who had been co-chair of Chicago Action for Soviet Jewry for eight years.

Chicago Action traces its roots to a talk given at West Suburban Temple Har Zion in River Forest, Illinois, by Chicago attorney Joel Sprayregen, who had jumped at the chance to visit the USSR on a trip organized by the American Civil Liberties Union in early 1970.[76] He returned highly motivated after meeting Soviet Jews who were eager to live in Israel, "some of the bravest and most brilliant people I have ever known." Sprayregen organized a mass demonstration at the 20th Pugwash Conference on Science and International Affairs that was held in Fontana, Wisconsin, in September 1970. His goal was to confront the Soviet delegates over the issue of emigration. Although some leaders of the Chicago Jewish Federation attempted to prevent the demonstration, the Community Council of Jewish Organizations of Chicago and the Milwaukee Conference on Soviet Jewry sponsored the rally that they called "Operation Exodus."[77] In the *Congressional Record* Congressman Sidney Yates (D-IL) reported that 1200 people participated in the "program of prayer, music, speeches, and reading of Jewish freedom letters smuggled out of Russia."[78]

Lorel Abarbanell of Chicago (then Lorel Pollack of Oak Park, Illinois) was at Har Zion when Sprayregen held up a list of refuseniks' names, addresses and telephone numbers, and urged everyone to let Soviet Jews know they were not alone. Abarbanell turned to a friend and said, "We can do that." Their first session, a small Sunday morning letter-writing and phone-in breakfast, with a Russian speaker standing by, led to weekly phone calls and more letters. When the women of West Suburban Hadassah agreed to hold a letter and phone-call session at an Oak Park home, Chicago's CBS-TV affiliate sent a crew to film the event expecting nothing more than a nice local human-interest story.

What they got was a scoop, breaking news from Russia that they transmitted nationwide. Abarbanell's weekly Moscow contact, Lydia Korenfeld, speaking in English from a gathering of refuseniks at Alexander Lerner's apartment, reported that ten minutes earlier the militia had taken away a U.S. congressman who had been visiting with them. "James Scheuer of New York," said Korenfeld, and in clear, measured tones she added, "call your State Department." The women in Oak Park decided it would be faster to call *The New York Times*.[79] As soon as the news spread, the militia released Scheuer, who met with the international press in his hotel lobby, and upon returning to Washington maintained his strong support for Soviet Jewry. Alexander Lerner later noted that after the Scheuer incident every United States senator and congressman visiting Moscow made it a point to meet with refuseniks.[80]

The Chicago-area group began to expand. Information

collected by phone and from USCJ mentors, as well as publicity from the Scheuer incident and an article in *People* magazine encouraged Abarbanell to found Chicago Action for Soviet Jewry. An office at Chicago's Spertus College of Judaica became its initial headquarters. With Abarbanell as its first chairman, the group affiliated with the UCSJ and established close ties with Sisters Ann Gillen and Margaret Traxler of the newly formed Interreligious Task Force on Soviet Jewry, which was also headquartered in Chicago.

Chicago Action pressed members of Congress to speak out on behalf of refuseniks, mounted campaigns for Prisoners of Conscience, and organized one of the earliest grassroots efforts to enact the Jackson-Vanik Amendment. Abarbanell recalls how teams of Chicago Action members produced and distributed material about the amendment including addresses of relevant lawmakers and suggestions of how to write to them and to local newspapers. Abarbanell added, "We traveled to Washington often, telling our story in office after office, visiting representative after representative; and back home and throughout Illinois we spoke everywhere we could wangle an invitation. No group or synagogue was too small and no district was too remote." With few exceptions every member of the Illinois Congressional Delegation, Democrats and Republicans alike, not only voted in favor of Jackson-Vanik, but continued to support Soviet Jewry after the amendment passed and as was signed by Ford.[81]

Three decades later, one of Abarbanell's most treasured memories involved first lady Betty Ford. Chicago Action received an urgent letter addressed to Betty Ford from Anna Belopolskaya, a refusenik who had undergone surgery for breast cancer. In the same envelope were instructions, "Please do not mail the letter; put it directly into Mrs. Ford's hands." Mrs. Ford had also suffered from breast cancer, and Belopolsky called her a "sister in adversity" in the letter appealing for help in the Belopolsky family's struggle to emigrate. The letter was handled by Dorothy Jaffe, a Chicago Action volunteer from South Bend, Indiana who had been a campaign worker for Indiana senator Birch Bayh. Jaffe asked if Bayh's wife, Marvella, also a "sister in adversity", would be willing to add her own note and have the letter delivered to Mrs. Ford. Mrs. Bayh agreed, and Mrs. Ford informed the Soviet Embassy about the Belopolsky family situation.[82] Several weeks later, during Chanukah 1975, Abarbanell was in Lydia Korenfeld's apartment in Moscow when in burst Leonid Belopolsky with the miraculous and wonderful news that he and his family had just been granted exit visas.[83]

In 1974, unaware of Lorel Abarbanell and Chicago Action's activities, Pamela Cohen, on Chicago's North Shore, scoured American Jewish weeklies, searching for news about the oppression of Jews in the USSR, after learning of the arrest and trial of Dr. Mikhail Shtern. With information from the Jewish weekly out of Philadelphia, she launched a letter writing campaign, pulling together local activists from the North Shore branch of the National Council of Jewish Women. Their high profile campaigns for refuseniks were calculated to notify Soviet officials – from KGB apparatchiks censoring Western mail to the highest levels of the Kremlin – that concerned Americans maintained a wide base of information on the persecution of Soviet Jews, and that there was broad-based U.S. support for refuseniks. The rationale for projects such as "Americans United for Lev Blitshtein", a long-term refusenik, was to deliberately create a striking impression of the grassroots support that would also encourage the advocacy of U.S. elected officials. Cohen's activities soon found the road to Abarbanell and Chicago Action.

Abarbanell was pulling out of Chicago Action in 1978. Unwilling to see it close, Cohen, a mother of three young children, turned to Marillyn Tallman, a teacher of Jewish history and prominent figure in Jewish philanthropy, and Carol Boron, who had demonstrated a strong interest in Soviet Jewish advocacy, to join her in taking the reigns of Chicago Action leadership.[84] Tallman had traveled to Moscow, Kiev and Leningrad with her husband in 1968. At that time the Jews that they met denied that there was anti-Semitism in the Soviet Union. Only after the publication of an emotional letter to the United Nations, from eighteen Georgian Jewish families who wanted to live in Israel, did Tallman realize that Soviet Jews were in danger.

Thrust into the forefront, they worked energetically to develop a growing and diverse grassroots organization. They also moved the office from downtown Chicago to North Shore's Highland Park, to access the large concentration of young Jewish families. They quickly were able to bring in much-needed volunteer activists to process refusenik case data, develop refusenik case histories, send out press releases, and develop an adopt-a-family program that provided refusenik families with advocacy and direct links to members of Congress.[85]

That year Cohen brought to Chicago a prominent former refusenik who had been aided by Chicago Action in his struggle to emigrate. She asked him, "What could we do better?" He responded, "Why didn't you come?" Cohen immediately booked her first of many trips to the Soviet Union, and visited refuseniks in five cities, asking what they needed and arranging for fulfillment via other tourists after she returned.[86] When Leonid Volvovsky, a Hebrew teacher, asked for specific books, Cohen would buy a second copy for herself. She regards him as her "first Hebrew teacher."[87]

One of Cohen's talks at a Chicago Federation event inspired trial lawyer Harvey Barnett to travel to Moscow and meet refuseniks. Upon his return, he spoke frequently to recruit others into activity and financial donations for Chicago Action. After his second trip to the USSR in 1983, Barnett organized the Soviet Jewry Legal Advocacy Center to deal with issues of separated families and anti-Semitic discrimination. He and his associates filed lawsuits in Chicago and New York courts against the Soviet government for violations of international law. Although no monetary damages came of the suit, the press publicity highlighting Soviet violations of human rights was valuable to the movement. The Soviet Jewry Legal Advocacy Center also maintained a telephone liaison relationship with the Vladimir Kislik and the Refusenik Legal Seminar in Moscow.[88]

Photographs taken by Betty Kahn, who traveled with Barnett to the Soviet Union in 1980, became part of slide shows for Chicago Action presentations and for "Let My People Go," a 160-page curriculum developed by Marillyn Tallman for teaching Russian Jewish history, with emphasis on the modern emigration movement and the plight of refuseniks. Tallman, who had revisited Russia in 1978, focused on briefing other tourists, each of whom received nine hours of detailed instruction.

In 1986, just prior to Reagan's summit with Gorbachev in Reykjavik, Senator Chic Hecht (R-NV) called Tallman, whose brother is married to Hecht's sister. Hecht said that Reagan had offered to present a list of the most desperate refuseniks to Gorbachev. Tallman immediately called the UCSJ office in Washington and received a list of 1,100 – the longest-waiting cases.[89] Reagan handed the list to Gorbachev, and when the two leaders were alone, Gorbachev told Reagan that as long as there was no publicity about it, the Jews on the list would be quietly released.[90]

One Jew who had waited as a refusenik for fourteen years joyously returned to Chicago saying, "It's wonderful to be here. This is my hometown. I love Chicago." Abe Stolar was born in Chicago, but as a teenager during the Depression went with his Russian-born parents to help build Communism in the Soviet Union. Stolar served in the Red Army, and worked as a translator and announcer for Radio Moscow. After retiring, he applied to emigrate but Soviet authorities repeatedly broke their promises to him. Senator Paul Simon (D-IL) met Stolar in Moscow in 1980 and urged Soviet officials to release him. Freedom finally came after a special request to Gorbachev from Reagan who, like Stolar, was born in Illinois in 1911.[91]

UCSJ PHILOSOPHY AND PROGRAMS

From its early days when Rosenblum, Light and Frumkin agreed to contact Soviet Jews and solicit their opinions, the UCSJ valued the judgment of refuseniks whose lives were on the line, and incorporated expert information obtained from them into UCSJ policy. The briefers in each council formed a network and asked their tourists to find out how refuseniks felt about key issues. Responses were compiled at UCSJ headquarters. In the late '70s two questions were "Should the Jackson-Vanik Amendment be waived?" and "Should we advocate boycotting the Moscow Olympics?" Refuseniks responded negatively to the former and positively to the latter.

Taking the pulse of the refusenik community was in line with the UCSJ's non-paternalistic approach that often ran counter to the attitude of "We know what's best for Soviet Jews," which prevailed in the Lishka and with its loyal followers in establishment organizations. However, the UCSJ was careful to avoid public condemnation of the Israeli government and the organized Jewish establishment. The UCSJ felt that it was essential that the Soviet government not perceive the Soviet Jewry movement in the West as being divided.[92] Morey Schapira recalls that the establishment didn't reciprocate.[93]

In the early '80s, as it became more difficult for Americans to obtain tourist visas to enter the Soviet Union, and telephones in the apartments of prominent refuseniks were being disconnected, the UCSJ had to find innovative ways of communicating with Soviet Jews. A group of religious Christians from Finland who were frequently traveling to Leningrad came to the rescue. They were willing to act as couriers for messages and microfilms to and from refuseniks. An underground network of trust was established. Pamela Cohen and Marillyn Tallman arranged for documents to be photographed in Chicago with negatives sealed in what appeared to be fresh containers of unexposed film. The refuseniks developed the film and duplicated them for distribution to other refuseniks throughout the Soviet Union. Refuseniks used the same channel and technique to send their documents to the UCSJ.[94]

Through the late '80s the American Jewish community was

solidly united in support of Soviet Jewry and membership in the
UCSJ soared to nearly 100,000 by 1988. Although some in the
Israeli government considered the UCSJ to be anti-Zionist, ties
to Israel were very strong. Lynn Singer instituted a program of
convening a UCSJ biennial international meeting in Israel and included de-briefings of newly emigrated refuseniks, consultations
with separated families, and meetings with Knesset members and
the Israeli press.[95] A small core of newly arrived Soviet Jewry activists, sensitive to the need of grassroots pressure on the Israeli
government, with financial support from UCSJ and its councils,
formed the grassroots organization in Jerusalem called the Soviet
Jewry Education and Information Center.[96]

Early in 1987 Cohen hired Micah Naftalin, who had been
working for Elie Wiesel at the United States Holocaust Memorial
Council, to become national director of the UCSJ. Cohen and
Naftalin were a very successful duo who brought the UCSJ into
the mainstream of the human rights movement. But their most
troublesome episode was the attempt by Morris Abram, chairman
of both the NCSJ and the Council of Presidents of Major Jewish
Organizations, and Edgar Bronfman, president of the World Jewish Congress, to negotiate, in behalf of Israel, with Soviet officials
on emigration numbers, direct flights to Israel and waivers of the
Jackson-Vanik Amendment.[97] Refusenik activists reported their
outrage to Cohen. Abram and Bronfman were negotiating various
interests without consulting the very Jews whose futures they were
trying to determine.[98] Former Prisoner of Conscience Yosef Mendelevich, who was a founder of the SJEIC, was most vociferous in
lambasting Abram and Bronfman over their proposal which he
believed would make things worse for long-term refuseniks.[99] It
turned out that the Soviets were not interested in any deal, leaving Abram and Bronfman embarrassed not only by the Soviet
indifference, but by the united protest of refusenik leaders who
felt that Abram and Bronfman were patronizing them rather than
treating them as partners.[100]

In June 1987 the Israelis convened a "Soviet Jewry Presidium" meeting in London. The official U.S. representative organization at these annual meetings was the NCSJ, but in an effort to improve relations with the UCSJ, Cohen and Naftalin were invited to participate. Their op-ed piece, "Give Soviet Jews a Choice," had just been published in the *New York Times* and spelled out the UCSJ's objections to coercive elements in Israel's plan for direct flights from Moscow to Tel Aviv.[101] The UCSJ policy advocating freedom of choice so upset representatives of the Lishka, the French delegation, and Abram that a whole day's agenda was lost as they condemned and threatened the UCSJ leaders.[102] Abram furiously screamed at Cohen and Naftalin that the Soviet Jewry movement was exclusively an aliyah movement, not a human rights movement. "Jews wanted to emigrate to America," he said, "to buy two refrigerators, not because they were refugees [fleeing anti-Semitism]". However, at a press conference, he switched to the UCSJ position, speaking at length about the human rights dimension of the movement.[103]

The squabble over the contentious issue of aliyah-only versus freedom of choice was just one of the profound philosophic differences between the UCSJ and Lishka-oriented establishment organizations such as the NCSJ. The Israeli government bought into the Kremlin's insistence that to pursue aliyah it must eschew advocacy of human rights and confrontations regarding anti-Semitism. The UCSJ exercised no such constraints, and developed policies with refusenik leaders, that involved support from allies among the dissidents and the international human rights movement.[104]

Cohen and Naftalin applied for visas to travel to Russia during Reagan's 1988 summit meeting in Moscow with Gorbachev. They were initially turned down and expected to be able to go no further than Helsinki, Reagan's first stop and the venue of his major foreign policy speech. In Helsinki where they were working with the international press, the UCSJ leaders learned that thanks to the intervention of Colin Powell, Reagan's national security advisor, they would be allowed to go to Leningrad during the week of the summit and to Moscow the following week.[105] Cohen had memorized only one refusenik phone number in Leningrad, that of Evgeny and Irina Lein. She called them on a phone borrowed from one of the Helsinki press people.[106] Irina answered the phone and had breaking news to report. Cohen got her telephone amplified so that other reporters could listen as Irina reported that refuseniks who had been invited by the American Embassy to meet with Reagan were being harassed, and others were detained after boarding trains bound for Moscow. "Here are Gorbachev's perestroika, glasnost and openness for you," Irina heatedly shouted.[107]

More front-page publicity for Soviet Jewry emanated from Helsinki thanks to the efforts of sssj activists Rabbi Avi Weiss and Glenn Richter. They set up a mock jail in a public square and sat inside wearing prison garb and holding Torah scrolls.[108]

When Cohen and Naftalin arrived in Leningrad they found that the Leins had arranged for meetings from morning to night with refuseniks from all parts of the USSR and representing a variety of histories, points of view and priorities. Naftalin recalls that they came to "express their gratitude to Pamela – whom they regarded as the 'voice of refuseniks in America' – and the ucsj, and to confer with us about their common situation and the strategies best calculated to achieve their freedom. Pamela Cohen knew scores of them personally, and she had extensive knowledge of hundreds of specific cases. "Beyond the sheer power of this universal response, I was struck most by the phenomenon of selflessness; in all the hundreds of interviews we conducted during those two weeks, not a single refusenik or prisoner's family advocated on behalf of his or her own case. Such was their commitment to the unified cause."[109]

Cohen and Naftalin also used the meetings to inform the refuseniks about the infrastructure of the Soviet Jewry movement in the United States, and how information given to one activist from England or America could be rapidly faxed to every other council in the West. They explained the roles of congressmen and

CSCE members, and the UCSJ's systematic and political approach to dealing with them.[110]

A year later the UCSJ pushed the envelope by choosing Moscow as the site of its annual meeting. It would be a test of a Soviet-American agreement to hold a human rights conference in Russia. Would refuseniks be allowed to participate? Would delegates from Israel be given visas? Cohen insisted on these conditions and was backed up by Alexander (Sandy) Vershbow, who directed the State Department's Office of Soviet Union Affairs, and by Petrus Buwalda, Holland's ambassador to the Soviet Union.[111] Nearly 100 delegates from the free world met openly in the first-ever public human rights conference in the USSR, and celebrated Shabbat dinner with about 200 refuseniks in a remarkable display of unity and equality never before seen in the Soviet Union.[112]

One of the refuseniks at the meeting was Leonid Stonov, a Moscow agrobiologist who had studied Soviet law and succeeded Vladimir Kislik as leader of the Refusenik Legal Seminar.[113] In addition to being a refusenik leader, Stonov had been a member of the Sakharov/Orlov/Sharansky group of dissidents in Moscow. With twenty other refuseniks he organized a public committee for monitoring OVIR. Twice each week they would go to the OVIR office to counsel new applicants for exit visas and help prepare appeals for those who were refused. They called themselves the "Public Committee to Aid the Work of OVIR" and with some pressure from the U.S. State Department they managed to operate.[114] But even in the era of glasnost they were often thrown out by the militia, reviled in newspapers, and embarrassed by OVIR officials. Stonov prepared lists of refuseniks and delivered them to the U.S. Embassy. Thanks to support from former President George H.W. Bush, Stonov received permission to emigrate in April 1990.[115] He traveled to Copenhagen two months later where he attended the Conference on the Human Dimension as a representative of nongovernmental organizations. That conference led to the idea of setting up a human rights bureau for the UCSJ in Moscow that would be a joint venture of refuseniks and the UCSJ.[116] Stonov postponed his emigration and went to work as head of the Soviet-American Bureau on Human Rights, an organization officially registered with the Moscow City Council.[117] Since then, in addition to the Moscow office, Human Rights Bureaus were established by the UCSJ in eight major cities of the former Soviet Union.[118]

As restrictions on emigration loosened, Stonov put a high priority on monitoring anti-Semitism that was manifesting itself not from the government, but from nationalist organizations like *Pamyat* ("Memory"). Pamela Cohen described Stonov's role in seeking ways to combat anti-Semitism, as the UCSJ's face to the Soviet Union.[119] In late 1990 Stonov accepted Cohen's offer to work for her in the Chicago Action office as the UCSJ International Director.[120]

After ten years as UCSJ president, Cohen, described by Naftalin as "the most charismatic, strategic, non-paternalistic and knowledgeable Soviet Jewry leader in the [free] world,"[121] summed up her view of the UCSJ's contribution to the rescue of Soviet Jews:

"Our dream was inviolate and unshakable. We were defiant and unrelenting and stubborn, and we fought on every front. We fought when Jews were fired from their jobs after they applied to emigrate, and we fought when they were stripped of their academic degrees in public humiliation. We fought when they were denied medical attention, and we fought for the rights of our people in the prisons and labor camps. We fought anti-Semitic article by anti-Semitic article and we knew that every battle was a skirmish that had to be won. We understood that we had to demand the delivery of every letter, the successful completion of every phone and tourist contact, and the release of every refusenik and prisoner of conscience. We knew that our momentum and determination would eventually crescendo into a force that would ultimately rip open the gates."[122]

Valery and Galina Panov in their Leningrad apartment/ ballet studio with Zev Yaroslavsky in 1974. Photo credit: Si Frumkin.

SFCSJ helium balloon launched at Cape Canaveral in 1975. Photo credit: SFCSJ.

*In 1984 UCSJ leaders convened a "Think Tank" in Washington to develop
strategies for approaching the Andropov regime. Left to right: Bob
Gordon, Ruth Newman, Lynn Singer, former National Security Advisor
Zbigniew Brzezinski, and Pamela Cohen. Photo credit: UCSJ Archives.*

*Rabbi David Oler, surrounded by other members of the Washington
Board of Rabbis, reading from an open Torah scroll in front
of the Soviet Embassy. Photo credit: UCSJ Archives.*

In 1973 the South Florida Conference on Soviet Jewry, in cooperation with Donnelly Advertising Corp., erected billboards on behalf of oppressed Soviet Jews. Pictured left to right are Congressman William Lehman; Dr. Robert Wolf, SFCSJ chairman; Yosef Yanich, American Jewish Congress Southeast regional director and a founder of SFCSJ; Robert Cochrane, Donnelly Advertising vice president; and Richard Siegel, SFCSJ vice-chairman. Photo credit: SFCSJ.

CHAPTER EIGHTEEN

Support from American Christian and Jewish Clergy

They marched with Martin Luther King Jr. in Selma, cheered the Vatican's announcement of *Nostra Aetate*, and protested the Vietnam war. Could they possibly have the energy to champion yet another human rights cause? Absolutely! These liberal-minded, spirited women and men of the cloth – Catholic, Jewish and Protestant – were ready to let the world know that Soviet anti-Semitism, repression of religious freedoms, and restrictive emigration policies must end.

SISTER ROSE THERING

Growing up as one of ten children on a Wisconsin dairy farm is an unlikely beginning for someone who would overturn centuries of Roman Catholic doctrine, but Rose Thering was not one to do what was likely. As a child she asked, "Jesus was a Jew and we love him, so why don't we love the Jews?" But she received no definitive answers from her parents or teachers.[1] During her years as a Dominican nun and an elementary- and high-school teacher she was appalled and "almost got ill" reading the church's teachings about Jews. Again and again she found school texts saying, "Jews killed the Messiah." Her doctoral dissertation at Saint Louis University in 1961, on the subject of the treatment of Jews in Catholic textbooks, was used as evidence during the ecumenical council that issued *Nostra Aetate* (In Our Time) which declared that Jews were not responsible for the death of Jesus.

Sister Rose didn't stop there. As a teacher of Jewish-Christian studies at Seton Hall University in New Jersey she helped pass a bill making instruction on the Holocaust and genocide mandatory in every primary and secondary school in New Jersey.[2] She led over fifty Christian study missions to Israel and participated in hunger strikes in support of Soviet Jews. She summed up her passion by saying,

> Once we acknowledge this whole history of discrimination against Protestants, Jews and Muslims, then we can move forward together. But even then tolerance is not enough. We must not just tolerate, but understand and eventually love people of other faiths. We are children of God, striving to understand God in our own ways.[3]

SISTER MARGARET TRAXLER

Sister Margaret Traxler, a nun who was totally aligned with Sister Rose Thering's beliefs, and had marched with Martin Luther King Jr. in Selma, Alabama, served as executive director of the National Catholic Conference for Interracial Justice in Chicago. In 1971 Eugene DuBow, who directed the local office of the American Jewish Committee, was startled to read that a Catholic nun had given a speech on behalf of Soviet Jews. Soviet Jewry, to this point, had been a matter mostly for Jews. After several meetings with her and the assistance of Gerald Strober of the AJC Interreligious Affairs Department staff, an interreligious gathering in Chicago was held. Rabbi Marc Tanenbaum, the director of interreligious affairs of the American Jewish Committee, Sister Traxler and a number of other noted Christian and Jewish leaders agreed to form a National Interreligious Task Force on Soviet Jewry in March 1972. The NITFSJ was the first attempt to turn the problems of Soviet Jewry from an internal Jewish matter into one of international human rights. The inclusion of high profile non-Jewish religious leaders did just that.

The purpose of the task force was to raise awareness in the Christian community about oppressed minorities in the Soviet Union and promote interreligious activities on their behalf. Sister Margaret recruited R. Sargent Shriver, the first director of the Peace Corps and the Democratic candidate for vice president in 1972, to be honorary chairman.[4]

As Nixon was preparing to visit the Soviet Union in May 1972, 700 people attended the concluding assembly of the task force's first conference and heard calls for him to speak to Brezhnev in support of Soviet Jews.[5] Archbishop Fulton J. Sheen, in an emotional "Summary of Conscience," urged:

> President Nixon, as the representative of the American people, to convey in clear and forthright terms to the Soviet authorities…the expectation of the American people…that these discriminations and denials of Soviet Jewry and others must be stopped now, and that fundamental human rights be granted now.[6]

SISTER ANN GILLEN

Sister Margaret was succeeded by Sister Ann Gillen as executive director of the task force. Sister Ann was originally from Texas and at age 51 had begun studies for a doctorate at Dropsie College of Hebrew Cognate Learning in Philadelphia. The combination of what she learned there about the plight of Soviet Jews and the publication of *Nostra Aetate* fueled her determination to do something to end the oppression of Soviet Jews.

Sister Ann had no fear about taking on the Communist superpower. She traveled throughout North America and Europe to bring the "Let My People Go" message to thousands of people in synagogues, churches and government offices as well as at international meetings in Belgrade, Brussels, Jerusalem and Madrid.[7] Wearing a Star of David around her neck, she lobbied the United Nations, the U.S. Congress, the White House and State Department. Many Soviet embassies were venues for her frequent picketing.[8]

Rabbi A. James Rudin, who succeeded Rabbi Tanenbaum as interreligious director of the American Jewish Committee, accompanied Sister Ann on many visits to congressional offices. The sight of a nun and a rabbi pleading for the same cause was both unnerving and exhilarating; no congressman or senator dared to ignore them or throw them out. They traveled together to the conferences in Belgrade and Madrid, joined by two eminent Protestants: Professor Andre LeCocque of Chicago Theological Seminary, a native of Belgium, whose parents had sheltered Jews from the Nazis, and Rev. John Steinbruck, a Lutheran pastor and outspoken advocate for the homeless of Washington, D.C.

In 1973 Sister Ann visited Russia and worked with the Red Cross to get a Bible for Natasha Fedorova, the wife of Yuri Fedorov, who was imprisoned for his role in the foiled hijack plot.[9] Five years later she traveled there again for sixteen days with Sister Gloria Coleman of Philadelphia. They visited thirty refuseniks and activists including Ida Nudel a few days before her trial on charges of "malicious hooliganism."[10] When they arrived at Nudel's apartment Sister Ann told her that she had had a premonition that she would need to go to Russia and had hastily applied for a visa. On the day the visa arrived at her home in Chicago she received a phone call from Viktor Elistratov, a friend of Nudel's, who said he was conveying Nudel's appeal for help. Nudel told the nuns that she would soon be on trial and was awaiting the dossier of accusations to prepare her defense. Her crime was hanging a banner on her balcony that read: "KGB GIVE ME MY VISA FOR ISRAEL." KGB agents tailed the nuns after that visit and subjected them to body searches, questioning, and confiscation of their notes and films at the airport in Moscow prior to their departure.

A week later Nudel was sentenced to four years of internal exile in Siberia.[11] Halfway through her term Sister Ann made a stunning announcement. In Copenhagen for the 1980 International Women's Conference, she offered to go to Siberia in place of Nudel for the next two years. Her rationale: "We exchange spies; why not friends?" Soviet officials ignored the offer.[12]

Later that year Sister Ann led a delegation of American religious leaders to the Madrid Conference on European Security and Cooperation to press Soviet leaders for full compliance with the human rights provisions of the 1975 Helsinki Final Act. Sister Ann spoke out again on behalf of Ida Nudel as well as Naftali Tsitverbilt, a 16-year-old boy who had been severely beaten by KGB thugs in Kiev. Other members of the delegation brought up the cases of Soviet Christian prisoners of conscience.[13]

As the Soviet regime under Yuri Andropov grew more repressive in the early 1980s Sister Ann pointed out at a rally in Houston that her contacts in the Soviet Union were saying that "the '60s was KGB's decade of searching for spies; in the '70s political dissidents were the top priority; and now the '80s will be a decade of going after religious groups." She asserted that religious persecution was on the rise in an effort to make the nation ethnically homogeneous.[14] Twenty Soviet church leaders were sent to the United States in 1984 on exchange visits in an attempt to refute such characterizations. But Sister Ann maintained that considerable persecution of Soviet religious leaders persisted, citing Lithuania where outspoken Catholic priests had recently been jailed and a Catholic church was converted into a concert hall. She urged Americans to express concern for religious freedom to the visiting Soviets.[15]

She returned to Houston in September 1986 to launch Project Co-Adoption. Her premise was that there were 400,000 Soviet Jews who wanted to emigrate (having received letters of invitation from Israel) and that it would have a tremendous impact if 400,000 non-Jews would adopt them.[16] "Imagine letters and cards from Christian Americans to Jews in Russia! We would also like synagogues to adopt Christian prisoners of conscience." A month later she and Sister Gloria Coleman took off for Iceland and participated in a press conference on the eve of the Reagan-Gorbachev summit in Reykjavik.[17]

In 1989, as emigration rates began to increase, Sister Ann felt that her work was finished and closed her Chicago office. Later that year she was diagnosed with cancer and underwent surgery. Although her condition did not improve, she continued writing and kept up contacts. She even returned to Russia before she passed away on January 14, 1995.[18] At her funeral Rudin, who worked with her for over twenty years, recalled how relentless and indefatigable she was in pursuing her mission to save the Jews of the Soviet Union.[19]

FATHER ROBERT F. DRINAN

At the Interreligious Task Force's first conference, Father Robert F. Drinan, the only Catholic clergyman to serve in Congress, urged passage of a proposed bill to give Israel $85 million to help absorb 40,000 immigrants.[20] He recalled that during his first trip to Israel, as a Jesuit priest and dean of the Boston College Law School, he had visited the tomb of Theodor Herzl and had been moved to hear his tour guide remark that "one of the purposes of the founding of Israel was to serve as a homeland for the two or three million Soviet Jews when and if they could escape."[21] Now, nine years later, he was working to make that dream a reality.

Drinan had upset some members of the Jesuit hierarchy by announcing his candidacy as a Democrat for a seat in Congress from a suburban Boston district. Ultimately he received permission to run in 1970 from the Jesuit order and from Cardinal Cushing of Boston. When he won the election he informed Father Pedro Arrupe, the Father General of Jesuits worldwide, that he viewed his entry into politics as fully in keeping with Jesuit commitment to social justice. As a congressman he applied for a visa to visit the USSR and was turned down twice.[22] Finally in 1975 he was allowed to enter as part of a congressional delegation. During this trip he went with Sharansky to meet Andrei Sakharov, who told him that "only the Christians of America could liberate the Jews of Russia." Drinan "witnessed firsthand the heartrending condition of Jews…in Leningrad, Moscow and other cities…and saw how more profoundly than ever before the mysterious ways in which the God of Abraham, Isaac and Jacob speaks to those born in that biblical tradition." The following year Drinan joined forty Christians and 1,300 Jews at the Second World Conference on Soviet Jewry in Brussels and was part of a group that declared:

> We Christians…keenly aware of the plight of all persons of conscience in the USSR and especially pained by the harassment and persecution of our Christian brothers and sisters, nonetheless are convinced that the oppressed condition of our Jewish brothers and sisters is unique and in all specifics more rigorous that that faced by the Christian communities.

Golda Meir was greatly moved by the declaration and said, "On the issue of Soviet Jews we have always been alone…now there is a promise that this generation of Christians will not be silent… in the struggle to prevent the cultural and spiritual annihilation of the Jews in the Soviet Union."[23]

After his 1975 trip to the Soviet Union, Drinan's congressional office became the focal point for support of Soviet Jews.[24] Additionally, in 1977 when Sharansky was charged with treason and held incommunicado, Drinan created an international committee to fight for his release. He also hosted Avital Sharansky's visits to Washington and introduced her to his colleagues in Congress, who were glad to enter statements in the *Congressional Record* in support of her husband, the world's best-known prisoner of conscience.[25]

Drinan went far beyond serving his constituents, becoming a national spokesman and raising awareness for Soviet Jews. During his ten years in Congress Drinan's concerns for human rights extended beyond Soviet Jewry; he expressed concern for victims of persecution in Latin America, the Middle East and South East Asia.[26] Speaker Thomas P. (Tip) O'Neill described Drinan as "the most indefatigable crusader in the House of Representatives...to those who have firmly believed in the right of all people to 'life, liberty and the pursuit of happiness,' Father Drinan has been the wayshower."[27] Unfortunately, in May 1980 he received an order from Pope John Paul II, which he chose to follow, telling him not to run for reelection. It is believed that the order was not because of his international human rights efforts but due to his pro-choice voting record on the issue of abortion.[28]

Drinan's commitment to the cause of Soviet Jewry did not end when he left Congress and resumed teaching law at Georgetown. He continued to speak out on the subject at every possible opportunity, and in the fall of 1980 he traveled to the Helsinki Accords review meetings in Madrid where the Union of Councils for Soviet Jews set up the Robert F. Drinan Human Rights Center. This was the "voice and conscience of human rights" during the meeting, a focal point for dissemination of information to conference delegates and the press, as well as a venue where human rights activists, including relatives of refuseniks and prisoners, could publicize their concerns.[29]

RABBI SHELLY LEWIS AND REVEREND DOUG HUNEKE

While Father Drinan was in Congress as a lawmaker hundreds of activist clergymen were descending upon Washington, New York and San Francisco as lawbreakers. They were demonstrating within the separation zones that surrounded the Soviet Embassy, UN Mission and Consulate buildings in those cities. In front of press photographers they would be handcuffed and taken to jail by local policemen and then, thanks to understanding judges, their cases would be dismissed.

Rabbi Shelly Lewis was one of the demonstrators arrested for picketing outside the Soviet Consulate in San Francisco in 1979. His history in the Soviet Jewry movement goes back to 1964 when he was a student at the Jewish Theological Seminary and was active in the Student Struggle for Soviet Jews. He renewed his commitment to the cause when he returned from duty as a chaplain in Vietnam to assume the pulpit at Congregation Kol Emeth in Palo Alto, California. The activities of the Bay Area Council for Soviet Jews caught his attention and he decided to make social action, especially freedom for Soviet Jews, a high priority for himself and his congregation.

When Lewis told BACSJ director David Waksberg that he wanted to visit refuseniks in the Soviet Union, Waksberg suggested that a rabbi who had been arrested in front of the Soviet Consulate would be more likely to obtain an entry visa if he indicated some other profession and was traveling with a group of gentiles.[30] Waksberg introduced him to Reverend Doug Huneke of Westminster Presbyterian Church in Tiburon, California. Huneke's interest in Soviet Jewry arose from his research at Yad Vashem in the '70s, and his writings on the moral and spiritual development of Christians who had rescued Jews in Nazi-controlled countries of Europe. Huneke's friend and neighbor, Rabbi Michael Barenbaum, had visited the Soviet Union in 1982. Huneke was eager to go there himself and enjoyed the full support of his congregation. Waksberg briefed Lewis and Huneke in April 1983 and gave them a list of refuseniks to visit, as well as medicine, books and material aid that filled four large suitcases.

Lewis and Huneke planned to claim that "we were college roommates traveling together as we did periodically and we had never been to Russia." The medicine Lewis was carrying was provided by a San Francisco physician, improperly labeled intentionally, so that to customs inspectors it would appear to be a prescription for Lewis, claiming to be a diabetic. But it was actually for a pregnant woman refusenik in Odessa suffering from kidney failure. She had been told that if she withdrew her application for an exit visa she would be given the medical care she needed. She refused to submit to this outright blackmail.

The customs inspector at the airport in Moscow found the

hypodermic syringes with the medicine and immediately called KGB agents. Lewis insisted that if he didn't take the medicine and had a diabetic seizure he would die and it would be the Russian government's fault. He had been told by the San Francisco doctor, "If you have to take the medicine, you might be a little uncomfortable, but it won't harm you and it's certainly not life-threatening." Fortunately, they didn't test it on him.

True to Andropov's oppressive policies, Lewis and Huneke were threatened at every airport, followed to nearly all contacts, and intimidated by militia and KGB officers at will. When they arrived in Odessa, on their way from their hotel to the apartment of someone who would bring the medicine to the refusenik patient, KGB agents tried to enter their taxicab. Lewis pushed two of them away while Huneke slammed the door on another. Within five minutes two truckloads of militia men pulled the cab over and took the American tourists to jail. Lewis was still able to make the case that it was his medicine and was allowed to keep it.

Lewis and Huneke were interrogated and told that they were being charged with espionage. When Huneke was asked who had sent them to the Soviet Union he didn't want to implicate David Waksberg, so he made up a name and affiliation: "Rabbi Moses Malone, San Francisco Jewish Federation." After the interrogation Lewis said to Huneke, "When we get back, I want to take you to a basketball game." Huneke asked, "Why a basketball game?" To which Lewis replied, "I think you'd be interested in seeing the six-foot, nine-inch, African-American, Baptist center of the Philadelphia 76ers. His name is Moses Malone." They were thankful that there were no fans of American basketball among their KGB interrogators or the staffs of the Odessa and Moscow newspapers who later wrote up their story!

Huneke and Lewis were kept under house arrest until the charges were amended to "malicious hooliganism", and they were escorted by guards throughout the flight to Moscow, where they were able to connect with someone who knew the woman who needed the medicine and was able to take it from Lewis for her.

About a year later they got a letter sent indirectly with a traveler from Boston saying that the woman and her baby had survived and that they were in good health.[31]

In 1988 Huneke and Lewis organized an Interreligious Task Force for Soviet Jews involving clergy and lay leaders of various faiths in the San Francisco Bay Area. Its program was successful in activating congregants to initiate letter writing campaigns, petition drives, adopting families and interfaith missions to the Soviet Union. The Task Force pointed out that although emigration was on the rise, the trends of increasing anti-Semitism, the loss of leadership in the refusenik community, and further erosion of religious liberty were major concerns.[32]

In 1989, inspired by Gorbachev's *glasnost* policy, the Task Force sponsored an unprecedented conference of clergy in Moscow and Leningrad. Huneke and Lewis chaired a delegation of Catholic, Jewish and Protestant leaders in meetings and exchanges of papers with thirteen Russian leaders and scholars of the Evangelical, Jewish and Orthodox communities on "Human Dignity in the Jewish and Christian Traditions." Doug Kahn, executive director of the San Francisco Jewish Community Relations Council, supported by Lucie Ramsey of the Bay Area Council for Soviet Jews, orchestrated the event and presented a paper on "Cooperation and Non-Cooperation with Authority in the Jewish Tradition." It was clear that glasnost had made an impact when one realizes that Huneke and Lewis, who had been arrested and treated as criminals in the Soviet Union only six years earlier, were now welcomed and encouraged to talk and exchange ideas with their Russian colleagues in the Geographic Society Auditorium, located within sight of the Kremlin. Refuseniks were allowed to meet with the delegation at their hotel and while riding in their tour bus. The conference ended with a declaration on "Human Dignity and Religious Freedom" urging the leaders of the Soviet Union to amend the Soviet Constitution to allow people of all faiths to freely practice and teach their traditions, allow freedom of emigration, allow religious leaders to maintain contact with their counterparts in other countries, and eliminate anti-Semitism and all forms of religious intolerance.[33]

Lewis found that the goals of the declaration were being met as he revisited Russia in 2004, leading a delegation from his congregation for a celebration as they delivered a Torah scroll to the Jewish community of Pskov, an ancient city 175 miles southwest of St. Petersburg. He observed that a spark of Jewish survival and commitment still burned within the thousand Jews of Pskov who had been deprived of the opportunity to learn about their heritage, and now were thrilled to have their own Torah.[34]

CHAPTER NINETEEN

European Activism
for Soviet Jewry

As in America, Christians in Western Europe, both clergy and lay people, were extremely supportive of the campaigns in behalf of Soviet Jewry. Throughout the United Kingdom church members of various denominations joined demonstrations in solidarity with the Women's Campaign for Soviet Jewry.[1] Although only 30,000 Jews live in Holland, the Solidarity Committee for Soviet Jews circulated a petition through churches and obtained one million signatures.[2] In France 75% of the members of the Comité des Quinze were non-Jews.[3] While these three activist organizations originated after 1968 under very different circumstances, they were aligned strategically and tactically with the UCSJ and generally supported both human rights and the Soviet Jewry struggle. However, prior to 1968, European support for Soviet Jewry tended to be influenced by the Lishka in Israel and the Jewish establishment.

EARLY SUPPORT FOR SOVIET JEWRY
Anna Rock, who chaired the Women's International Zionist

Organization (WIZO) branch in Stockholm, and was fluent in Russian, traveled to the Baltic states in 1949. The Israeli Embassy in Stockholm then sent her as a translator for other Swedes (Jews and non-Jews) who were on numerous secret missions to Moscow, Leningrad, Minsk and Kiev to make contact with Soviet Jews and to bring them Jewish books and religious articles from Israel.[4] In the late 1960s Torsten Press, a telecommunications business executive, frequently traveled to Moscow and founded a small Soviet Jewry support group that was linked to the Jewish community of Stockholm and also had indirect contact with the Lishka.[5]

An important aspect of Lishka strategy in the 1960s involved enlisting influential European leaders who were friendly to the Soviet regime as signatories on appeals to Khrushchev in behalf of Soviet Jewry. One such appeal in 1963 that argued against executions for economic crimes was signed by Dowager Queen Elisabeth of Belgium, Lord Bertrand Russell, Dr. Albert Schweitzer, and François Mauriac.[6]

After witnessing the plight of Soviet Jews in the 1950s when he accompanied his wife and her fashion show to Russia, London-based writer Emanuel Litvinoff launched a campaign against anti-Semitic persecution. He edited a newsletter called *Jews in Eastern Europe*.[7] In 1966 a group of students in London formed the Universities Committee for Soviet Jewry and marched one thousand strong to the Soviet Embassy. The Board of Deputies of British Jews took a dim view of public protest and tried to prevent the march. They argued that overt activities by British Jews would be counterproductive.[8] Following the precedent set by its president, Sir Barnett Janner, who had sent a letter to the Kremlin in 1964 requesting that Jews be allowed to bake matzot, the Board had its Foreign Affairs Committee write a letter of concern to Soviet Premier Alexei Kosygin.[9] That committee convened a Conference on Soviet Jewry in June 1969, and in 1971 formed a Soviet Jewry Action Committee which held numerous meetings but with so little action that activists called it "The Inaction Committee."[10]

HOW MICHAEL SHERBOURNE'S BET
PAID OFF TWENTY YEARS LATER

One of the activists was Michael Sherbourne, a London school-teacher. In 1949 Sherbourne returned to his native London and enrolled in a teacher's training college after working on a kibbutz, serving in the Royal Navy during World War II, and fighting in the Israel Defense Forces during its War of Independence. At the college library Sherbourne and his friend Jack Weltman spotted a book called *Teach Yourself Russian*. Weltman turned to Sherbourne and said, "I bet you couldn't teach yourself Russian." Sherbourne, who had no prior knowledge of Russian whatsoever, replied, "I bet I will." For the next four years Sherbourne studied and became proficient enough in the language to receive a degree with second-class honors from the London University School of Slavonic Studies. He had no practical use for the language other than taking a school party to Russia in 1962. At that time he was unaware of a Jewish problem even when meeting Jews at the synagogue in Leningrad.

Sherbourne's eyes were opened to the reality of the situation in 1968 when he attended a meeting in London of the Association of Jewish Ex-Servicemen (AJEX) featuring two Jewish women who had immigrated to Israel from Russia. After the meeting one of the attendees remarked, "We didn't do enough during the Holocaust to help our fellow Jews. Let's form a committee to do something to aid Soviet Jews." Sherbourne and his wife, Muriel, offered to join them, and the organizers were thrilled to learn that Sherbourne knew Russian. He was given names and telephone numbers of Soviet Jews who wanted to be called, and made four to six calls each evening, tape recording all of them. Ida Nudel was one of his key contacts; she provided details on the conditions of the prisoners she had been monitoring.[11] Sherbourne helped relieve the stress she was experiencing from KGB surveillance and her overwhelming concern for the welfare of the prisoners and other refuseniks. He would tell her, "Don't get upset, Ida. We'll do everything we can."[12]

Sherbourne coined the term refusenik during a 1971 phone conversation with Gabriel Shapiro of Moscow, who called himself an *otkaznik* in Russian and then translated it as *siruvnik* in Hebrew from the verb "to refuse." Sherbourne, then said, "Aha, in English you would be called a refusenik!"[13] He frequently used the term in his communications with activists in England and America and its usage spread quickly and entered English dictionaries as "a Soviet citizen, usually Jewish, who has been denied permission to emigrate from the Soviet Union."[14]

He also coined the term "Office with No Name" for the Lishkat HaKesher during one of his contentious meetings with Nechemia Levanon, whom he had known since 1939 when they both were at Kibbutz Kfar Blum. Sherbourne was frustrated that much of the information and many documents from refuseniks that he had sent to Israel disappeared, because, "the Israelis, in their arrogance, decided what should and should not be published."[15] For example, news of demonstrations staged by refuseniks in Moscow in 1972 that Sherbourne gave the Israeli Embassy was either never released or published in a distorted version – the Israelis were quick to play down activities that could be construed as anti-Soviet. When Sherbourne received information that refuseniks wanted published in the West, he translated the documents and passed them on to activists in England and America, via his own bulletin and daily calls to Rae Sharfman in Detroit and other activists who relayed the material through the UCSJ network.[16] Within days, refuseniks who could listen to the BBC or Voice of America would hear their news being broadcast. Sherbourne also boosted the morale of refuseniks by telling them about rallies staged by activists in the West.

When the KGB searched Nudel's apartment in 1973 they confiscated a photo that Sherbourne had sent her of himself. It soon appeared on Soviet TV and he was referred to as "British Lord Sherbourne, one of three fascists in the West who are waging a vicious anti-Soviet campaign." The other two "fascists" were

Congressmen Robert Drinan and Dante Fascell. The three of them would, a few years later, be linked in fervent support for Sharansky and advocacy of human rights.

Sherbourne got to know Sharansky early in 1974 and usually spoke with him at length, sometimes for an hour if there was considerable activity to report.[17] These calls and about 5,000 more that Sherbourne placed over a twelve-year period were paid for by Cyril Stein, a prominent British businessman and philanthropist.[18] Sherbourne recalls calling Sharansky after his two-week jail term in 1975. Sharansky asked:

"Can you call my wife in Jerusalem?"

"I didn't know you had a wife."

"Neither did I – until a few days ago!"

Sharansky then explained the unusual circumstances of his release from jail and Avital's departure deadline that dictated the date of the wedding. Sherbourne instituted a phone and message service for the newlyweds that lasted until March 1977 when Sharansky was arrested. Andrei Sakharov phoned Sherbourne to inform him of the arrest, and Sherbourne gave that information to Nechemia Levanon's second-in-command, Tzvi Netzer. But the message disappeared as the Lishka disavowed any support for Sharansky, whom they regarded as a dissident. Sherbourne met Avital and her brother Misha when they came to London soon after the arrest, on a trip paid for by Stein, and helped organize the campaign for Sharansky,[19] in defiance of the Lishka's attempts to influence the Jewish establishment in England that Sharansky was "a naughty boy for mixing with dissidents" and implied that he was a spy.[20]

In April 1978, at the first UCSJ meeting held in Jerusalem, Sherbourne openly accused Levanon of sabotaging the campaign and of failing to give activists information on refuseniks. Levanon refused to budge on the issue, and also resented Sherbourne's support for freedom of choice with regard to where Soviet Jews would settle once they received permission to emigrate. Furthermore,

Sherbourne felt that by not painting a grim picture of the plight of Soviet Jewry, Levanon failed to arouse public opinion in Israel to support their struggle for freedom.

As the Soviet Jewry movement grew in the West there were additional Russian speakers who were willing and able to call, and many refuseniks spoke English, so Sherbourne stopped calling in 1983 and went with Muriel to live in Israel for a year. He returned to Jerusalem in 1986 to meet Natan and Avital Sharansky a week after their reunion. Elation over the release of a prisoner or a refusenik was the inspiration that kept Sherbourne calling and working 30–40 hours each week for over a dozen years.[21]

UNITED KINGDOM – THE 35S

The group with which Michael Sherbourne was most closely associated was the Women's Campaign for Soviet Jewry, or the 35s, as they were often called. The press gave them that numeric nickname on May Day 1971 when nearly thirty-five of them, about thirty-five years of age, demonstrated and fasted outside the Soviet Embassy in London on behalf of Raiza Palatnik, a thirty-five-year-old Odessa librarian who had been arrested and whose whereabouts were unknown.[22] Within twelve hours of the demonstration the 35s were secretly informed by an Israeli Embassy staffer that she had been moved to a regular prison and would stand trial.[23]

A month later Palatnik was convicted on charges of anti-Soviet slander. At the suggestion of Joan Dale, one of their founders, the 35s were dressed uniformly in black during their silent demonstrations, following the example of the Black Sash women of South Africa who protested apartheid. Additional founders were Rita Eker, Doreen Gainsford, Zelda Harris, Barbara Oberman and Sylvia Wallis. The 35s' immediate goal was to deliver a petition to the wife of the Soviet Ambassador, signed on behalf of all the thirty-five-year-old Jewish women of Britain. Embassy officials angrily refused to accept it so the 35s tried again daily, except for Shabbat, for the next two weeks. They carried a massive banner that read KGB STOP TORTURING RAIZA PALATNIK as they marched to the office of *The Times*. The next day there was massive press coverage of the campaign, and Raiza Palatnik's parents heard where she was being held.[24]

Before they acquired their nickname some of the group's early members had marched in December 1970 on behalf of the Leningrad prisoners who had been sentenced to death and long prison terms. Amelie Jakobovits, the wife of Britain's chief rabbi, led the march.[25] Cyril Stein also tried to get some publicity for the Leningrad prisoners by entering the Soviet Consulate with some students and 35s in a ploy to request visas to visit Russia. Inside the consulate they found anti-Semitic literature that they removed before KGB agents threw them out. Television crews waiting outside filmed the action and the hateful literature.

Like the activist students, the 35s faced stern opposition from the Board of Deputies and other Jewish establishment organizations for their public demonstrations.[26] The Board favored the National Council for Soviet Jewry, which was like the NCSJ in America in promoting the Lishka policies. The Board of Deputies also published an informative weekly bulletin called *Jews in the USSR*, that was influenced by the Lishka and edited by Colin Shindler and Nan Greifer.[27]

Zelda Harris remembers how the women in black also faced taunts from anti-Semites and Communist sympathizers, and that women who slept on the street outside the Soviet Embassy shocked their families. "No middle-class Jewish women had ever done such a thing in London," she recalls.[28] They were energized by thoughts of Raiza Palatnik and Sylva Zalmanson (Chapter 8), and in later years, Ida Nudel and other women prisoners. And because many of the 35s' grandparents had come from Russia, they adopted the motto, "There, but for the grace of God, go I."[29] The 35s were also concerned about refuseniks and regarded life in the limbo of refusal, as imposed upon them by the Soviet system, as a form of psychological torture.[30]

The 35s were elated and vindicated in 1975 when Raiza

Palatnik emigrated to Israel and told interviewers from Amnesty International that public awareness of her suffering led to improvement of her prison conditions and an early release.[31] By that time the 35s had grown to have a network of nineteen groups throughout the British Isles and affiliates in Europe, Canada, Australia, New Zealand and Israel.[32] Women from Canada, Denmark, France, Ireland, Sweden, the u.s. and West Germany joined with Doreen Gainsford as the International Women's Committee for Soviet Jewry lobbied delegates at a session of the Committee on Security and Cooperation in Geneva that preceded the Helsinki Accords meeting. In Helsinki Gainsford and five other women were arrested for greeting Brezhnev with banners that read: USSR HONOR THE AGREEMENT – GIVE HUMAN RIGHTS TO SOVIET JEWS.[33]

Manchester had a twin-cities relationship with Leningrad since 1963 and 35s members sought to cultivate that relationship to publicize the Soviet Jewry issue. However the city council was dominated by left-wingers who were hostile to demonstrations by the 35s that would embarrass visitors from Leningrad. The 35s offered to call off their demonstrations if twenty prisoners and refuseniks from Leningrad were released. Eventually ten of them received exit visas, but not until an enormous demonstration took place in Manchester with women in black coming from all over England.[34] Barbara Portner, a 35s activist from Manchester, had a harrowing time during her 1980 visit to Russia and was detained at Leningrad's airport prior to departure, but as soon as she produced a letter from the lord mayor of Manchester wishing her a good trip and looking forward to hearing about it, the KGB agents apologized and allowed her to board the plane.[35]

The 35s' built relationships with their local members of Parliament, who then lobbied on their behalf to help Soviet Jews. Greville Janner, the son of Lord Barnett Janner, promoted human rights and Jewish causes upon being elected to Parliament in 1970. He formed the All-Party Parliamentary Committee for the Release of Soviet Jewry in 1972 and worked closely with the

35s in support of many individual cases.[36] He was encouraged by prime minister Harold Wilson who wrote, "Demonstrate as much as you like as long as there is no violence. The more you demonstrate the more strength it gives your arm and gets the Russians to do what we want."[37]

One unusual demonstration took place to protest the Soviet education tax. Emulating Lady Godiva's naked ride through Coventry in 1057 to persuade her husband to cancel an onerous tax,[38] a beautiful young woman from the 35s donned a flesh-colored body stocking and a long blonde wig, and rode on horseback in the middle of London.[39]

Two years before the 1980 Olympic Games the 35s started a campaign of demonstrations against holding them in Moscow, and a boycott of the games was debated in the House of Commons. Although Great Britain sent athletes to compete in Moscow a great deal of public consciousness of the plight of Soviet Jewry had been aroused by the 35s' campaign, especially when news reports told of dissidents being expelled from Moscow to avoid embarrassing demonstrations during the Olympic Games.[40]

The 35s quickly mastered communications skills and created events that would generate media coverage.[41] They even borrowed a vacant shop across the street from the Soviet Embassy and installed a neon sign that read "Save Our Sharansky".[42]

Like the Soviet Jewry supporters in America, the 35s organized person-to-person contacts with refuseniks through direct visits. Every week travelers from Britain, briefed by the 35s, and loaded with medicine, clothes, books and tapes, were on their way to the Soviet Union to meet refuseniks and bring back their latest information.[43] Bar and bat mitzvah twinnings took place as early as March 1976 with a ceremony involving twenty boys outside the Soviet Embassy who acted as proxies for Sasha Roitburd, the son of Lev Roitburd, a Prisoner of Zion.[44] The program continued through the 1980s, lifting the morale of refusenik families as their sons and daughters came of age and received congratulatory messages from supporters in the u.k. and America.[45]

During the 1980s Margaret Thatcher served as Britain's prime minister and the Soviet Jewry movement was fortunate to have her support. She embraced the cause of human rights upon entering Parliament and frequently wrote appeals to Soviet authorities on behalf of Prisoners of Zion. As prime minister she met with Avital Sharansky and leaders of the 35s. In meetings with Gorbachev she often brought up human rights concerns and the cases of specific individuals for whom the 35s were campaigning.[46] During the Thatcher-Gorbachev meeting on December 7, 1987, Gorbachev got a preview of what he would be hearing in Washington from Reagan the next day, as 35s groups demonstrated and a truck bearing a huge placard that read LET MY PEOPLE GO in English and Russian was driven through London.[47]

As the Soviet Union collapsed and emigration soared, the 35s, led by Rita Eker and Margaret Rigal, changed their direction and launched a one-on-one program of giving financial aid to needy Soviet Jews in Israel. By then most of the original leaders had made aliyah to Israel.[48] In 1992, when it became apparent that many Jews were remaining in the states that succeeded the Soviet Union and were suffering from poverty and a revival of anti-Semitism, the 35s set up a network of trusted contacts in each major city of the FSU and began distributing medicine, clothing, and kosher food through them.[49]

FRANCE – THE COMMITTEE OF FIFTEEN

Across the English Channel another organization with close ties to Michael Sherbourne and the 35s emerged to aid refuseniks and dissidents in the Soviet Union. *Le Comité des Quinze* (The Committee of Fifteen) was the brainchild of David Selikowitz, an American expatriate living in Paris and working in the business office of *Women's Wear Daily*. In 1976 as Selikowitz and his friend Michel Giberstein prepared to go on a vacation trip to Samarkand and Tashkent, another friend asked them to visit some Jewish families in Moscow. On a snowy winter night they walked past an array of KGB and police cars into Alexander Lerner's apartment. They were surprised to find a large group of Americans from Omaha along with eleven refuseniks, including the Lerners, Ida Nudel and Anatoly Sharansky, as well as four non-Jewish political dissidents. When Selikowitz and Giberstein returned to Paris in January 1977 they decided that they had to do something for the fifteen endangered families that they had met in Lerner's apartment.

While Giberstein, who was active in the French Jewish community, preferred to support only the refuseniks, Selikowitz insisted on aiding both refuseniks and dissidents. Selikowitz prevailed and the Comité des Quinze was established with the aim of enabling those fifteen families to get out of Russia, and if not, to at least give them material and moral support. Fifteen was a number that Selikowitz thought they could handle, and each time a family emigrated they would be replaced by another refusenik or dissident. Because of the committee's support for dissidents mainstream Jewish organizations in France, influenced by the Lishka, distanced themselves from the committee, but the four Reform synagogues in France did provide funds and support.[50]

The *International Herald Tribune* described the committee as "an adoption agency for Soviet refuseniks". To qualify for adoption a family had to have applied for exit visas and helped others emigrate. To facilitate contacts with the committee the adoptees had to be living in Moscow or Kiev, and able to speak English, French or German. The committee printed postcards with photos of the adopted refuseniks and messages of support for them. The cards were sold for five francs ($1) each as a fundraiser and mailed to the refuseniks in Russia. Although Ida Nudel received only one card out of 10,000 sold, it was clear to Soviet authorities that she had thousands of supporters in France. The committee encouraged members of the French National Assembly to visit refuseniks on trips just as American congressmen had done. In the first year of its existence four of the adopted families received exit visas. The permission granted to Gregory Schudnovsky of Kiev could be traced to publicity stemming from the visit of a French deputy.[51]

After visiting refuseniks in Moscow and Leningrad in June 1978, Patty Pyott, a committee member, recommended a campaign "of showing the world and the Soviet Union that holding the Olympic Games in Moscow in 1980 would be as much a travesty as it was to hold them in Berlin in 1936." She also proposed an economic boycott of the Soviet Union and working with Soviet Jewry groups in England and America to hold simultaneous demonstrations at the Soviet Embassies in Paris, London and Washington.[52]

By 1985 the committee that had started with only twenty members in Paris had grown to over 1,000, 250 of whom were active. And seventeen of the adopted families, fifty people in all, had emigrated.[53] Sadly, Inna Meiman, one of the first fifteen to be adopted, died in February 1987. Her husband, Nahum Meiman, was still in refusal in Moscow while she was allowed to travel to Georgetown University Hospital in Washington for cancer treatment. His exit visa application was denied because he had worked for Sakharov on Soviet nuclear projects in the 1950s.[54] Selikowitz was visiting and chatting with Inna Meiman in Washington when she passed away.[55]

After fourteen years in refusal Nahum Meiman emigrated to Israel in 1988. By 1990 all of the adopted families had left the Soviet Union and the committee disbanded. Its final publication, a souvenir journal in January 1993, had the headline *Le Comité des 15, mission accomplie* (The Committee of 15, mission accomplished).[56]

HOLLAND – THE SOLIDARITY COMMITTEE FOR SOVIET JEWS

In 1968 Ephraim Tari, a Paris-based envoy of the Israeli government, told Awraham Soetendorp about the plight of Soviet Jews. As Tari explained how Jews in Russia were fearful of expressing their Jewishness, it was as if the clock had been turned back a quarter century to the time when Soetendorp, a rabbi's son, survived as a hidden child in Nazi-occupied Amsterdam. Awraham

Soetendorp grew up to become the rabbi of the Liberal Jewish Community in The Hague and head of the European Region of the World Union for Progressive Judaism. He identified with the "Jews of Silence" in Russia and began organizing a committee in the Netherlands to support them.

A meeting in April 1970 at the Portuguese Synagogue in Amsterdam drew a capacity crowd of over 3,000 – the largest gathering there since the end of World War II. Simon Wiesenthal, Lord Barnett Janner and Emanuel Litvinoff were the featured speakers and motivated the attendees to sign a petition to Soviet authorities. Soetendorp brought it to the Soviet Embassy and told one of the officials that it was painful to realize that Russians who had helped liberate the death camps were now suppressing Jews. The official reacted by clenching his fist and warning Soetendorp against continuing the demonstrations.

Soetendorp and the Solidarity Committee for Soviet Jews were undeterred and held their first Simchat Torah rally. Orthodox and Reform Jews danced together in a spirit of -Jewish unity that would pervade the movement for the next two decades. The Simchat Torah rallies grew each year until they had 20,000 people participating in the early 1980s. When Sharansky was freed he pushed for a massive demonstration in the United States, arguing that if a Jewish community of 30,000 could have a rally with 20,000, couldn't a million Americans come out for a rally? The answer was that a large number of non-Jews in Holland were aligned with the struggle and were very willing to demonstrate their support.

Another huge demonstration took place in Amsterdam after Dymshitz and Kuznetsov were sentenced to death on Christmas Eve in 1970. Soetendorp's radio appeal to the Dutch people was, "Having survived and always living with the horror and the loneliness of survival, we cannot accept that Jews will be executed and the world will just stand by."

In 1981 Soetendorp launched a campaign called "One million signatures for Soviet Jews." When asked on national television if he really expected to get a million signatures on a petition, he replied, "I know the heart of the Dutch people and I know that we will be able to do it." He wrote a heartfelt letter to every school and church in Holland telling how he lived with the memory of having been saved by the compassion and solidarity of the Dutch people. After over a year of day-and-night effort, the Solidarity Committee had a million signatures, and Soetendorp went to the Soviet Embassy with Jaap Littooy, a pastor of the Dutch Reformed Church, who headed an organization of non-Jews for Jews in the Soviet Union and Arab countries.

The Soviet Ambassador acknowledged the power of million signatures but commented, in keeping with Cold War rhetoric, "The power is wrongly directed; it should be directed against the United States which is waging a war against us and against human rights." What the ambassador didn't realize was that many of the signers were active in the peace movement, hoping for rapprochement between East and West and opposed to NATO's placement of neutron bomb sites in Europe.[57] On a visit to Israel, Soetendorp pointed out to prime minister Menachem Begin that the million signatures had been collected with the help of the mostly left-wing peace movement. Begin interrupted him and said, "Young man, you have not lived through Munich," and warned him of the dangers involved in working with the forces of appeasement. Soetendorp replied that he had been a hidden child who had lived with the experience of the few who acted to save them and the silent majority who did nothing, and that now wide coalition was needed, maybe including people who were critical of some U.S. policies. The Solidarity Committee's demonstrations were the only ones in Holland in which the peace movement and mainly right-wing Protestant religious parties marched side-by-side.[58]

Petrus Buwalda, who served as the Dutch ambassador to Moscow from 1986 to 1990, wrote about the Dutch support for Israel (whose interests in the Soviet Union were represented by the Dutch Embassy from 1967 to 1990) and for Soviet Jews. He states that "in 1967 the Netherlands, next to the United States, was

Israel's best friend." And many Dutch Calvinists welcomed the founding of Israel as fulfillment of biblical prophesies.[59]

When Sharansky was on trial Soetendorp arranged for Avital to meet Dutch prime minister Andreas van Agt. She spoke in Hebrew and Soetendorp translated. But he hesitated when she asked van Agt to stop all trade with the Soviet Union if they continued with the trial. Soetendorp told her that she could not ask that of the head of a democratic state. At van Agt's insistence, Soetendorp translated Avital's request, to which van Agt replied, looking at Avital, "You're so right. I feel that I am with you. Unfortunately, I haven't the power, but I will never forget the responsibility put in my hands."

The Solidarity Committee held an International Tribunal for Sharansky in 1980 that was modeled after the International Tribunal for Mikhail Shtern (Chapter 14) that was to be held in Amsterdam in 1977.[60] The Soviets released Dr. Shtern a week before the event was scheduled when they learned that Jean Paul Sartre and Simone de Beauvoir had agreed to participate in it.[61] Even though the Sharansky tribunal had testimony from notable figures including prime minister Mario Soares of Portugal and u.s. ambassador to the United Nations Andrew Young, the Soviets would not release Sharansky.

The Solidarity Committee maintained daily contact with the 35s and coordinated their campaigns with them, as well as with the ncsj and ucsj in America. The Israelis asked Soetendorp to tell Dutch students not to demonstrate at the Soviet Embassy. The Israelis feared that such demonstrations could backfire and affect the work of the Dutch Embassy in Moscow that was representing Israel's interests. Demonstrations went on as planned and were well-publicized. The only problem was one complaint from the Soviet Embassy saying that the road to their building had been blocked during a demonstration in 1971, and that the event received twenty minutes of television coverage. The secretary-general of the Dutch Foreign Office laughed off the Soviet complaint, saying, "They don't understand free expression of the press. But do me a favor, and next time just make sure people don't block the road." He didn't say anything about demonstrations affecting the Dutch Embassy in Moscow.

In 1991 the Solidarity Committee turned from campaigns for the release of refuseniks and prisoners to helping Soviet Jews find Judaism. Soetendorp spent three months in the Soviet Union assisting in the establishment of the first Reform congregation there. The Solidarity Committee collected funds for it as well as for assisting Soviet Jews in Israel. Two years later Soetendorp joined Mikhail Gorbachev as one of the founders of Green Cross International, an organization devoted to preserving the Earth's environment, and headed a committee that welcomed Gorbachev on his first visit to Holland. They embraced each other when Soetendorp told him that "in 1985 I was on the other side [demonstrating] and now we are working together for a better world.[62]"

SWITZERLAND – ACTION COMMITTEE FOR JEWS IN THE SOVIET UNION

Like Holland, Switzerland has a small Jewish population. Nevertheless, nearly all of the 18,000 Swiss Jews were involved in supporting their Soviet brethren. For about ten years community members sent Rosh HaShanah cards that were especially designed by Dan Rubinstein, Marion Richter and other Swiss artists, to refuseniks. Synagogues all over Switzerland twinned with refusenik families. Torchlight parades were held during the week of Chanukah in Basel, Bern and Zurich. Fifty pairs of well-briefed tourists (married couples, two women or two men) were sent on trips to the USSR to meet with refuseniks.[63] All of these activities were coordinated by the Action Committee for the Jews in the Soviet Union that was started in 1979 by Chana Berlowitz and Werner Guggenheim. It maintained a headquarters office in Zurich until 1996 when it shifted its office to Basel, and changed its purpose to the sending of relief packages to destitute Jews in Minsk.[64] Werner Rom was the first president of AJS and was instrumental in establishing a Parliamentary Committee for the rights of Soviet Jews.

The committee made numerous depositions to the Red Cross in Geneva and Bern.[65]

Ask Ruth Bloch how many times she's been to the Soviet Union, and this Jewish educator from Zurich will tell you "four and a half because the KGB kicked me out on my last trip!" Bloch was inspired to do something for Soviet Jews after reading Elie Wiesel's *The Jews of Silence*. In 1974 she joined a group of Jewish students from England, Holland and Switzerland on a tour of Prague, Budapest, Moscow, Leningrad and Kiev. She visited refuseniks and after returning to Zurich phoned them frequently to assess their needs and find other tourists who could visit them. She found Jewish Swissair pilots and flight attendants who were willing to bring in Judaica, including large volumes of the Talmud, and other contraband that would have surely been confiscated if they had been found in the luggage of ordinary tourists.

Her fifth trip was with a group from East Germany, and the KGB became immediately suspicious of her because her suitcases were full and weighed over 40 pounds while the East Germans were traveling very light. She was searched and her Talmud cassettes were confiscated. In Leningrad she called Aba Taratuta to advise that she would be coming, but his telephone was bugged and the KGB awaited her arrival. She was searched and questioned. The next day she had high hopes of enjoying Simchat Torah with the Jews of Leningrad, but the KGB and police had other ideas. They came for her, seized her visa, and at gunpoint, took her to railroad station. As she screamed, they put her on a train bound for Helsinki. She wanted to jump off the train but the train conductor held her passport. The story of her expulsion appeared in a Leningrad newspaper and refuseniks later told her how they admired her fearlessness.[66] Lishka operatives, however, were dismayed and concerned that she had put refuseniks in danger. They expressed similar thoughts about some British tourists who were sent by the 35s without adequate briefing about how to behave in the Soviet Union.[67]

When Bloch got back to Zurich she gave lectures all over

Switzerland and worked with Chana Berlowitz to set up an AJS office, and organized "Free Sharansky" demonstrations in front of the Aeroflot office.[68] As AJS grew to have hundreds of members it began publishing a monthly news bulletin in German called *Juden in der UdSSR*. Susanna Merkle, who had first heard of AJS through Amnesty International when she was a student, edited the publication, as well as participating in demonstrations. Information for *Juden in der UdSSR* came from contacts in the Soviet Union, Israel, the 35s in London, the Committee of 15 in Paris, and the UCSJ in Washington.[69]

AJS cooperated with the Lishka and Student Struggle for Soviet Jews in holding a mass demonstration in Geneva during the 1985 Reagan-Gorbachev Summit.[70] In 1986 there was a conference of European activists in Bern,. Berlowitz, Merkle, Soetendorp, and leaders of the 35s and the Committee of 15 participated in sharing information on the Helsinki Process, campaign techniques, travel reports, evaluation of the first year of Gorbachev's regime, and the continuing problems that refuseniks were facing. Refuseniks who could hear broadcasts of The Voice of Israel were delighted to learn about the conference and the names of participants.[71]

Merkle traveled to Moscow and Leningrad in 1984 and impressed refuseniks with her fluency in Hebrew, English, French, German, Italian and Hungarian. She, in turn, was impressed by the solidarity amongst the refuseniks, describing them as "one big family linked together, eager to help each other under any circumstances." She wrote that she and her traveling companion, Charlotte Herz, were told by Evgeny Lein (Chapter 10) that "a well-known Leningrad refusenik, Yuri Kolker, and his wife and son would be leaving Leningrad for Vienna. They might be on the same plane with us. Sitting on the plane our excitement grew. Would we see the Kolkers? As soon as we were able to leave our seats, we searched the plane for them and found them. All we said then was 'Shalom'; their eyes were full of tears and Yuri kissed our hands…How wonderful it was to leave the Soviet Union and accompany at least one refusenik family to the Free World! In

Vienna we asked where their destination was. 'Ben-Gurion Airport,' Yuri answered proudly."[72]

The 35s' initial protest in 1971, against the holding of Russian Prisoner of Zion Raiza Palatnik, a 35-year-old librarian. Photo credit: Courtesy.

CHAPTER TWENTY

Support from the Medical
and Scientific Communities

W hile statesmen from the free world were negotiating with Soviet officials, and American legislators were hammering out trade policies that linked favorable terms to unrestricted emigration, physicians and scientists in the West organized ad-hoc professional groups that would have an impact on their counterparts in the USSR and on the Soviet leadership. Three that began in the 1970s and remained active in the quest for human rights and support of refuseniks and prisoners until the collapse of the Soviet Union were the Medical Mobilization for Soviet Jewry, the Committee of Concerned Scientists, and Scientists for Sakharov, Orlov and Shcharansky.

MEDICAL MOBILIZATION FOR SOVIET JEWRY

Two first-year medical students, Paul Appelbaum and Carl Schoenberger, showed up at a Student Struggle for Soviet Jewry event in Boston and told Morey Schapira, the New England chapter's president, that they would like to help but had limited time. Schapira's response was, "Gee, you're in medical school, why don't we set up an organization that's focused on the medical community? We need something like that because there could be great potential leverage considering the Soviets' interest in advanced medical information from America." Furthermore, there was the opportunity to attract Jews who were not yet activists to a cause that would be relevant to them emotionally and professionally.[1] Appelbaum and Schoenberger agreed and started contacting doctors who were on synagogue mailing lists. Soon these doctors spread the word among their professional associates and wrote letters to the editors of medical journals.[2] Saralea Zohar, an energetic nurse, brought other nurses to meetings of the group that called itself the Medical Mobilization for Soviet Jewry.[3]

The organization took off much faster than Schapira had expected from a generally very conservative community. He now believes the Soviets contributed to this rapid growth by their egregious and abusive medical policies, giving the MMSJ three areas of focus. People who applied for exit visas or expressed dissident views were often thrown into psychiatric asylums. Political prisoners in Siberia were subjected to inhumane conditions with little or no access to medical treatment.[4] Soviet Jewish physicians were subjected to anti-Semitic persecution, the most notable being endocrinologist Dr. Mikhail Shtern in Ukraine who was demonized and imprisoned in 1974 in a revival of the ancient libel of Jews drawing blood from gentile children for religious rites. People in the West were shocked and 1,500 doctors signed a petition that appeared as a full-page ad in the *New York Times*.[5]

Letters published in medical journals, citing cases of persecuted Jewish doctors, brought contributions and petition signatures from gentile and Jewish doctors and health-care professionals. MMSJ sent out update mailings every three or four months with instructions for circulating petitions, writing letters of protest, and corresponding with refuseniks. The mailings at the season of the High Holy Days in 1975 and 1976 were particularly poignant, reminding the readers how Prisoners of Zion in the gulag were suffering.

Good news, however, appeared in early 1977 when the mailing featured a photo of Dr. Mikhail Shtern, newly released and standing alongside MMSJ members, thanks to all the resolutions and petitions issued on his behalf. Other former refusenik doctors who were permitted to emigrate were invited to speak at forums in America arranged by MMSJ.[6] American doctors traveling to the Soviet Union were briefed by MMSJ and encouraged to contact refuseniks who wished to meet visitors from the West. They often assessed the refuseniks' needs for medical help and medicines that were not readily available in the USSR. Other tourists would carry these drugs with them on subsequent trips.[7] On a trip to the USSR, Congressman William Lehman (D-FL) carried a heart valve for a Soviet Jew in need. Lehman had been briefed by Joel Sandberg, a physician who resided in Lehman's district and was the MMSJ southeastern coordinator.[8] These activities eventually were undertaken by the UCSJ, and as the MMSJ grew, new chapters were established wherever there was a UCSJ-affiliated council. In 1978, a part-time staffer, shared with Boston Action for Soviet Jewry, was hired to meet the growing need for assistance.

OTHER MEDICAL SUPPORT GROUPS

Protesters with picket signs appeared outside the Royal College of Physicians in London during the 1972 Symposium on Schizophrenia of the World Psychiatric Association. They were calling attention to the forced incarceration of refuseniks and political prisoners as "schizophrenics" in Soviet mental institutions.[9]

The 35s in England set up a group called the Medical Committee for Soviet Jewry in 1982, following the visit to Moscow of Rita Eker when she met Dr. Lev Goldfarb and other refuseniks, who pointed out that the most common ailment among refuseniks was stomach ulcers.[10] Goldfarb volunteered to order and dispense medicines brought by travelers to the refuseniks in need. Goldfarb, a neurologist, had been in refusal since late 1979, when emigration of scientists and engineers was drastically reduced to stem the brain drain. Upon applying for exit visas he and his wife, Inna, were dismissed from their research positions and found lower paying jobs in hospitals for alcoholics and tuberculosis patients. Until he and his family emigrated in 1986, Goldfarb secretly cared for 90 patients in 36 refusenik families. Knowing that searches of people who had been arrested turned up lists of refuseniks, he kept no written list of patients but committed their phone numbers to memory. He frequently consulted with visiting physicians from the West and followed their recommendations.[11]

One of them was Dr. Victor Borden, a New Jersey obstetrician/gynecologist and son of Polish Jews who survived the Holocaust in Russian labor camps. This background piqued Borden's interest in doing something to alleviate the situation for Russian Jews. The NCSJ gave him refusenik profiles and briefed him for an eight-day trip to Moscow and Leningrad in the summer of 1985. At a refusenik biological/medical seminar he gave the first presentation on HIV-AIDS in the Soviet Union. He returned to New Jersey resolved to devote most of his free time to Soviet Jewry and, having concluded that the UCSJ was more activist than the NCSJ, he offered his services to the UCSJ for directing medical support that would be carried by tourists from the West to refuseniks. Borden and other doctors observed that in the Soviet Union modern medical equipment and quality care were reserved for high-ranking Party members, but for the masses care was abysmal.[12]

Linda Opper, who had been briefing tourists in the UCSJ Chicago office, started the International Physicians Commission in 1985 after hearing horror stories of how refuseniks and prisoners who were terribly ill were being neglected; they often lacked what they needed and sometimes, because several tourists brought the same medication, they had too much of what they didn't need. The IPC's mission was to expedite delivery of what was needed and avoid unnecessary duplication. Opper became the one-person clearinghouse for all medical requests. UCSJ-affiliated councils would call her saying, "I have a tourist going to this city. What's needed there?" She would then call upon doctors in eight countries to provide medicines from their own supplies or donations from pharmaceutical companies, and arrange for the tourists to bring exactly what was needed. At first all of IPC's patients were Jewish, but that rapidly changed as there was no way to deny help to anyone who needed it. IPC worked with anyone who a refusenik said was deserving of support.[13]

In November 1987 Borden and six other physicians with a variety of specialties including cardiology and oncology, from New Jersey and Tennessee, traveled to Russia to set up clinics for refuseniks. They brought over $20,000 worth of medical equipment and drugs, including a pacemaker and diabetic equipment. Drs. Inna and Igor Uspensky, who succeeded Goldfarb as Moscow coordinator of medical aid to refuseniks, arranged for clinics to be set up in apartments in Moscow in which the doctors examined 110 patients during their week-long visit and gave advice. Dr. Alla Kelman, a pediatrician who had been distributing donated medicine to refuseniks in Leningrad, organized similar clinics and enabled forty people to be examined there. Borden recalls how he had to use kitchen gloves and a flashlight for his examinations. After examining over a hundred people, he was exhilarated upon returning and remarked, "This is what medicine is all about." The seven physicians were never hassled during their week in Russia, but five of them were arrested in New York, in front of the Soviet UN Mission, for demonstrating in support of a cancer patient who had been refused an exit visa. The charges were quickly dismissed but the incident helped fuel the growing publicity effort for Soviet Jewry just prior to the March on Washington and the Gorbachev-Reagan Summit meeting of December 1987.[14]

Doctors from abroad could not visit prisoners and even distributing vitamins to them was prohibited, but the Uspenskys and their associates arranged for children's vitamins, disguised as candy, to be taken to the prisons by the prisoners' wives.[15]

Other physicians who were not involved with IPC often went to the Soviet Union as private tourists or with other groups and rendered medical assistance to refuseniks. Michael Dohan, a Boston cardiologist active in both the Physicians for Social

Responsibility and the International Physicians for the Prevention of Nuclear War, went to Moscow, Kiev, Tbilisi and Leningrad and secretly met with a few refuseniks in 1985, and to Moscow in 1987, when Igor Uspensky arranged for him to treat activists Ben Charney, who had severe hypertension, and Yuri Chernyak (Chapter 11) who had suffered a heart attack. Dohan recruited other IPPNW physicians, Jewish and gentile, to bring in medicines in 1987. A refusenik doctor, Josef Brodsky, who was denied permission to join the Russian counterpart of IPPNW, complained and was arrested. Dohan organized a protest campaign on Brodsky's behalf that resulted in his release and emigration to Israel.[16]

Borden's next trip to the Soviet Union was in 1989. He met refuseniks in Kiev, Leningrad, Moscow, Tallinn, and Vilnius. With the opening of the gates to emigration he realized Soviet Jewish doctors might not be readily accepted as physicians in Israel, so he went to Israel and met with absorption officials and with the dean of the Medical School in Beersheba to develop a program for retraining former Soviet doctors. [17]

COMMITTEE OF CONCERNED SCIENTISTS

When Jack Cohen read the "I am a Jew" letter to Brezhnev written by Boris Kochubievsky (Chapter 7) he felt compelled to do something. Cohen, a biochemist at the National Institutes of Health, went to the Jewish Community Center in Rockville, Maryland, and, speaking as the newly appointed chairman of its Soviet Jewry Committee, persuaded the group to name the JCC entrance "Kochubievsky Square." The rationale was that Soviet Jews coming out of the closet were in grave danger and having their names known and publicized in the West could be a source of protection.

Cohen went to Moscow in August 1972 to participate in the International Biophysics Conference. During his free time he attended a session of the weekly seminars organized by Alexander Voronel (Chapter 11) for refusenik scientists and saw firsthand the harassment that they were experiencing. Cohen also met the

Slepaks (Chapter 9) while they were in a friend's apartment, where they were awaiting a phone call from British MP Greville Janner as their own telephone had been disconnected. Benjamin Levich, who had been dismissed from his position as a department head at the Institute of Electrophysics, also had his phone cut off a few days after his son, Yevgeny, was dragged from the car he was driving, beaten and arrested by the KGB. Benjamin Levich had been a member-correspondent of the USSR Academy of Sciences, the highest official level of all refusenik scientists. Cohen wrote a letter to the conference protesting this incident and also Levich's exclusion from the conference. Levich provided Cohen with a list of refusenik scientists whom he called "Slaves of the Twentieth Century," as well as a letter describing the newly introduced and infamous "education tax".[18]

When he returned to Washington, Cohen and his NIH colleague Robert Adelstein took Levich's letter to the *Washington Post* and an op-ed piece bashing the education tax was published.[19] Recalling Mark Azbel's (Chapter 11) advice that "Soviets value their international scientific contacts and concern expressed by friends from abroad would be a tremendous asset to Soviet Jews who were trying to emigrate,"[20] Cohen met with like-minded scientists in New York, notably Fred Pollak, a physics professor at CUNY, and organized an ad-hoc group called the Committee of Concerned Scientists. The group's purpose was to translate their concern about the persecution of their Jewish colleagues in the Soviet Union into meaningful constructive action. They enlisted support from associates throughout American scientific and academic communities on behalf of Soviet scholars and scientists who had been denied their human rights.[21] Pollak and Mel Pomerantz, an engineer at IBM, were the first co-chairs of CCS. Vice-chairs were elected in the areas of astronomy, chemistry, computer science, engineering, mathematics, medical sciences and physics.[22]

In 1974 Cohen testified in behalf of CCS in congressional hearings on détente at the House Sub-Committee on Europe of the Foreign Affairs Committee. He brought recently released refusenik scientists including Alexander Voronel to his meetings with congressmen and senators.[23]

Levich was allowed to emigrate in 1975, the highest-ranking Soviet scientist to be released up to that time, and held dual appointments as Albert Einstein Professor of Science at the City College of New York and as professor of physics at Tel Aviv University.[24] The New York Academy of Sciences held a reception in his honor soon after his arrival. Joel Lebowitz, a mathematics professor at Rutgers University who had survived Auschwitz, attended the event, and moved by Levich's remarks about the plight of refusenik scientists, started a human rights committee within the New York Academy of Sciences. Three years later Lebowitz became that organization's president and from the mid-1980s to the present time he has been a co-chair of CCS. Lebowitz estimates that until the collapse of the Soviet Union 80–90% of its activities were devoted to refusenik scientists.[25] CCS eventually grew in size and scope in response to the oppression of its colleagues in other countries.[26]

In 1975 Jack Minker, the vice-chair of CCS for computer science, became concerned that the International Joint Conference on Artificial Intelligence was scheduled to be held in Tbilisi in Soviet Georgia. Would Soviet scientists who were refuseniks or dissidents be barred from attending? Would the Soviet government allow Israeli scientists to enter the USSR to attend the conference? Minker arranged for CCS to assure that the conference would be open to all scientists by inviting Alexander Lerner to be on a proposed panel on "Artificial Intelligence and Cybernetics." Since Lerner's phone had been disconnected and postal service was unreliable, Minker wrote to him inquiring if he would be interested in being on such a panel, and brought the letter to Irene Manekofsky of the Washington Council on Soviet Jewry (Chapter 14). She entrusted the letter to a congressman who was about to travel to Moscow and was willing to deliver it to Lerner. After Lerner responded affirmatively, Minker worked with key members of the Western Organizing Committee of IJCAI to make certain that Lerner would be on the panel. When Lerner received his invitation, he applied for permission to travel to Tbilisi for the conference but the KGB intervened and his application was turned down. When Minker read about the KGB action he discussed it with his colleagues on the organizing committee, and then sent letters out to the membership of the Special Interest Group on Artificial Intelligence, polling them on whether they wanted the conference moved out of the USSR. The response was 400 in favor of moving the conference to only six for keeping it in Tbilisi. This gave the Western members of the IJCAI organizing committee leverage to deal with their Soviet colleagues. The Soviets retreated and granted Lerner permission to go to Tbilisi to attend IJCAI. The turnaround in Soviet behavior was a significant success for CCS.[27]

Soon other professional societies, including the American Association for the Advancement of Science and the National Academy of Sciences, were establishing support groups for refusenik scientists and engineers. On a mostly quiet basis, NAS President Phillip Handler provided crucial support for Sakharov and other oppressed scientists.[28] Organizations similar to CCS were springing up outside the United States. The Canadian group was headed by Eric Fawcett, a non-Jewish physics professor who, after attending a refusenik seminar in Moscow in 1976, said, "I was struck by the persecution of Jewish scientists in the USSR and the tremendous potential being lost."[29]

In 1977 CCS hired Dorothy Hirsch as its executive director. Until her retirement in 2003 she played a pivotal role in supporting refusenik and dissident scientists by staging press conferences, issuing press releases, organizing human rights sessions at scientific meetings and circulating petitions.

Lebowitz and his colleague Jim Langer of Carnegie Mellon went to Leningrad and Moscow in December 1978 as part of a CCS tour group that was invited to attend "The Third International Conference on Collective Phenomena," an expanded version of the unauthorized refusenik seminars held in private apartments.

Mark Azbel initiated the first international conference in 1974 and had been jailed for his efforts. Langer described his experience of meeting with Sakharov and other courageous scientists at the home of Irina and Victor Brailovsky in an article for *Physics Today*.[30]

Six months later Lebowitz revisited the USSR for a mathematics conference in Tbilisi and a meeting in Moscow with Anatoly Alexandrov, the president of the Soviet Academy of Sciences. Their dialogue was rather predictable:

Lebowitz: 'There are some obstacles to scientific cooperation due to the fact that many American scientists are disturbed by anti-Semitism in Soviet mathematics.'

Alexandrov: 'There is discrimination against blacks and other minorities in the United States but Soviet scientists do not protest about that. Jews occupy some important scientific positions in the USSR.'

Lebowitz: 'I'm concerned about scientists like Alber, Alpert, Brailovsky, the Goldstein brothers and others who have been prevented from leaving for very long periods of time, more than five, some for over seven years.'

Alexandrov: 'For what reason would we want to keep people in this country who do not want to be here?'

Lebowitz: 'This is exactly what we don't understand.'

Alexandrov: 'Sakharov certainly could not be let out because of the secret work he has done.'

Lebowitz: 'I'm talking about others who have been connected with secret work only in a marginal way or not at all, and some of whom have received clearance from their labs – surely after so many years these people possessed no secrets.'

Alexandrov: 'Levich the electron chemist was let go after his work was no longer secret. Sending telegrams and applying pressure to let a particular individual go can be counterproductive. People who protest are trying to disrupt Soviet-American cooperation.'[31]

The refusenik seminars continued until 1981, although with more KGB harassment. One problem the refusenik scientists faced was publication of the technical papers they wrote. No Soviet journal would accept an article submitted by an out-of-work refusenik. Lebowitz came to the rescue with periodic issues of special editions of New York Academy of Sciences publications that were devoted to smuggled refusenik papers.[32] Jack Minker arranged for the Institute of Electrical and Electronic Engineers to publish a paper authored by Victor Brailovsky just before he was arrested in 1980.[33]

Several volumes of refusenik manuscripts were published by Neil Bradman, a British genetic anthropologist and businessman who owned a publishing company and was chairman of the National Council for Soviet Jewry in the U.K. Bradman also raised several thousand dollars for the purchase of scientific books chosen by refuseniks and carried in by visitors to Russia. This program, coordinated in Moscow by Alex Ioffe, for several years thwarted the KGB's efforts to deprive refuseniks of access to new scientific information.[34]

When Lebowitz returned to Moscow in 1981 he found that the refusenik seminar participants were being called in for talks at local police stations, prominent seminar leader Victor Brailovsky (Chapter 11) had been exiled to Kazakhstan, and the international conference had to be postponed indefinitely.[35] Jack Minker and Nobel laureates Arno Penzias (Chapter 11) and George Wald were eager to go to Moscow that year to participate in the international conference with refuseniks, but they were denied visas. Attending a lecture on Soviet science policy given by the Soviet scientific attache in Washington, Minker protested, "How can denying visas to American scientists help Soviet-American relations?"[36]

Lebowitz challenged CCS to come up with appropriate

actions to influence a country whose behavior often appeared to be inconsistent and contradictory. One CCS innovation was support for the biological/medical seminars initiated in 1983 by Drs. Lev Goldfarb, Yosef Irlin, Mark Tarshis, and Igor Uspensky. At first they attracted a dozen refuseniks to the bimonthly meetings, which often featured presentations by scientists from America, England and Sweden. By 1989 there were more thirty attendees at each session.[37]

Through the dark years of Andropov's and Chernenko's regimes the Soviet Union seemed impervious to pressure from the West. With Gorbachev's ascent to power in 1985 there were new opportunities. The Swiss government invited all the states that were signatories to the Helsinki Accords to a meeting to explore ways to achieve the objectives of the "human contacts" provisions of the Helsinki Final Act. At the meeting of experts that took place in Bern during April 1986 CCS provided a list of 782 Soviet Jewish scientists, physicians and engineers whose applications for exit visas for family reunification in Israel had been refused. There were 93 on the list who had been waiting for over ten years. CCS backed up its report with a study that stated, "Many have been demoted or dismissed outright from their jobs, denounced by co-workers at open meetings, barred from attending professional meetings, shunned by their neighbors and vilified in the media. In addition, their mail has been intercepted and their telephones have been disconnected."[38]

CCS followed up with petition campaigns, press conferences, protests, human rights sessions at scientific meetings, and participation in the revived refusenik seminars. Its members walked arm-in-arm among the 250,000 people who rallied in the March for Soviet Jewry from the White House to the Capitol on December 6, 1987. Jack Minker recalls how he remarked to his friends, "Too bad such demonstrations were not carried out in the 1930s and 1940s." A day after the rally Reagan and Gorbachev held their summit meeting and Reagan reiterated his request that prominent long-term refuseniks be given permission to emigrate. Two weeks later Minker was elated to receive a phone call from Alexander Lerner's daughter with the good news that her father had finally received his exit visa, and thanked Minker for all of his efforts on his behalf.[39]

Lebowitz and other leaders of the CCS were on hand for the final international conference of the refusenik seminar that took place in three Moscow apartments in December 1988.[40] It was a joyous occasion as nearly all the refuseniks present had received either permission to emigrate or some sort of assurance that they would soon receive their long-desired visas.[41]

CCS continues to support scientists who are facing human rights issues in all parts of the world and is campaigning against attempts to boycott Israeli universities and scholars. Its annual report for 2005 lists summaries showing how CCS "raised its voice on behalf of scholars in twenty-eight countries on five continents."[42]

SCIENTISTS FOR SAKHAROV, ORLOV AND SHCHARANSKY

A group called Scientists for Sakharov, Orlov and Shcharansky had its start in Berkeley, California, in 1977 when Denis Keefe, a physicist at the Lawrence Berkeley Labs became distressed to learn that his colleague and personal friend, Yuri Orlov, had been imprisoned, and Anatoly Shcharansky was placed on trial for treason. Keefe and Moishe Pripstein, another physicist at LBL, approached Andrew Sessler, the director of LBL, who agreed that it was time to get scientists together to demand human rights for scientists in the USSR. Their field of high energy physics, like most scientific endeavors, is truly international with considerable exchange among scientists of various countries, but it was perverted by the Soviets who were not permitting some of their scientists to attend conferences in the West to which they had been invited; only those approved by the Communist Party were allowed to travel abroad. Keefe, Pripstein and Sessler proposed denying invitations to them.

The idea of a boycott was not new to Pripstein. In 1970 he had become incensed at the systematic exclusion of Israeli scientists from international conferences in the USSR. The Soviet organizers would issue invitations, but not visas, to Israeli scientists. After 1967, when the USSR severed diplomatic relations with Israel, the Israeli invitees would be told to pick up their visas in Vienna before entering the Soviet Union, but when they arrived in Vienna they were told that there were no visas for them. Pripstein and his colleagues threatened to boycott the prestigious High-Energy Conference that was scheduled to be held in Kiev, unless visas for the Israeli invitees came through before their arrival. Sure enough the Soviet officials provided the visas and displayed an Israeli flag along with those of all the other participating nations at the conference site. On Shabbat a group of Jews walked across the city of Kiev from the synagogue to the Palace of Culture and were elated to see an Israeli flag waving over Soviet soil.

Pripstein invited his colleagues to his home for meetings to determine what to do about Orlov's incarceration in the gulag and Shcharansky's life in the hands of the Soviet justice system. They agreed to organize as a group to do something for their endangered colleagues but debated whether it would be wise to support both Orlov, a non-Jewish dissident, and Shcharansky, a Jewish refusenik. Would linkage of the two harm other refuseniks? The Bay Area Council for Soviet Jews strongly advocated the linkage as it would enlarge the community of people concerned about human rights in the Soviet Union. With that blessing the group organized itself as "Scientists for Orlov and Shcharansky" (SOS).[43]

Whereas CCS had scientists from a wide variety of disciplines, nearly all of the founding members of SOS were physicists with the exception of Paul Flory, a Nobel laureate and Stanford chemistry professor, and Philip Siegelman, who had taught Chinese and Soviet politics and classical Marxist theory at San Francisco State University for twenty-five years.

In one of its first actions SOS raised money among its

members to bring Avital Shcharansky from Israel to America to arouse public awareness of her husband's persecution and to testify at Congressional hearings. Nobel laureate Owen Chamberlain, a member of the SOS board, also flew to Washington to testify. Additional funds were used for the placement of small advertisements in *Nature* and *Science* magazines stating "If you want to defend persecuted scientists in the Soviet Union join SOS and sign the following pledge." The pledge read:

> In response to the unjust trials and harsh sentencing of our colleagues Yuri Orlov and Anatoly Shcharansky, we the undersigned members of the American science and engineering community, pledge ourselves to the following actions:
>
> 1. We shall not attend international conferences in the Soviet Union.
> 2. We shall collaborate with and attend lectures by Soviet visitors only if they are invited.
> 3. We shall oppose any enlargement of scientific and technical exchange programs between the Soviet Union and the United States.
> 4. We shall campaign against the transfer of sophisticated Western technology to the Soviet Union and against the granting of most-favored-nation trading status to the USSR.
>
> We intend to continue this course of action until the Soviet government provides tangible proof that it has curtailed its persecution and harassment of our Soviet colleagues."[44]

On March 1, 1979, SOS issued a press release stating that "Over 2,400 U.S. scientists, including 13 Nobel laureates, announced today their pledge to severely restrict their cooperation with the Soviet Union. No step of this magnitude has ever been taken by American scientists. These restrictions have already had a serious impact on U.S.-Soviet scientific relations."[45] Ten days later Nahum Maiman and Andrei Sakharov wrote to SOS expressing their encouragement and joy at hearing about the pledge.[46]

When Flory signed the pledge he announced that he would be canceling his participation in a meeting on polymer chemistry that was to take place in Tashkent. Polymer chemistry was very important to the Soviets and they desperately wanted Flory at that meeting, hoping to establish a working relationship with him. Although he was flooded with requests that he reconsider, some from the highest levels of the Soviet Academy of Sciences, he firmly refused to participate.[47] An associate of Flory's at Stanford, Yuri Yarim-Agaev, was an exiled dissident who brought a unique expertise to SOS meetings and helped define the group's strategies and campaigns.[48]

The Soviet government was perturbed by the boycott as evidenced by a CPSU document uncovered by former dissident Vladimir Bukovsky after the collapse of the Soviet Union. He revealed the minutes of a meeting in which Brezhnev demanded to know who the SOS group was and what could be done about them. The scientific attaché of the Soviet Consulate in San Francisco invited the officers of SOS to a luncheon meeting in hopes of getting the boycott called off, but no agreement was reached and SOS continued to participate in rallies (usually organized by local Soviet Jewry councils) and to gather additional support for the moratorium.[49]

In 1980 after the Soviet invasion of Afghanistan and Sakharov's exile to Gorky, the group changed its name to "Scientists for Sakharov, Orlov and Shcharansky" and cabled a letter of protest to the Kremlin.[50] By the end of 1980 SOS counted more than 8,000 scientists and engineers in forty-four countries, including thirty-two Nobel laureates, who had signed the moratorium pledge.[51] The moratorium campaign was widely discussed during the 1980 Helsinki Accords follow-up meeting in Madrid with the Soviets claiming to be the aggrieved party in a Western violation of the Accords.[52] Western European support for the moratorium

grew, and in 1983 the governing council of the European Laboratory for Particle Physics (CERN) refused to renew CERN's exchange
agreement with the Soviet Union, thus barring Soviet scientists
from access to one of the world's most important centers for high-
energy physics research. Other international organizations such as
the Association for Computing Machinery were very supportive
and also refused to sponsor joint conferences with the Soviets.[53]

In 1984 when Yelena Bonner applied to the Soviet government for permission to travel abroad for medical treatment, and
her husband, Andrei Sakharov, was on a hunger strike (Chapter
12), SOS proposed a plan whereby fifty-five prominent Western scientists would serve as "good-faith witnesses" in the Soviet Union
until Bonner returned and to guarantee that her journey would
be for medical, not political, purposes. The fifty-five scientists
were from thirteen countries and included six Nobel laureates.[54]
During the Chernenko regime Soviet authorities wouldn't even
respond to the proposal, but in late 1985, with Gorbachev firmly
in control, Bonner was given permission to travel to her family
and receive medical treatment in the United States.

With the onset of glasnost and Shcharansky's release, a group
called the Center for Peace and Freedom tried to convince SOS to
suspend the moratorium and start participating in meetings in the
Soviet Union, but as long as Sakharov and Orlov were still in exile SOS would not yield.[55] At the end of 1986, when Sakharov was
back in Moscow and Orlov was living in the United States, most
SOS people were ready to suspend the moratorium. Siegelman,
however, reminded them that other scientists were still in the
gulag. And when he visited with SOS officers in Berkeley, Orlov
asked then not to quit. He was certain that a lot of people still
needed support. In 1989, SOS finally gave up its post office box
and turned its bank account over to the International Helsinki
Foundation.[56]

A decade later, for his role in founding SOS and all his unrelenting efforts in taking on the Soviet Union on behalf of his
imprisoned colleagues, Moishe Pripstein was presented with

the New York Academy of Sciences Heinz Pagels Human Rights Award. Upon accepting the award, Pripstein reflected on the imprisoned scientists who ultimately won their freedom: "The greatest thing that amazed me about these people was their sense of humanity and compassion. Each of them had suffered terribly, each in his own way – either by long incarceration or actual torture. After all they went through I figured they'd come out with deep psychological scars and be really embittered. Instead they were filled with compassion for their fellow men and totally lacking in bitterness."[57]

A "troika" of activists. Left to right: Moishe Pripstein, SOS President; Father Robert Drinan. Member of Congress; Morey Schapira BACSJ President. Photo Credit: BACSJ Archives.

344

CHAPTER TWENTY-ONE

HIAS Support for Soviet Jews Going to America

*I*t was inevitable. During the years 1967 through 1970 only 4,000 Soviet Jews were allowed to emigrate and every one of them gladly made aliyah. But in 1971, when the gates of the USSR opened to 14,000 Jews, fifty-eight of them dropped out and chose to go to America. They were called *noshrim* (dropouts in Hebrew) and grew in number in subsequent years, especially after the 1973 Yom Kippur War, when 24% of the émigrés sought refugee status in the United States rather than life in Israel.[1] Clearly many of the émigrés wanted to leave the Soviet Union and live where they would not be discriminated against as Jews, but they were not fervent Zionists. Economic considerations and the desire to avoid living in a war zone influenced their decision. One woman, aghast to learn that she would not be able to have a private room in Israel, opted for America. She said she had shared a bathroom in Moscow with twenty-four people and now sought a little privacy.[2] Based on negative propaganda, others feared that Israel was a desert where life would be hard and that they would have to endure absorption center conditions indefinitely.[3]

FROM VIENNA TO ROME TO AMERICA

It was in Vienna that the Soviet Jews with exit visas could make their decision. When they arrived in Vienna they would be met by representatives of the Jewish Agency for Israel who checked that they were Jewish and wanted to go to Israel. If they wished to go to the United States, Canada or Australia they would be re-ferred to representatives of HIAS (Hebrew Immigrant Aid Soci-ety, founded in 1881 to help new arrivals who were teeming into New York).[4] The U.S. government policy established by attorney general John Mitchell in 1971 was to allow "political refugees to come into this country without a specific quota, provided that the sponsoring agency in the United States assumed responsibil-ity for the newcomers."[5]

Because the U.S. Immigration and Naturalization Service had its headquarters for Europe in Rome, HIAS set up facilities there. Émigrés were transported from Vienna to Rome where they would be interviewed by HIAS caseworkers and translators who helped them fill out their INS forms. People who had been Com-munist Party members were required to write explanations of the circumstances under which they joined the party.[6]

David Harris (Chapter 15) was teaching English to Soviet Jews in New York in 1973. His students often praised the assistance they had received from HIAS in Rome. Two years later he walked into the HIAS office in Rome and became one of its Russian-speak-ing caseworkers. In order to fully grasp the experience of a Soviet Jewish émigré he boarded a train in Vienna with eighty-three of them and rode for eighteen hours to Rome. He observed how well HIAS had coordinated security and transportation arrangements with the Austrian and Italian governments, and how the Soviet Jews were amazed that a voluntary Jewish agency was organized to help them bridge the divide between Soviet and Western cultures.[7] Harris also described how supportive the Italian people were to the thousands of Soviet Jews who were living in transit in Rome and its environs. On the other hand, Arab terrorists were deter-mined to make life miserable for Soviet Jews. There were attacks on Jewish and American offices in Rome in 1976; four people were injured by a bomb that exploded near a place where Soviet Jews gathered in 1981; the following year bombs were found at HIAS offices in Rome and an attack at the main synagogue killed a child and injured forty people; and worst of all was the 1985 attack at the El Al counter in Rome's Fiumicino Airport that killed sixteen people.[8]

When Hedva Boukhobza started working as secretary to the director of the HIAS Rome office in 1970 there was a trickle of Jews from Poland and Romania who were en route to America. The procedure for them and for the small number of Soviet Jews emigrating to the United States in the early 1970s took about four weeks. But while the numbers of noshrim escalated, the INS staffing remained constant and backlogs grew so that several months would pass before an émigré received a U.S. visa.[9] The American Joint Distribution Committee (JDC or "The Joint") provided funds for housing and feeding the émigrés, in keeping with its tradition that dates back to its founding at the beginning of World War I, to provide aid to "Jews in need wherever they are."[10] The JDC had had a presence in the Soviet Union until 1953, when it was accused of collaborating with Western Jewish organizations and Soviet doctors (mostly Jewish) in a plot to murder Soviet leaders.[11]

THE CLASH OF IDEALS: ZIONISM VS. HUMAN RIGHTS

The JDC felt obligated to help the Jews who wanted to immigrate as refugees to the United States even though its CEO since 1976, Ralph Goldman, argued that they were not really refugees because Israel guaranteed them asylum as Jews under the Law of Return. The dilemma facing the JDC was one of the most controversial issues in the history of the Soviet Jewry movement.

The Zionist view was that Soviet Jews who received vysovs from Israel and used them to obtain exit visas were morally bound to immigrate to Israel and defection from Jewish nationalism was a selfish slap at the Jewish state. Furthermore, from a political standpoint Zionists feared that Soviet authorities would ultimately react to excessive abuse of the Israeli vysovs by cutting off emigration entirely.[12]

Genya Intrator, who emigrated from Moscow in 1934, grew up in Israel and settled in Canada in 1950, was enlisted by Nechemia Levanon and the Lishka to make phone calls in Russian to Soviet Jews in 1971. She became a driving force in the Canadian Soviet Jewry movement.[13] But in 1978, when Levanon asked her to help only Jews who were going to Israel, she was outraged and replied, "Soviet Jews have suffered so much. No way will I turn my back on other Jews just because they want to go somewhere other than Israel." She became active in the UCSJ, which advocated freedom of choice, and later became a board member. On a visit to Vienna she was appalled to observe refugees being interrogated by a committee and ridiculed when they said they wanted to join relatives in America.[14]

HIAS, through its president, Carl Glick, wholeheartedly advocated "freedom of choice," and launched programs to welcome Soviet Jews to America. They were supported by the American Jewish Committee and the National Jewish Community Relations Council.[15] However, the Presidents' Conference, following the wishes of the Israeli government regarding Soviet Jewry, was opposed to supporting the noshrim, and the Zionist Organization of America strongly opposed a bill in Congress that would have granted 30,000 entry visas to Soviet Jews. According to William Orbach in *The American Movement to Aid Soviet Jews*, the ZOA accused HIAS and the JDC of "hijacking Jews to the United States by offering them greater benefits."[16]

The perfect solution for Israel would have been direct flights from Moscow to Tel Aviv, but the Soviet Union was unwilling to upset its Arab clients by directly aiding the growth of their enemy. Instead the Israeli government formed a "Committee of Ten" that unsuccessfully tried to persuade Americans to stop aiding the noshrim.[17] A poll in 1976 showed that 46% of Israelis favored freedom of choice and 43% were opposed.[18] Austrian chancellor

Bruno Kreisky declared his opposition to any attempt to limit the movement or destination of transmigrants. He told reporters, "Whoever comes to Austria to emigrate somewhere will not only be admitted, but we watch also that his right to choose the country to which he wants to go should be respected."[19]

Orbach summarized the key questions facing the Soviet Jewry movement at the end of the 1970s over the noshrim issue. If Zionist concerns were addressed, forcing all Soviet Jews to go to Israel, would the movement alienate international opinion? On the other hand, would allowing Soviet Jews freedom of choice result in assimilation in the Diaspora? And what if non-Jewish ethnic groups in the USSR demanded their rights, wouldn't Soviet authorities clamp down on all who wanted to emigrate?[20]

In 1979, 66% of the 50,000 Soviet Jews arriving in Vienna chose the United States, Canada, Europe, Latin America, Australia and New Zealand. The debate over Zionism vs. human rights soon became moot as emigration was drastically curtailed by the Soviets, first to stem the brain drain, and then in early 1980 as a counter-reaction to American outrage over the Soviet invasion of Afghanistan.[21]

As permission to emigrate started increasing again under glasnost in 1987 the controversy was rekindled and Jewish Agency officials were heard commenting, "If HIAS didn't exist more people would go to Israel."[22]

SUPPORT IN AMERICA

HIAS remained true to its mission to assist Jews and others whose lives are in danger, derived from the teaching *Kol Yisrael arevim zeh bazeh* (all Jews are responsible for each other, see Chapter 2). HIAS worked closely with agencies throughout the United States to assure resettlement assistance to the Soviet Jews, and to advocate for U.S. policies that would provide generous, humanitarian support. In 1976 HIAS, along with the Council of Jewish Federations and National Association of Jewish Vocational Services, sponsored a national symposium at the Baltimore Hebrew College on the integration of Soviet Jews into the American Jewish community.

From 1974 through 2006 HIAS assisted over 410,000 Jewish refugees from the former Soviet Union in finding new homes in America. More than 185,000 or 45% of them settled in New York City, especially in the Brighton Beach neighborhood of Brooklyn where Russian is heard and bilingual signs are seen on every street. The area's nickname, "Little Odessa", is most appropriate because both Brighton Beach and Odessa, Ukraine, are situated on seashores and about half of the Soviet Jewish émigrés in America came from Ukraine. Chicago, Los Angeles, San Francisco, Philadelphia and Boston became home to 90,000, or 23% of the refugees. Over the three decades of resettlement Jews from the former Soviet Union settled in nearly every state.[23]

Omaha, Nebraska, was a success story. After grassroots activist Shirley Goldstein visited Russia in 1972 and 1973 she formed Omaha's Free Soviet Jewry Committee, served on the UCSJ board of directors, and worked with the local Jewish Federation, the media and members of Congress in the campaign to enable Jews to get out of the Soviet Union.[24] Declaring, "If we're going to get them out, we ought to get some here," she launched a program to resettle Soviet Jews in Omaha. Miriam Simon worked with her in that program and they secured support from the Jewish Federation to sponsor a few émigré families in 1975. Simon recalled, "As many families as we said we would take, HIAS would send. In the beginning, the families that came had no relatives here. They didn't know a soul. They couldn't find us on a map." Local residents welcomed the newcomers at the airport, donated clothing, furniture and basic needs for their new apartments, and also helped them learn English and find jobs.[25] Over the past thirty years 250 families from the former Soviet Union have settled in Omaha and, aided by Jewish Family Services, integrated with the 2,000 Jewish families who already resided there.[26]

Other Jewish communities eagerly welcomed Soviet Jews and,

from 1979 through 1989, received federal funding in the form of matching grants of up to $1,000 per refugee, which was increased to a $50 weekly cash allowance for each adult refugee in 1998.[27] Prior to the establishment of that program some Jewish communities were strapped for funds and limited acceptance of refugees to those who had first-degree relatives in the community.[28]

Newly arriving Soviet Jews were met at Kennedy Airport by HIAS Port Reception team members who were there for the arrival of every flight from Rome and Vienna. In keeping with a tradition that was unbroken since the inception of HIAS, they made sure each émigré had home hospitality in New York before heading for the community where they would resettle. In 1990, when Soviet Jews were allowed to choose the country to which they would emigrate in Moscow, buy their own tickets and fly from there to various American cities, crises of misinformation and misunderstanding were commonplace. To remedy the situation HIAS developed a database of emergency phone numbers for every Jewish community in the United States. That system worked successfully for about two years until the International Organization for Migration arranged charter flights of HIAS-sponsored refugees to America and provided information on all arrivals.[29]

Jews from the FSU who immigrated to Canada were assisted by Jewish Immigrant Aid Services of Canada, which was founded in response to the massacres of Jews in pogroms in Russia and Ukraine in 1918 and 1919. According to a Jewish census taken in 2001 there were 28,000 Jews from the FSU or 7.5% of the Canadian Jewish population of 370,000. Most had settled in Toronto, Montreal and Vancouver.[30]

DEALING WITH THE INS

Since 1980 the INS has defined a refugee as a person who is outside his or her country "and who is unable or unwilling to return… because of a well-founded fear of persecution, on account of race, religion, nationality, membership of a particular social group, or political opinion."[31] From 1980 to 1988 the INS, in a practice called presumptive eligibility, accepted as refugees all Soviet Jews who wanted to immigrate to the United States.[32] But getting an entry visa to the United States was far from instantaneous; processing INS forms, fingerprinting, and medical exams could take months. The émigrés would stay in boarding houses in Rome for two weeks and then be taken to the seaside resort towns of Ladispoli and Santa Marinella, where they could find apartments at moderate cost.[33]

From August 1988 through September 1989 delays increased as the INS reviewed every application for refugee status and interviewed each applicant.[34] The INS was staffed to handle about 8,000 applications a year, but three times that number were languishing in Ladispoli. Furthermore, visa rejections at the U.S. Embassy in Rome were increasing – 36% of those who applied were turned down in March 1989. Approvals and rejections appeared to be subjective, depending on which INS officer handled the case. Many of the officers were unfamiliar with conditions in the Soviet Union and doubted whether Jews were really being persecuted.[35] Others didn't believe that some applicants had been compelled to join the Communist Party.[36]

Congressman Barney Frank, who succeeded Father Drinan (Chapter 18) called the overcrowded situation in Ladispoli "appalling." Jewish leaders met with attorney general Dick Thornburgh to convince him that there was enough historical evidence to prove that Soviet Jews had well-founded fears of persecution. Thornburgh disavowed the charges and asserted that the U.S. government had insufficient funds and refugee slots. By October 1989 the backlog of visas and interviews reached 40,000.[37]

Dorit Grossman Perry, a young attorney from San Francisco, was hired by HIAS in 1989 as European legal counsel to work in Rome and prepare a special request to the INS to treat all Soviet Jews as a part of a class certified to have a well-founded fear of persecution.[38] Concurrently a team of attorneys representing the Soviet Jewry Legal Advocacy Center and the Union of Councils for Soviet Jews testified in Congress that Jews and non-Jews who wished to emigrate from the Soviet Union were branded as "traitors," had been persecuted and had a well-founded fear of persecution. They recommended establishment of an additional 25,000 refugee slots and $100 million to fund them.[39]

In November an amendment, initiated by Senator Frank Lautenberg (D-NJ) and supported by American Jewish leaders, was enacted and immediately required immigration officers to grant refugee status to Jews and Evangelical Christians from the Soviet Union with no requirement to demonstrate proof of persecution on an individual basis.[40] The INS also implemented a new practice which required Soviets holding exit visas issued after October 1, 1989, and seeking to immigrate to the United States to apply at the American Embassy in Moscow, not in Vienna or Rome.[41] This procedure combined with the Lautenberg Amendment resulted in an approval rate of 90% for Soviet Jews applying in Moscow for refugee status.[42] In 1990, as Soviet Jews started flying directly from Moscow to the United States, apartments in Ladispoli were vacated and some of the HIAS offices in Rome were shut down.[43]

POST-SOVIET DEVELOPMENTS

The uncertainty that prevailed in 1991 and 1992 as the Soviet Union unraveled led to the greatest migration of Soviet Jews to the United States. HIAS supported 46,000 arrivals in 1992 and, in a concerted effort to resettle them outside New York, worked with 150 Jewish community federations.[44] The Lautenberg Amendment received extensions every year and enabled nearly 470,000 Soviet Jews, Evangelical Christians and other religious minorities to gain refugee status in the United States.[45] But after passage of the Immigration Act of 1996, which provided harsh penalties for illegal immigrants, the INS started scrutinizing all applicants for refugee status more closely than in earlier years. The denial rate for Jewish applicants had been 4% in 1996 and rose to 41% in 1998. An "unconscionable" example of INS action was a case cited by William Cohen, president of the Center for Human Rights Advocacy, based in Boulder, Colorado. Gena and Luba Magidin immigrated to the United States after their home in Belarus had been smeared with anti-Semitic graffiti on several occasions, but Luba's parents were denied refugee status because they couldn't prove that they were the targets of anti-Semitism. The INS offered "parole" status to applicants who didn't qualify as refugees and had families in the United States, but the Magidins' combined income was not sufficient to qualify as sponsors at that time.[46]

According to Cohen, "since the economic crisis and the collapse of the ruble which struck Russia in August 1998, anti-Semitic expressions by leading politicians and elected officials, aimed at demonizing and scapegoating Jews, and, ultimately, at driving them out of Russia, have dramatically accelerated." He also pointed out that "militantly anti-Semitic groups such as Russian National Unity have grown in size and popularity." Cohen criticized the "impotence and indifference of law enforcement agencies" in Russia, leaving Jews vulnerable to anti-Semitic discrimination, violence and persecution.[47]

Mindful of the risks facing Jews in the former Soviet Union, HIAS began operating in Moscow in 1994 to assist refugees in the FSU bound for the United States and other countries. HIAS personnel in Moscow and Kiev provide classes and counseling in Russian to assist refugees in INS (now Department of Homeland Security) procedures and prepare them for resettlement in America.[48]

Part Five

American Legislative & Diplomatic Support 1972–2007

.

CHAPTER TWENTY-TWO

u.s. Congressional Action Links Trade to Emigration

Nixon was on a roll. His trip to China in February 1972 – the first by an American president – was the highlight of his career and his most enduring success. Now he was ready to move in the direction of détente with the Soviet Union. The world was eager to see it happen after witnessing the horrors of the Vietnam War and fearing a nuclear holocaust. Could the u.s.a. and ussr find a peaceful solution to the Cold War and stop draining their resources in an escalating arms race? And how about normalization of bilateral trade? But senator Henry Jackson had other ideas. He questioned the rationality and morality of trusting an oppressive regime that would not trust its own people.

LINKING TRADE AND HUMAN RIGHTS – AN AMERICAN TRADITION

In *The American Movement to Aid Soviet Jews*, William Orbach points out that "since the American revolution, pressure groups have played an influential role in u.s. politics."[1] Efforts on behalf of Russian Jewry go back to Abraham Lincoln's administration when trade restrictions were imposed on Russia in response to pogroms perpetrated against Jews.[2]

In 1869 protests from former President Ulysses S. Grant persuaded tsar Alexander II not to expel 20,000 Jews from Bessarabia (then part of southwestern Russia, now part of Moldova). Ten years later Congress, prompted by tsarist restrictions on ownership of land by Jews, adopted a resolution calling upon the president to amend treaties between the United States and Russia.[3] A grateful Russian Jew wrote to congressman Samuel Cox, the resolution's sponsor, "In this hour of all but hopeless misery, groaning under the yoke of cruel and heartless despotism, we turn to the West..." Reacting to the pogroms and expulsions of Jews that had "shocked the moral sensibilities of the Christian world," in 1892 Congress refused to allocate funds for transporting food to Russia.

The American Jewish Committee, established in 1906 out of concern for Jews who were being persecuted in Russia, campaigned for abrogation of the 1832 Russo-American Commercial Treaty. But, in a preview of what would occur six decades later, former President William Howard Taft and secretary of state Philander Knox in 1911 argued for "quiet and persistent endeavor" rather than harming American commercial interests and subjecting Russian Jews to the risk of additional hardship. Congress overwhelmingly voted to abrogate the treaty and Russian officials reacted with anger and astonishment, failing to understand how "a moralistic crusade could dictate political action."[4]

SOVIET BLUNDERS AND CONGRESSIONAL REACTION

Totally disregarding the worldwide outrage that would follow, a Soviet court in Leningrad on Christmas Eve in 1970 imposed death sentences on two Jews, and harsh prison sentences to their nine associates (Chapter 8) for a hijacking that never got off the ground. Their desperation to emigrate and the continuing history of discrimination against Jews in the Soviet Union inspired the u.s. House of Representatives to adopt, by a vote of 360–0, with 70 abstentions, a resolution calling upon the president to "request the Soviet government to permit its citizens the right to emigrate."

The Union of Councils for Soviet Jews announced its support for legislation that would include a guarantee of the right of free emigration in any exchange or agreement with the Soviet Union. Following up on a request from UCSJ Board member Si Frumkin (Chapter 16), congressman Thomas Rees (D-CA) proposed an amendment to the Export Administration Act that would authorize the president to prohibit export of commodities or information to any nation that prohibited freedom of religion or emigration. While the UCSJ lobbied to get the Rees Amendment into both Democratic and Republican party platforms during the 1972 conventions, Jerry Goodman of the National Conference on Soviet Jewry told Rees that he could not support the bill. Although Rees had thirty sponsors his amendment died in the House Banking and Currency Committee.[5]

On August 3, 1972, the Soviet regime decreed that persons wishing to emigrate would have to pay a tax ranging from $5,000 to $25,000 depending on their educational level. It had a twofold purpose: to discourage emigration since few Soviet citizens could afford the exorbitant fee, and to generate foreign currency if Jews in the West were willing to pay the ransoms. Protests from the free world immediately followed, along with pledges to boycott the ransom that brought back memories of Nazi tactics. However, some prominent refuseniks like Herman Branover (Chapter 2) were able to emigrate once their taxes were paid for by Western donors. Pablo Picasso gave art critic Igor Golumshtock about $20,000 so that he could emigrate.[6]

The NCSJ viewed the education tax as one of the most onerous acts they had ever seen. Emergency leadership meetings were held in September 1972 with the staffs of key congressmen including senators Jackson, Javits and Ribicoff. Richard Perle of Jackson's staff argued for legislation that would link trade benefits to emigration.[7] Jackson personally came to the meeting in Washington to whip up support in the Jewish community, passionately imploring the 120 people at the session to "Get behind my amendment!" and "Let's stand firm!"[8] NCSJ executive director Jerry Goodman and chairman Richard Maass supported the proposal as the most effective way to get the Soviets to rescind the education tax.[9]

SENATOR HENRY JACKSON INTRODUCES
AN "AMENDMENT WITH TEETH"

Henry "Scoop" Jackson, born in Everett, Washington, the son of Norwegian immigrants, was elected to the U.S. Senate in 1952 and served in that body until his death in 1983.[10] As a young congressman in the closing days of World War II he traveled to Europe and witnessed the liberation of Buchenwald. This made an indelible impression on him that affected him for the rest of his life.

Jackson was an unswerving adversary of the Soviet Union and an advocate of a strong national defense, often at odds with many of his fellow Democrats. A trip to the Soviet Union in 1956 left him with the notion that the "Soviets would act like hotel burglars trying any doors that were open but passing those that were locked." He also stated, three decades before Reagan and Shultz came to the same conclusion, that "the essence of the Soviet dilemma [is that] the Kremlin must grant some freedom in order to maintain technological growth, but allowing freedom undermines Communist ideology and discipline."[11]

Jackson was also an ardent supporter of Israel and the right of Soviet Jews to emigrate, and often spoke at Soviet Jewry rallies, including the 1971 Chanukah event at New York's Madison Square Garden that filled 20,000 seats.[12] When Soviet leaders enacted the education tax he was outraged and declared, "If Norway had had the same policies as the Soviets, my father would never have been able to come to America."[13]

Jackson formally introduced his amendment "with some teeth in it" to the East-West Trade Relations Act of 1971 on October 4, 1972. He had seventy-three co-sponsors. The amendment would prohibit granting "Most Favored Nation" status or participation "in U.S. credit and investment guarantee programs unless that country permits its citizens the opportunity to emigrate to the country of their choice" and would require the president to judge and report on each nation's compliance.[14] In the next congressional session Jackson reminded his colleagues that the Universal Declaration of Human Rights holds that "everyone has the right to leave any country, including their own…" as he reintroduced his amendment on the Senate floor on March 15, 1973.[15]

A group of former Soviet Jews who had immigrated to Israel and called itself the "Action Committee of Newcomers from the Soviet Union" wrote a letter of support to Jackson, declaring that "your amendment…is the proper way to obtain free emigration from the USSR, and today stands alone against the quiet diplomacy recommended by circles in both American and Israeli governments". They pointed out that they had sent a cable to Nixon expressing their hope that he "will be remembered in history as the rescuer of three million Jews."[16]

In the House of Representatives a similar bill was introduced by Rep. Charles Vanik of Ohio (Chapter 5) in early January 1973 with 144 co-sponsors.[17] Mark Talisman, one of Vanik's aides, met with Richard Perle and Morris Amitay, an aide to Ribicoff, to coordinate strategy. Wilbur Mills, the powerful chairman of the House Ways and Means Committee, was brought on board as a co-sponsor by Vanik and the measure became known as the Jackson-Mills-Vanik Amendment (Chapter 5). The NCSJ sent letters to 1,000 Jewish leaders nationwide, who in turn solicited letters of support from their contacts.

THE BATTLE OVER JACKSON-VANIK

At the end of 1972 it became clear to the Kremlin that they would not get any favorable trade deals as long as the education tax was in force. They first announced that applicants over the age of 55 would be exempt from the tax and the rates were being reduced for others according to their ages.[18] In March 1973 George Shultz, then secretary of the Treasury, met with Brezhnev in Moscow and learned that Soviet Jews were now being permitted to leave without paying the tax.[19] The minutes of a Politburo meeting on March 20, 1973, reveal that Brezhnev was furious that his instructions to stop collecting the tax were not carried out, and that Zionists in America "have incited a campaign around the Jackson Amendment and around the bill on granting us most favored nation status." He then gave Andropov orders to: "Let out 500 individuals of secondary importance, but not academicians. Let them say they weren't charged anything. Take a couple of engineers with higher education, with no relation to secrets, for instance from the food industry, and let them go, but not from the defense industry. Let them go for free. This is a temporary tactical maneuver."[20]

Enabling Soviet Jews to emigrate without paying the tax convinced the Nixon administration to agree to lend the Soviets $200 million from the Export-Import Bank for purchases of industrial equipment, as well as the signing of a protocol on joint scientific projects. Furthermore, administration officials started trying to persuade senators that quiet diplomacy would be more effective than the Jackson-Mills-Vanik Amendment. They even suggested to Jackson that his home state of Washington could benefit by the sale of Boeing jet planes to the Soviets. Perle viewed this effort as "crude blackmail". Senators who had supported Jackson remained committed to the amendment but, in the House, Mills was satisfied that the education tax had been rescinded and withdrew his co-sponsorship.

Nixon turned to his closest friends in Jewish leadership circles, Max Fisher and Jacob Stein, and called them to a White House meeting with a dozen other Jewish leaders on April 19, 1973. Nixon tried to assure the group that emigration would continue at rates of 32,000 to 35,000 per year.[21] Fisher, Stein, and Charlotte Jacobson, who headed the American Section of the World Zionist Organization, followed up with a statement applauding Nixon's efforts to get the education tax suspended, as well as his concern for the plight of Soviet Jews, but didn't include any reference to the Jackson-Vanik Amendment.[22]

Perle contacted his friends and received immediate support from Malcolm Hoenlein of the GNYCSJ (Chapter 15) as well as from the SSSJ (Chapter 6), and UCSJ (Chapter 17).[23] Within the Jewish establishment, Goodman and Maass of the NCSJ remained committed to the Jackson-Vanik Amendment and were encouraged to do so by Nechemia Levanon (Chapters 3 and 15). However, they had to await the conclusion of a heated meeting of the Presidents' Conference (of which Stein was chairman) before announcing their support.[24] According to Glenn Richter (Chapter 6), some Jewish establishment leaders were thrown out of Jackson's office after they asked him to compromise on the amendment.[25]

Jackson's campaign was bolstered in September 1973 when he inserted a letter from Andrei Sakharov into the *Congressional Record*. The letter to Congress expressed unequivocal support for the Jackson Amendment and asserted that the amendment would not "imperil international détente." Sakharov warned, "The abandonment of a policy of principle would be a betrayal of the thousands of Jews and non-Jews who want to emigrate, and of the hundreds in camps and mental hospitals, of the victims of the Berlin Wall. Such a denial would lead to stronger repressions on ideological grounds. It would be tantamount to total capitulation of democratic principles in face of blackmail, deceit, and violence. The consequences of such a capitulation for international confidence, détente and the entire future of mankind are difficult to predict."[26] Sakharov was denounced in *Pravda* for opposing Soviet policies, and received threats against himself, his children and his grandchild.[27]

While the Jewish world was distressed by the Yom Kippur War in Israel, Kissinger met with Fisher, Stein and Maass and told them Congress should eliminate all trade bill restrictions because he needed Soviet cooperation to achieve a cease-fire. Some Jewish leaders also feared that support for the Jackson-Vanik Amendment could jeopardize arms shipments to Israel. Jackson invited them to a meeting and denounced Nixon's exploitation of Jewish leaders.

Vanik's amendment passed in the House on December 11, 1973, by a 319–80 vote, and the administration's strategy turned to negotiating with the Senate. After a meeting with Gromyko in May 1974, Kissinger told Jackson and Ribicoff that the Soviets would allow 45,000 Jews to emigrate annually. Jackson asked for 60,000.[28] On August 9, Nixon, facing impeachment over the Watergate scandal, resigned and Gerald Ford was sworn in as president. In his first meeting with the new president, ambassador Anatoly Dobrynin told Ford in confidence that the Soviet government was willing to give him an unwritten guarantee that 50,000 Jews would be able to emigrate each year. Ford met with Jackson, Javits and Ribicoff and told them of the confidential offer. After Jackson demanded written assurance, Kissinger wrote a letter indicating that the Soviets would permit 60,000 Jews to leave each year. Jackson released Kissinger's letter to the press, igniting anger in the Kremlin and indignation from Ford and Kissinger toward Jackson.[29]

As Congress was nearing adjournment for 1974, the Trade Reform Act with the Jackson Amendment intact passed in the Senate by a vote of 77–4. A House-Senate Conference Committee recommendation to accept the Senate version was approved by both houses on December 21. Former President Ford signed it on January 3, 1975.[30]

Vanik described the legislative action as "a clear mandate on the part of the Congress in the United States in support both for human rights and decency." Jackson declared, "I hope the loud and clear message of the House will be heard in Moscow and that the Soviet government will come to realize that the American people, above all, are committed to a human détente – to the free movement of men and ideas on which a more stable and lasting peace must be based."[31]

RAMIFICATIONS OF THE JACKSON-VANIK AMENDMENT

The Jackson-Vanik Amendment can be summarized as prohibiting certain commercial relations with a country that engages in practices prohibiting or severely restricting free emigration of its citizens and specifically identifies such practices as:

1. denying its citizens the right or opportunity to emigrate;
2. imposing more than a nominal tax on emigration or documents required for emigration;
3. imposing more than a nominal tax or other charge on a citizen as a consequence of his desire to emigrate to the country of his choice.

Other than being modified by specific new legislation, the JVA prohibition can be temporarily rendered inoperative, and remain so, by Executive action if the president reports to Congress either:

1. that the country does not engage in any of the listed practices (i.e., fully complies with JVA freedom-of-emigration requirements), and resubmits such reports semiannually;
2. or, that he has determined that a waiver of the prohibition will substantially promote the objectives of JVA and that he has received the country's assurances that its emigration practices will lead substantially to those objectives, and, under an annually renewable waiver authority, issues such waivers.[32]

News of the passage of JVA thrilled refuseniks like Mark Azbel, who wrote, "Who would have thought it possible that one of the great superpowers would take serious economic risks for the sake of a disinterested ideal? Our hopes had soared: we were practically positive that now the emigration would be much simplified."[33] But official reaction from Kremlin leaders came quickly. Viewing JVA as an insulting stick rather than a carrot, they repudiated the trade agreement of 1972 and suspended repayment of the Soviet Lend-Lease debt to the United States. Furthermore, emigration figures for 1974 fell by 42 percent to 20,000 compared to 35,000 the previous year, and the pace of permissions fell off even more in 1975 when only 13,000 were allowed to emigrate. Petrus Buwalda, the Dutch ambassador to the USSR, concluded that JVA "in the short run failed in what was, after all, its purpose: to increase the flow of emigration of Jews from the Soviet Union."[34]

Although the Soviet leaders rejected JVA, president Nicolae Ceausescu of Romania accepted its provisions and entered into a trade agreement with the United States in April 1975. Ford exercised his waiver authority to grant MFN status to Romania after its government approved the emigration of 1,250 of its citizens and resolved issues of divided American-Romanian families.[35]

The adoption of JVA was a great boost to Jackson's aspirations to become president of the United States. He campaigned for the Democratic nomination in 1972 and 1976 with strong Jewish support, especially among activists in the UCSJ like Irene Manekofsky (Chapter 14). Ambassador Dobrynin complained that "Jackson kept escalating his demands in an appeal to the Jewish constituency for his presidential aspirations."[36] But Jackson was out of touch with the post-Vietnam cultural revolution within the Democratic Party, underestimated Jimmy Carter's popularity, and lost the 1976 nomination battle to him.[37]

THREE DECADES OF JACKSON-VANIK

While Carter campaigned for the presidency claiming to share Jackson's "deep concern over the protection of human rights and freedom of emigration in the Soviet Union and throughout the world," within his first year as president, officials of the Carter administration asked Congress to alter JVA to eliminate the requirement of Soviet emigration assurances.[38] The American Jewish Congress in 1978 supported a bill that would allow credits to the Soviet Union for the purchase of American grain. This bill was opposed by all the Soviet Jewry support groups, and they reprimanded the AJCongress for abandoning JVA at a time when Sharansky and other prominent dissidents and refuseniks were being imprisoned and placed on trial.[39]

In 1979 Congress voted to extend MFN status to China and Hungary, but not to the Soviet Union. However, Senator Adlai Stevenson III introduced a bill that would modify JVA by authorizing the president to grant a waiver for five years if he decided that emigration had increased sufficiently. Emigration of Soviet Jews was increasing appreciably with 31,000 exit visas issued in 1978 and 230 a day in mid-1979. It appeared that the USSR was carrying out a two-pronged policy: easing up on emigration in hopes of winning trade concessions and derailing JVA, but clamping down on dissidents who were monitoring human rights abuses (Chapter 13). Stevenson's bill was designed to mollify Soviet sensitivity with respect to interference in their internal affairs. Activists in the United States and refusenik leaders like Alexander Lerner in the Soviet Union were adamant in their opposition to any softening of JVA.[40] There was also the question of Senate ratification of the Strategic Arms Limitation Talks (SALT II) treaty that Carter and Brezhnev had signed in June 1979. Both issues were removed from the Senate agenda in the wake of the Soviet invasion of Afghanistan six months later.[41]

The thawing of the Cold War during Gorbachev's regime brought JVA back to life. As emigration rates started increasing from about 1,000 a year through the early 1980s to 9,000 in 1987 and 26,000 in 1988, the NCSJ board voted to support a one-year waiver of JVA if the Soviets agreed to sustain the high emigration level, settle outstanding refusenik cases, and legislate a reformation of emigration procedures. The SSSJ and UCSJ denounced the NCSJ decision and demanded that Soviets be judged on deeds rather than words. No waiver was granted to the Soviets until December 1990, when emigration was at a rate of 12,000 a month. And even at that rate, the administration of George H.W. Bush held the USSR to only a six-month waiver.[42]

After the Soviet Union collapsed in 1991 Russia and the other successor states were granted MFN status on an annual basis; JVA served to assure continued compliance with unrestricted emigration policies.[43] Russia's "full compliance" was formally recognized in September 1994 by former President Bill Clinton. Russian president Boris Yeltsin was delighted to be granted MFN status and Export Import Bank credits without annual review. [44]

Dobrynin published his autobiography the following year, and in it called the education tax a "stupid political move" that had "only helped stir up the debate in the United States linking Jewish emigration to trade with the Soviet Union."[45] Furthermore, he admitted, "Our biggest mistake was to stand on pride and not let as many Jews go as wanted to leave. It would have cost us little and gained us much. Instead, our leadership turned it into a test of wills that we eventually lost."[46]

In 2002 the administration of President George W. Bush asked Congress to legislate the exemption of Russia from JVA, but Congressman Tom Lantos (D-CA), the chairman and founder of the House Human Rights Caucus, expressed serious concerns. He insisted that Russia first adopt procedures assuring the right of its citizens to emigrate and travel freely, and also to outlaw hate crimes and combat incitement to violence against ethnic groups.[47] In April 2007 U.S. trade representative Susan Schwab said that "Congress does not see fit to lift the Jackson-Vanik Amendment and that the World Trade Organization is not prepared to admit Russia".[48] Meanwhile Ukraine has fared better. On March 23, 2006, Bush signed a bill that authorized permanent normal trade relations with Ukraine, including removal of JVA requirements. In his address at the signing ceremony, Bush recognized Ukraine's "Orange Revolution" as "a powerful example of democracy for people around the world."[49]

The Orange Revolution began in November 2004 after the Ukrainian presidential election had been compromised by massive corruption, voter intimidation and election fraud. Hundreds of thousands of orange-clad protesters demonstrated in Kyiv (Kiev) until Ukraine's Supreme Court annulled the election results and ordered a revote that would be monitored by international observers. The revote resulted in a resounding victory for Viktor Yushchenko, who was favored by the protesters.[50] The

Orange Revolution showed that international pressure and non-violent protest could help restore the rule of law and human rights to a totalitarian regime just as the Jackson-Vanik Amendment and the Soviet Jewry movement had done during the previous generation.

CHAPTER TWENTY-THREE

The Congressional Human Rights Caucus

Kathryn Cameron Porter was furious. Before being allowed to depart from Leningrad she was strip-searched. All of her body orifices were inspected. As she boarded the plane, bruised, and feeling violated and abused, she wondered, "If Soviet authorities could do this to me, an employee of president Reagan's administration and the wife of a congressman, what could they do to someone else?"

In 1982 Porter was a special assistant for international affairs to the secretary of energy; her husband, John Edward Porter, was serving his first term as a Republican member of the House of Representatives from Illinois. Lynn Singer, then president of the UCSJ, asked the Porters if they would be willing to join a group of other congressmen and their wives and staff members on a mission to the Soviet Union.[1] John Porter recalled that during his election campaign in 1980, Congressman Tom Corcoran, another Illinois Republican, had mentored him and said, "When you get to Congress you really ought to look into the situation involving

Human rights in the Soviet Union, especially the inability of people who want to emigrate to leave that place."

The Porters joined the group and were moved by the plight and courage of the refuseniks they met in Moscow and Leningrad. Their group was harassed and followed by the KGB in both cities. When the militia tried to disrupt a meeting in a Leningrad apartment, claiming there were scandalous things going on, the fearless refuseniks quipped: "Yes, free speech is going on here. It's very scandalous!"[2]

On departure day at the Leningrad airport terminal Kathryn Porter tried to protect a female member of the tour group who was being meticulously searched and badgered by Soviet agents. She linked arms with her and yelled for assistance from the American Consulate. A consular official arrived and helped the woman get on the plane but Porter was taken to a small cement block building and put through the strip-search ordeal.

Once they were aloft and out of the clutches of the "Evil Empire", the Porters pondered their options. How could they bring the power of the U.S. Congress to bear to prevent further abuses of human rights?[3] John pointed out that "there are a lot of caucuses in Congress, but no caucus for the thing that is the essence of what America stands for, and that's human rights." They agreed that a caucus was needed to help the people they had just visited, as well as others across the world who were being abused. They also felt that a human rights caucus would be most effective if it were bipartisan, and that Tom Lantos of California, the only Holocaust survivor ever elected to Congress, would be the most appropriate Democrat to approach to co-found the caucus.

Lantos enthusiastically agreed to co-chair the Congressional Human Rights Caucus with John Porter.[4] It was set up in early 1983 to defend the rights of individuals as defined in the United Nations Declaration of Human Rights.[5] Lantos and Porter buttonholed their colleagues and got ten members to join the caucus, the minimum number required for official status with its own office and staff. It wasn't easy. Human rights was not yet a popular issue for many congressmen and the American Jewish establishment's aversion to activism discouraged some Jewish members of the 98th Congress from joining the fledgling caucus.[6]

The caucus augmented the work of the Commission on Security and Cooperation in Europe (CSCE, often called the "Helsinki Commission") which was created in 1976, and included a bipartisan contingent of nine senators and nine members of the House of Representatives, as well as liaison members from the State Department.[7] They were responsible for official U.S. diplomacy at the "Humanitarian Basket" (Chapter 13) international meetings of the Helsinki Process, and often brought NGO representatives including NCSJ and UCSJ leaders into their delegations. In the late 1980s the combination of NGO monitoring and advocacy and relentless pressure from the State Department was extremely effective in achieving the release of prisoners and refuseniks.[8]

Unlike the Helsinki Commission, the caucus didn't have jurisdiction to write legislation or hold hearings with sworn testimony, but it was authorized to hold briefings on human rights issues for members of Congress.[9] The CHRC briefings were held weekly, often with notable outside witnesses such as the Dalai Lama, since the scope of the caucus was global.

From its inception the CHRC was highly focused on Soviet Jewry and worked closely with the UCSJ. Since 1976 the UCSJ had sponsored the "Congressional Call to Conscience" in the form of a weekly insertion of a refusenik case history into the *Congressional Record* by a member of Congress.[10] The UCSJ also supported the work of the CHRC by publishing the "Congressional Handbook for Soviet Jewry" in 1988 and 1989. This resource provided details on contacting refuseniks and their relatives in America, writing to Soviet officials, and stimulating activity within the State Department on behalf of specific refuseniks.[11]

Members of the CHRC became personally involved, often telephoning individual refuseniks from their offices, visiting them during trips to the Soviet Union, and meeting with Soviet officials and diplomats in Moscow, Washington, New York or San

Francisco to appeal for the release of prisoners and for exit visa for refuseniks.[12] According to Lantos, "the possession of a congressman's business card could serve as the only means of protection that a Soviet Jewish family had against harassment and intimidation."[13] His colleague Representative Steny Hoyer (D-MD) who chaired the Helsinki Commission, points out that anonymity was dangerous for refuseniks and dissidents, but if they were well known and the West raised their issues to high visibility, it was more difficult for the Soviet Union to act adversely against them.[14]

As the CHRC grew, the wives of twenty-five of its members organized the Congressional Wives for Soviet Jewry, whose purpose was to "adopt" refusenik families. Annette Lantos adopted the Sharansky family because Avital had been a role model when Tom and Annette Lantos initiated their campaign on behalf of Raoul Wallenberg, who had saved not only their lives, but the lives of thousands of other Hungarian Jews. Wallenberg, a young Swedish diplomat posted to Budapest during World War II, courageously issued Swedish passports to Jews who otherwise would have been sent to Auschwitz. When the Soviet Army occupied Hungary Wallenberg was arrested and never heard from again. Annette Lantos organized the International Free Wallenberg Committee in 1978 with the thought, "If Avital could make Sharansky a household name, maybe I could do the same for Wallenberg."[15]

Like the Senate Wives for Soviet Jewry that had started in 1978, the Congressional Wives for Soviet Jewry strived to bring the pressure of public opinion to bear on the Soviet government to live up to its commitments regarding human rights. Both groups held letter-writing campaigns, conducted silent vigils in front of the Soviet Embassy, and met with refuseniks in the Soviet Union.[16] In April 1984 they met with their counterparts from Canada, Israel, the Netherlands and the United Kingdom in Washington at the International Conference of Parliamentary Spouses for Soviet Jewry.[17] Tom Lantos was the chairman of a congressional committee that met with members of European parliaments twice a year. The refusenik issue was frequently on his agenda for these sessions.[18]

By the mid-'80s the CHRC grew to over 230 members, Democrats and Republicans of all persuasions, and was the second largest caucus in the House of Representatives.[19] During 1987 all 435 members of the House participated in some activity in support of human rights. In addition to its concerns regarding Soviet Jewry, the CHRC monitored, reported and protested election abuses in Haiti, political executions in Tibet, and persecution of Hungarian minorities in Romania. Briefings were also held on abuses in numerous countries such as forced prostitution and child soldiers.[20]

After the first three years of the Gorbachev regime, while there were encouraging improvements in human rights in the USSR there were new concerns of anti-Semitic activities as manifested by the desecration of Jewish cemeteries and threats of programs voiced by the Pamyat organization that claimed to have 20,000 members in Moscow alone.[21] The CHRC held a press conference at the Capitol in 1988, with former refusenik Lev Shapiro as a witness, to condemn the ominous trend and urge the Soviet government to condemn Pamyat's anti-Semitic campaign.[22]

The following year the Porters returned to Moscow with a delegation headed by Steny Hoyer for the U.S. Helsinki Commission, and found the human rights environment somewhat warmer than they had expected.[23] There was a reception at the American Embassy that was attended by several dozen refuseniks and dissidents who spoke at length to members of Congress about their frustrations dealing with the bureaucracy.[24] Kathryn Porter was moved to tears by the plight of an elderly woman with health problems who was told she couldn't leave and see her children in Israel because her husband had been a nuclear scientist decades earlier. Porter screamed at a Soviet official, "Is this what your policy is all about; that you won't let this woman go?"[25]

John Porter brought a list of 704 refuseniks and said, "These people have been refused exit visas for years, some of them for up to fifteen years. What you can do is release them." All of them received their exit visas before the delegation left Moscow.[26] One by one, the Congressional Wives for Soviet Jewry joyously welcomed their adopted families and organized receptions for them when they visited Washington.[27] Senator Barbara Boxer (D-CA) recalls the "great joy when Judith Ratner was given permission to emigrate to Israel and rejoin her husband, Leonid, after 15 or 16 years of waiting, and when Boris Kelman was given permission to leave the Soviet Union and come to America after a similar wait. When you see the results of your work and the happiness in the faces, it's a wonderful feeling."[28]

The CHRC faced a new internal challenge in 1994 when the Republicans regained control of Congress. Motivated by his "Contract With America" campaign to reduce the size and scope of government and to limit the influence of lobbyists on Capitol Hill, incoming Speaker of the House Newt Gingrich (R-GA) abolished twenty-eight congressional caucuses, including the CHRC.[29] Gingrich, however, admired the work of the CHRC and agreed to "look the other way" as Lantos and Porter designated one staff member in each of their offices to run the caucus without a budget. Unfortunately the CHRC files were not digitally archived and most caucus records were lost in the transition.

When Porter retired from Congress in 2001 he was replaced as co-chairman of the CHRC by Frank Wolf (R-VA).[30]. In November 2003 Lantos co-founded the bipartisan Russia Democracy Caucus to "focus congressional attention on the vanishing vestiges of freedom in Russia." The arrest in Moscow of business leader Mikhail Khodorkovsky, described by Lantos as a pioneer in "Western-style corporate transparency and governance", triggered Lantos's action.[31]

The CHRC became a bicameral institution in 2006 with Senators Sam Brownback (R-KS) and Tim Harkin (D-IA) joining Lantos and Wolf as co-chairmen. The enlarged caucus also established working groups for two major issues of concern: Russia and international religious freedom. Lantos vigorously pursued these issues until he died of cancer on February 11, 2008.

Looking back at the work of the CHRC a quarter century after the fateful flight from Leningrad, John Porter recalls that his most rewarding experience in Congress was his involvement with the Zunshine family.[32] In 1984 Zachar Zunshine was sentenced to three years in prison camps for anti-Soviet slander because he had written to Soviet authorities and traveled to Moscow to stage a public demonstration to demand permission to emigrate after being refused in his hometown of Riga.[33] His wife, Tatiana, worked relentlessly to secure his release, and her situation came to Porter's attention in 1986. When he phoned her, Tatiana said that she was certain that the KGB was following her and had bugged her telephone line. Porter then declared, "Whoever is listening: This is John Porter, a member of the United States House of Representatives and I will go to the floor of Congress to tell all that I have heard." When he got the name and telephone number of the warden of the prison where Zunshine was held, Porter, together with Senator Paul Simon (D-IL), telephoned the warden and said, "We know you're holding Zunshine on trumped-up charges and we're going to do everything we can do to get him released." CHRC people kept at it until Zunshine was out of prison.[34]

The Zunshine family arrived in Israel in March 1987 and visited Porter in Washington five months later.[35] Porter accompanied them to see president Reagan proclaiming the 200th anniversary of the signing of the United States Constitution. With tears streaming down their faces, the newly freed Zunshines and Congressman Porter heard Reagan declare that the U.S. Constitution was "the oldest written instrument of democratic rule in the world still in use, and it continues to proclaim and to shape a peaceful revolution toward freedom and prosperity for all mankind."[36]

Co-sponsors of the Congressional Fast and Prayer Vigil confer with Avital Sharansky after a press conference. Left to right: John Edward Porter (R-IL), Edward Mrazek (D-NY), Avital Sharansky. Photo credit: UCSJ Archives.

Congressional wives attempt to deliver flowers to the Soviet Embassy on behalf of Jewish women refuseniks on International Women's Day. The Soviets refused to accept the flowers. Left to right: Kathryn Porter, Annette Lantos and Jane Gephardt. Photo credit: UCSJ Archives.

CHAPTER TWENTY-FOUR

Advocacy from Reagan's State Department

C aptain Ronald Reagan was absolutely appalled by the films he was viewing. As World War II drew to a close the future president was producing training films for the Army Air Force and his assignment included editing films of the death camps that were shot by military cameramen and correspondents who accompanied the American liberators. This was his introduction to the Holocaust and his gut feelings told him that these horrors must never happen again and must not be denied.[1] Disregarding military regulations, he took copies home to show to any skeptics. Indeed, four years later he felt compelled to show the films to a house guest who questioned the stories of the Holocaust. As president, Reagan confided this incident to secretary of state George Shultz and expressed his intention to be strongly involved in the cause of human rights.[2]

AMBASSADOR KAMPELMAN GOES TO MADRID

While Reagan was campaigning for the presidency, former President Jimmy Carter asked Max Kampelman, a lawyer in private practice – a strong civil rights advocate with a staunch anti-Soviet outlook – to go to Madrid as head of the u.s. delegation to the Helsinki Review meeting commencing on November 11, 1980. Kampelman had come to Washington in 1949 to serve on Senator Hubert Humphrey's staff and while in that office they both became interested in the cause of Soviet Jewry.[3]

Former secretary of state Henry Kissinger told Kampelman, "You shouldn't go to Madrid; it's just a Soviet operation." Arthur Goldberg, who had served on the u.s. Supreme Court and as u.s. Ambassador to the United Nations, advised him, "My time in Belgrade (in 1977) was the most miserable experience of my political life. Max, don't go." Despite the negative advice, after reading the Helsinki Final Act, Kampelman agreed to go to Madrid.[4] When Reagan was elected president, Kampelman, as an ambassador, submitted his resignation. The secretary of state designate Alexander Haig then told him that both he and the president-elect wanted Kampelman to continue leading the delegation in Madrid.[5]

At preliminary meetings Kampelman served notice on both NATO allies and leaders of the Soviet delegations that he would be quite specific about Soviet aggression in Afghanistan and human rights violations. At first the Soviets objected to bringing up particular violations of human rights, but they soon complained about what they considered human rights violations in the United States, thus legitimizing discussion of the topic. In Belgrade, at the previous CSCE meeting only the United States had been willing to mention the names of victims of Soviet repression. Three years later in Madrid, thanks to Kampelman's persuasion, twenty-three of the thirty-five participating nations named specific victims. Even the foreign minister of neutral Sweden came forward to cite the name of his country's courageous victim – Raoul Wallenberg.[6] During the course of the meeting Kampelman and his delegation brought up over one hundred cases of Soviet human rights violations[7] including jailed Helsinki Watch Group monitors and such high-profile refuseniks as Brailovsky, Lerner, Nudel and Shcharansky.[8]

When Kampelman first went to Madrid he expected the meetings to be concluded in about three months; they actually dragged on for three years, during the tenures of three secretaries of state: Edmund Muskie, Alexander Haig and George Shultz.[9] On a visit to Washington in 1982, Kampelman told Shultz that he felt the Soviets were losing their campaign for public opinion against NATO's deployment of Pershing and Cruise missiles in Europe, and that he thought the Soviets, wanting to end the Madrid meeting soon, would be willing to accept our NATO proposals. Kampelman then added, "But I'm not satisfied any longer with what we've asked for." Shultz replied, "Explain yourself; what would satisfy you?" "Getting people out of jails, out of mental hospitals and out of the Soviet Union," was Kampelman's answer. Shultz retorted, "Am I hearing you correctly? Do you want to change the rules in the middle of the game?" They agreed that there was risk that America's allies, especially West Germany, would object and the Soviets would explode.[10] Shultz pondered the issue for a minute and then said, "It's above my pay-grade, Max."

After a phone call to Reagan the two were on their way to the Oval Office. Reagan heard the proposal and said, "All right, we'll go with it."[11] He mentioned that he was eager to see the release of the seven Siberian Pentecostal Christians who had taken refuge in the U.S. Embassy in 1978 after being harassed by the Moscow police and denied the right to freely practice their religion.[12] Reagan also pointed out that upon assuming the presidency, in his first meeting with Soviet Ambassador Dobrynin, he had suggested that if the Soviets wanted to have good relations with him, safety of the Pentecostals would be the appropriate signal. His suggestion was ignored. As Shultz and Kampelman were leaving, the president pulled a sheet of paper from a drawer and said, "Max, see what you can do to help these people." It was a list of Jewish refuseniks.[13]

Kampelman returned to Madrid and immediately went to talk privately with KGB General Sergei Kondrashev, the No. 2 man in the Soviet delegation. Kondrashev spoke English well and got along amicably with Kampelman. As expected, he exploded in anger when Kampelman said, "I have a message for you to deliver to Moscow from the president of the United States..."[14] Kondrashev apparently did deliver the president's message to Soviet general secretary Yuri Andropov via his KGB channel, rather than through the Foreign Ministry, and a few days later informed Kampelman that he was authorized to negotiate on the condition that only Kampelman, Shultz and Reagan would be involved. Furthermore, no other delegation, and no Soviet officials, including Ambassador Dobrynin and foreign minister Gromyko, would be informed.

Kampelman was able to give Kondrashev a list of the names of the seven Pentecostals in the embassy and eighty members of their families in Siberia. The negotiations went smoothly and all the Pentecostals on the list were allowed to leave the Soviet Union for Germany via Israel in July 1983. Additionally, a large number of human rights activists were released from prison and hundreds were permitted to emigrate.

Reagan kept his part of the bargain and did not crow about the successful resolution of the thorny Pentecostal issue that had persisted for five years. He and Shultz wondered if it represented a desire on the part of Andropov for improved relations between the superpowers. A month later the Madrid conference concluded with all thirty-five nations signing an agreement that included a statement that future meetings would deal with human rights including family reunification. It seemed to Kampelman and Shultz that the Soviets were willing to engage in real negotiations and that there was now a "minithaw" in the cold war.[15]

One thing Kampelman and Kondrashev could not accomplish in Madrid was to get Natan Shcharansky released from prison. After many meetings Kondrashev proposed that Shcharansky sign a letter saying, "I hereby request that I be released from prison on the grounds of poor health." Kondrashev also agreed to arrange for Ida Milgrom, Shcharansky's mother, who had not seen her son for eighteen months, to bring the letter to him in prison. The Soviets set a date for her, as well as Shcharansky's brother

Lenya, to visit. She called Andrei Sakharov and he recommended that Shcharansky sign the letter as the Soviets were not asking for an admission of guilt. Avital, however, consulted rabbis in Israel and they were against his signing any letter.[16] When Milgrom brought the letter to Shcharansky he asked how Avital felt, and Milgrom truthfully revealed that Avital was opposed. Shcharansky then said he would not sign because that would have been a "terrible blow to our spiritual unity." Asking the authorities to show humanity, he continued, meant acknowledging that they represented a legitimate force that administered justice.[17]

Although Shcharansky remained in prison until well after the end of the Madrid meetings, Kampelman proved that the Iron Curtain was not impenetrable. Through his diplomatic savvy and negotiating skills Kampelman drilled a few pilot holes that would be enlarged in subsequent years, culminating in the collapse of the Soviet Union.

GEORGE SHULTZ PUTS HUMAN RIGHTS ON THE AGENDA

George Shultz came into the office of secretary of state with a familiarity of the Soviet Jewry issue and a track record of accomplishment in removing an obstacle to emigration. As secretary of the treasury in 1973 he met with Brezhnev in Moscow and while extending a loan of $101 million from the Export-Import Bank, asserted that further progress in trade and credit would be dependent upon Soviet liberalization of emigration. Shultz reported that Soviet officials showed "both the spirit to try to solve the problems and the willingness to tackle them in very real terms."[18] A week after the meeting the Soviets announced that forty-four Soviet Jews with college degrees would be allowed to emigrate without paying the onerous education tax and that, in fact, the tax would no longer be levied.[19]

Soon after he became secretary of state, Shultz met with Avital Shcharansky, finding her "intense and compelling." He was frustrated that he could not promise her anything other than saying "The president and I will never give up on pressing the cause of human rights and the case for your husband's release."

In preparation for meetings in New York with foreign minister Gromyko, Shultz gathered information on human rights issues, especially the situations of refuseniks and prisoners of conscience. During their initial meeting Shultz brought up the human rights issues of Jews, dissidents, divided families, and imprisoned Helsinki Watch Group monitors. Gromyko responded, "Is it so important that Mr. or Mrs. or Miss so-and-so cannot leave such-and-such a country? I would call it a tenth-rate question." Gromyko, or "Mr. Nyet," as he was nicknamed in the West, continued by lecturing Shultz on dealing with the internal affairs of a sovereign nation.[20]

Nevertheless, Shultz felt that human rights had a place in his diplomatic efforts and developed a "four-part agenda" for future meetings with Gromyko and Yuri Andropov, who had just become general secretary after Brezhnev's death. The agenda consisted of arms control, bilateral issues, regional issues and human rights. Reagan, keenly interested in progress on all four broad items, encouraged Shultz to apply the agenda to his meeting with Gromyko in Stockholm in January 1984.[21] During this meeting Gromyko again accused Shultz of trying to interfere in Soviet "internal affairs" after Shultz brought up human rights and cited the cases of Shcharansky, Nudel, Begun and Sakharov. However, for the first time in their meetings Gromyko actually listened to what Shultz was saying.[22]

A year later, after the deaths of Andropov and Chernenko, the Politburo chose Mikhail Gorbachev as general secretary. Shultz and vice president George H.W. Bush attended Chernenko's funeral where they had an opportunity to meet Gorbachev who, according to Shultz, made a good first impression as a man who "displayed a breadth of view and vigor."[23] In reporting to Reagan they endorsed prime minister Margaret Thatcher's view that Gorbachev was "a man one could do business with." [24]

Reagan and Gorbachev agreed to hold a summit meeting in Geneva in November 1985 and Shultz went to Moscow to meet

Gorbachev's new foreign minister, Eduard Shevardnadze. Shultz raised the issue of human rights at the start of their first session. Shevardnadze listened attentively and, unlike his predecessor, without expressing any resentment. The summit in Reykjavik the following year was considered a failure because no arms control agreement was signed, but Shultz considered it a breakthrough because there was a verbal agreement that human rights would be recognized as a regular part of the agenda for future meetings.[25] Shevardnadze told Shultz, "We might do some of the things you want, but not just to please *you*, but only if it makes sense from *our* standpoint."

Shultz thought about that remark and talked it over with Reagan. At their next meeting Shultz said to Shevardnadze, "The world is changing; we are moving into a knowledge and information age. In a closed, compartmented society you won't be able to take advantage of all that it has to offer. In order to be part of a new age you have to loosen up; you have to change the relationship between the state and the people in the state and allow more interaction not only within your country but with people in other countries. The right to emigrate is something connected with that. But you should let them have a freer situation where people don't particularly want to emigrate. I know people prefer to live in their own country if they can."[26]

While Shultz and Shevardnadze were beginning to develop a warm relationship, they each faced considerable opposition from leaders in their respective capitals. Shultz had differences with secretary of defense Caspar Weinberger, CIA director William Casey and others in the National Security Council. At the Kremlin Shevardnadze constantly fought with defense and KGB chiefs as well as his colleagues in the Foreign Ministry. Both Shevardnadze and Gorbachev saw themselves as the vanguard of liberal thinking against the entrenched Politburo. Shevardnadze, as foreign minister, accumulated considerable face time with Western leaders and Gorbachev was greatly influenced by Shevardnadze's reports on their ideas.[27]

Shultz had the additional requirement of convincing America's allies to support his administration's positions. He skillfully sold his NATO colleagues on a strategy of linking human rights to arms control that could yield significant progress at an upcoming CSCE conference in Vienna.[28]

After two days of meetings with Shevardnadze in Moscow in April 1987, Shultz went to Spaso House, the American ambassador's residence that had been a mansion in the days of tsar Nicholas II, for a Passover Seder with about forty refuseniks. Donning a white kippah, he greeted each one warmly.[29] For some, like the Slepaks, he brought photographs of grandchildren in America they had not yet seen. He was moved and inspired to be with all these courageous people who obviously could be identified with the Israelites who had been enslaved in Egypt, and declared, "You are on our minds; you are in our hearts. We never give up, we never stop trying, and in the end some good things do happen. But never give up, never give up. And please note that there are people all over the world, not just in the United States, who think about you and wish you well and are on your side."[30] At the end of the Seder the traditional refrain, "Next Year in Jerusalem" was amended by the refuseniks to "This Year in Jerusalem." And by Passover 1988 nearly all of those present at the Spaso House Seder had finally received permission to emigrate – a miraculous achievement that no one had dared to predict.[31]

The event was broadcast worldwide by the American press and TV corps in Moscow. Wyatt Andrews of CBS was there and recalls that he "felt proud to be an American" that evening.[32] Gorbachev was well aware of the presence of refuseniks at the American Embassy Seder, and when Shultz brought up human rights at a meeting the next day, Gorbachev steamed, "You always meet with those lousy Jews! We have some good Jews here. Why don't you meet them?" Shultz replied, "Well, if you think they're lousy Jews, have I got a deal for you! I've got a great big airplane over there and every one of my staff and the reporters would gladly give up his or her seat to let me take them off your hands if you don't want them. No problem!" Gorbachev had no response other than a standard Soviet attack on the treatment of minorities in the United States.[33]

Five months later it was Shevardnadze's turn to come to Washington for meetings that would follow the four-part agenda, including an agreement on intermediate-range nuclear forces and the resolution of conflicts in Afghanistan, Angola, Cambodia and Nicaragua. With regard to human rights, Shevardnadze didn't need to be prodded; he stated that Soviet policy had changed and he asked Shultz to "give me your lists [of people who wish to be allowed to emigrate] and we'll be glad to look at them."[34] Shultz was gratified to hear that and provided lists given to him by Morris Abram, the chairman of the National Conference on Soviet Jewry, whom Shultz considered to be "his rabbi" on Soviet Jewry.[35]

Ida Nudel's name had been on a list that Shultz gave Shevardnadze in 1986 during the negotiations to secure the release of journalist Nick Daniloff. Shultz had met her sister, Lena Fridman, in Jerusalem several times. Moved by her plea, he told Fridman, "Only among Jews would a sister – not a mother or a wife – fight so devotedly and desperately for the freedom of her sister." On October 15, 1987, Shultz took a phone call from Jerusalem and heard the voice of Ida Nudel saying, "I'm in Jerusalem! I'm home."[36] Shultz recalls: "I could hardly speak for the rush of emotion I felt. This was one of the most moving moments in my years as secretary of state."[37]

At the beginning of 1988, as more and more refuseniks and prisoners were being released, restrictions against religious practice were being removed, broadcasts from the West were no longer jammed, and freedom of expression internally was growing under glasnost, it was clear that the Soviet attitude on human rights was moving in the right direction. Shultz went to Moscow to continue negotiations and to prepare for the Moscow summit scheduled for May 30. He also visited Andrei Sakharov and Elena Bonner in their walk-up apartment. Sakharov told Shultz that he "must insist on Soviet departure from Afghanistan and on the release of prisoners of conscience. Then you should welcome a human rights conference in Moscow. Such a meeting, lasting several weeks, would call real attention to this subject in Moscow, where the attention could make a difference."[38]

Shultz retired at the end of the Reagan administration and his last trip as secretary of state was in January 1989 to the concluding session of the CSCE review meeting in Vienna where he signed a treaty on conventional arms in Europe and agreed to a conference on human rights in Moscow.[39] His efforts over seven years in that position resulted in enormous progress in Soviet human rights.

Two years later Shultz was honored with the Paul Flory Flynn Humanitarian Award by the Bay Area Council for Soviet Jews. In his acceptance speech he reflected on meeting with refuseniks and talked of them as "people who are oppressed and who are not getting a fair shake." He continued, "I want to buck them up in every way that I can, or at the minimum let them know that people are paying attention, and want to help, and won't give up, will keep after it. And by the time you get through, you have a different attitude entirely. You find that these people have lifted *you* up, because what you feel is a strength of character, a spirit, a set of inner convictions that nobody can repress, and it gives you faith and courage and lifts you up yourself."[40]

RICHARD SCHIFTER – SHULTZ'S POINT MAN ON HUMAN RIGHTS

Like his law firm partner, Max Kampelman, Richard Schifter was a liberal Washington D.C. attorney with family roots in Czernowitz, Ukraine.[41] Schifter was tapped by his good friend, conservative U.N. ambassador Jeane Kirkpatrick, to serve as a member of the U.S. delegation to the U.N. Commission on Human Rights in 1983. Two years later he was appointed assistant secretary of state for humanitarian affairs, succeeding Elliott Abrams, who had served during the first Reagan administration.[42]

Schifter's initial counterpart in the Soviet Union was Yury Kashlev, appointed by Shevardnadze to head the newly created Department of Humanitarian and Cultural Affairs within the Foreign Ministry. Kashlev wasted no time in showing the West that the Soviets were taking a new tack on emigration. He traveled to Washington and announced a new policy that allowed emigration for persons who had a spouse, parent, child or sibling living abroad.

In another reorganization of the Foreign Ministry, Shevardnadze appointed deputy foreign minister Anatoly Adamishin to negotiate with Schifter on human rights issues. Schifter met him in Moscow just prior to the Seder attended by Shultz and his entourage, and found Adamishin hard-nosed but civilized; they soon became cordial colleagues. Adamishin's expertise had been in African affairs, so Schifter's concerns about political prisoners in the Gulag and in psychiatric hospitals, and limits on emigration and freedom of religion, were all new to him.

Four months later Schifter returned to Moscow for consultation with Adamishin in preparation for the next Shultz-Shevardnadze meeting on arms control and human rights. Adamishin advised him to discuss matters of emigration at the Foreign Ministry's Office of Consular Affairs. At that office Schifter was able to get a status report on the case of each individual who had relatives in the United States and wanted to emigrate to the United States. However, when he brought out his list of people interest in emigrating to Israel he was told that the cases of those who wished to emigrate to a third country were no business of the United States. Schifter protested that the first person on his list, Prof. Nahum Meiman, had a daughter who had emigrated to the United States and was living in Colorado. They then pulled out Meiman's file and said his refusal was due to possession of classified information. Schifter's response that Meiman hadn't worked with classified matters for thirty-five years (Meiman had done mathematical calculations for Sakharov's H-Bomb project) didn't change the situation. Schifter then returned to Adamishin's office and told him that Shultz would be unhappy to hear about what transpired at the Consular Affairs office. Schifter asserted that when someone wanted to emigrate, the Helsinki Final Act guaranteed that right, regardless of where the person wanted to live.

The next day, when Schifter was leaving Moscow, a junior official from the Foreign Ministry named Oleg Krokhalev greeted him at the airport terminal in perfect English (with a Brooklyn accent) and escorted him to the VIP lounge for tea. Krokhalev said, "That list of names which you wanted to discuss at the Foreign Ministry, please let me have a copy." Schifter was certain that Krokhalev had been sent by his superiors, and on the plane Schifter composed a cable to Shultz about his meetings at the Foreign Ministry and the surprise visit from Krokhalev. His bottom line was "I think they just blinked," invoking secretary of state Dean Rusk's phrase from the 1962 Cuban missile crisis.[43]

Schifter's assumption proved accurate at the September meeting when Yuri Reshetov, another Foreign Ministry official, told him, "We have decided that if a Soviet citizen wants to separate himself from the motherland and live abroad, it is no longer a domestic case. It is therefore a case which we can discuss with you." It was clear that Shevardnadze had convinced Gorbachev that progress on arms control was too important to be impeded by obstinacy on human rights. Reshetov, however, advised Schifter against overloading the bureaucracy with long lists of refuseniks, and also asked him to make sure American negotiators avoided harsh criticism that would embarrass Soviet diplomats. The Foreign Ministry was now becoming the advocate within the Soviet government for freer emigration.[44] Shevardnadze's intervention accomplished a relaxation of the requirement that a *vysov* (letter of invitation) come from a close relative. Schifter found that Shevardnadze's team was willing to work on the cases of long-term refuseniks and that the Foreign Ministry was an ally engaging in battles with the real adversaries in the Defense Ministry and the

KGB, especially if the American envoys provided credible talking points for special cases.[45]

A typical day for Schifter in Moscow found him in two roles. During business hours he would be going head-to-head with Soviet Foreign Ministry officials in hard-nosed negotiations, and in the evening he would visit refuseniks – with a warm and caring heart, acting as a surrogate rabbi or psychiatrist to those who continued to be denied exit visas after years of waiting.[46]

But one case just wouldn't go away and Schifter decided to concentrate on it at a meeting with Shevardnadze in May 1989. The foreign minister's jaw dropped when Schifter told him about Slava Uspensky, a nineteen-year-old from Moscow, who was refused permission to emigrate because his grandmother allegedly possessed state secrets. Irina Voronkevich, the grandmother, was a professor of biology who had worked on plant diseases for the Agriculture Ministry until her retirement in 1976. She never did classified work, but the institute in which she worked housed a biological warfare laboratory and this proximity may have tainted her and caused the KGB to put a special label on her file: "Neither she nor any member of her family should ever leave the country."[47] The continued refusals were in violation of a new decree that put a five-year limit on refusals for security reasons.[48] Two months later Shevardnadze's intervention resulted in exit visas for Slava (now Hillel) and for his parents, Igor and Inna Uspensky. Prof. Voronkevich was refused permission to emigrate twice after that but was able to travel to Israel as a tourist and never returned to Russia.[49]

Schifter continued to serve in the foreign policy positions until 2001 and observed the new administration under former President George H.W. Bush and secretary of state James Baker, initially taking a harder line with the Soviets. Shevardnadze visited Baker's ranch in Jackson Hole, Wyoming, during the summer of 1989. They bonded and were able to revive the spirit of cooperation that had been evident when Shultz was in office.[50]

Reflecting on the events from a historical perspective, Schifter concluded that in 1989 "basic steps were taken which dismantled the system of government created by Lenin, elaborated on by Stalin, and maintained by Stalin's successors."[51]

President Reagan welcomes Natan Sharansky to the White House in 1986. Official White House photo.

George Shultz, a staunch supporter of the State of Israel, at the "Israel Corner" of his office in the Hoover Institution, Stanford, California, 2003. Photo credit: Philip Spiegel

Part Six

Post-Soviet Campaigns
1991–2007

CHAPTER TWENTY-FIVE

Help My People Go

The dominoes finally fell, but they were East Bloc dominoes falling to the West; not, as every American president since Eisenhower had feared, democracies of the Free World being drawn into the orbit of Communism.[1] During 1989 the Soviet government allowed Poland and Hungary to legalize multiparty systems, and renounced its habit of intervening in the internal affairs of its Warsaw Pact allies. By the end of the year the Warsaw Pact had collapsed and the Berlin Wall was demolished. It quickly became clear to Soviet Foreign Ministry officials that all of Eastern Europe would "go." Indeed the spirit of "socialism with a human face" that Czechoslovakia had experienced briefly in 1968 was re-emerging throughout the region. To Communist diehards in the Kremlin who accused him of "losing" Eastern Europe, Shevardnadze, with Gorbachev's endorsement, argued that democracy in Eastern Europe and improved relations with the West were in Moscow's interest.[2]

The departure from Moscow's influence was contagious. In Lithuania, which borders on Poland and had been independent from 1918 until 1940, the Communist Party voted to break its ties with the Soviet party in 1989, and declared its independence in

1990. Gorbachev's visit to Lithuania was to no avail; its leaders were determined to pursue an autonomous course.[3] The Kremlin recognized Lithuania, Latvia and Estonia as independent states on September 6, 1991, a few days after the attempted coup that nearly toppled Gorbachev's regime. Later that year Ukraine, Armenia, Georgia and Moldova moved to detach themselves from the Soviet Union, and leaders of Belarus, Russia and Ukraine met secretly to disband the USSR and create the Commonwealth of Independent States. By the end of the year Gorbachev announced that he would step down as Soviet president. Over the Kremlin the new white, blue and red flag of Russia replaced the old hammer and sickle.[4]

A PARADIGM SHIFT FOR THE SOVIET JEWRY MOVEMENT

During those two tumultuous years of breakup in the Soviet Union an unprecedented 400,000 Jews were permitted to emigrate. Diplomatic relations with Israel were restored, and, after twenty-three years, the Netherlands Embassy in Moscow ended its task of issuing Israeli visas. The staff of the newly established Israeli Consular Mission was phased into the process and handled an overwhelming average of 915 visas each day.[5]

But how many of the visas would actually be used for aliyah? In 1989 only 15% of the 85,000 Soviet Jews who arrived in Vienna with Israeli visas immigrated to Israel.[6] Where Soviet Jews should reside was the subject of countless debates between Israeli and American Jewish leaders. The Israeli view expressed by Mendel Kaplan, the chairman of the Jewish Agency for Israel Board of Governors, was, "We, in Israel, do not believe in Soviet Jews going to America – moving them from one diaspora to another. To us, the freedom of choice that American Jews spoke about was a negation of Jewish leadership. I believe that Jews should have a right to move anywhere they want. But they should not use public Jewish funds to do it. The Soviet Jews were being referred to as refugees, which means that the person is politically persecuted and has nowhere else to go. But every Jew in the world does have a place – Israel. The word "refugee" is offensive to us because Israel is their home." On the other hand, Martin Kraar, the Council of Jewish Federations executive vice president, stated, "The position that the majority of us took was that Soviet Jews were entitled to decide where they wanted to live. We may have preferred that they go to Israel, but we were not going to rescue them from an oppressive society, bring them into a free one, and then make their first personal decision for them. Nor once they entered the United States were we going to allow them to become destitute. Our mandate is to help Jews and so our services were made available to them."[7]

The debates simmered down somewhat when it was determined that the United States government would accept no more than 40,000 Soviet Jews as refugees each year. The burden then shifted to Israel to absorb the rest. Furthermore, there was no time to lose because of the great uncertainty over the possibility of the entire emigration enterprise being overturned by a KGB-backed coup or a nationalist retrenchment accompanied by a resurgence of repression and anti-Semitism.[8] The mantra of the Soviet Jewry movement was no longer *Let My People Go*; it now was a desperate cry of *Help My People Go*.

THE RIDE TO FREEDOM

In a June 1990 phone call to the Boston Action for Soviet Jewry office, Ida Nudel quantified the logistical problem. She reported that only 200 to 300 Jews were being taken out of the USSR while thousands were waiting for transportation; some of them were sleeping on the floor of the airport in Moscow. Nudel offered a possible solution involving buses taking Jews from Kishinev to Bucharest at a cost of only $87 per person, and asked if ASJ could provide funds for the project.[9] The Ride to Freedom project was originally the brainchild of several individuals working in the *Gush Emunim* (Bloc of the Faithful movement, religious Zionists who advocated settlement in the West Bank) including Uri Ariel, Yehuda Etzion, and Yisrael Harel. A committee headed by Natan

Sharansky (at the time a leader of the Soviet Jewry Zionist Forum in Israel) along with Shmuel Azarkh (also of the Zionist Forum), as well as several Israeli army officers was set up to provide oversight and critical support.[10]

Zale Anis, a transportation expert and ASJ board member, reviewed the plan and summarized it in a memo to the UCSJ. He revealed that Elie Weiss, the owner of Tour Tevel, an Israeli company that specializes in travel to Eastern Europe with offices in Kishinev and Chernovtsy, had negotiated with Soviet authorities for Intourist buses to carry passengers from Kishinev to Bucharest, KGB security for the buses within Soviet territory, and police vans preceding and following each bus convoy. There were also trucks transporting the household belongings of each family. Weiss was prepared to treat impoverished Soviet Jews with the same respect and consideration his firm extended to well-heeled clients.

Anis also pointed out that the Jewish Agency was spending $300 per person to fly Jews from departure points in the USSR to Budapest or Bucharest, where they would be turned over to agency representatives who would facilitate their boarding of El Al planes bound for Tel Aviv. Although the $87 per person cost of getting out of the Soviet Union by bus was a real bargain the agency refused to underwrite the operation. Anis then called upon the UCSJ to provide funds for the "Ride to Freedom" and also for underwriting the costs of shipping each family's household belongings.[11] The UCSJ responded by campaigning relentlessly for the Ride to Freedom program.[12] ASJ raised $100,000 for the project during its first year.[13] Additional funding came from the Greater New York Conference for Soviet Jewry.[14]

Anis heard from his contacts in Israel that the Lishka enthusiastically supported the project. Lishka officials apparently felt that the Jewish Agency's efforts to facilitate emigration were not sufficiently effective. The Ride to Freedom project was seen to have distinct advantages. One feature was the ability of the émigrés to take personal belongings with them. The agency had restricted the amount of baggage that the *olim* (new immigrants) could take out. Many Soviet Jews, concerned that they would face economic deprivation in Israel, wanted to bring with them items they could sell to help support themselves in their new home. Ride to Freedom's ability to transport belongings was therefore seen as something that would help Soviet Jews who were "on the fence" to make the jump.[15]

However, the Jewish Agency and the Lishka were rivals, and the agency's chief financial officer, Zvi Barak, attempted to discredit the project and limited agency support to only $20 per person, payable when the passenger manifests were verified by the agency.[16] The agency also tried to organize its own busing operation.[17] In essence it was following the successful pattern that Elie Weiss had set up of using local contacts, but lacking Weiss's competence, it chose the wrong local contacts and wound up dealing with criminals. The Jewish Agency's emigration route also failed to provide for transport of household belongings.[18]

The Ride to Freedom program became operational on July 11, 1990, with two buses from Kishinev and two railcars from Chernovtsy.[19] In the next twelve months Ride to Freedom transported 40,000 Soviet Jews out of the USSR to transit points in Eastern Europe, and reached a capacity of 7,000 a month, accounting for about one third of all Soviet Jews making aliyah.[20] Embarkation points were added to accommodate the large Jewish populations in various cities throughout Ukraine, eliminating the need for them to travel to Moscow.[21]

EXITING RUSSIA BY PRIVATE AUTOMOBILE

Buses and trains were not the only means of land transport out of the Soviet Union; some Jews exited in private automobiles. Boris Chernobilsky, a fourteen-year refusenik and Prisoner of Zion, owned a car and wanted to be able to use it in Israel.[22] He had been active in demonstrations with Ida Nudel in the 1970s and helped her when she was exiled to Siberia.[23] He was also involved in human rights, working with Sakharov after the Nobel laureate returned to Moscow at the end of 1986.

Chernobilsky's widow, Leah, recalled that when the family finally got permission to emigrate in 1989, they could sell their apartment but couldn't take out the money. They decided to keep the car and Boris would drive it out while Leah and the children flew to Israel. He exited the Soviet Union via Hungary, continued to Yugoslavia and Greece and then boarded a ferry for Haifa. The drive took a month and enabled Chernobilsky to prolong his newfound feeling of freedom.[24]

While Chernobilsky had permission and proper papers when he drove across the Soviet border, the border crossing for Michael Shapiro and his wife was an illegal escape. Shapiro had a Ph.D. and was a section head in a high-temperature physics laboratory at the Moscow Institute of Technology when he first applied for an exit visa in 1987. Some friends had gotten permission so Shapiro decided to try his luck. At the end of that year he received permission and celebrated. But his joy was short-lived; the permission was for a different Michael Shapiro. He reapplied a few months later and was told that there would be no chance of him leaving the USSR until 1993 at the earliest. Devastated by the prospect of another five years in Russia, Shapiro obtained refugee status from the U.S. Embassy in Moscow, and began to develop a plan to escape.

He and his wife, Irina, became involved with other refuseniks in Moscow and through them met visitors from the Bay Area Council for Soviet Jews, including its executive director, David Waksberg. In 1989, in the privacy of his car, he told Waksberg that he was planning to escape without an exit visa. Over the next fifty weeks, spending about eight hours each day thinking through every aspect of his route and procedure, Shapiro worked out a detailed plan.

He would still be Michael Shapiro, but with a different biography. A Jewish friend in Leningrad who owned a computer business hired him as a technician, and over three months created a new work document that showed a fictitious birth date and birthplace and indicated that Shapiro had not completed college.

The new document was inserted in his passport replacing the original document that showed his degrees, actual work history and his refusals. Shapiro's wife reverted to her maiden name and was also hired by the computer company.

The escape had to take place on a Saturday night when the lowest-level border guards, without computer access, were on duty. The director of the computer firm drove the Shapiros across the Belarussian-Polish border at Brest, claiming to be on a business trip. The Shapiros spent three days in Poland where they met supporters from the human rights movement. Meanwhile the director drove his car back to the USSR a week later via a crossing into Ukraine where there was no record that he had a couple of passengers who had exited the USSR with him at Brest the previous week.

From Poland the Shapiros went to Czechoslovakia, Hungary and finally, freedom in Austria, and at David Waksberg's invitation, immigration to the United States. In all, forty-one people in seventeen countries supported and kept secret the Shapiros' unique and daring escape adventure that ended successfully in November 1990.[25]

THE VOYAGES FROM ODESSA TO HAIFA

Support for about 100,000 Soviet Jews emigrating to Israel came from an unexpected source: generous Christians. Gustav Scheller, a Swiss-born Briton, was inspired by reading the prophecy of Jeremiah 16:15, "But the Lord liveth, that brought up the children of Israel from the land of the north, and from all the lands whither he had driven them; and I will bring them again into the land that I gave unto their fathers." At an Intercessory Prayer Conference in Jerusalem in 1991 Scheller realized that "the land of the north" was the Soviet Union, and he believed he heard God telling him, "Now you can begin helping my people come home."[26]

After traveling throughout Russia, Scheller and his wife, Elsa, founded the Ebenezer Emergency Fund (EEF), and arranged for use of the Russian vessel *Dmitri Shostakovich* to transport Jews from Odessa on the Black Sea to Haifa, a four-day voyage. Jews were also flown from Kazakhstan to connect with Jewish Agency flights to Israel, and from Armenia to connect with sailings from Odessa.[27] Contributors to EEF supported its workforce of 350 and the $150,000 cost of each voyage.[28]

Between 1991 and 2004 EEF made 165 sailings from Odessa to Haifa, and also brought Jews from the former Soviet Union to Israel by airplane.[29] EEF is in partnership with the Jewish Agency, which estimates that 100,000 Jews arrived in Israel with aid from EEF. Scheller, who traveled to Israel more than sixty times, has always declined credit for his enormous humanitarian effort, saying, "All we've done is God's doing. I've just been a tool in His hand."[30]

OPERATION EXODUS

In addition to transporting Jews from the Soviet Union to Israel there was the huge and costly task of absorbing them into the country. The Jewish population of Israel was about four million in 1990. Bringing a million new olim to Israel would be the equivalent of the United States absorbing the entire population of France. Imagine what it would be like to educate, build housing and infrastructure, and create jobs for all of them.

A special General Assembly of the CJF was convened in Miami Beach in February 1990 for the purpose of embarking on a massive fund-raising campaign to help settle Soviet Jews in Israel. The campaign was dubbed Operation Exodus and had a goal of $420 million. Max Fisher, who made his fortune in oil and real estate and had been an advisor to four U.S. presidents, was instrumental in launching Operation Exodus at a breakfast meeting the following month. Prior to the meeting he received a phone call from ambassador Walter Annenberg, a close friend from the Nixon and Ford administrations. Annenberg was eager to help, pledged $5 million a year for three years, and agreed to let Fisher announce his donation at the meeting. Fisher recalled that "Walter's pledge was a real spark. I made the announcement, and by the time coffee was poured, $58 million was pledged to

Operation Exodus."[31] As Soviet Jews in record numbers arrived in Israel, prime minister Yitzhak Shamir exclaimed to Fisher, "It's a miracle!"[32] and Mendel Kaplan announced to the Jewish Agency Board of Governors that "in one decisive step Max Fisher changed the course of Jewish history."[33]

In Israel the huge absorption effort was administered by the Jewish Agency, led by Simcha Dinitz from 1988 to 1994. Dinitz was also chairman of the World Zionist Organization and had been Israel's ambassador to the United States during the Yom Kippur War and the Camp David negotiations.[34] He promoted a change in the way Soviet olim were acclimated to Israel, moving them directly into housing rather than placing them in absorption centers. In May 1991 Dinitz headed Operation Solomon, the single-day airlift of 14,000 Ethiopian Jews to Israel.[35]

Mindful of the uncertainties and delays faced by Soviet Jews who wanted to reunite with family members in America, several former refuseniks living in the United States joined Lithuanian-born former UCSJ president Si Frumkin to create the American Emergency Committee to Save Soviet Jews in February 1991. The ECSSJ declared its intention to set up a database of Soviet Jews who wanted to emigrate to the United States, collect information about regions of greatest danger for Soviet Jews with a view to evacuating them, and to work with Congress and the American Jewish community to expedite the process of family reunification for an estimated 250,000 Soviet Jews. The committee's proposal was supported by the UCSJ, but denounced by Israeli and American establishment organizations, who perceived the proposal as an attempt to undermine the aliyah of Soviet Jewry to Israel. Natan Sharansky, who had been a supporter of UCSJ ideology and tactics, including freedom of choice, criticized the plan, saying that it would only confuse Soviet Jews who might put off aliyah thinking that there was a chance to go to the United States. Yuli Kosharovsky was even more vehement in his rhetoric, declaring that the UCSJ evacuation plan "will accomplish what the Iraqi Scud missile attacks were unable to do: halt Soviet emigration to Israel. They somehow are acting in the same direction as Saddam Hussein. They don't understand what they are doing." By October 1991 the UCSJ had reconciled itself to abandoning the rescue plan.[36]

Aliyah of Soviet olim actually exceeded all expectations of the architects of Operation Exodus. The original goal of needing $420 million was predicated on a need to absorb 250,000 people over five years. Instead 320,000 olim arrived in just two years.[37] Operation Exodus ultimately raised about $950 million and supported the absorption of a million olim over fifteen years.[38]

ON WINGS OF EAGLES

Robert Gottstein, an Anchorage entrepreneur, sold ice to Alaskans. Surely he could convince every Jew in Alaska to contribute to Operation Exodus. As anti-Semitism increased in Russia after Glasnost, Gottstein became determined to do whatever he could to get Jews out of danger. The words "Never Again" profoundly impacted him for two personal reasons[39]: his stepmother, Rachel Gottstein, was a Holocaust survivor, and as an Alaskan Jew, he deeply regretted that a bill to admit 10,000 Jews from Nazi Germany and settle them in Alaska died in a Congressional committee in 1940.[40]

Gottstein and the Alaska Council for Soviet Jewry produced a fifteen-minute videotape for Operation Exodus in 1990. It opened with Rachel Gottstein articulately describing the beatings she received and the horrors she witnessed as a five-year-old in Nazi-occupied Poland. There was recent footage of Soviet Jews, fearing pogroms and anti-Semitic incidents, expressing their anxiety and eagerness to leave the Soviet Union. Holocaust survivor and Congressman Tom Lantos exhorted viewers to contribute to Operation Exodus to fulfill "the greatest experiment in aliyah ever tried."[41] The videotape and postage cost $2.50 a copy, and Gottstein mailed one to each of the 500 Jewish households in Alaska. One hundred families responded with a total of $50,000 in contributions.

Gottstein modified the tape with help from Lantos to produce a version for every state with a Jewish population of more than 100,000, and offered it to the United Jewish Appeal. However its bureaucracy and "Not Invented Here" attitude resulted in rejection of Gottstein's innovation [42]

At a subsequent policy meeting of the American Israel Public Affairs Committee Gottstein met Rabbi Yechiel Eckstein[43], a fourth-generation Orthodox rabbi and graduate of Yeshiva University, who was also interested in supporting Operation Exodus. After organizing conferences with Christian clergymen he founded the International Fellowship of Christians and Jews.[44] In 1986 IFCJ rallied for the release of Soviet Jews.[45]

When Gottstein told Eckstein how frustrated he was over the UJA's rejection of his videotape, Eckstein commiserated and shared how he was also frustrated with the UJA because it was unwilling to accept a $100,000 contribution for Operation Exodus from Eckstein's friend, Rev. Pat Robertson. Eckstein had proposed using Robertson's donation for reaching out to a broad Christian audience and enlisting support for Operation Exodus over Christian television throughout the United States. Gottstein became enthralled with Eckstein's ideas of inspiring evangelicals, and got the project going by contributing $35,000 and masters of his videotape.[46]

The IFCJ project was called "On Wings of Eagles",[47] and its thirty-minute infomercial, "While the Door is Still Open", was hosted by popular singer and television personality Pat Boone. It used footage of Rachel Gottstein and Soviet émigrés from Gottstein's tape and added a historical review of centuries of anti-Semitism in Russia starting with the dreadful reign of Ivan the Terrible in the sixteenth century. Rev. Jerry Falwell invoked Jeremiah's prophecy, and Robertson predicted that the exodus from the north (Soviet Union) would eclipse the exodus from Egypt. Eckstein, in dialogue with Boone, explained that the cost of the aliyah was about $600 a person. Boone said that "this is an extraordinary opportunity that we as Christians can respond to. Jews are returning to the land of Abraham, Isaac and Jacob." He urged viewers to pick up their phones, dial the number on the screen and say, "I *am* my brother's keeper."[48]

The response was excellent, breaking records in ministry television fund-raising, which generally received average gifts of $30; the average gift to the On Wings of Eagles campaign was $130. In 1992 the IFCJ sponsored its first airlift of Russian Jews to Israel. Since the inception of the program 400,000 American Christians have contributed over $100 million toward the resettlement of Soviet Jews in Israel. The contributions were transferred to the Jewish Agency's budget for immigration and initial absorption.

Eckstein, a member of the Board of Governors of the Jewish Agency, travels to the former Soviet Union several times each year. In 1995 he brought a Torah scroll to Uzbekistan, the first one openly delivered to that republic since the Communist Revolution. The IFCJ has also taught Christian leaders how to fight for religious freedom in places like China and Sudan, based on the successful Soviet Jewry model.

In 1997 IFCJ launched the Isaiah 58 program to provide food, clothing, medical help and other lifesaving aid for orphans and elderly Jews who remain in the former Soviet Union. Its name is derived from the passage that is read in synagogues as the Yom Kippur morning *haftarah* (a selected reading from the books of Prophets): "And if thou draw out thy soul to the hungry, and satisfy the afflicted soul; then shall thy light rise in darkness, and thy gloom be as the noonday." Isaiah 58 operates in conjunction with the Joint Distribution Committee and to date has donated nearly $30 million to JDC.[49] Eckstein insists that contributions to the Isaiah 58 and On Wings of Eagles programs come with no strings attached. He refuses to work with anyone who targets Jews for conversion. Eckstein points out that many of the donors to IFCJ programs are firm believers in Genesis 12:3, in which God promises Abraham that He will bless those who bless the Jews.[50]

CHAPTER TWENTY-SIX

Let My People Know

Getting out of the Soviet Union was just the physical or geographic part of the journey to a new home in Israel or America. For many there would also be a spiritual journey back to their Jewish roots. They would learn that being Jewish meant more than having the word *Yevrei* on their identity cards. And for Jews who remained in Russia or the other states that succeeded the Soviet Union, the elimination of an ethnicity line on the cards created a new challenge.[1] Mikhail Chlenov, the president of Va'ad, the Jewish Federation of Russia, called the change "a step toward gradually changing the nature of the Jewish community here." He said, "Now it is going to be a community of Jews-by-choice."[2]

Chlenov is a linguist and ethnographer who joined an ulpan to learn Hebrew in 1971 and started teaching Hebrew in Moscow the following year.[3] He was Sharansky's first Hebrew teacher and he hosted the first Seder Sharansky ever attended.[4] Although he was closely associated with refuseniks and actively supported them, Chlenov never applied to emigrate because his wife is non-Jewish and did not want to leave Russia. He and Lev Gorodetsky remained in Moscow teaching Hebrew and Jewish culture.[5]

In 1989 Chlenov became the co-chairman, consensus leader

and spokesman of the Va'ad of Jewish Organizations and Communities in the USSR that was created to support the growing Jewish revival movement.[6] Following the break-up of the Soviet Union, Chlenov became president of the Russian Va'ad in 1992, and since 2002 has been secretary general[7] of the Euro-Asian Jewish Congress, a body that serves as a umbrella for 1,500 Jewish organizations and 2.3 million Jews in the CIS (Commonwealth of Independent States), the Far East, the Pacific region and Australia. With links to international Jewry the group is developing educational and exchange programs as well as monitoring anti-Semitism. Chlenov has expressed his desire to see the Euro-Asian Jewish Congress foster dialogue and organize interfaith programs, especially with Muslims in the CIS.[8]

Like Chlenov, Zeev Shakhnovsky began learning and teaching Hebrew in Moscow in the early '70s. He and his wife, Leah, were part of a group of young Jews who were energized by Israel's victory in the Six-Day War. They studied Hebrew day and night, not as just another foreign language, but as a "special thing." Inspired by their study of the Torah, the Shakhnovskys became more observant. Keeping kosher meant becoming vegetarians. They made kosher wine from raisins for their friends and themselves. For the prisoners that she was visiting, Zeev gave Ida Nudel Jewish calendars and all the Jewish items he could get his hands on that were brought to the Moscow synagogue by tourists.[9] The Shakhnovskys became refuseniks in 1972 and were not allowed to emigrate until 1989. Once in Israel they began teaching Hebrew to newcomers and beginners.

The Shakhnovksys were part of the minority of about 7% of the Soviet Jewish population who considered themselves religious in a survey of 1,500 Jews compiled by Benjamin Fain in 1976, with assistance from Chlenov. Fain had been a leader of the Tarbut movement and organized a Symposium on Jewish Culture in December 1976. He made aliyah in 1977 and analyzed the data smuggled out of the USSR to Israel.[10] He and Mervin Verbit published the findings seven years later.[11] The data revealed that there was significant interest among Soviet Jews to return to their cultural roots. But as could be expected after generations of spiritual and cultural deprivation, the data predicted that over 900,000 out of a million olim from the former Soviet Union would be secular and lacking in knowledge of Jewish traditions and culture.[12] Feelings of alienation and bewilderment were expressed in a letter to a relative in Moscow from one of the 185,000 Soviet Jews who arrived in Israel in 1990:

> "You know, Tanya, at first these Shabbats were very annoying. Imagine, for two days you sit in your house like an idiot, you don't know where to put yourself. And then one day a friend came over and we decided to go for a walk. He promised to show me a pretty place. The place really was fantastic…We heard singing coming from somewhere. We saw the corner of a table covered with a white cloth. There were candles. We saw well-dressed people in white shirts, slowly singing and dancing. And you know, at that moment I was jealous to the point of tears, that we don't know something important, we don't understand it, we don't feel it, and because of that, we don't appreciate it. Something very important is happening right next to us, but we have no connection to it."

A variety of individuals and organizations are committed to meeting the challenge of educating and inspiring this large population in Israel, as well as the Soviet Jews who immigrated to America and those who remained in the CIS.[13] The situation in the CIS is especially daunting, as a survey of 3,000 Jews in Russia and Ukraine in 1997 found that Judaism was named by only 3% of the respondents as being an important ingredient of Jewish identity, and fewer than 3% of those between the ages of sixteen and twenty-nine identified themselves as religious.[14]

CHABAD – UP FROM THE UNDERGROUND

For over seventy years Chabad maintained a clandestine network of *yeshivas and cheders* in Uzbekistan and other Central Asian republics. Parents who sent their children to these schools knew that they would not receive telephone calls or letters from the undisclosed locations. When asked by neighbors about their absent children, they would fib, "Oh he's out of town visiting relatives."[15]

Rabbi Naftali Estulin, the director of the Chabad Russian Synagogue in Los Angeles, attended his father's secret cheder with seven other boys in one room of their house in Samarkand. Nutrition was minimal but strictly kosher – a diet of potatoes and herring. Estulin's education prepared him for challenges he would meet after emigrating to America, such as inspiring the growth of Chabad religious, social, vocational and summer camp programs available to the 40,000 Soviet Jewish immigrants who now reside in Los Angeles.[16]

There were also Soviet Jewish adults who met covertly with Chabad rabbis and steeped themselves in Chassidic tradition. Rabbi Moshe-Leib Kolesnik is a native of Ivano-Frankivsk in western Ukraine. Prior to becoming a rabbi he was a teacher of Russian. Because his father was a Communist Party official, he was privileged to be sent to Moscow for further studies in Russian in 1984. There he met Rabbi Israel Kogan and for five years secretly studied Judaism.[17] Kolesnik soon became fervently observant, and after Ukraine became independent he returned to Ivano-Frankivsk to serve as rabbi and Chabad emissary for more than 400 Jews in the city and about 25 surrounding communities.[18] Kolesnik managed to get restitution of the city's old synagogue, which earns some revenue by renting part of the building as a jewelry store.[19]

In 1991 the Joint Distribution Committee embarked on a program to financially support and coordinate the restitution of about 1,000 confiscated synagogues in the CIS. They enlisted lawyers, engineers and architects in eight cities, and historian Michael Beizer in Jerusalem to implement the program. More than half of the synagogues were too dilapidated to be maintained or were in towns where no Jews remained. By law synagogues could be turned over only to religious associations, so Chabad was in a good position to regain control of several synagogues in Belarus, Russia and Ukraine.[20]

It takes more than synagogue buildings to revive Jewish communities that had been barred from religious observance for more than seventy years. In 1992 Chabad formed the Rabbinical Alliance to work in partnership with the communities to provide a wide array of educational, cultural and humanitarian services. Fifteen years later the Rabbinical Alliance counted ninety members in thirteen countries.[21] The Federation of Jewish Communities of the CIS became an umbrella group in 1998 to support Chabad activities by building an infrastructure of synagogues, community centers and day schools throughout the CIS.[22] By 2007 the number of FJC-supervised day schools in the CIS had grown to seventy-two (from none in 1989). Additionally, the FJC, with support from the Ohr Avner Foundation established by FJC president Lev Leviev, oversees fifty-four kindergartens, twelve high schools and five universities. The total enrollment of these schools, located in sixty-five cities of the CIS, is 15,000.[23] Leviev made aliyah from Tashkent in 1971 as a teenager, and until his move to London in 2007, was reputed to be the wealthiest man in Israel, having established an international network of enterprises in diamonds, shopping malls, transportation and real estate.[24]

Directing all these educational activities is Rabbi Berel Lazar, the chief rabbi of Russia and the chairman of the Rabbinical Alliance. Born in Milan, Italy, and ordained by the Central Lubavitch Yeshiva in 1987 at age twenty-three, Lazar was dispatched to Russia by the Rebbe, Menachem Mendel Schneerson. His mission was to run the underground yeshivas and religious classes. As the reforms of perestroika and glasnost went into effect, with Zev Kuravsky in 1989 he opened the first Jewish day school in Moscow. During that year he became rabbi of the Marina Rostcha Synagogue in Moscow.[25]

Since 2000 Rabbi Lazar has been considered the chief rabbi of Russia by the FJC and the Chabad movement, and is recognized as such by the Russian government of President Vladimir Putin .

However, Rabbi Adolf Shayevich is regarded as the chief rabbi of Russia by the Russian Jewish Congress, which was established in 1996 to unite about fifty regional Jewish communities. Shayevich was born in 1938 in Birobidzhan, the autonomous region near China, established for Jews by Stalin. As a youth Shayevich was a secular member of the Communist Youth League, but in his thirties, living in Moscow, he became interested in Judaism and was allowed to go to Hungary to attend the only official rabbinic seminary in a Communist country. In 1980 he returned to Moscow and became rabbi of the Moscow Choral Synagogue.[26] Refuseniks despised him as a tool of the KGB, and some referred to him as "the colonel."[27] But in 1988 Shayevich used his influence with the Kremlin to welcome the re-entry of the Joint Distribution Committee to Moscow after an absence of nearly fifty years. Taking advantage of the climate of perestroika and glasnost, the JDC focused its efforts on importing books for teaching Hebrew and Jewish history, setting up Judaica libraries and holding concerts of Jewish music that attracted thousands of people.[28] By 2005 the JDC helped create 184 libraries throughout the CIS with collective holdings of close to a million books, and assisted in the expansion of Jewish studies at 100 state-sponsored universities and at the Jewish universities in Moscow and St. Petersburg.[29]

Further compounding the rivalry between Lazar and Shayevich is Rabbi Pinchas Goldschmidt, and the Moscow Jewish Religious Community, which he has headed since 1996, and calls him the chief rabbi of Moscow. Goldschmidt, originally from Switzerland, came to Moscow from Israel to head the Choral Synagogue. In 1991 he and his wife opened Moscow's largest Jewish day school and started building a network that now includes a rabbinical court, burial society, two cemeteries, two yeshivas, two kosher restaurants, three soup kitchens and a weekly Torah seminar. As infighting flared among the chief rabbis and their supporters Goldschmidt was denied a visa to return to Russia from a trip to Israel in 2005.[30] Following an international lobbying campaign he was given a one-year visa in January 2006.[31]

In Israel, Colel Chabad, which was established in 1788 and is the oldest continuously operating charity in the country[32], has launched a series of programs for the benefit of Russian-speaking Jews. A yeshiva in Migdal HaEmek trains young rabbis who will lead Jewish communities in Israel and other countries. Bar and bat mitzvah preparations enable 1,000 Russian Jewish children to participate in a mass bar/bat mitzvah each year. Free Seders for Soviet olim are held in 100 locations throughout Israel and led by Colel Chabad volunteers, enabling over 10,000 olim annually, many just beginning to learn about Jewish traditions, to celebrate Passover.[33]

Tens of thousands of Soviet Jews who immigrated to America and Australia have participated in programs run by Friends of Refugees of Eastern Europe (FREE), an organization founded in 1969 by Rabbi Schneerson. Its Adult Education Division teaches basic Judaism. FREE's Yeshivat Ohel Dovid, named in memory of Rabbi Dovid Okunov, an émigré who had attended underground yeshivas in Ukraine, educates boys of Russian parentage. He was murdered in a robbery on a Brooklyn street in 1979. For Soviet Jews unfamiliar with Jewish holidays, FREE publishes Russian-language holiday guides and distributes them to 50,000 households throughout the United States. Since 1972 FREE has performed circumcisions on over 13,000 child and adult refugees, including an eighty-two-year-old.[34]

RABBI ELIYAHU ESSAS AND THE RUSSIAN RELIGIOUS JEWS

Unlike the competing chief rabbis of Moscow, Eliyahu Essas, who now resides and teaches in Jerusalem, never aspired to be a rabbi. Ordination was thrust upon him in 1982 by the Lishka, who realized that he was the most prominent teacher of Judaism within the refusenik community. He reluctantly agreed to accept the certification, and kept it secret until 1986 when he received his exit visa and arrived in Israel. He said, "I liked to teach and couldn't care less about *smicha* (ordination) or diplomas."

Essas was born in Vilnius, Lithuania, in 1946. His father, Tzvi Hirsch Essas, was a Zionist who had received a British visa to immigrate to Palestine, but his plans were thwarted by the Nazi invasion of Lithuania. Tzvi and his wife, Sonya, applied to emigrate in 1956 but were refused and waited until the 1970s to reapply.[35] They made aliyah in 1975, but Eliyahu (then called Ilya) and his wife, Anya, were refused permission because of Anya's one year of employment in the missile industry. They became part of the Moscow refusenik community, enthusiastically studying Hebrew, attending the synagogue, and speaking English to tourists and foreign correspondents.[36] Rabbi Pinchas Teitz of Elizabeth, New Jersey, who frequently traveled to Moscow, was Essas's first rabbinic mentor, and encouraged him to study and participate in the Jewish *t'shuvah* (repentance, return) movement. Enthralled with learning all aspects of Torah and Talmud, Essas enrolled in the yeshiva that was reopened in Moscow at the time of Nixon's visit to Moscow in 1972. He was expelled after nine months when the faculty discovered that he wanted to go to Israel. They considered this a criminal offense and stated that they didn't teach criminals. An exception among the teachers was Lev Gurevich, who was a friend of young refuseniks and taught Judaism in the yeshiva until he became very ill.

Essas had his first group of fifteen students, aged sixteen to thirty, in 1977. He multiplied his effectiveness by having each of his students agree to teach to others whatever they learned from him. Nine years later, Essas had teachers in various Soviet cities and a total student body of over 300 men and women.[37]

One of the teachers was Grisha Wasserman from Leningrad, who had been transformed from a vodka-drinking college student to a religious leader in 1979.[38] Upon becoming a refusenik and losing his job as an electrical engineer, Wasserman found work as an elevator technician. He studied Jewish texts while riding up and down in the elevators.[39]

Wasserman was eager to learn Essas's methods of teaching and visited him in Moscow on a yearly basis.[40] As they walked for hours on deserted streets in Moscow, Essas shared his experience of how to get Jewish books and kosher food, how to conduct a Seder, what to teach, all without drawing the ire of the KGB.[41]

But the KGB soon became more vigilant and aggressive in its efforts to seek out and eliminate religious activities. In December 1980 the KGB staged a "pogrom" at one of Essas's study sessions. Most of his forty students were taken to the police station, and religious books were confiscated.[42] Similarly, a seminar conducted by one of Wasserman's students in Leningrad was raided by four uniformed militia men in May 1981[43] (Chapter 10). Friends in the West learned about the harassment of the seminars from Ruth Bloch, who telephoned Essas from Switzerland on a regular basis for over six years. Her reports of the conversations were circulated to Soviet Jewry groups throughout Europe and America. They included news of the refusenik community and requests for literature needed for the religious classes that Essas was teaching.[44]

Another source of support from the West was Ernie Hirsch, a London jeweler who first visited Russia in January 1980 in hopes of educating Soviet Jews in Jewish traditions.[45] Hirsch and his friend Ivor Katz contacted Essas and Yuli Kosharovsky and learned how desperately the refuseniks were in need of help. Hirsch organized three additional groups of London Jews to go to Moscow later that year, and with some of the travelers, founded a charity organization called Russian Religious Jews. The Hirsch home became headquarters of RRJ and Hirsch spent all his non-working hours arranging for groups of volunteers to travel to the Soviet Union every three or four weeks. They had two objectives: sending material aid and teaching Judaism. Most of their efforts were concentrated on support for Essas and his students.

The volunteers had to be sincerely Orthodox, knowledgeable about Israel, and Hebrew-speaking. A "pleasant and communicative personality" was also one of the requirements for RRJ volunteers. From 1980 to 1990 a total of 246 travelers including fifty-five rabbis went on 153 trips. They were amazed by the thirst for learning demonstrated by the refuseniks, and did their best to encourage them.[46] Some of the travelers spent eighteen to twenty hours a day on a teaching visit. For a young man who wanted to become a *sofer* (Torah scribe) the RRJ arranged for a British sofer to train him as the only sofer in Russia was eighty years old and not in position to teach. Another man wanted to learn to be a *shochet* (ritual slaughterer) and a large knife was brought in for him. The traveler confidently told the Soviet customs agent that it was for slicing the salami that was also in his luggage.[47]

Essas received permission to emigrate as part of a goodwill gesture soon after the first Reagan-Gorbachev meeting (in Geneva in November 1985).[48] A few months after settling in Israel, Essas flew to America to thank many of his supporters, including Esther Feuerstein Zemelman, who attended the weekly seminars of the renowned Rabbi Joseph Soloveitchik of Boston and managed to send her notes to Essas who, of course, would pass them on to his students.[49] In 1989 he returned to Moscow as an Israeli delegate to the International Book Fair. What a turnaround to be a visitor, rather than one being visited! It was a great opportunity to meet students he had left behind.[50]

In Jerusalem Essas develops Russian-language programs for teaching Torah to olim from the Soviet Union at Yeshiva Ohr Somayach and the Neve Yerushalayim Seminary for Girls.[51] He points out that before the collapse of the Soviet Union "there were fewer than 1,000 observant Jews in the USSR, including his 300 students, and now we have about 50,000 outside of the FSU including Israel and America. It's tragic that there are 950,000 secular Soviet Jews in Israel." Essas is using the Internet to bring Torah knowledge to a worldwide audience. His Russian-language site offers real-time on-line lectures on Judaism and a variety of questions and answers daily.

When asked for his views on religious pluralism, Essas replied, "I don't like the word 'Orthodox'; I prefer 'Normative Judaism' for the ideals of standard Judaism…I believe the Torah was given on Mount Sinai by the Almighty and passed on from generation to generation. Reform and Conservative Judaism are man-made religions, but all Jews are my brothers."[52]

ZEEV DASHEVSKY – REACHING OUT TO TWO CAMPS

Zeev Dashevsky, the founder and President of *Machanaim* (a term from the Book of Genesis meaning two camps, and in recent times referring to Moscow and Jerusalem) appears to take somewhat broader view. His organization's mission is to provide Jewish education to Russian-speaking olim in Jerusalem and to Jews who are still in the CIS. Dashevsky and his associates are Orthodox, but not aligned with any specific group or rabbi. Martin Buber, Abraham Isaac Kook and Joseph Soloveitchik are among the thinkers and rabbis who have influenced Machanaim.

Dashevsky was a secular Jew when he studied theoretical physics, specializing in general relativity and cosmology at Odessa University and while he earned his doctorate at Moscow University, under Academician Yakov Zendovich (a colleague of Andrei Sakharov). From childhood he was interested in Israel, and whenever they could, Dashevsky and father would listen to the Voice of America and the Voice of Israel. During the Six-Day War he decided to learn about his Jewish heritage. Fascinated by the story of Jacob and Esau that he had heard on a Christian broadcast one Sunday, he wanted to read the Bible, but didn't know Hebrew. He purchased a small Russian-Hebrew dictionary that had been copied by a group in Kishinev, and eventually got hold of a nineteenth-century *Chumash* (Five Books of Moses) with text in Russian and Hebrew. He would read from it to his infant daughter, and as she grew he taught her everything he learned.

Dashevsky first applied for permission to emigrate on Lenin's birthday, April 22, 1977, and was a "waitnik" for two years, and then refused for eleven. On the same date in 1990, he and his family made aliyah. Like other secrecy refuseniks, Dashevsky was never given an official reason for his refusal. Nearly thirty years later, he thinks that the real reason was ordained from Heaven; he needed to embark on a new career to teach Soviet Jews about Judaism and have them pass their education on to others.

Although he earned a living by private tutoring in physics to candidates for university entrance exams, his real work was studying Hebrew and Torah. His study was not just academic; it demanded a change in lifestyle, and in late 1979 he started observing the Sabbath. During the early 1980s visitors from America and Europe came to the synagogue in Moscow, covertly under the auspices of the Lishka, and led monthly seminars for Dashevsky and his associates. Ernie Hirsch and the RRJ provided material support and a steady stream of well-informed visitors.

Each of the ten people in Dashevsky's underground group in 1980 had his own group of students. By 1987 the entire network had 200 students, many of whom were getting exit visas and making aliyah. The realization that a huge number of Soviet Jews in Israel were illiterate in Jewish tradition led to the formation of a center in Jerusalem and the name Machanaim for the overall group. The Israeli Ministry of Religious Affairs provided modest financial support including the use of telephones for a weekly seminar conducted by Rabbi Yaakov Filber in Jerusalem and heard on speakerphones in Moscow.[53]

Isi Leibler visited Dashevsky in Moscow in October 1988 to learn about Machanaim and what help was needed to expand the study groups. In his report Leibler described Machanaim as a bridge between the Orthodox and the secular cultural activists, and recommended investing "financial and manpower resources to sustain this group, otherwise Lubavitch, for whom I have the greatest respect and admiration, will remain the only religious movement left in the Soviet Union."[54]

Of the 200 people who had been in the Machanaim group in 1987, Dashevsky was the last to make aliyah. From his new base in Jerusalem he worked on getting support for the movement. Elie Wiesel, who met Dashevsky in 1987, spoke highly of Machanaim to Rabbi Michael Melchior, the chief rabbi of Norway[55], and in 1994 Machanaim started receiving aid from "Help Jews Home", a Norwegian initiative dedicated to Christian and Jewish collaboration and support for Israel.[56]

In April 2005 Dashevsky, who is on the faculty of Bar-Ilan University, participated in a videoconference with fifty Jewish educators in the CIS that was the first in a series of interactive videoconference lectures. Distance learning over the Internet reaches several thousand students, many of whom are teachers in all parts of the CIS. Dashevsky claims that with dozens of courses and online consultations, Machanaim has the biggest Russian language website for teaching Jewish tradition.[57]

THE LEGACIES OF LENINGRAD

In the late 1970s, while Essas and Dashevsky were forming their underground networks in Moscow, Lev Utevski, the chief of a fibers research laboratory, started giving lectures about Jewish history to friends in Leningrad. He was an amateur artist and produced a series of graphical illustrations on Biblical themes that were exhibited privately.

In 1979 he joined Grigory Wasserman and Grigory Kanovich in organizing the seminar on "Jewish History, Culture and Traditions", and lectured on Judaism and Jewish history. The participants had no doubt that the KGB would know about the seminars and decided to be completely open, rather than hide their gatherings.[58] The seminars were open to any Jew, refusenik or not. KGB raids on the seminars involved collection of the participants' passports, followed up by reprimands in their workplaces, and dismissal from their jobs in some cases. These measures did not stop the seminars.[59]

Utevski unexpectedly received permission to emigrate in 1980, and gave his last lecture, "The Great Revolt Against Rome", to 100 people packed into an apartment. Utevski wanted to take his Biblical art with him when he left the Soviet Union but was told, "It's forbidden to take religious propaganda abroad." Fortunately, Michael Elbert, a friend in Kiev, photographed the artwork and gave the negatives to tourists from Chicago Action for Soviet Jewry, who ultimately sent them to Utevski in Israel. These artworks gave rise to further activity and the publication of three trilingual books by Utevski: *Back to Roots* in 1982, *Still Small Voice* in 1999, and *I will not Bow or Stoop before Time* in 2004.[60]

Wasserman and his students continued to lecture at the seminars until the KGB raid in May 1981 at which Evgeny Lein was arrested (Chapter 10). Wasserman was fined fifty rubles (half a month's salary) and had to restrict his lessons to small groups. Until he received permission and made aliyah in January 1988, he had only ten devoted students[61], but they took on the laborious task of copying books on Judaism by photographing each page and developing the images in their own darkroom. They would also translate English texts into Russian and type each page on a typewriter. Over forty publications were produced and delivered to refuseniks throughout the Soviet Union.[62] Forced dispersal of the seminars did not prevent further Jewish activity in Leningrad. Teaching of Hebrew continued; Leonid Kelbert produced Jewish plays; Michael Beizer taught Jewish history; Boris Deviatov organized youth groups; and Yuri Kolker published a Jewish almanac.[63]

After settling in Israel, Wasserman joined the faculty of *Shvut Ami* (Return, my people), as its emissary in Haifa. Shvut Ami trains Russian-speaking educators who teach olim from the FSU, provides educational programs in the CIS, and publishes Russian- language educational materials.[64] It was founded in 1978 by Shimon Grilius, a former Prisoner of Zion who had learned Hebrew from Yosef Mendelevich when they were in the same labor camp.[65] The Shvut Ami Communities Program operates a variety of educational, cultural and recreational activities to attract unaffiliated olim through its branches in Bat Yam, Karmiel and Petach Tikvah.[66] Thousands of Jews in the CIS are benefiting from Shvut Ami programs in St. Petersburg, Riga and Kiev.[67]

"Let My People Know" is the slogan on Jakov Gorodezky's business card as president of the Society for Education of Russian Jews. Gorodezky became one of Wasserman's Hebrew students back in 1980, and when Utevski went to Israel, Gorodezky began lecturing.[68] Gorodezky was a leading organizer of the Leningrad Society for Jewish Culture and applied for legal registration of the organization in 1983, much to the consternation of the KGB.

They intimidated everyone who signed the registration papers and threatened Gorodezky that his wife and daughter would be harmed. He was seized on the street, brought to KGB central headquarters in Leningrad and pressured to sign a prepared confession that portrayed him as an agent of international Zionism, hired to damage the image of the Soviet Union. He refused and was released with warnings that the KGB could bring him to his knees.[69]

In addition to his efforts to promote the revival of Jewish culture in Leningrad, Gorodezky was busy publicizing the abusive treatment inflicted upon prisoners, and actively campaigning for the right of Jews to renounce their Soviet citizenship and demand repatriation to Israel.[70] He was severely harassed and vilified in the Soviet press for all these activities.

Although he was nearly forty years old and could not pass the army physical exam due to poor eyesight, he was told to prepare to be drafted.[71] Fortunately he was allowed to emigrate in early 1986, and from Israel, as well as during a tour of the United States, he called for a massive campaign against Soviet anti-Semitism.[72] Twenty years later and based in New York, Gorodezky is engaged in a fund-raising campaign to enable SERJ to bring Jewish identity and spiritual heritage to Russian-speaking adolescents in Israel through after-school classes, Jewish holiday programs, and summer day camps.[73]

The LSJC arranged memorial gatherings at Jewish cemeteries on Holocaust Remembrance Day. With tape recorders donated by the Bay Area Council for Soviet Jews, Gennady Farber and other members of the Holocaust Research Group within the LSJC went to *shtetls* outside of Leningrad and interviewed Jews who had survived the Holocaust. Their findings were displayed in an exhibit called "We Will Never Forget". They also worked on preserving the common graves at sites where mass murders of Jews took place. Soviet authorities tried to cover up these sites and pretend that Jews were not victimized.[74] The group got permission to set up a monument in Pushkin, a town not far from Leningrad, on

October 13, 1991, the fiftieth anniversary of the massacre of an estimated 800 Jews by the Nazis.[75]

Boris Kelman joined the LSJC after he and his wife, Alla, became refuseniks in 1979. He had a Ph.D. in naval engineering and she was a pediatrician. Attending a Passover Seder sparked their interest in Judaism. Kelman worked closely with Michael Beizer, who studied the history of the Jews of St. Petersburg, conducted walking tours based on his research and wrote a book on the subject. When LSJC chairman Aba Taratuta got permission and made aliyah, Kelman took over.[76] In 1988 he also became the editor of the journal of the Leningrad Chapter of the USSR-Israel Friendship Society. In a meeting with Isi Leibler he stressed the importance of using legal processes to obtain official recognition for the expression of Jewish culture.[77]

The following year the LSJC opened the Leningrad Jewish University offering evening classes in Hebrew, Torah and commentaries, Jewish history and Jewish literature. In 1991, when the city's name reverted to St. Petersburg, the university was renamed St. Petersburg Jewish University and had an enrollment of 150 part-time students.[78] The LSJC evolved into the Jewish Community Center of St. Petersburg and grew from a 3,000-square-foot rented basement to a fully owned 20,000-square-foot building. Its success is largely the result of a core of leaders, including Alexander Frenkel and Evgenya Lvova, who have served the community for two decades. A highlight of the revival of Jewish culture in St. Petersburg is the Klezfest that has featured traditional Yiddish and Klezmer music every July since 1999. The concert hall holding about 500 people is always sold out and additional post-Klezfest performances are held in other major cities of the FSU.[79]

Although his refusal for security reasons stated that he was not to leave the USSR until 2007, Kelman was allowed to travel to the United States on a tourist visa in 1990, and surprisingly received permission to emigrate for the family later that year. David Waksberg sponsored them and invited Boris to work for the BACSJ, which he did for several months before starting a business.[80] Kelman joined a Reform synagogue, Congregation Beth Am in Los Altos Hills, California, and became an active participant in the Émigré program that was founded in 1988 by Peggy Shapera and Rabbi Richard Block to provide a gateway into Jewish communal and religious life by offering programs in Russian and English. Over 600 families have been assisted in resettlement by the program and about 180 of them are members of the congregation. Kelman is the chairman of the Émigré Council and a member of congregation's board of directors.[81] He says that the program is vital because "it's important not to lose the émigrés to assimilation."[82]

Gennady Farber succeeded Kelman as head of the LSJC when Kelman emigrated, and as the Jewish community in Leningrad became more established, the LSJC received legal recognition and support from the Joint Distribution Committee as well as the Russian Va'ad, BACSJ, and the Israeli government. Farber and his family emigrated in January 1992 and were sponsored by Waksberg and Kelman to settle in the San Francisco Bay Area. Gennady and his wife, Masha, became very active in the Congregation Beth Am Émigré program. Masha teaches classes on Torah and Jewish traditions in Russian for adults and families. The Farbers say that they are motivated to be involved in the program because they want a better future for their children.[83]

Rabbi Block recalls that for several years virtually every week at least one new family from the FSU came to Beth Am for their first Shabbat service in America, often the first time they had been in a synagogue in their lives. After the conclusion of services he would open a Torah scroll for them, and each time, he adds, "they would begin to cry, and then I began to cry."[84]

Every émigré who came to Beth Am was interviewed by Peggy Shapera, and she was particularly impressed by the personal involvement, support and devotion of Inna Benjaminson, who had arrived from St. Petersburg in 1993. Benjaminson, fluent in English, had volunteered to drive elderly émigrés to physicians and hospitals and interpreted for them. Shapera invited

Benjaminson to work in Beth Am's Émigré program and she has been doing that for nearly fourteen years, with funding from the Jewish Family and Children's Services. In addition to providing translations of the rabbi's High Holy Day sermons into Russian, she composed trilingual prayer books for Kabbalat Shabbat and shiva services with the Hebrew portions transliterated into Cyrillic print.[85] These resources and her innovative family-oriented programs called "My Jewish Discovery" and "Gan Haggim" are leading to increased participation and membership by émigrés in Beth Am, and are being shared with other Reform congregations.[86]

THE REFORM MOVEMENT TAKES ROOT IN THE FSU

In 1998 Rabbi Block moved from California to Jerusalem and became the executive director of the World Union for Progressive Judaism, a worldwide umbrella agency for about two million Jews in the Reform and Reconstructionist movements. He succeeded Rabbi Richard Hirsch, who was retiring after holding the position for twenty-five years.[87]

Hirsch had a long history of involvement with Soviet Jewry, commencing with his marriage in 1954. His wife, Bella, is a native of Russia who was able to emigrate with her family in 1946 after her older sisters married Polish citizens.[88] Her knowledge of Russian was extremely useful on a trip with Hirsch to the USSR in 1969 during which they met hundreds of Jews, including a young man who said his name was Moise (Moses) but knew nothing of the Biblical Moses. Hirsch, through Bella, then related the story of Moses and the Exodus as he had done countless times in kindergarten classes. Moise, weeping, thanked them profusely and said, "At last now I have something Jewish to transmit to my child."

As founding director of the Reform Movement's Religious Action Center in Washington from 1962 to 1973, Hirsch had an office around the corner from the Israeli Embassy and became very friendly with envoys of the Lishka who were posted there. Hirsch played a role in the formation of the NCSJ[89], and also informed Irene Manekofsky, who worked for him at RAC, regarding the plight of Soviet Jews. She was inspired to take an activist approach and became president of the UCSJ several years later.[90]

Hirsch maintained his close ties with the Lishka upon moving to Israel to head the WUPJ in 1972. David Bar-Tov, a close personal friend who directed the Lishka from 1986 to 1992, visited Hirsch in 1987 and predicted that Gorbachev's reforms would result in many Jews getting out and religious freedom for those who stayed. Bar-Tov commented that although Chabad had a monopoly as the established Jewish movement in Russia, there could be an opportunity for the Reform movement to offer an alternative that would be more appealing to those who had grown up in a communist anti-religious environment.

Hirsch led a fact-finding mission of WUPJ lay leaders to Moscow and Leningrad in 1988 and verified Bar-Tov's assessment.[91] The opportunity to enable Soviet Jews to regain their Jewish consciousness inspired all forty mission participants into contributing to a fund for the development of Progressive Judaism in the Soviet Union. They met Zinovy Kogan of Moscow[92], who had started a progressive Jewish prayer group in his kitchen in 1983.[93]

In the 1980s, Kogan, then a construction engineer who had studied in Eliyahu Essas's secret yeshiva, met rabbis Maynard Bell of Phoenix, Arizona, Hugo Gryn of London, and Earl Kaplan of Los Angeles, and from them learned about Reform Judaism. Bell gave Kogan a Reform prayer book written by Betty Golomb for *Kabbalat Shabbat* (service welcoming the Sabbath) in Russian and Hebrew with some parts transliterated. Kogan's kitchen minyan grew to nearly thirty participants who liked most of the ideas in the Reform prayer book.[94]

Lacking a traditional shofar, Kogan improvised one out of a deer's antler that he had found on the Kola Peninsula in northern Russia and kept for over twenty years[95]. In 1985 he took his shofar to the Ovrashky Forest for the annual Sukkot gathering of hundreds of refuseniks and "blessed" them with its sound.

Kogan's minyan became Congregation Hineini, literally meaning, "Here I am, God", and signifying a declaration that "we are here, we have arrived, and we will continue to believe in ourselves and the Jewish tradition." Hineini was welcomed as the first Russian congregation to join the WUPJ and was registered as the first congregation of Reform Judaism in Russia. Kogan became its spiritual leader in 1993.[96]

Kogan attended the 1990 WUPJ Convention in London and electrified the delegates at the West London Synagogue by reciting the Ten Commandments in Russian. Rabbis from the WUPJ and the Israel Movement for Progressive Judaism traveled to Moscow to conduct community-building seminars before Passover, Rosh HaShanah and Chanukah every year from 1991 to 1997. In 1993 the WUPJ established the Institute of Modern Jewish Studies, better known as the *Machon* (institute), to train native rabbinic students for the Progressive movement with a full year curriculum of forty hours a week in Moscow. From 1997 to 1999 the Machon held its classes in Kiev and supported the establishment of Congregation HaTikva there.[97] Beginning in 1997 native-born rabbis conducted the seminars with Russian as the primary language of instruction, fulfilling a WUPJ goal of having indigenous leaders to assume responsibility for the movement. By 1999 there were native-born rabbis teaching at the Machon.[98]

In 2002 Steve Bauman, the chairman of WUPJ's FSU Committee, went to Moscow, St. Petersburg and Kiev to meet with Jewish leaders and government officials to develop a strategy for building an indigenous, autonomous, and democratic liberal Jewish movement in the FSU. He also visited Germany where over 200,000 Soviet Jews had settled. It became clear to him that elders who tried to teach Orthodox Judaism were being rejected by younger Jews, who wanted a more liberal and egalitarian approach and were willing to drive a new movement that would help them find their Jewish identity. The huge number of intermarried Jews also preferred the American Reform movement's recognition of patrilineal, as well as matrilineal, descent to define who is a Jew, over the strict conversion procedure demanded by the Orthodox rabbis for those whose mothers were not Jewish.

Bauman, who became WUPJ chairman in 2005, believes that the keys to achieving the goals set out for the Reform Movement in the FSU involve reaching out to the oligarchs for funding, and to the intelligentsia to raise the level of intellectual discourse. To support the latter, the WUPJ has commissioned a Torah commentary based on the works of Rabbi Gunther Plaut to be published in Russian.[99] There is also an extensive effort to educate Jewish youth through kindergartens, day schools and summer camps throughout the FSU, introducing them to pluralistic egalitarian Judaism.[100] Netzer Olami, the international Progressive youth movement, held twelve camps for 1,300 young people in 2007.[101]

The number of Progressive congregations in the FSU has grown to over sixty, spanning the vast area from the Baltic Sea to the Sea of Japan. Six indigenous rabbis are leading some of the congregations, and other Russian-speaking rabbinic students are being trained at Leo Baeck College in London and Abraham Geiger Kolleg in Berlin. The WUPJ celebrated its fifteenth anniversary of association with the Progressive congregations of the FSU by holding its 32nd international convention in Moscow during the summer of 2005. It was attended by 350 delegates, 300 of whom traveled from twenty-four countries for the event.[102] Alex Kagan, the director of WUPJ Programs in the FSU, regards reaching financial self-sufficiency, with local sponsors or "oligarchs" donating money to buy synagogues in the major cities, as the greatest challenge faced by the Progressive movement in its effort to provide the opportunity to live a liberal Jewish life.

There are no activists screaming, "Let My People Come Back", but 70,000 Soviet Jews who had emigrated to Israel returned to live in the FSU.[103] Most of them (called *olim-yordim* in Hebrew) are concentrated in Moscow and claim that they returned because of economic opportunities in Russia, along with social difficulties in adapting to Israeli society.[104] Some of these returnees are participating in programs offered at Reform congregations.[105]

The rapid growth of the Progressive movement in the FSU has been dismissed by Chabad Chief Rabbi Berel Lazar as a "God-less,

Torah-less American import." In 1991 the Moscow District Court approved Congregation Hineini's request to use the nineteenth-century Polyakov Synagogue in central Moscow. But Chabad challenged that decision a few weeks later, and after hoodlums had forcibly removed the Hineini Torah scroll (a gift from Ralph Goldman of the JDC) and its furniture, Chabad took over the building. Hineini retrieved its Torah and moved to the Moscow Memorial Synagogue.[106]

In Belarus, which once had a strong Orthodox tradition, Chabad's large synagogue is deserted, while the Progressive movement led by Rabbi Grisha Abramovich, a native of Minsk, is thriving, and the Association of Progressive Jewish Communities of Belarus has become the largest Jewish organization there.[107]

OTHER SOURCES OF JEWISH LEARNING IN THE FSU

Camp Ramah-Ukraine is sponsored by the Masorti (Conservative) movement in Israel. Located near Kiev, it hosts 200 children each summer, most of whom are among the 1,000 pupils in Midreshet Yerushalayim (Schechter Institute) schools in the renascent Jewish communities of Ukraine. An additional 1,000 Soviet olim participate in Midreshet Yerushalayim activities in Israel.[108]

Young adults from the FSU are among the 145,000 Jews from fifty-two countries who have been given free ten-day trips to Israel since 1999 in a unique program called Taglit-birthright Israel, run by a consortium of benefactors, local Jewish federations and the Jewish Agency for Israel.[109] As of October 2007, 17,500 young adults from the FSU have come to Israel on this program and nearly 40% of them have made aliyah.[110]

The Jewish Agency, which had been concerned with aliyah as its primary reason for having a presence in the FSU, has recently added educational, cultural and recreational programs aimed at attracting participants who have no intention of moving to Israel.[111]

Hillel in the FSU, as on campuses elsewhere in the world, provides stimulating programs for college students. Hillel's president,

Wayne Firestone, whose exploits to heighten awareness about the plight of Prisoners of Zion were described in Chapters 10 and 17, reports that since 1994 twenty-seven Hillels have been established across ten time zones of the FSU. He was excited to return to Moscow in 2007 for a Limmud conference[112] for 800 participants organized by indigenous alumni of Hillel and the Taglit-birthright Israel programs. Limmud started in London in 1981 and has spread globally as a model of pluralistic, cross-communal, volunteer-led, dynamic Jewish education.[113] ORT now operates a network of technological schools serving 27,000 people in seven FSU countries and provides support for Jewish education in partnership with the Jewish Agency and Israel's Ministry of Education. The organization was founded in St. Petersburg in 1880 but had been forced to close its schools for over fifty years during the Soviet era.[114]

THE PROGRESSIVE MOVEMENT
REACHES OUT TO SOVIET OLIM

In Israel, an estimated 300,000 of the million Soviet olim are considered to be non-Jews. The Israel Movement for Progressive Judaism, unlike the Progressive Movement outside of Israel, recognizes only matrilineal descent to define a Jew, forcing many Soviet olim to convert if they want to be considered Jewish. The conversion process required by Reform rabbis in Israel requires considerable study and a test administered by a *Beit Din* (a court of three rabbis). However, the commitments required are far less daunting than those required by the Orthodox establishment. For example, a female athlete who wanted to have an Orthodox conversion was appalled to learn that she would have to agree to never wear shorts in public – a career-limiting prohibition![115] In 2002 the Israeli Supreme Court ruled that Israeli citizens converted by Conservative or Reform rabbis in Israel or abroad must be registered as Jews by the Interior Ministry.[116]

Iri Kassel, the executive director of IMPJ, regards the conversion activity the movement's No. 1 priority and greatest success among its activities for new immigrants. He estimates that about 2,000 Soviet olim have been converted by Reform rabbis since 1993. Another IMPJ function that benefits about 5,000 olim each year is the free legal aid provided by the Israeli Religious Action Center.

Kassel is looking forward to increasing the number of Soviet olim joining Reform congregations throughout Israel. The approach is to integrate them into existing congregations rather than setting up new congregations exclusively for Russian speakers. Such a congregation was started by and for Soviet olim in Ashdod, but it disbanded after a few years of organizational disputes. IMPJ is finding that most effective in the effort to attract Soviet olim to Reform synagogues are various study programs that introduce them to Judaism intellectually and help them adjust to Israeli society and culture.[117]

Eliyahu Essas lecturing to refuseniks including Yuli Kosharovsky, Ida Nudel, Vladimir Prestin, and Natan Sharansky, at a Lag b'Omer picnic in a forest near Moscow in 1975. Photo credit: Reproduced from Silent Revolution by Miriam Stark Zakon with permission from the copyright holders Artscroll/Mesorah Publications, Ltd.

430

Lev Leviev, a former student of the Lubavitch underground in Uzbekistan, established the Ohr Avner Foundation in memory of his father, Rabbi Avner Leviev, a leader of the Bukharan Jewish community in Tashkent, and later in Israel. Photo Credit: Chabad.org/Israel Bardugo.

CHAPTER TWENTY-SEVEN

Let My People Live

"My mother used to say, 'Be sure to eat everything on your plate because there are people starving in Europe.' Well, there are people starving in Europe now – they're in the former Soviet Union. It's time to re-remember these people under siege." These were the opening lines of a fund-raising videotape called "Re-Remembering" that was produced in 2002 by Chicago Action for Jews in the Former Soviet Union. The video continued with Marillyn Tallman (Chapter 17), the chair of Chicago Action, telling viewers that after thirty years of crying "Let My People Go" and helping refuseniks, Chicago Action had re-evaluated its goals and its mission. With the fall of the Soviet Union the survival of Jews who remained was being jeopardized by poverty, sickness, isolation, rising anti-Semitism and persecution. Chicago Action and other councils of the UCSJ had to step into the breach with programs to enable the Jews of the FSU to live in dignity.

THE JOINT RETURNS TO THE SOVIET UNION

Preceding Chicago Action and other grassroots organizations in the role of bringing aid on a large scale to the Jews of the FSU was the Joint Distribution Committee. In 1989 the Joint returned to the Soviet Union, fifty years after Stalin had expelled the organization. Compounding the challenge of setting up programs in the FSU were the budgetary problems inherent in caring for the needs of thousands of transmigrants who were leaving the country. Ralph Goldman, its honorary executive vice president, who for decades had been the heart and soul of JDC, insisted that the JDC focus its efforts on caring for Jews who remained in the FSU. He emphasized the importance of working with local partners, like Yad Ezra, a Moscow Jewish social service organization, to distribute food packages from JDC to needy recipients. In this endeavor Rabbi Adolf Shayevich and Mikhail Chlenov, who had been at odds in earlier years, worked together recruiting volunteers at the Choral Synagogue and empowering Yad Ezra to grow into a well-regarded welfare provider.[1]

Many of the welfare clients were "double victims" who had suffered Nazi persecution followed by Soviet oppression. During the decades of Soviet rule they were unable to receive any compensation that was available to Holocaust survivors living in Western countries. Finally, in 1995 the Conference on Jewish Material Claims against Germany (Claims Conference) partnered with the JDC to provide funding for welfare services to Jewish victims of Nazi persecution in the FSU, and in 2001 JDC received grants resulting from litigation brought against Swiss banks by Holocaust survivors.[2]

Using $24 million a year from the Claims Conference to augment its own budget, and with the aid of 14,000 volunteers in a network of *Hesed* (social service with compassion) centers, the JDC has been enabling the elderly (who otherwise would have been starving on pensions of about $15 per month) to survive.[3] The JDC has also discovered intense needs among Jewish children, and through its Children's Initiative provided food, therapy, and early childhood assistance to more than 21,000 Jewish children in fifty communities during 2004.[4] The JDC maintains seventeen field offices that serve Jews in over 3,000 cities, towns and villages of the FSU, forging partnerships with all sectors of the communities, while avoiding interference in local affairs and remaining impartial and non-partisan.[5]

THE BOSTON-DNIPROPETROVSK PARTNERSHIP

In 1990 there was no JDC presence in Dnipropetrovsk, Ukraine, a region with 70,000 Jews, making it the fourth largest Jewish community in the FSU.[6] Because of its intercontinental ballistic missile plant it was a closed city and the Jews there were neglected as they never met foreign tourists.[7] To rectify this situation, twenty-five-year-old Rabbi Shmuel Kaminezki, born in Israel and educated in the United States, was sent by the Chabad Lubavitcher Rebbe, Rabbi Menachem Schneerson. Kaminezki enthusiastically worked to revitalize Dnipropetrovsk's Jewish community. He found a synagogue in shambles that was open only on Shabbat, serving as a refuge for old men, and transformed it into a place for daily worship and activities for all age groups. He also established a Jewish day school that several years later became one of the largest in Europe with 650 students.[8] In 2000 Kaminezki led the Jewish community in reclaiming the Golden Rose Synagogue. It had been used as a coat factory for seventy years under communism and now serves as a spiritual, cultural, and educational center.[9]

When the USSR collapsed and Dnipropetrovsk became open to foreign visitors, Betsy Gidwitz and Judy Wolf traveled there on behalf of the NCSJ and the Boston JCRC.[10] The Boston JCRC and UCSJ's Action for Post Soviet Jewry in Boston followed up on their visit and established a Kehilla project with Dnipropetrovsk in 1992. Representatives from various Jewish agencies in Boston went to Dnipropetrovsk to assess the needs of the Jewish community and launched specific programs over the next few years.[11] Bob Gordon (Chapter 17), a former UCSJ president and the CEO of Store 24, solicited food donations from his suppliers and used his company's warehouse for storage prior to shipment to Dnipropetrovsk.[12]

A non-sectarian ambulatory clinic for women and children was founded in 1997 in response to appalling medical conditions, and is supported in conjunction with hospitals in the Boston area.

A resource center for children with special needs who otherwise would not receive schooling was set up at the Beit Hana Women's Teacher College in Dnipropetrovsk.[13]

Betsy Gidwitz helped the Jewish community of Dnipropetrovsk to convince the JDC to become more supportive in the region. Subsequently the JDC sent one of its employees to live there and supervise the refurbishing of a building.[14] Dnipropetrovsk became the administrative center of JDC operations in eastern Ukraine where over forty hesed centers delivered food parcels and meals on wheels to about 25,000 clients in the region.[15] In recent years JDC funds for these programs were reduced and in some cases clients were required to pay for services. APSJ is providing increased support and also helped to set up a pharmacy and has provided support to physicians in Dnipropetrovsk.[16]

On a visit in 2003 Judy Patkin (Chapter 17), APSJ's executive director, found that even with help from the JDC elderly pensioners were still struggling to survive, especially as they were developing the chronic ailments that are common with advancing age.[17] APSJ's "Adopt-a-Bubbe (grandmother) or Zayde (grandfather) program reaches out to these elderly Jews in Dnipropetrovsk and nearly fifty other cities and villages in Ukraine, Belarus and Moldova. Food, medicine, clothing, eyeglasses, hearing aids and utility payments are provided under the direction of volunteers in the major cities. APSJ also supports the formation of Warm Houses, apartments of housebound seniors who act as hosts for other elderly friends who can enjoy meals together, celebrate Jewish holidays, and have discussion groups.[18]

YAD L'YAD PARTNERSHIPS

Sandy Cantor, who had chaired Florida Action for Jews in the former Soviet Union since 2000, traveled with Patkin to Ukraine and Belarus in 2003 to visit communities supported by UCSJ's Yad l'Yad (hand to hand) program. About 100 congregations, Jewish schools, and charitable organizations in ten republics of the FSU are partnered with councils of the UCSJ, often with direct support from specific American congregations. The national program is currently co-chaired by Marillyn Tallman and Hinda Cantor (Chapter 17), a long-time South Florida activist. In addition to providing material support, the Yad l'Yad partners have developed strong personal and spiritual bonds, especially evident when a congregation in the FSU warmly receives a Torah scroll from its American partner, or when representatives of paired communities visit each other.[19]

In Europe the Swiss Action Committee for the Jews in the Soviet Union (AJS) was reconstituted as "Aid to Jews in White Russia" and has been functioning since the mass exodus of Soviet Jews. Martina Frank coordinates its efforts in collecting and shipping truckloads of clothing, food and medical supplies from Basel to Minsk three times a year. The Swiss-Belarus relationships stems from trips made by Jacques and Chana Berlowitz (Chapter 19) and other Swiss Action Committee members to Belarus for meetings with activists during the Soviet era, and subsequent visits by Jewish educators from Switzerland who were sent to Minsk to teach Jewish subjects.[20]

RAMPANT ANTI-SEMITISM

Along with welcome news of the growth of summer camps for Jewish youth, meals-on-wheels programs and successful distribution of vitamins and medicine, the Yad l'Yad partners have been reporting alarming outbreaks of anti-Semitic violence in their communities. The March 2005 issue of *Lifeline*, Chicago Action's newsletter, carried the headline, "Skinheads Attack Jews in Simferopol, Ukraine", and described attacks on Jews and vandalism of synagogues and Jewish cemeteries in Moscow and thirteen other cities of the FSU. Although the anti-Semitic acts were not state-sponsored the local authorities often refused to do anything about them. In the Simferopol incident two Jewish girls had to be hospitalized but the local police refused to declare the attack a hate crime, and instead labeled it ordinary "hooliganism".

The Russian Orthodox Church allowed the notoriously

libelous *Protocols of the Elders of Zion* to be published in its Eka-
terinburg diocese in 2002. Mikhail Chlenov, as general secretary
of the Euro-Asian Jewish Congress, appealed to the leadership of
the church, requesting that they publicly condemn anti-Semitism
and declare the publication "a harmful and disgusting falsifica-
tion".[21] Chlenov never received a written response, and the publication was not withdrawn, but some local priests were orally
criticized.[22]

In 1990 Leonid Stonov (Chapter 17) alerted the UCSJ to "a
wild outburst of anti-Semitism in this country" involving racist
and neo-Nazi groups who were allowed to function freely and in-
cite anti-Jewish violence. He pointed out that in many cities there
had been acts of violence against Jewish families that "might at
any time grow to pogroms."[23] Five years later, Stonov, working for
the UCSJ in Chicago, expressed concern about election results in
Russia which indicated a possible coalition of Communists and
ultranationalists coming to power, stopping democratic reforms,
and even limiting emigration.[24] Although such a coalition never
materialized because the Communists became very weak, Stonov
remains concerned about the neo-Nazis. Since 2002 they have
become the most dangerous force in Russia, with at least 50,000
skinheads throughout the country.[25] Stonov believes that skinheads were responsible for the murder, in St. Petersburg in 2004,
of ethnographer and anthropologist Nikolai Girenko, who had
been an expert witness in trials involving extremist nationalists.
The Moscow Bureau for Human Rights and Rule of Law, supported by the UCSJ, estimated that twenty to thirty people die
each year from racially motivated assaults committed by neo-
Nazi gangs.[26]

THE CLIMATE OF TRUST

Pamyat was the initial post-Soviet Russian nationalist group es-
pousing anti-Semitism. As this group fizzled out, in northwestern
Russia two neo-Nazi groups, Russian National Unity and "Dead
Water", began sending threatening notes to Jews in Borovichi, a

city near Novgorod where 500 Jews resided.[27] In 1998 Dead Water sponsored anti-Semitic television ads calling for the "good Christians of Borovichi to pick up arms and kill at least one Jew a day." Local Jewish leaders protested to Mayor Vladimir Ogon'kov and the governor of the Novgorod region, Mikhail Prusak, and succeeded in halting the broadcast of these ads.[28]

The Light Center (Chapter 16) in St. Petersburg, which was supported by the Bay Area Council for Jewish Rescue and Renewal, proposed the "Climate of Trust" as a series of local seminars for training teachers to address the anti-Semitic threats. The program was successful and BACJRR considered similar seminars for police officers in response to the situation in Borovichi. San Francisco's Police Department already had programs for combating hate crimes and agreed to go to Russia and share its experience with its counterparts there. A Russian delegation subsequently went to San Francisco for a week of workshops and discussions. The visits were followed by the establishment of Regional Tolerance Centers in St. Petersburg, Ryazan, Kazan, and Stavropol. At these centers police officers, city administrators, ethnic and religious community leaders are able to meet regularly to promote dialogue and prevent conflict.[29]

Pnina Levermore, who became executive director of the BACJRR in 1997, was instrumental in driving the Climate of Trust as the organization's primary activity. [30]Together with Rabbi Doug Kahn, executive director of the San Francisco JCRC, and Daniel Grossman, who had served in the U.S. Consulate in Leningrad, she met with Russian Consul General Yuri Popov in San Francisco. They pointed out that the Jewish community unfortunately had a lot of experience dealing with hatred, and since these neo-Nazis were a danger not only to the Jews but to all of Russian society, they would be pleased to work together with the Russians in confronting them. Popov arranged for meetings in Moscow with the Ministry of Justice and the General Procurator's Office that led to the initiation of the Climate of Trust program. Levermore describes the program as a prophylactic approach to dealing with intolerance and is proud to report that in 2005 and 2006 there were no hate crimes in Borovichi. The BACJRR changed its name to the Climate of Trust Council in 2006 and has received grants from the U.S. State Department and the Agency for International Development.[31]

UCSJ IN THE POST-SOVIET ERA

The post-Soviet era demanded new strategies for the UCSJ, whose clients in previous decades were Jews trying to leave. Now the UCSJ is supporting Jews who are trying to stay. The UCSJ considers protecting the Jews of the FSU from anti-Semitism as its No. 1 priority. In addition to monitoring anti-Semitism, the UCSJ is concerned with xenophobia, racism, and religious persecution.[32] Its 2001 report, "Anti-Semitism, Xenophobia and Religious Persecution in Russia's Regions," concluded that the violation of human rights inherent in anti-Semitism and neo-Fascism, "including the persecution of non-Jewish ethnic and religious minorities, has a pernicious effect on the safety of the Jewish community." Excerpts from the report include the following "snapshots of hate":

'Ryazan officials never condemned the previous [arson] attack against the Jewish school.'

'In Saratov nowadays it has become unsafe. Over the past year the Jewish cemetery has been attacked five times.'

'Young members of the RNU and other pro-Fascist organizations regularly break the windows of the Jewish school... located next door to the main police station of the Sovetsky District.'

'Despite the clear incitement of hatred contained in Governor Mikhaylov's comparison of the Russian Jewish Congress to "filth" in December 2000, the Procurator General's Office refused to bring charges against him.'

'Every single African student I know has been beaten at least once in Moscow.'

'In August 2001 the Pentecostal bishop in Izhevsk reported to a religious freedom watchdog group that a 'massive anti-Pentecostal and anti-Protestant campaign in the republic's media had led to local Pentecostals being murdered
and kidnapped.'

The report was read by Russian President Vladimir Putin, and
according to Yossi Abramowitz, the president of the UCSJ who
succeeded Pamela Cohen (Chapter 17), Putin complained to the
regional governors about the human rights violations cited in UCSJ
reports. His predecessor, Boris Yeltsin, had created human rights
congresses, and officials of Yeltsin's administration met with UCSJ
representatives, saying, "We need money and training and we'll be
your partners."[33] USAID has been funding the Climate of Trust for
several years, as it supported UCSJ and Moscow Helsinki Group
from 1999 to 2001 in its program of monitoring human rights and
anti-Semitic/xenophobic hate crimes in Russia. In 2002, responding to an open competition to respond to anti-Semitism by the
European Commission (the action arm of the European Union)
UCSJ National Director Micah Naftalin (Chapter 17) prepared the
winning proposal that led to a three-year, 1.4 million euro grant
to UCSJ's Moscow Bureau on Human Rights with collateral support to MHG. The grant included provisions for a hate crime "hot
line" and legal advice to victims.[34]

But the case of Alexander Nikitin showed that Russia's post-
Soviet path to acceptance of its human rights obligations would
not be smooth and straightforward. Nikitin, a captain and chief
engineer of a nuclear submarine, left the Russian Navy to work for
the Bellona Foundation, a Norwegian environmental organization, in 1994. He contributed to a shocking report two years later
that detailed the rundown condition of Russia's Northern Fleet
and the hazards that threatened the Arctic Ocean's ecology due to
improper storage of nuclear waste on Russian submarines. Nikitin was arrested in St. Petersburg and charged with high treason,

even though the Russian constitution prohibits classifying environmental information as secret.[35] He was denied the right of due process, detained for ten months before his trial, had secret and retroactive decrees applied against him during the trial that were not made available to him or his attorneys, and put through a second trial that ended in 1999 with a full acquittal.[36] Nevertheless, Putin has labeled environmentalists as spies, and a journalist named Grigory Pasko whose videotape of a Russian Navy ship dumping nuclear waste into the Sea of Japan was broadcast on Japanese television was imprisoned for twenty months on treason charges. Stonov used the Nikitin and Pasko cases to show that "official secrecy paranoia, a defining aspect of Soviet life, never quite went away."[37]

In testimony to the CSCE, Stonov pointed out that Putin accepts and approves nationalistic and chauvinistic forces, including some known anti-Semitic ideologues.[38] A year after 9/11 Naftalin testified before the CSCE, declaring, "Raging racism demonstrates a dangerous breakdown of rule of law that threatens Russia's economic and political stability and vulnerability to extremism and terrorism. It calls out for American vigilance and assistance." He stated that while Putin makes positive gestures toward Russia's Jewish community and employs the appropriate rhetorical remarks against chauvinism, nationalism and religious intolerance, his government allows regional authorities to openly collaborate with neo-Nazis.[39]

The UCSJ publicized Nikitin's case and campaigned on his behalf. Yossi Abramowitz led a fact-finding trip to Moscow during the summer of 1997 and confronted Russian officials about the Nikitin case. He said, "Nikitin isn't Jewish, but this case is a litmus test of who is in charge in Russia. Is it the remnants of the KGB or is it the democrats?"[40] Abramowitz was no stranger to human rights activism. As a Boston University student he had been the driving force of the anti-apartheid movement. In 1987 he was in Israel, and led the World Union of Jewish Students (of which he was president) in a hunger strike in support of Prisoner of Zion

Alexei Magarik (Chapter 10). He also organized a thousand Ethiopian children at the Dutch Embassy in Tel Aviv in a "Let My People Go" rally on the day of the huge Soviet Jewry demonstration in Washington that year.[41] In 2004 he was the keynote speaker at Russia's national human rights convention.[42]

The UCSJ and the Moscow Helsinki Group, chaired by Ludmilla Alexeeva, one of the founders of Sakharov's original Helsinki Watch Group, in consultation with thirty other religious freedom and human rights NGOs in Belarus, Russia and Ukraine, formed the "Coalition Against Hate" in 2007. Their unprecedented bilingual website, *www.coalitionagainsthate.org*, provides monitor-based facts and opinions about anti-Semitism, xenophobia, fascism, and religious persecution throughout the FSU. Naftalin views the Soviet Jewry movement as a prelude to today's challenges in the FSU. He points out that "Belarus remains the surviving totalitarian dictatorship in the FSU; in Ukraine civil society has not caught up with the promise of the Orange Revolution, and anti-Semitic events reached record highs [in 2007], surpassing in numbers of incidents even Russia. Meanwhile Russia devolves back into totalitarian/oil-rich rule: oppressing its citizens, threatening its near neighbors, intimidating the West, especially Europe, and supporting such enemies of Israel and democracy as Iran, Syria, Hezbollah, and Hamas."[43]

THE CAUCASUS NETWORK – AIDING JEWS IN FORGOTTEN PLACES

Skinheads and Russian nationalists were not the only perpetrators of hate crimes in the republics of the FSU. In Uzbekistan, authorities including the police, prison guards, and the republic's procurator general all issued anti-Semitic slurs against Ioisif Koenov, a Jew arrested on trumped-up murder charges.[44] He was released in 1995 after Uzbek authorities received 25,000 letters on his behalf from supporters who responded to a campaign coordinated by the UCSJ and numerous meetings involving Uzbek officials and U.S. and foreign diplomats.[45]

Several months later another Tashkent Jew, Dmitri Fattakhov, was falsely accused of murdering an Uzbek whose dismembered body was found in a river. The u.s. State Department reported that Fattakhov was "beaten nearly to the point of insanity by police to obtain a confession.[46]" Instead of dropping charges against Fattakhov and releasing him, the judge ordered him to be detained in a mental hospital for an indeterminate period.[47]

Fattakhov's case was taken up by New York attorney Helene Kenvin, who was the founder and president of The Caucasus Network. Kenvin, whose parents had visited the Soviet Union to meet Jews in 1963, started this organization after traveling to the Soviet Union with her husband in 1984. Their trip included meetings with Jews in the Caucasus republics of Armenia, Azerbaijan and Georgia. Kenvin collected numerous requests for help from people she met there, and organized CN because it appeared that the existing Soviet Jewry support organizations were overwhelmed by the needs of refuseniks in Russia and the other republics in the western part of the USSR and lacked the time or resources to attend to the needs of the estimated 300,000 to 500,000 Jews in outlying areas. Eventually CN expanded to include support for Jews living in Chechnya and Dagestan (politically part of Russia, but geographically in the Caucasus) and the republics of Central Asia as well as for tourists going to these regions. Kenvin created master lists of thousands of Jews in these areas, and disseminated information about the conditions of Jews in these republics to other Soviet Jewry groups and government officials in America and Europe.[48] For two decades CN primarily worked on helping tens of thousands of Jews to emigrate, but in recent years its mission has shifted to keeping abreast of Muslim terrorism in the Caucasus and Central Asian republics.

Until the Koenov case CN assiduously shunned publicity to avoid calling attention to Jews in republics whose populations are predominately Muslim (six of the eight republics and Chechnya and Dagestan where CN works).[49] Daniel Palanker, whose family spent their refusenik years in Yerevan, Armenia, recalls how Kenvin and other tourists from CN were extremely helpful by arranging secret visits and bringing them Jewish religious articles.[50] CN also gave considerable support to the Jews of Baku, Azerbaijan, who maintained an ulpan and were eager to leave as quickly as possible because they feared that Muslim nationalism, exacerbated by the dispute between Armenia and Azerbaijan over the region of Nagorno-Karabakh, was growing in the late 1980s.[51] Kenvin and CN were well respected by the Israeli government, and she was able to put émigrés from Baku on a "shortlist" for expeditious entry into Israel.[52]

Kenvin could not go to Tashkent to fight for Koenov's or Fattakhov's release because her people in Central Asia had discovered that she had a thick KGB file due to her activities on previous visits, and they could no longer guarantee her safety. Instead, she enlisted international support from veteran Soviet Jewry advocates including UCSJ, the 35s in England and Jacob Birnbaum in New York. American, British, and German diplomats were convinced to put pressure – including possible withholding of most-favored-nation trading status – on Uzbekistan's officials. Finally, in February 1996, Fattakhov was released and allowed to leave with his mother for Israel.[53] In both the Fattakhov and Koenov cases CN had strong support from UCSJ and its constituent councils. CN also worked with NCSJ, and was not exclusively aligned with either major umbrella organization, and on occasion served as a conduit for communication between them.[54]

NCSJ – ADVOCATING FOR THE JEWS OF THE FSU

"We won't turn our backs on those who stay," says Mark Levin, NCSJ's executive director, about his organization's 1992 decision to make a transition from promoting aliyah to political advocacy on behalf of the Jewish communities in the FSU. Israelis and Zionist groups criticized what NCSJ considered to be a realistic step. Levin, who had been on the NCSJ staff since 1980, became its executive director in 1992.[55]

The current mission of NCSJ is to safeguard the individual

and communal political rights of Jews living in the FSU and to secure their religious and political freedoms. NCSJ actively monitors compliance by the governments of the FSU in the areas of free emigration and religious and cultural rights, and also monitors developments related to anti-Semitism in the Soviet successor states. NCSJ works closely with all branches of the U.S. government, particularly the White House, State Department, and CSCE in order to further its goals. Operation Lifeline provides a flow of material support, including kosher food and religious and cultural objects, to Jews in the FSU.[56] Levin views the NCSJ as more focused on Jewish issues than the UCSJ, which has a broader mandate to tackle a wide variety of human rights issues in the FSU.

He is especially concerned about former Ku Klux Klan leader David Duke, who is regarded as a folk hero in Ukraine where he is a frequent visitor, agitating expulsion of "Jewish extremists – the Zionists". Duke has been a featured speaker at MAUP, the Inter-Regional Academy of Personnel Management in Kyiv, which awarded him a doctorate.[57] In 1991 the current NCSJ president, Lesley Israel, campaigned in Louisiana to defeat Duke, who was running for governor as a white supremacist.[58] Fifteen years later, with support from the NCSJ, the State Department described MAUP as the "leading purveyor of anti-Semitic material in Ukraine" and alleged that Middle Eastern governments funded the school. Jewish organizations and the U.S. and Israeli embassies in Kyiv lobbied the Ukrainian government to dismiss the school's leadership.[59] In October 2006 the Ukrainian Ministry of Education denied official recognition of diplomas awarded by MAUP, and ordered the closure of thirty regional MAUP offices, but MAUP declared its intention to sue the Ukrainian government for "political persecution inspired by Zionist forces."[60]

NCSJ is also responding to the requests from Jewish communities in the FSU for connections with "sister" communities in America through its program of Kehilla Projects. Paired community projects supported by NCSJ and listed on their website are Washington-Moscow, Baltimore-Odessa, Western Connecticut-

Kazan, St. Louis-Riga, Boston-Dnipropetrovsk, and Chicago-Kyiv.[61]

Levin has pointed out that the nature of activism has changed since the days of "Let My People Go". "It's not letter writing, marching, sign waving; it's a much more subtle but no less significant form of activism," he said. "Today's activism," he continued, "involves working closely with the U.S. State Department, representatives in the former Soviet Union, and international human rights monitoring groups. It also involves myriad relations with the Jewish groups that are re-establishing a vibrant Jewish life in those countries."[62]

NOMINATION FOR THE NOBEL PEACE PRIZE

"It would be terrific if they could get it," Levin commented regarding the possibility of the 2007 Nobel Peace Prize being awarded to the UCSJ and MHG, and the presentation of the prize coinciding with Chanukah and the twentieth anniversary of the massive rally for Soviet Jewry in Washington.[63] On February 10, 2007, *The Jerusalem Post* reported that the two human rights monitoring groups had been nominated to share the 2007 Nobel Peace Prize. The article quoted Natan Sharansky, "There's no doubt these groups played a central role in advancing the release [of prisoners in the Soviet Union]. The two organizations conducted grassroots activism, each in its own way. The UCSJ connected housewives with international activism, and refuseniks with the international community. The Moscow Helsinki Group, meanwhile, turned the articles of the Helsinki Accords, including the human rights commitments that were initially considered [worthy of] mere lip service by Soviet leaders, into a central element of activism."

An important point made in the *Post* article was "while the Nobel nomination comes for the two groups' past successes in advocating for Soviet Jewish refuseniks and human rights generally in areas under Soviet influence, it also seeks to shine the spotlight on the troubles human rights NGOs are currently experiencing in the FSU."[64]

Yossi Abramowitz excitedly described the nomination – the third time the two groups received this recognition – as: "It's wild and a big honor."[65] That statement could also describe the feelings of every activist in the campaigns that brought about "a great moment in Jewish history"[66] – the saving of endangered Jews in perhaps the greatest example of a successful liberation since Moses, combined with the revival of religious and cultural traditions that had been stifled for three generations.

CONCLUDING THOUGHTS

Unlike the biblical Exodus, there was no solitary Moses to lead two million Jews out of the Soviet Union. This modern-day triumph over tyranny was achieved by the determination of countless heroic Jews in the Soviet Union who refused to cower under communist oppression and by thousands of their partners in courage throughout the free world who refused to abandon their brethren. All of them were heeding the cry "Never Again!" that arose out of the ashes of the Holocaust.

Whether they realized it or not, they were also responding affirmatively to the three questions posed by Hillel in the *Pirke Avot* (Ethics of the Fathers). He first asked "If I am not for myself, then who is for me?" The Jews of Riga defied Soviet authorities by erecting a memorial to the Jews murdered in the Rumbula Forest. Yasha Kazakov entered the Israeli Embassy in his quest for Hebrew books and information about the Jewish state. In Kiev Boris Kochubievsky stood up to cast his vote against an anti-Israel resolution. Risking their lives, the plotters of the aborted Leningrad hijacking demonstrated their overwhelming passion to emigrate and, by their action, ignited support worldwide support for Soviet Jewry.

Hillel's second question, "If I am only for myself, what am I?" was echoed by Elie Wiesel in *The Jews of Silence*. Ida Nudel demonstrated her compassion by visiting prisoners while she was conducting her own visible and vociferous campaign to emigrate.

And prisoners like Yosef Mendelevich and Natan Sharansky, upon their release, spoke out for others who were not yet free.

Finally, there are numerous examples showing fulfillment of Hillel's third question, "If not now, when?" They include Aryeh Kroll organizing a secret army of tourists to bring material, educational and spiritual aid to refuseniks, Michael Sherbourne telephoning refuseniks on a daily basis, Scoop Jackson legislating trade agreements tied to free emigration, and George Shultz negotiating for human rights along with disarmament and an end to the Cold War.

Climate of Trust exchange in St. Petersburg. Left to right: Father Fiofan, Bishop of Stavropol; Valery Tishkov, Commission on Tolerance and Religious Freedom; Alexander Kucherena, Commission on Control over Law Enforcement; Leroy Baca, Los Angeles County Sheriff; Pnina Levermore, Climate of Trust Executive Director. Photo Credit: Climate of Trust.

Aliyah Activist Memorial in Israel

They came from all over Israel. Some of them had vivid memories of refusenik picnics in the Ovrashky Forest outside Moscow. Others had made aliyah from the former Soviet Union before those picnics began in 1976. There were also the children and grandchildren of Soviet Jews who had struggled to emigrate. All of them, gathered for a picnic in the Ben Shemen Forest, midway between Tel Aviv and Jerusalem, were proud to be Israelis.

In addition, as at some of the Ovrashky gatherings, in 2003 at Ben Shemen there was a sprinkling of foreign tourists who were friends of refuseniks. Chana and Jacques Berlowitz and Ruth Bloch were visiting from Zurich, and the author and his wife, Carolyn, had recently arrived from California.

Since 1996 former refuseniks have been coming to Ben Shemen during the Sukkot festival. The site with its birch trees is reminiscent of Ovrashky. Photographs of prior gatherings in Ovrashky and Ben Shemen were strung from wires between trees. Absent, but not missed, however, were the KGB men who lurked behind the birch trees with their cameras, and the noisy tractors whose only purpose was to harass the Jews.

The birch trees in Ben Shemen were among 1,000 planted

in 2001 as part of the project spearheaded by Natan and Yona Shvartsman to create the Aliyah Activists Park in cooperation with the Jewish National Fund, which administers Ben Shemen. The Shvartsmans collected contributions from aliyah activists in Israel and friends abroad. These funds also enabled the erection of a playground, and a monument to commemorate the exodus from the USSR as a symbol of the activists' struggle and eventual victory.

The monument was designed by Boris Lobovikov, a long-time refusenik, who prior to applying for an exit visa had been the chief engineer responsible for the restoration of the tsars' Peterhof Palace near St. Petersburg. The monument in Ben Shemen was Lobovikov's last project, and after his death it was completed by his son, Michael, an architect in Haifa. It was unveiled at a dedication ceremony on October 17, 2003, and consists of two massive boulders separated by a stone staircase upon which a heavy broken and rusted chain is resting. Inscribed in Hebrew, Russian and English are the words of Jeremiah 31:16: "and your children shall return to their border."

The dedication on the base of the monument, read to the audience at Ben Shemen by Jacques Berlowitz in English is:

> For those, who struggled for the right to live in their own land
>
> For those, who returned home from all corners of the earth
>
> For those, who in their quest to return, made the ultimate sacrifice

Rabbi Eliyahu Essas expressed his thoughts about this newly dedicated monument. It reminded him of the pillar of stones built by Jacob and Laban at Mount Gilead, the midway point on Jacob's return home to the land of Canaan (Genesis 31:52). To Essas the aliyah activists' monument is a sign that the journey is only half complete. He asserts that those who have made the geographic journey from the former Soviet Union to Israel must journey further, spiritually, to return to their roots and traditional Jewish values.

Knesset member Yuri Shtern, who had been a Hebrew teacher in Moscow, and after making aliyah in 1981, founded the Soviet Jewry Education and Information Center, the Council of Immigrants Association, and the Soviet Jewry Zionist Forum, was a keynote speaker. He spoke about the wind of Jewish history that had brought Soviet Jews to the Land of Israel, and how had they made a reality of Theodor Herzl's famous words, which Shtern enunciated in Hebrew, "*Im tirtzu, ein zo aggadah*" ("If you will it, it is not a dream").

Aliyah activists monument in Ben Shemen Forest, Israel. Photo by Philip Spiegel.

GLOSSARY OF ABBREVIATIONS
AND FOREIGN WORDS

ACLU, American Civil Liberties Union
AJC, American Jewish Committee
AJCSJ, American Jewish Conference on Soviet Jewry
AJEX, Association of Jewish Ex-Servicemen (United Kingdom)
Aleph-bet, Hebrew alphabet
Aliyah, Immigration to Israel; literally, going up
AJS, Action Committee for the Jews in the Soviet Union
    (Switzerland)
APSJ, Action for Post-Soviet Jewry (Boston)
ASJ, Action for Soviet Jewry (Boston)

BACJRR, Bay Area Council for Jewish Rescue and Renewal (San
    Francisco)
BACSJ, Bay Area Council on Soviet Jewry (San Francisco)
Beriozka, Soviet state-run shops for foreign tourists with hard
    currency only
Bolshevik, member of the Communist Party
Brit, Brit Milah, ritual circumcision

CCS, Committee of Concerned Scientists

455

CCSA, Cleveland Committee on Soviet Anti-Semitism
CJF, Council of Jewish Federations
Chabad, Lubavitch Chassidic movement
Chamah, an international charitable organization supporting
    Russian-speaking Jews
Chassidut, Chassidic philosophy
Cheder, Jewish elementary school, usually a single room
Cheka, the Soviet state security organization from 1917 to 1922
CHRA, Center for Human Rights Advocacy
Chuppah, marriage canopy
Comité des Quinze, Committee of Fifteen (France)
CPMAJO, Conference of Presidents of Major American Jewish
    Organizations)
CPSU, Communist Party of the Soviet Union
CSCE, Commission on Security and Cooperation in Europe
CSSJ, California Students for Soviet Jews

Dacha, a country house
Druzhinniki, people's guard, police auxiliary
Duma, parliament

Gabbai, synagogue official
Geula, Redemption
Glasnost, openness
GNYCSJ, Greater New York Conference on Soviet Jewry
GPU, the Soviet state security organization from 1922 to 1934
Gulag, the network of Soviet prisons and camps

Haftarah, a reading from the Prophets
Havdalah, ritual at end of the Sabbath
HIAS, Hebrew Immigrant Aid Society (United States)
Histadrut, General Federation of Jewish Labor (Israel)

INS, Immigration and Naturalization Service (United States)
IOM, International Organization for Migration

IPC, International Physicians Commission
IPPNW, International Physicians for the Prevention of Nuclear War
IWCSJ, International Women's Committee for Soviet Jewry

JCRC, Jewish Community Relations Council
JDC, American Jewish Joint Distribution Committee
JDL, Jewish Defense League
JIAS, Jewish Immigrant Aid Services of Canada
JLC, Jewish Labor Committee (United States)
JVA, Jackson-Vanik Amendment
JWAR, Jewish Women Against Refusal
JWESR, Jewish Women for Emigration and Survival in Refusal

Kaddish, Jewish prayer for the dead
KGB, Soviet state security organization from 1954 to 1991
Kippah, skullcap worn by observant Jewish men
Kolkhoz, collective farm
Komsomol, Union of Communist Youth

Lag B'Omer, a joyous holiday 33 days after Passover that commemorates the breaking of a plague that afflicted the students of Rabbi Akiva in the 1st century
LICSJ, Long Island Committee for Soviet Jewry
Lishkat HaKesher, Lishka, Israeli liaison bureau for contacts with Soviet Jews
L'shana Haba B'Yerushalayim, Next Year in Jerusalem
Lubavitcher, A member of Chabad

Magen, Shield, an advocacy organization in Israel for Soviet Jews
Magen David, Star of David
Mashpiya, mentor
Mazkir hakibbutz, Kibbutz secretary
Menshevik, a minority faction of the Russian revolutionary movement

MFN, Most Favored Nation

Minyan, a quorum of ten Jews necessary for certain communal prayers

Mitzvah, commandment, good deed

MMSJ, Medical Mobilization for Soviet Jewry

Mohel, practitioner of ritual circumcision

Mossad, Israel's intelligence service

Nativ, path, a branch of the Lishkat HaKesher involving tourists to the USSR

NATO, North American Treaty Organization

NCSJ, National Conference on Soviet Jewry

NJCRAC, National Jewish Community Relations Advisory Council

NKVD, Soviet state security organization from 1922 to 1954

Noshrim, dropouts, people who chose not to immigrate to Israel

Olim, immigrants to Israel

Otkaznik, see Refusenik

OVIR, the Soviet Visas and Registration Department

Pamyat, Memory, an anti-Semitic organization in Russia created in 1985

Parasitism, the crime of living without official employment

Perestroika, restructuring, liberalization of the Soviet economic system

Prisoner of Zion, a prisoner of conscience who wanted to emigrate to Israel

Rebbe, spiritual leader, a Chassidic master

Refusenik, a Jew whose application to emigrate from the USSR was refused

Rosh HaShanah, Jewish New Year

SALT, Strategic Arms Limitation Talks

Samizdat, the clandestine copying and distribution of government-suppressed literature or other media in Soviet-bloc countries

SCCSJ, Southern California Council for Soviet Jews

Seder, Passover ritual meal

SFCSJ, South Florida Conference on Soviet Jewry

Shabbat, Sabbath

Shochet, ritual slaughterer of kosher meat

Shofar, a trumpet made of a ram's horn that sounded on *Rosh Hashanah* and at the conclusion of *Yom Kippur*

Shtadlanut, private and quiet negotiations with government leaders

Shtetl, a Jewish village in Eastern Europe

Simchat Torah, the festival of rejoicing with the Torah

Siruvnik, Hebrew term for refusenik

SJAG, Soviet Jewry Action Group (San Francisco)

SJEIC, Soviet Jewry Education and Information Center (Israel)

SOS, Scientists for Sakharov Orlov and Shcharansky

SSSJ, Student Struggle for Soviet Jewry

Tallit, prayer shawl

Tarbut, culture

Tefillin, phylacteries, leather prayer accessories

Tisha B'Av, a fast day recalling the destruction of the First and Second Temples

UCSJ, Union of Councils for Soviet Jews

Ulpan, Class for intensive study of the Hebrew language

Va'ad, Council

Voice of Israel, Israel's domestic and international radio service

Vyzov, Letter of invitation

WIZO, Women's International Zionist Organization Yad Vashem, the Holocaust Martyrs'and Heroes' Remembrance Authority (Israel)

Yad l'Yad, Hand to hand
Yad Vashem, the Holocaust Martyrs' and Heroes' Remembrance Authority (Israel)
Yeshiva, an institution of Torah learning
Yevrei, Jewish, the word indicating Jewish ethnicity on a Soviet passport
Yevsektsia, the Jewish section of the Communist Party
Yiddishkeit, Jewishness

ZOA, Zionist Organization of America

NOTES

PROLOGUE

1. Although the German word *Märchen* is properly translated as fable or fairy tale in English, this quote has been expressed by many writers and speakers as "If you will it, it is no dream."
2. Israel Cohen, *Theodor Herzl, founder of political Zionism* (New York: Yaseloff, 1959), p. 22
3. Ibid., pp. 31, 32
4. Ibid., p. 37
5. Allan Levine, *Scattered Among the Peoples* (Woodstock, N.Y.: Overlook Press, 2003), p. 248
6. Arthur Hertzberg, ed., *The Zionist Idea* (New York: Harper & Row, 1959), p. 202
7. Israel Cohen, *Theodor Herzl, founder of political Zionism*, p. 270
8. Walter Laqueur, *A History of Zionism* (New York: Schocken Books, 1976), p. xiii
9. Abram Leon Sachar, *A History of the Jews* (New York: Alfred A. Knopf, 1965), p. 367.
    The Balfour Declaration was issued by the foreign minister to Lord Rothschild and read, "His Majesty's Government view with favour the establishment in Palestine of a national home for the Jewish people, and will use their best endeavours to facilitate the achievement of this object, it being clearly understood that nothing shall be done which may prejudice the civil and religious rights of existing non-Jewish

communities in Palestine or the rights and political status enjoyed by Jews in any other country." Weizmann served as the first president of Israel from 1949 until his death in 1952.

10. Cohen, *Theodor Herzl, founder of political Zionism*, p. 329

11. Shari Schwartz, "Editor's Preface: The Making of a Martyr," 1992. http://www.shemayisrael.co.il/orgs/baiskaila/html/editor_s_preface__the_making_of_a_martyr.html

12. Petrus Buwalda, *They Did Not Dwell Alone* (Washington, D.C.: Woodrow Wilson Center Press, 1997), pp. 90–91

13. Grete Mahrer, "Herzl's Return to Judaism," *Herzl Year Book, Volume 11*, (New York: Herzl Press, 1959) pp, 28–29

14. Chaim Herzog, *Heroes of Israel* (Boston: Little, Brown & Company, 1989), pp. 90–91

CHAPTER ONE

1. Alexander Lerner in conversation with the author, Rehovot, October 28, 2003

2. Alexander Lerner, *Change of Heart* (Minneapolis, M.N.: Lerner Publications Co., 1992, p. 31

3. Edvard Radzinsky, *The Last Tsar*, trans. Marian Schwartz (New York: Doubleday, 1992), pp. 169–180

4. Ibid., p. 235

5. Zvi Gitelman, *Jewish Nationality and Soviet Politics* (Princeton, Princeton University Press, 1972), p. 69

6. Benjamin West, *Struggles of a Generation* (Tel Aviv: Massadah Publishing, 1959), pp. 7–8

7. Benjamin Pincus, *The Jews of the Soviet Union* (Cambridge, Cambridge University Press, 1988, p. 43

8. Zvi Gitelman, *A Century of Ambivalence* (Bloomington, Indiana University Press, 2001), pp. 64–70

9. Zvi Gitelman, *Being Jewish in Russia and Ukraine* (Talk at Visegradi Synagogue, Budapest, June 18, 2002, http://www.pestisul.hu/eddigi/2002-06-ZGit-Talk.html

10. Alexander Lerner, p. 33

11. Lionel Kochan, ed. *The Jews in Soviet Russia since 1917* (London: Oxford University Press, 1972), p. 64

12. Ibid., pp. 48–50

13. Benjamin Pincus, *The Jews of the Soviet Union*, pp. 58, 59. Yiddish was regarded as the language of the proletariat while Hebrew was considered by the *Yevsektsia* as the language of the Zionist bourgeoisie.

14. Zvi Gitelman, *A Century of Ambivalence*, p. 64

15. Zvi Gitelman, Jewish Nationality and Soviet Politics, pp. 224–226
16. Lester Samuel Eckman, *Soviet Policy Towards Jews and Israel 1917–1974* (New York: Shengold Publishers, 1974), pp.29–33
17. Zvi Gitelman, *Jewish Nationality and Soviet Politics*, p. 301. A Jew named Mendel Beilis was charged with killing a Christian child to obtain blood for baking Passover matzah.
18. *American Jewish Year Book*, 5683 (Philadelphia: Jewish Publication Society, 1922), p. 23
19. *American Jewish Year Book*, 5690 (Philadelphia: Jewish Publication Society, 1929), p. 68
20. Alexander Lerner in conversation with the author, Rehovot, October 28, 2003
21. Evan R. Chesler, *The Russian Jewry Reader*, (New York: Behrman House, 1974), p. 138
22. Zvi Gitelman, *A Century of Ambivalence*, p. 107
23. Martin Luther King, Jr., Address to the American Jewish Conference on Soviet Jewry, December 1966, http://www.ncsj.org/AuxPages/MLK.shtml#Address
24. Alexander Lerner, *Change of Heart*, p. 48
25. Ibid., p. 66
26. Ibid., pp. 59–60

CHAPTER TWO

1. Herman Branover and Abraham Naveh, *The Ultimate Jew*, trans. Mika Tubinshlak (Jerusalem: Shamir Publishing House, 2003) pp. 87–90
2. Ibid., pp. 65–83
3. Joseph Isaac Schneersohn, and trans. Alter B.Z. Metzger, *The Heroic Struggle* (Brooklyn, N.Y.: Kehot Publication Society, 1999), p.21
4. Branover and Naveh, p. 89
5. www.chabad.org/library/article.asp?AID=110490
6. Joseph Isaac Schneersohn, pp. 33–148
7. Ibid., p. 154
8. Ibid., p. 170
9. Branover and Naveh, pp. 91–93
10. Joseph Isaac Schneersohn, p. 171
11. Hillel Zaltzman in conversation with the author, New York, June 27, 2005
12. Rachel Levin Liberow in conversation with the author, London, March 24, 2004
13. Elchonon Lesches, *A Life of Sacrifice, The Life and Times of Reb Yitzchak Elchanon HaLevi Shagalow* (New York: Elchonon Leches, 2003)

14. Anthony Polonsky, *Jews in Eastern Poland and the USSR, 1939–46* (New York: St. Martin's Press, 1991) p. 26

15. A.D. Faigelson, *Reb Mendel* [in Hebrew] (Kfar Chabad: Kehos Publishing House, 1997) Excerpts were translated by Chana Berman of Palo Alto, CA.

16. Yossel Liberow in conversation with the author, Kfar Chabad, July 15, 2004, and November 23, 2005

17. Sue Fishkoff, *TheRebbe's Army* (New York: Random House, 2004) pp. 143–144

18. http://www.sichosinenglish.org/books/keeping-in-touch-2/rosh-hasha-nah.htm

19. Yechezkel Brod, trans. Daniel Goldberg, *Chassidic Light in the Soviet Darkness*, (Brooklyn, NY: Yechezkel Brod, 1999), pp. 143–158

20. Hillel Zaltzman in conversation with the author, New York, May 3, 2004

21. American Jewish Year Book 5718 (American Jewish Committee, 1957), p. 318

22. David Hollander, in telephone conversation with the author, May 12, 2004

23. Yaacov Ro'i, *The Struggle for Soviet Jewish Emigration 1948–1967* (Cambridge, England: Cambridge University Press, 1991) pp. 116–121

24. Hillel Zaltzman in conversation with the author, New York, May 3, 2004

25. Daniel Schorr, *Staying Tuned* (New York: Pocket Books, 2001) pp. 142–144

26. http://www.vaadua.org/VaadENG/JosefEng/Emmigration.htm

27. Rabbi Yosef Brod, in telephone conversation with the author, July 18, 2007

28. Herman Branover, *Return, The Spiritual Odyssey of a Soviet Scientist*, trans. Mika Tubinshlak (Jerusalem: Shamir Publishing House, 2002) pp. 80

29. Herman Branover in conversation with the author, New York, May 2, 2004

30. Herman Branover in telephone conversation with the author, March 1, 2004

CHAPTER THREE

1. Golda Meir, *My Life* (New York: G.P. Putnam's Sons, 1975), p. 245

2. Ibid., pp. 251–252

3. Jonathan Brent and Vladimir P. Naumov, *Stalin's Last Crime* (New York: HarperCollins, 2003), p. 96

4. Leonard Schroeter, *The Last Exodus* (Seattle, WA: University of Washington Press, 1979), p. 23

5. Yaacov Ro'i, *The Struggle for Soviet Jewish Emigration 1948–1967* (Cambridge, Cambridge University Press, 1991) pp. 34–35

6.   Michael Sherbourne, interviewed by Lou Rosenblum, London, May 15, 1987

7.   Alexander Luntz in conversation with the author, Jerusalem, October 26, 2003

8.   *American Jewish Year Book*, 5709 (Philadelphia: Jewish Publication Society, 1949), pp. 337–339

9.   Golda Meir, p. 248

10.   Geoffrey Martin and Natan Herzl, *A Matter of Priorities: Labor Zionism and the Plight of Soviet Jewry, 1917–1996* (Jerusalem: Diamond Books, 1996), pp. 31–32

11.   Israel Foreign Ministry, et al., *Documents on Israeli Soviet Relations, 1941–53* (London: Frank Cass Publishers, 2000) p. 29

12.   Murray Friedman and Albert Chernin, eds., *A Second Exodus* (Hanover, N.H.: Brandeis University Press, 1999), p. 227

13.   Geoffrey Martin and Natan Herzl, pp. 13–50

14.   Yaacov Ro'i, pp. 91–92

15.   Jonathan Brent and Vladimir P. Naumov, pp. 3–4

16.   Leonard Schroeter, pp. 126–127

17.   Yaacov Ro'i, p. 101

18.   Ibid., p. 157

19.   Ibid., p. 102–105

20.   Murray Friedman and Albert Chernin, pp. 71–75

21.   Geoffrey Martin and Natan Herzl, pp. 83–85

22.   Petrus Buwalda, *They Did Not Dwell Alone* (Washington, D.C.: Woodrow Wilson Center Press, 1997), p. 36

23.   Anshel Pfeffer, "Jerusalem & Babylon / Gleaning more from the Struggle for Soviet Jewry," www.haaretz.com, December 7, 2007

24.   Yaacov Ro'i, p. 285

25.   Meir Rosenne, in conversation with the author, Jerusalem, October 29, 2003

26.   Yaacov Ro'i, p. 138

27.   William Korey in conversation with the author, Bayside, NY, March 1, 2005

28.   http://cms.education.gov.il/EducationCMS/Units/PrasIsrael/Tashas/ArieKroll, (Hebrew, translated for the author by Natasha Ratner)

29.   Itchie Fuchs in telephone conversation with the author, August 31, 2005

30.   Seth Jacobson in telephone conversation with the author, May 19, 2004

31.   Dennis Prager in telephone conversation with the author, June 28, 2005

32.   Rami Aronzon in telephone conversation with the author, November 1, 2005

33.   Zale Anis in telephone conversation with the author, July 9, 2003

34.   Yosef Raday in telephone conversation with the author, March 20, 2006

35. http://cms.education.gov.il/EducationCMS/Units/PrasIsrael/Tashas/ ArieKroll, (Hebrew, translated for the author by Natasha Ratner)
36. http://nechemia.org/avney%20oderech_e.html
37. http://nechemia.org/writings/interview2_e.html
38. Murray Friedman and Albert Chernin, p. 77
39. Leonard Schroeter, pp. 122–129
40. http://nechemia.org/avney%20oderech_e.html
41. Murray Friedman and Albert Chernin, p. 231
42. William Orbach, *The American Movement to Aid Soviet Jews* (Amherst, MA: University of Massachusetts Press, 1979), p. 38
43. Ibid., p. 79
44. Daphne Gerlis, *Those Wonderful Women in Black*, (London: Minerva Press, 1996), pp. 22, 120
45. Leonard Schroeter in conversation with the author, Seattle, Washington, September 15, 2003
46. http://nechemia.org/writings/interview6_e.html
47. Murray Friedman and Albert Chernin, p. 81
48. Petrus Buwalda, p. 176
49. http://nechemia.org/writings/nativ2.html

CHAPTER FOUR

1. http://www.jewishlabor.org/JLC_Basic_History.pdf
2. http://www.ajc.org/site/c.ijITI2PHKoG/b.789093/k.124/Who_We_Are. htm
3. William Orbach, *The American Movement to Aid Soviet Jews* (Amherst, MA: University of Massachusetts Press, 1979), p. 18
4. Moshe Decter in conversation with the author, New York, May 5, 2004
5. Charles McGrath, "A Liberal Beacon Burns Out," *New York Times*, January 23, 2006
6. Douglas Martin, "Moshe Decter, 85, Advocate for Soviet Jews, Dies," *New York Times*, July 5, 2007
7. Yaacov Ro'i, *The Struggle for Soviet Jewish Emigration 1948–1967* (Cambridge, Cambridge University Press, 1991) pp. 161–162
8. Murray Friedman and Albert Chernin, eds., *A Second Exodus* (Hanover, N.H.: Brandeis University Press, 1999), p. 33
9. Moshe Decter in conversation with the author, New York, May 5, 2004
10. Yaacov Ro'i, pp. 122–125
11. Moshe Decter in telephone conversation with the author, September 26, 2006
12. Murray Friedman and Albert Chernin, p. 75
13. Susannah Heschel, "The Legacy of Abraham Joshua Heschel: Religion

and Politics," presented at The South Bay Institute for Jewish Living & Learning, Los Gatos, CA, March 16, 2006

14. http://www.ujc.org/content_display.html?ArticleID=5206
15. Reuven Kimelman, " Abraham Joshua Heschel: Our Generation's Teacher", http://www.crosscurrents.org/heschel.htm
16. Gershon Jacobson, "An Interview with Prof. Heschel about Russian Jewry", *Day Morning Journal*, September 13, 1963
17. Andrew Harrison, *Passover Revisited* (Madison, NJ: Fairleigh Dickinson University Press, 2001), p. 27
18. "Assembly Defends Heschel, Attacks 'Dismayed Rabbis,' *Long Island Jewish Press*, Hempstead, NY, June 1966
19. Elie Wiesel, in conversation with the author, Boston, MA, September 12, 2005
20. Elie Wiesel, *Memoirs – All Rivers Run to the Sea* (New York: Alfred A. Knopf, 1995), p. 365
21. Elie Wiesel, trans. Neal Kozodoy, *The Jews of Silence* (New York: Holt, Rinehart and Winston, Inc., 1966), pp. 18–21
22. Ibid., pp. 83–84
23. Ibid., p.127
24. "The Solomon Mykhoels Cultural Center," Executive Council of Australian Jewry on behalf of the World Jewish Congress, February 1989, p. 234
25. Elie Wiesel, *Memoirs – And the Sea is Never Full*, New York: Alfred A. Knopf, 1999), p. 88
26. Glenn Richter, in telephone conversation with the author, August 6, 2006
27. Wendy Eisen, *Count Us In* (Toronto: Burgher Books, 1995), pp. 13–22
28. Ibid., p. 46
29. William Orbach, p. 46
30. Elie Wiesel, *Memoirs – And the Sea is Never Full*, pp. 200–202
31. http://www.pbs.org/eliewiesel/nobel/index.html
32. Elie Wiesel, in conversation with the author, Boston, MA, September 12, 2005
33. Isi Leibler, in conversation with the author, Jerusalem, June 21, 2006
34. Isi Leibler, "Soviet Jewry – Report on Visit to Moscow (September 20–29, 1987)", p.
35. Yaacov Ro'i, p. 169
36. Isi Leibler, *Soviet Jewry and Human Rights* (Melbourne,: Human Rights Publications, 1965), pp. 6–7
37. Ibid., pp. 48–52
38. William Orbach, p. 98
39. Isi Leibler, in conversation with the author, Jerusalem, June 21, 2006
40. Isi Leibler, "Soviet Jewry – Report on Visit to Moscow (September 20–29, 1987)", pp. 36–57

41. Robert Pullam, *Bob Hawke: A Portrait*, (Sydney, Methuen of Australia, 1980), pp. 142–143

42. Stephen Mills, *The Hawke Years: The story from the inside* (Ringwood, Victoria, Australia: Viking, 1993), pp. 166–178

43. Isi Leibler, "Soviet Jewry – Report on Visit to Moscow (September 20–29, 1987)", pp. 39–257

44. Stephen Mills, pp. 176–179

45. Isi Leibler, "Report on Mission to Moscow October 16–25, 1988", p. 121

46. Ibid., p. 135

47. Jonathan Brent and Vladimir Naumov, *Stalin's Last Crime* (New York: Perennial, 2004), p. 94

48. Charles Hoffman, "Breakthrough for USSR Jews", *Jerusalem Post*, October 28, 1988

49. Esther Fein, "Lasting Faith of Jews Moves Wiesel," *New York Times*, February 13, 1989

50. Isi Leibler, in conversation with the author, Jerusalem, June 21, 2006

CHAPTER FIVE

1. History of Beth Israel – The West Temple, www.uahc.org/congs/oh/oho20/history.html

2. Lou Rosenblum, in conversation with the author, Middleburg Heights, OH, June 12, 2003

3. "Charges Reds Fear Anti-Semitism Debate", Cleveland *Plain Dealer*, November 29, 1963

4. William Orbach, *The American Movement to Aid Soviet Jews* (Amherst, MA: University of Massachusetts Press, 1979), p. 39

5. Archives of the Cleveland Council on Soviet Anti-Semitism, Western Reserve Historical Society, Cleveland, OH, Container 1, Folder 2

6. Lou Rosenblum

7. Archives of the Cleveland Council on Soviet Anti-Semitism, Western Reserve Historical Society, Cleveland, OH

8. Lou Rosenblum

9. Rabbi Moshe Sachs, in conversation with the author, Jerusalem, June 27, 2006

10. William Orbach. p. 42

11. Lou Rosenblum

12. Moshe Sachs, *Brave Jews*, unpublished manuscript, August 2005

13. Lou Rosenblum letter to the Honorable Charles A. Vanik, "On the 25th Anniversary of the Jackson-Vanik Amendment", March 26, 2000

14. Ellen Harris, "Celebrating 30 Years of Jackson-Vanik Amendment", Cleveland *Jewish News*, December 28, 2004

15. Lou Rosenblum
16. Anatoly Dobrynin, *In Confidence: Moscow's Ambassador to America's Six Cold War Presidents* (Seattle: University of Washington Press, 2000), pp. 267–268
17. Lou Rosenblum

CHAPTER SIX

1. "Honoring the Life of Jacob Birnbaum," Congressional Record, U.S. House of Representatives, June 18, 2007. www.govtrack.us
2. Jacob Birnbaum, "The Seminal Activity of the Student Struggle for Soviet Jewry (SSSJ) 1964–1966", unpublished manuscript, September 18, 2005
3. Rabbi Yitz Greenberg, in telephone conversation with the author, March 22, 2005
4. Rabbi Shlomo Riskin, in telephone conversation with the author, June 6, 2005
5. Rabbi Yitz Greenberg
6. Jacob Birnbaum, "The Seminal Activity of the Student Struggle for Soviet Jewry (SSSJ) 1964–1966"
7. Jacob Birnbaum, "U.S. Jewish Student Activism for Soviet Jewry in the 1960s", unpublished manuscript, October 2002
8. Bernard Kabak, in telephone conversation with the author, May 18, 2003
9. Jacob Birnbaum, "The Seminal Activity of the Student Struggle for Soviet Jewry (SSSJ) 1964–1966"
10. Glenn Richter, in conversation with the author, New York, May 18, 2003
11. Jim Torczyner, in telephone conversation with the author, May 8, 2005
12. Rabbi Arthur Green, in telephone conversation with the author, May 24, 2005
13. Jacob Birnbaum, "U.S. Student Activism for Soviet Jewry in the 1960s", unpublished manuscript, October 2002
14. Jacob Birnbaum, "The Seminal Activity of the Student Struggle for Soviet Jewry (SSSJ) 1964–1966"
15. William Orbach, *The American Movement to Aid Soviet Jews*, (Amherst, MA: University of Massachusetts Press, 1979), p. 28
16. Irving Spiegel, "Jews' Treatment by Soviet Scored", *New York Times*, October 19, 1964
17. Glenn Richter, email to the author, May 19, 2005
18. "The Seminal Activity of the Student Struggle for Soviet Jewry (SSSJ) 1964–1966"
19. Glenn Richter, email to the author, May 19, 2005
20. Jacob Birnbaum, "Dear Friend" letter on Student Struggle for Soviet Jewry letterhead, circa March 1965

21. Sue Cronk, "Jewish Students Picket Reds", Washington *Post*, May 21, 1965

22. Yossi Klein Halevi, *Memoirs of a Jewish Extremist*, (Boston: Little, Brown & Co., 1995)

23. "The Seminal Activity of the Student Struggle for Soviet Jewry (SSSJ) 1964–1966"

CHAPTER SEVEN

1. Yuri Chernyak, email to the author, December 12, 2003

2. Chaim Herzog, *Israel's Finest Hour*, (Jerusalem, Maariv Book Guild, 1967), p. 36

3. William Korey, *The Soviet Cage*, (New York: Viking Press, 1973), p. 5

4. Iver Peterson, "Soviet Jew who Got Out After 11 Years Tells How Difficult It Was," *New York Times*, December 6, 1969

5. Baruch Ashi, in conversation with the author, Jerusalem, June 23, 2006

6. Leonard Schroeter, *The Last Exodus* (Seattle, WA: University of Washington Press, 1979), pp. 44–46

7. Baruch Ashi

8. Allan Levine, *Scattered Among the Peoples* (Woodstock, NY: Overlook Duckworth, 2002), pp. 385–386

9. Murray Friedman and Albert Chernin, eds., *A Second Exodus* (Hanover, N.H.: Brandeis University Press, 1999), p. 56

10. Natasha Ratner email to the author, September 25, 2006

11. Baruch Ashi

12. Rivka Alexandrovich, in telephone conversation with the author, May 22, 2005

13. Leonard Schroeter, p. 82

14. Ibid., p. 227

15. Rivka Alexandrovich

16. Leonard Schroeter, pp. 231–237

17. Rivka Alexandrovich

18. Leonard Schroeter, p. 340

19. S.O.S. Soviet Jewry, Newsletter of the Student Struggle for Soviet Jewry, Vol. VI, #1, Fall-Winter 1969–1970, pp. 2–3

20. Yaakov Kedmi, in conversation with the author, Jerusalem, June 20, 2006

21. Leonard Schroeter, pp. 88–90

22. Yaakov Kedmi

23. Wendy Eisen, *Count Us In* (Toronto: Burgher Books, 1995), pp. 28–29

24. William W. Orbach, p. 88

25. Ehud Barak in an interview with *Pravda*, March 29, 2004

26. Yaakov Kedmi

CHAPTER EIGHT

1. http://www.charleslindbergh.com/history/index.asp
2. Hillel Butman, *From Leningrad to Jerusalem: The Gulag Way*, trans. Stefani Hoffman, (Berkeley, CA: Benmir Books, 1990), p. 77
3. Si Frumkin, *Prisoner of the Month – May: Mark Dymshitz*, (Los Angeles: Southern California Council for Soviet Jews, 1977)
4. Hillel Butman, pp. 78–98
5. Yuri Fedorov in conversation with the author, New York, July 19, 2003
6. Leonard Schroeter, *The Last Exodus* (Seattle, WA: University of Washington Press, 1979), p. 150
7. Yosef Mendelevich, in conversation with the author, Jerusalem, October 21, 2003
8. Hillel Butman, pp. 99–106
9. Ibid., pp. 116–130
10. Rami Aronzon, in telephone conversation with the author, November 1, 2005
11. Leonard Schroeter, pp. 189–192
12. Rebecca Rass and Morris Brafman, *From Moscow to Jerusalem* (New York: Shengold Publishers, 1976) pp. 168–169
13. Boris Morozov, *Documents on Soviet Jewish Emigration* (Portland, O.R.: Frank Cass, 1999), pp. 84–85
14. Hillel Butman, pp. 154–157
15. Rebecca Rass and Morris Brafman, pp. 170–179
16. Murray Seeger, "Episode in Leningrad", *Present Tense*, Autumn 1975, p. 31
17. Leonard Schroeter, pp. 149–169
18. Ibid., p. 206
19. Murray Seeger, p. 32
20. Rebecca Rass and Morris Brafman, p. 199
21. Richard Lourie, *Sakharov* (Hanover, N.H.: Brandeis University Press, 2002), p. 228
22. Leonard Schroeter, p. 159
23. Ibid., pp. 181–183
24. Rebecca Rass and Morris Brafman, pp. 201–206
25. Edward Kuznetsov, *Prison Diaries*, trans. Howard Spier (Briarcliff Manor, NY: Scarborough Books, 1975) pp. 217–254
26. Andrei Sakharov, *Memoirs*, trans. Richard Lourie (New York, NY: Alfred A. Knopf, 1990), p. 323
27. Israel Zalmanson in conversation with the author, Fairlawn, NJ, March 6, 2005
28. Richard Lourie, *Sakharov*, pp. 228–229
29. Leonard Schroeter, pp. 174–177
30. Glenn Richter, email correspondence with the author, September 7, 2006

31. Wendy Eisen, *Count Us In*, (Toronto, ON: Burgher Books, 1995), p. 35
32. Murray Friedman and Albert Chernin, eds., *A Second Exodus* (Hanover, NH: Brandeis University Press, 1999), p. 207
33. Leonard Schroeter, pp. 201–206
34. William W. Orbach, *The American Movement to Aid Soviet Jews*, (Amherst, MA: University of Massachusetts Press, 1979), pp. 158–159
35. Murray Seeger, pp. 34–37
36. Sylva Zalmanson, in conversation with the author, Ashdod, June 27, 2006
37. Murray Friedman and Albert Chernin, p. 177
38. Carol Golfus and Naomi Ballas, "Prisoner of Zion – Ida Nudel", http://w3.kfar-olami.org.il/reed/resources/landmark/aliyah/INUDEL.htm
39. "April 27, 1987 Ida Nudel is 56 Years Old Today", Washington Committee for Soviet Jewry
40. Yosef Mendelevich, in conversation with the author, Jerusalem, October 21, 2003
41. William Korey, *The Promises We Keep*, (New York: St. Martin's Press, 1993), p. 128
42. Yosef Mendelevich
43. Yuri Fedorov in conversation with the author, New York, July 19, 2003

CHAPTER NINE

1. Natan Sharansky, *Fear No Evil*, trans. Stefani Hoffman (New York: Random House, 1988), p. 61
2. Mark Ya. Azbel, *Refusenik*, (Boston: Houghton Mifflin, 1981), pp. 435–436
3. http://www.jewishvirtuallibrary.org/jsource/History/Human_Rights/refuseniks.html
4. Theodore Shabad, "Soviet Lists 8 Jews Who It Says Can't Leave," *New York Times*, February 22, 1987
5. Chaim Potok, *The Gates of November* (New York: Alfred A. Knopf, 1996), pp. 111–140
6. Ibid., pp. 102–103
7. David K. Shipler, *Russia* (New York: Times Books, 1983) pp. 148–149
8. David K. Shipler, "Vladimir Slepak: Like His Father and Sons a Russian Dissident, Now Isolated From Both," *New York Times*, November 26, 1977
9. Chaim Potok, p. 109
10. Ibid., pp. 141–155
11. Wendy Eisen, *Count Us In* (Toronto: Burgher Books, 1995), p. 39
12. Chaim Potok, pp. 160–164

13. Vladimir Slepak in conversation with the author, Kfar Saba, October 24, 2003

14. Leonard Schroeter, *The Last Exodus* (Seattle, WA: University of Washington Press, 1979), pp. 337–339

15. Chaim Potok, pp. 191–204

16. Vladimir Slepak in conversation with the author, Kfar Saba, October 24, 2003

17. Daphne Gerlis, *Those Wonderful Women in Black* (London: Minerva Press, 1996), p. 97

18. Chaim Potok, pp. 226–227

19. Vladimir Slepak in conversation with the author, Kfar Saba, October 24, 2003

20. Chaim Potok, pp. 230–231

21. Alexander Lerner, *Change of Heart*, (Minneapolis: Lerner Publications, 1992), p. 11

22. Mark Ya. Azbel, p. 251

23. Alexander Lerner, *Change of Heart*, pp. 16–23

24. Alexander Lerner in conversation with the author, Rehovot, October 28, 2003

25. Leonard Schroeter, p. 317

26. Petrus Buwalda, *They Did Not Dwell Alone*, (Washington, D.C.: Woodrow Wilson Press, 1997), pp. 67–68

27. Mark Ya. Azbel, pp. 410–413

28. Alexander Lerner, *Change of Heart*, pp. 195–203

29. Ibid., p. 213

30. Helsinki Agreement Watchdog Committee, London, Case Sheet on Lerner, October 1981

31. Alexander Lerner, *Change of Heart*, pp. 201–227

32. David Bezmozgis, "Alexander Yakob Lerner, Refusenik," *New York Times Magazine*, December 26, 2004

33. Yuli Kosharovsky in conversation with the author, Jerusalem, October 30, 2003

34. Leonard Schroeter, pp. 289–291

35. Yuli Kosharovsky

36. Haskel Lookstein, in conversation with the author, New York, September 15, 2005

37. Mark Ya. Azbel, p. 430

38. Martin Gilbert, *The Jews of Hope* (New York: Penguin Books, 1985), pp. 95–97

39. Women's Campaign for Soviet Jewry, London, Case sheet on Yuli Kosharovsky, November, 1981

40. Martin Gilbert, pp. 100–103

41. Yuli Kosharovsky, email to the author, June 30, 2006
42. Yuli Kosharovsky in conversation with the author, Jerusalem, October 30, 2003
43. David Harris, *In the Trenches* (Hoboken, NJ: KTAV Publishing House, 2000), p. 51
44. Yuri Chernyak, in conversation with the author, Waltham, MA, May 22, 2003
45. Petrus Buwalda, *They Did Not Dwell Alone*, (Washington, DC: Woodrow Wilson Press, 1997), p. 221
46. Martin Gilbert, "Orphans of Glasnost," *Hadassah Magazine*, May 1988, pp. 22–23
47. "25 to Run in Bay to Breakers for Soviet Jews," *Northern California Jewish Bulletin*, May 6, 1988, p. 6
48. "Yuli Kosharovsky's Address to President Ronald Reagan," Soviet Jewry Education and Information Center, Jerusalem, Israel, May 31, 1988
49. Union of Councils for Soviet Jews, Soviet Jewish Refusenik Case History – Yuli Kosharovsky, August, 1988
50. Susan Birnbaum, "Kosharovsky and Four Others Win Permission to Emigrate from USSR," *Daily News Bulletin, Jewish Telegraphic Agency*, December 15, 1988
51. Hugh Orgel, "Kosharovsky Arrives in Israel After 18-Year Wait for Freedom," *Daily News Bulletin, Jewish Telegraphic Agency*, March 13, 1989
52. Yuli Kosharovsky in conversation with the author, Jerusalem, October 30, 2003

CHAPTER TEN

1. Vladimir Prestin, in conversation with the author, Tel Aviv, June 19, 2006
2. Michail Beizer, *The Jews of St. Petersburg*, trans. Michael Sherbourne, (Philadelphia: Jewish Publications Society, 1989), p. 270
3. Vladimir Prestin
4. Michael Prestin, in conversation with the author, Sunnyvale, CA, January 18, 2004
5. Leah Prestin-Shapiro, *Slovar Zapreshchennogo Laxyka*, (Minsk: MET, 2005)
6. Vladimir Prestin
7. Ida Nudel, *A Hand in the Darkness*, trans. Stefani Hoffman (New York: Warner Books, 1990), pp. 16–18
8. Ibid., pp. 33–34
9. Leonard Schroeter, *The Last Exodus* (Seattle, WA: University of Washington Press, 1979), p.338

10. Vladimir Prestin
11. Genya Intrator, "The Legends of Our Time," Beth Tzedec Bulletin, Toronto, August 1978
12. Boris Morozov, *Documents on Soviet Jewish Emigration* (Portland, OR: Frank Cass, 1999), pp. 141–145
13. Wendy Eisen, *Count Us In* (Toronto: Burgher Books, 1995), p. 95
14. Natan Sharansky, *Fear No Evil*, trans. Stefani Hoffman (New York: Random House, 1988). p. 188
15. Petrus Buwalda, *They Did Not Dwell Alone* (Washington, DC: Woodrow Wilson Press, 1997), p. 122
16. Daphne Gerlis, *Those Wonderful Women in Black* (London: Minerva Press, 1996), p. 47
17. Helsinki Agreement Watchdog Committee, London, "Soviet Jewish Prisoner of Conscience" October 1983
18. Martin Gilbert, *The Jews of Hope* (New York: Penguin Books, 1985), pp. 128–129
19. Yosef Begun, in conversation with the author, Jerusalem, October 29, 2003
20. Martin Gilbert, "Andropov and the Jews", http://www.angelfire.com/sc3/soviet_jews_exodus/English/JewishHistory_s/JewishHistoryGilbert.shtml
21. Boris Morozov, pp. 244–245
22. Union of Councils for Soviet Jews, Information, No. 101, Iosif Begun, POC, October 17, 1983
23. "Soviet Crackdown on Dissidents Seen," *Washington Post*, October 15, 1983
24. Jacob Birnbaum, in telephone conversation with the author, September 19, 2006
25. Ronald Reagan, "Statement on Soviet Human Rights Policies, October 18, 1983, www.reagan.utexas.edu/archives/speeches/1983/101883b.htm
26. Petrus Buwalda, pp. 203–204
27. Wendy Eisen pp. 233–234
28. James O. Jackson, "A Day in the Depths of the Gulag", *Time*, March 9, 1987
29. Wendy Eisen, p. 234
30. Isi Leibler, "Soviet Jewry – Report on Visit to Moscow", September 20–29, 1987
31. "Begun Leaves Soviet, Ending 17-Year Emigration Struggle". *New York Times*, January 19, 1988
32. Martin Gilbert, *The Jews of Hope*, p. 138
33. Evgeny Lein, *Lest We Forget* (Jerusalem: Jerusalem Publishing Centre, 1997) cover jacket flaps

34. Martin Gilbert, *The Jews of Hope*, pp. 191–192

35. Evgeny Lein, email to the author, October 8, 2006

36. Evgeny Lein, *Lest We Forget*, pp. 1–5

37. Martin Gilbert, *The Jews of Hope*, pp. 1–6

38. Evgeny Lein, *Lest We Forget*, pp. 5–7

39. Evgeny Lein, in conversation with the author, Jerusalem, June 26, 2006

40. Greg (Zvi) Margolin, "Vladimir Albrecht: Democratic Senator Should Have Tried Gulag's Balanda, *Jewish Russian Telegraph*, Boston, MA, June 27, 2005

41. Evgeny Lein, *Lest We Forget*, pp. 8–11

42. Jakov Gorodezky, in conversation with the author, Brooklyn, NY, March 6, 2005

43. Martin Gilbert, *The Jews of Hope*, pp. 15, 16

44. Evgeny Lein, in conversation with the author, Jerusalem, June 26, 2006

45. Martin Gilbert, *The Jews of Hope*, pp. 18–31

46. Evgeny Lein, in conversation with the author, Jerusalem, June 26, 2006

47. Alexander Paritsky, in conversation with the author, Modi'in, Israel, October 23, 2003

48. Sharon Morton, "Yad l'Yad: Helping Hands Across the Ocean", March 2, 1998, http://www.fsumonitor.com/stories/yschernovtsy.shtml

49. Alexander Paritsky

50. Daphne Gerlis, p. 243

51. Alexander Paritsky

52. Yuli Edelstein, in conversation with the author, Jerusalem, June 22, 2006

53. Wendy Eisen, p. 174

54. Yuli Edelstein

55. Yuly Edelstein case sheet, Amnesty International, London, 1985

56. Yuli Edelstein

57. Wayne Firestone, in conversation with the author, San Francisco, October 8, 2007

58. Yuli Edelstein

59. Wendy Eisen, pp. 237–238

60. Yuli Edelstein

61. Natasha Ratner, in conversation with the author, Jerusalem, June 23, 2006

62. Vladimir Magarik, in conversation with the author, Jerusalem, October 19, 2003

63. Newsletter to UCSJ Member Councils, Union of Councils for Soviet Jews, Washington, DC, May 2, 1986

64. "Refusenik Cellist Sentenced to Three Years", News Release, Coalition to Free Soviet Jews, New York, June 9, 1986

65. News Release, Soviet Jewry Education and Information Center, Jerusalem, June 10, 1986
66. "Emergency Action Response Network (EARN): POC Alexei Magarik, Union of Councils for Soviet Jews, Washington, DC, December 4, 1986
67. Letter to Mikhail Gorbachev from Congressman Gary Ackerman, July 28, 1986
68. Lu Ann Briggs, "Soviet Campaign for son's release," *Indiana Daily Student*, September 11, 1986
69. News Release, Soviet Jewry Education and Information Center, Jerusalem, November 9, 1986
70. Hinda Cantor, "Helsinki review puts heat on Moscow," *Miami News*, December 24, 1986
71. Vladimir Magarik, in conversation with the author, Jerusalem, Israel, October 19, 2003
72. "Refusenik Update," Union of Councils for Soviet Jews, Washington, DC, February 13, 1987
73. "Refusenik Update," Union of Councils for Soviet Jews, Washington, DC, May 4, 1987
74. "Telephone Conversation with Alexei Magarik," Soviet Jewry Education and Information Center, Jerusalem, Israel, October 1, 1987

CHAPTER ELEVEN

1. Petrus Buwalda, *They Did Not Dwell Alone* (Washington, DC: Woodrow Wilson Press, 1997), p. 63
2. Dina Beilin, email to the author, December 27, 2004
3. Petrus Buwalda, p. 63
4. Mark Ya. Azbel, *Refusenik* (Boston: Houghton Mifflin, 1981), p. 239
5. Dina Beilin, email to the author, December 27, 2004
6. Ida Nudel, *A Hand in the Darkness*, trans. Stefani Hoffman (New York: Warner Books, 1990), p. 31–33
7. Dina Beilin, email to the author, November 15, 2006
8. Tony Barbieri, in telephone conversation with the author, January 14, 2007
9. Foundation for Documentary Projects, Interview with Alexander Luntz
10. Dina Beilin, email to the author, November 15, 2006
11. Yona Shvartsman, in correspondence with the author, August 21, 2006
12. Mark Ya. Azbel, p. 283
13. Alexander Lerner, *Change of Heart* (Minneapolis: Lerner Publications, 1992), p. 192
14. Jack Cohen, *Confessions of a Jewish Activist* (unpublished memoir sent to the author August 28, 2006)

15. Mark Ya. Azbel, pp. 301–311
16. Mark Azbel, in telephone conversation with the author, October 4, 2006
17. Boris Morozov, *Documents on Soviet Jewish Emigration* (Portland, OR: Frank Cass, 1999), pp. 197–199
18. Soviet Jewish Prisoner of Conscience: Dr. Viktor Brailovsky, Women's Campaign for Soviet Jewry, London, U.K., July 1981
19. Martin Gilbert, *The Jews of Hope* (New York: Penguin Books, 1985), pp. 140–141
20. Biography of Soviet Jewish Refusenik: Aba Taratuta, Women's Campaign for Soviet Jewry, London, August 1987
21. Foundation for Documentary Projects, Interview with Victor Brailovsky
22. Anthony Austin, "Police in Moscow Again Bar Meeting of Jewish Scientists," *New York Times*, November 30, 1980
23. Biography of Soviet Jewish Refusenik: Alexander Ioffe, Women's Campaign for Soviet Jewry, London, U.K., January 1984
24. Yuri Chernyak, in conversation with the author, Waltham, MA, May 22, 2003
25. Solomon Schimmel, "Report on Trip to the Soviet Union to Visit Jewish Refuseniks," http://www.angelfire.com/sc3/soviet_jews_exodus/English/WhoHelped_s/WhoHelpedSchimmel_1.shtml
26. Yuri Chernyak, interviewed by Aba Taratuta, Boston, June 2004, http://www.angelfire.com/sc3/soviet_jews_exodus/English/Interview_s/InterviewChernyak.shtml
27. Tony Barbieri, email to the author, July 18, 2007
28. Cheryl North, "Vladimir Feltsman Interview", Classical Music Column for ANG Newspapers Preview Section, June 14, 2002
29. Mark Berenfeld, in conversation with the author, New York, May 5, 2004
30. Vladimir Kislik, in conversation with the author, Jerusalem, October 22, 2003
31. Soviet Jewish Prisoner of Conscience: Vladimir Kislik, Women's Campaign for Soviet Jewry, London, June 1981
32. Ida Nudel, pp. 295–299
33. Foundation for Documentary Projects, Interview with Bella Gulko
34. Foundation for Documentary Projects, Interview with Vladimir Kislik
35. Natasha Chernyak "Jewish Women Movement in Moscow," March 7, 1988
36. Irene Lainer, et al, "Appeal to all Women's Organizations", undated attachment to email from Irene Lainer to the author, January 8, 2007
37. Dan Fisher, "Soviet Police Thwart Women's Protest", *Los Angeles Times*, March 9, 1978

38. Jim Gallegher, "Refusenik wives join fight to leave Russia," *Chicago Tribune*, June 30, 1978

39. Biography of Soviet Jewish Refusenik: Alexander Ioffe, Women's Campaign for Soviet Jewry, London, January 1984

40. Irene Lainer email to the author, January 8, 2007

41. Philip Taubman, "For Soviet-American Couple, Memories Dim After 11 Years," *New York Times*, November 10, 1985

42. Robin Toner, "After 11 Years Apart, Russian is Reunited with American Husband," *New York Times*, January 31, 1986

43. Irene Lainer in telephone conversation with the author, December 19, 2006

44. 1990 Calendar distributed by Bay Area Council for Soviet Jews, San Francisco

45. Yehudit Agracov, "We, Jewish Women...," http://www.angelfire.com/sc3/soviet_jews_exodus/English/Interview_s/InterviewJewishWomen.shtml

46. Natasha and Yuri Chernyak, in conversation with the author, Waltham, MA, May 22, 2003

47. Inna Uspensky, in conversation with the author, Jerusalem, Israel, October 17, 2003

48. Martin Gilbert, "A Family Divided," *Jerusalem Post*, October 7, 1987

49 : "Young Mother on Hunger Strike," *Outcry*, Bay Area Council for Soviet Jews, San Francisco, November, 1987

50. Vladimir Meshkov, in conversation with the author, Neve Daniel, Israel, June 23, 2006

51. The 1991 Congressional Call to Conscience Vigil (Senate – July 22, 1991) http://thomas.loc.gov/cgi-bin/query/D?r102:22:./temp/~r102mq78Wb

52. Anonymous former Poor Relative, email to Gennady Farber, Palo Alto, CA, September 21, 2004

53. Yuri Chernyak, interviewed by Aba Taratuta, Boston, June 2004, http://www.angelfire.com/sc3/soviet_jews_exodus/English/Interview_s/InterviewChernyak.shtml

CHAPTER TWELVE

1. http://www.coldwar.org/articles/40s/h_bomb.html

2. Richard Lourie, *Sakharov, A Biography* (Hanover, N.H.: Brandeis University Press, 2002), p. 113

3. ibid., p. 6

4. Andrei Sakharov, *Memoirs*, trans. Richard Lourie (New York: Alfred A. Knopf, 1990), p. 112

5. http://spinner.cofc.edu/~tmasters/public/amstory.htm

6. Richard Lourie, p. 131
7. ibid., pp. 135–143
8. ibid., p. 157
9. ibid. p. 194
10. http://www.aip.org/history/sakharov/cosmresp.htm
11. Petrus Buwalda, *They Did Not Dwell Alone* (Washington, DC: Woodrow Wilson Center Press, 1997), p. 237
12. Leonard Schroeter, *The Last Exodus* (Seattle, WA: University of Washington Press, 1979), p.384
13. Harrison Salisbury, editor, *Sakharov Speaks* (New York: Vintage Books, 1974) p. 68
14. Richard Lourie, pp. 210–214
15. ibid., pp. 220–221
16. ibid., pp. 222–227
17. Andrei Sakharov, *Memoirs*, pp. 321–324
18. Richard Lourie, pp. 238–242
19. Leonard Schroeter, p. 339
20. Andrei Sakharov, *Memoirs*, p. 344
21. ibid., p. 394
22. Richard Lourie, pp. 254–265
23. Andrei Sakharov, *Memoirs*, p 429
24. Gina Waldman in conversation with the author, Tiburon, CA, August 13, 2003
25. Yuri Tuvim, in telephone conversation with the author, January 4, 2006
26. http://www.aip.org/history/sakharov/humrt.htm
27. Henry Kissinger, *Years of Renewal* (New York: Simon & Schuster, 1999). pp. 638–639
28. Petrus Buwalda, pp. 119–120
29. Andrei Sakharov, *Memoirs*, p. 456
30. Paul Goldberg, *The Final Act* (New York: William Morrow & Co., 1988), pp. 219, 229
31. Richard Lourie, pp. 286–287
32. William Korey, *The Promises We Keep* (New York: St. Martin's Press, 1993), pp. 78–79
33. Richard Lourie, p. 293
34. Anatoly Dobrynin, *In Confidence* (Seattle, WA: University of Washington Press, 1995), pp. 512–513
35. Petrus Buwalda, p. 140
36. http://www.aip.org/history/sakharov/exile.htm
37. Andrei Sakharov, "A Letter from Exile," *New York Times Magazine*, June 8, 1980, p. 31
38. Elena Bonner, *Alone Together*, (New York: Alfred A. Knopf, 1986), p. 240

39. Richard Lourie, pp. 330–333
40. Anatoly Dobrynin, pp. 552–553
41. Richard Lourie, pp. 344–349
42. William Korey, p. 231
43. Jack Matlock, *Reagan and Gorbachev* (New York: Random House, 2004), p. 262
44. Richard Lourie, pp. 374–375
45. Carolyn Ekedahl and Melvin Goodman, *The Wars of Eduard Shevardnadze* (University Park, PA: Pennsylvania State University Press, 1997), pp. 245–246
46. Richard Lourie, p. 380
47. ibid., pp. 381–388
48. David Remnick, *Lenin's Tomb* (New York: Random House, 1993), pp 280–282
49. Yakov Alpert, *Making Waves* (New Haven, CT: Yale University Press, 2000), p. 198
50. David Remnick, p. 287

CHAPTER THIRTEEN

1. Anatoly Dobrynin, *In Confidence* (Seattle, WA: University of Washington Press, 1995), p. 345
2. Paul Goldberg, *The Final Act* (New York: William Morrow & Co., 1988), pp. 18–22
3. William Korey, *The Promises We Keep* (New York: St. Martin's Press, 1993), pp. 1–4
4. Petrus Buwalda *They Did Not Dwell Alone* (Washington, DC: Woodrow Wilson Center Press, 1997), pp. 115–116
5. William Korey, p. 14
6. Henry Kissinger, *Years of Renewal* (New York: Simon & Schuster, 1999). p. 639
7. William Korey, pp. 6–9
8. Murray Friedman and Albert Chernin, eds., *A Second Exodus* (Hanover, NH: Brandeis University Press, 1999), p. 125
9. Anatoly Dobrynin, p. 346
10. Martin Gilbert, *The Jews of Hope* (New York: Penguin Books, 1985), pp. 93–94
11. Daphne Gerlis, *Those Wonderful Women in Black* (London: Minerva Press, 1996), p. 51
12. Paul Goldberg, pp. 59–61
13. Ibid., p. 62

14. Yuri Orlov, trans. Thomas P. Whitney, *Dangerous Thoughts* (New York: William Morrow & Co., 1991), pp. 188–189

15. Paul Goldberg, p. 62

16. ibid., pp. 59–63

17. Murray Friedman and Albert Chernin, p. 127

18. Yuri Orlov, pp. 39–111

19. Ibid., pp. 118–122

20. Ibid., p. 136

21. Ibid., pp. 143–147

22. Ibid., pp. 160–162

23. Ibid., p. 168

24. Yuri Orlov in telephone conversation with the author, December, 8, 2005

25. Paul Goldberg, pp. 35–37

26. Yuri Orlov, pp. 189–191

27. Paul Goldberg, pp. 57–58

28. William Korey, pp. 50–51

29. Petrus Buwalda, p. 70

30. Natan Sharansky, trans. Stefani Hoffman, *Fear No Evil* (New York: Random House, 1988), p. 107

31. Jack Matlock, *Reagan and Gorbachev* (New York: Random House, 2004), p. 67

32. Petrus Buwalda, pp. 122–126

33. William Korey, pp. 61–88

34. Yuri Orlov in telephone conversation with the author, December, 8, 2005

35. Yuri Orlov, pp. 211–215

36. Tom Stoppard, *Tom Stoppard in Conversation* (Ann Arbor: University of Michigan Press, 1994), p. 109

37. Yuri Orlov, pp. 217–231

38. William Korey, p. 120

39. Petrus Buwalda, p. 181

40. Natan Sharansky with Ron Dermer, *The Case for Democracy* (New York: Public Affairs, 2004), p. 129

41. Paul Goldberg, p. 246–257

42. Yuri Orlov, p. 227

43. Natan Sharansky, pp. 246–252

44. Andrei Sakharov, "The Future of Human Rights," *Boston Globe*, September 18, 1980, p. 11

45. William Korey, p. 115

46. Jeri Laber, *"The Courage of Strangers"* (New York: Public Affairs, 2002), p. 182, 198

47. William Korey, pp. 101–170
48. Jack Matlock, pp. 197–211
49. Yuri Orlov, pp. 279–300
50. Jeri Laber, pp. 257–258
51. Yuri Orlov in telephone conversation with the author, December 8, 2005

CHAPTER FOURTEEN

1. David Shipler, *Russia: Broken Idols, Solemn Dreams* (New York: Times Books, 1983), p. 134
2. Natan Sharansky with Ron Dermer, *The Case for Democracy*, (New York: Public Affairs, 2004), p. 44
3. Natan Sharansky with Ron Dermer
4. Doublethink is a term meaning the acceptance of two contradictory ideas at the same time, coined in 1949 by George Orwell in his novel *1984*
5. Petrus Buwalda, *They Did Not Dwell Alone* (Washington, DC: The Woodrow Wilson Press, 1997), p. 68
6. Natan Sharansky, "The Lessons of Our Struggle," *Jerusalem Report*, May 17, 2004
7. Natan Sharansky, trans. Stefani Hoffman, *Fear No Evil* (New York: Random House, 1988), pp. xiv–xvi
8. Natan Sharansky, in conversation with the author, Jerusalem, June 13, 2006
9. Alexander Lerner, *Change of Heart* (Minneapolis, MN: Lerner Publications, 1992), p.192
10. Natan Sharansky, "The Lessons of Our Struggle,"
11. Jerusalem Post, *Anatoly and Avital Shcharansky: The Journey Home* (New York: Harcourt Brace Jovanovich, Publishers, 1986), pp. 3–6
12. Ibid., p. 33–39
13. Natan Sharansky, in telephone conversation with the author, April 19, 2007
14. Jerusalem Post, Anatoly and Avital Shcharansky: The Journey Home, pp. 40–41
15. Jerusalem Post, Anatoly and Avital Shcharansky: The Journey Home, p. 45
16. Natan Sharansky, trans. Stefani Hoffman, *Fear No Evil*, p. xix
17. Natan Sharansky, in conversation with the author, Jerusalem, June 13, 2006
18. Jerusalem Post, Anatoly and Avital Shcharansky: The Journey Home, pp. 54–57
19. Natan Sharansky, in conversation with the author, Jerusalem, June 13, 2006

20. Dina Beilin, in conversation with the author, Jerusalem, June 21, 2006
21. Dina Beilin, e-mail to the author, November 21, 2006
22. Natan Sharansky, "The Lessons of Our Struggle," *Jerusalem Report*, May 17, 2004
23. Dina Beilin, in conversation with the author, Jerusalem, June 21, 2006
24. Mark Ya. Azbel, *Refusenik* (Boston: Houghton Mifflin, 1981), p. 455
25. Dina Beilin, e-mail to the author, November 21, 2006
26. Natan Sharansky, "The Lessons of Our Struggle," *Jerusalem Report*, May 17, 2004
27. Alexander Lerner, pp. 198–199
28. Ida Nudel, trans. Stefani Hoffman, *A Hand in the Darkness* (New York: Warner Books, 1990), p. 134
29. Vladimir Shakhnovsky, in conversation with the author, Jerusalem, June 25, 2006
30. Paul Goldberg, *The Final Act* (New York: William Morrow & Co., 1988), pp. 243–244
31. Dina Beilin, e-mail to the author, November 21, 2006
32. Natan Sharansky, "The Lessons of Our Struggle," *Jerusalem Report*, May 17, 2004
33. Alan Dershowitz, *Chutzpah* (Boston: Little, Brown, 1991), p. 256
34. William Korey, "American Reaction to the Shcharansky Case," *American Jewish Year Book, 1980*, (New York: American Jewish Committee and Philadelphia: Jewish Publication Society, 1979), p. 120
35. Anatoly Dobrynin, *In Confidence* (Seattle: University of Washington Press, 1995), pp. 399–400
36. Natan Sharansky, trans. Stefani Hoffman, *Fear No Evil*, pp. 17–105
37. Avital Sharansky, in conversation with the author, Jerusalem, October 26, 2003
38. Natan Sharansky, trans. Stefani Hoffman, *Fear No Evil*, pp.106–121
39. Ibid., p. 113
40. Boris Morozov, *Documents on Soviet Jewish Emigration* (Portland, OR: Frank Cass, 1999), pp. 228–229
41. Natan Sharansky, in telephone conversation with the author, April 19, 2007
42. Kevin Klose in telephone conversation with the author, January 23, 2007
43. Natan Sharansky, trans. Stefani Hoffman, *Fear No Evil*, pp. 188–189
44. David Shipler, pp. 37–38
45. Glenn Richter, "More Light on the Sharansky Trial," Student Struggle for Soviet Jewry, New York, Press Release, September 12, 1978
46. Natan Sharansky, trans. Stefani Hoffman, *Fear No Evil*, p. 225
47. Paul Goldberg, pp. 275–276

48. Natan Sharansky, trans. Stefani Hoffman, *Fear No Evil*, pp. 229–235

49. Howard Tyner, "You can't see the gulag from here," Montreal *Gazette*, April 6, 1979

50. Natan Sharansky, trans. Stefani Hoffman, *Fear No Evil*, pp. 274–277

51. Ibid., p. 305

52. Natan Sharansky, Caravan for Democracy lecture at Stanford University, April 14, 2004

53. Wendy Eisen, *Count Us In* (Toronto: Burgher Books, 1995), pp. 118–119

54. Jerusalem Post, Anatoly and Avital Shcharansky: The Journey Home, pp. 101–102

55. Avital Sharansky, in conversation with the author, Jerusalem, October 26, 2003

56. Daphne Gerlis, *Those Wonderful Women in Black* (London: Minerva Press, 1996), p. 68

57. Alan Dershowitz, pp. 250–252

58. Ibid., pp. 252–255

59. Walter Ruby, "The Role of Nonestablishment Groups," in *A Second Exodus* (Hanover, NH: Brandeis University Press, 1999), p. 216

60. Ibid., p. 211

61. Aba & Ida Taratuta, interview of Glenn Richter, New York, September 2005, Remember & Save, http://www.angelfire.com/sc3/soviet_jews_exodus/English/Interview_s/InterviewRichter.shtml

62. Joan Baez, in telephone conversation with the author, January 23, 2006

63. Wendy Eisen, pp. 130–131

64. Ron Clingen, "PM tells Shcharansky's wife he hasn't forgotten," *Ottawa Journal*, March 21, 1979

65. Carla Hall, "Marking an Unhappy Anniversary," *Washington Post*, March 16, 1979

66. Doug Cahn, in telephone conversation with the author, April 7, 2006

67. William Korey, "American Reaction to the Shcharansky Case," *American Jewish Year Book, 1980* (New York: American Jewish Committee and Philadelphia: Jewish Publication Society, 1979), pp. 128–129

68. Walter Ruby, p. 208

69. Avi Weiss, in conversation with the author, Riverdale, NY, May 5, 2004

70. Natan Sharansky, trans. Stefani Hoffman, *Fear No Evil*, pp. 240–241

71. Natan Sharansky, lecture at Hoover Institution, Stanford, CA, April 14, 2004

72. Natan Sharansky, trans. Stefani Hoffman, *Fear No Evil*, pp. 305–308

73. Ibid., pp. 269–273

74. Ibid., pp. 310–322

75. Jerusalem Post, Anatoly and Avital Shcharansky: The Journey Home, p. 225

76. Natan Sharansky, "The Lessons of Our Struggle," *Jerusalem Report*, May 17, 2004

77. Craig Whitney, "Spy Trader," *New York Times*, May 23, 1993

78. Avi Weiss, *Principles of Spiritual Activism* (Hoboken, NJ: KTAV Publishing House, 2002, p. 154

79. Jerusalem Post, Anatoly and Avital Shcharansky: The Journey Home, pp. 230–231

80. http://www.age-of-the-sage.org/sharansky/biography.html

81. Jerusalem Post, Anatoly and Avital Shcharansky: The Journey Home, p. 232

82. Natan Sharansky, in conversation with the author, Jerusalem, June 13, 2006

83. Natan Sharansky, "The Lessons of Our Struggle," *Jerusalem Report*, May 17, 2004

84. http://www.age-of-the-sage.org/sharansky/biography.html

85. Nathan Guttman, "Sharansky To Resign From Politics," *Forward.com*, October 20, 2006

86. Ida Nudel, in conversation with the author, Karmei Yosef, Israel, October 27. 2003

87. Yuval Yoaz, "Sharansky awarded NIS 900,000 damages for libelous book." *Haaretz*, December 21, 2003

88. Nathan Guttman, "Sharansky To Resign From Politics," *Forward.com*, October 20, 2006

89. President's Remarks at Medal of Freedom Ceremony, Office of the White House Press Secretary, December 15, 2006

CHAPTER FIFTEEN

1. Murray Friedman and Albert Chernin, eds., *A Second Exodus* (Hanover, NH: Brandeis University Press, 1999), p. 173

2. William Orbach, *The American Movement to Aid Soviet Jews* (Amherst, MA: University of Massachusetts Press, 1979), pp. 65–66

3. Ibid., pp. 6–7

4. Murray Friedman and Albert Chernin, p. 38

5. William Orbach, p. 26

6. Murray Friedman and Albert Chernin, p. 44

7. William Orbach, p.46

8. Ibid., pp. 62–63

9. Jerry Goodman, in conversation with the author, New York, May 5, 2004

10. William Orbach, pp. 26–27

11. Murray Friedman and Albert Chernin, p. 174

12. Henry Feingold, *Silent No More* (Syracuse, NY: Syracuse University Press, 2007), p. 95

13. Jerry Goodman, in conversation with the author, New York, May 5, 2004

14. Jerry Goodman, interviewed by Aba & Ida Taratuta, New York, June 21, 2004, http://www.angelfire.com/sc3/soviet_jews_exodus/English/ Interview_s/InterviewGoodman.shtml

15. Murray Friedman and Albert Chernin, pp. 174–175

16. Jerry Goodman, in conversation with the author, New York, May 5, 2004

17. Jerry Goodman, interviewed by Aba & Ida Taratuta

18. William Orbach, p. 64

19. Jack Cohen, email to the author, January 10, 2008

20. William Korey, *The Promises We Keep* (New York: St. Martin's Press, 1993), p. 25

21. Murray Friedman and Albert Chernin, pp. 127–128

22. Foundation for Documentary Projects, Interview with Steny Hoyer

23. NCSJ Board of Governors Meeting, Washington, DC, October 27, 2003

24. "NCSJ Mourns Morris B. Abram," Press Release, March 16, 2000, http:// www.ncsj.org/AuxPages/abram031600.shtml

25. Murray Friedman and Albert Chernin, pp. 33–35

26. George Shultz in conversation with the author, Stanford, CA, February 5, 2003

27. Natan Sharansky, "The Lessons of Our Struggle," *Jerusalem Report*, May 17, 2004

28. Jerry Goodman, in conversation with the author, New York, May 5, 2004

29. Jerry Goodman, email to the author, January 29, 2008

30. David Harris, in telephone conversation with the author, August 1, 2003

31. David Harris, "A Moment That Made Jewish History" *New York Jewish Week*, November 30, 2007

32. David Harris, *In the Trenches* (Hoboken, NJ: KTAV Publishing House, 2000), pp. 83–90

33. Wendy Eisen, *Count Us In*, (Toronto, Burgher Books, 1995), p. 247

34. Henry Feingold, pp. 273–274

35. Evgeny Lein, *Lest We Forget* (Jerusalem: The Jerusalem Publishing Centre, 1997), p. 238

36. Murray Friedman and Albert Chernin, p. 180

37. William Korey, pp. 239–240

38. Ibid, pp. 280–281

39. Henry Feingold, p. 290

40. Wendy Eisen, p. 265

41. William Korey, pp. 319–326
42. Shoshana Cardin, in conversation with the author, Baltimore, MD, July 25, 2003
43. William Korey, p. 403
44. Shoshana Cardin
45. Malcolm Hoenlein, in conversation with the author, New York, July 17, 2003
46. Haskel Lookstein, in conversation with the author, New York, September 15, 2005
47. Zeesy Schnur, in telephone conversation with the author, November 15, 2005
48. Azriel Genack, in conversation with the author, New York, May 2, 2004
49. Glenn Richter, email to the author. January 31, 2008
50. Azriel Genack, email to the author, February 1, 2008
51. Zeesy Schnur
52. Henry Feingold, pp. 101–102
53. Malcolm Hoenlein, in telephone conversation with the author, August 23, 2007
54. Henry Feingold, p. 102
55. Murray Friedman and Albert Chernin, p. 209
56. Wendy Eisen, p. 111
57. Ibid, p. 209
58. Adam Dickter, "He Was a Good Friend," *Jewish Week*, New York, April 4, 2003
59. The Commission on Soviet Jewish Life, American Jewish Committee Archives, JAD 1970s, Box 205, Soviet Jewry, Greater NY Conference
60. Haskel Lookstein, in conversation with the author, New York, September 15, 2005
61. Report on Visit of Rabbi and Mrs. Haskel Lookstein to the Soviet Union, September 16 – October 2, 1975
62. Ramaz Mission & Legacy, http://www.ramaz.org/public/mission5.cfm

CHAPTER SIXTEEN

1. David W. Weiss, *The Wings of the Dove* (Washington: B'nai B'rith Books, 1987), p. 145
2. *25th Anniversary Issue, Outcry*, Bay Area Council for Soviet Jews, San Francisco, CA, October 1992, p. 8
3. David Weiss, pp. 140–142
4. David Weiss, in conversation with the author, Jerusalem, October 19, 2003
5. David Weiss, *The Wings of the Dove*, p. 143

6. David Weiss, in conversation with the author, Jerusalem, October 19, 2003

7. Bill Light, in conversation with the author, Santa Fe, NM, August 17, 2004

8. Edward Tamler, in conversation with the author, San Mateo, CA, January 22, 2003

9. Edward Tamler, "Early History of the Bay Area Council for Soviet Jews", unpublished essay

10. William Orbach, *The American Movement to Aid Soviet Jews* (Amherst, MA: University of Massachusetts Press, 1979), p. 32

11. *25th Anniversary Issue, Outcry*, Bay Area Council for Soviet Jews, San Francisco, CA, October 1992, p. 3

12. John Rothmann, in conversation with the author, San Francisco, CA, December 16, 2003

13. *25th Anniversary Issue, Outcry*, Bay Area Council for Soviet Jews, San Francisco, CA, October 1992, p. 9

14. Murray Friedman and Albert Chernin, eds., *A Second Exodus* (Hanover, NH: Brandeis University Press, 1999), p. 182

15. Harold Light Files, Papers of the Bay Area Council for Soviet Jews, Archives of the American Jewish Historical Society, New York

16. William Orbach, p. 45

17. Harold Light, "Confrontation? Yes! Violence? No!!!", *Exodus*, Soviet Jewry Action Group, San Francisco, December 3, 1970

18. Edward Tamler, "Early History of the Bay Area Council for Soviet Jews", unpublished essay

19. Will Stevens, "Tough Day for Russ Skipper," San Francisco *Examiner*, April 8, 1970

20. Bob Hirsch, in telephone conversation with the author, August 27, 2004

21. *25th Anniversary Issue, Outcry*, Bay Area Council for Soviet Jews, San Francisco, CA, October 1992, p. 11

22. Lillian Foreman, in conversation with the author, San Francisco, January 28, 2003

23. Edward Tamler, Remarks at the Funeral of Harold Light, Colma, CA, September 15, 1974

24. *25th Anniversary Issue, Outcry*, Bay Area Council for Soviet Jews, San Francisco, CA, October 1992, p. 14

25. Si Frumkin, in conversation with the author, Studio City, CA, February 25, 2003

26. Zev Yaroslavsky, in conversation with the author, Los Angeles, CA, April 21, 2003

27. Foundation for Documentary Projects, Interview with Zev Yaroslavsky

28. Si Frumkin, in conversation with the author, Studio City, CA, February 25, 2003

29. California Students for Soviet Jews, press release, March 17, 1972

30. Earl Raab, in conversation with the author, San Francisco, CA, February 10, 2003

31. Earl Raab, "Executive of the Jewish Community Relations Council, 1951–1987; Advocate of Minority Rights and Democratic Pluralism," oral history conducted in 1996 by Eleanor K. Glaser, Regional History Office, The Bancroft Library, University of California, Berkeley, 1998

32. Doug Kahn, in conversation with the author, San Francisco, CA, December 14, 2003

33. Si Frumkin, in conversation with the author, Studio City, CA, February 25, 2003

34. Harold Light Files, Papers of the Bay Area Council for Soviet Jews, Archives of the American Jewish Historical Society, New York, NY

35. Norm Schlossberg, in conversation with the author, San Francisco, CA, August 31, 2004

36. "Russian Fur Protest at I. Magnin," San Francisco *Chronicle*, November 25, 1972

37. Gina Waldman, in conversation with the author, Tiburon, CA, August 12, 2003

38. Murray Friedman and Albert Chernin, eds., pp. 188–189

39. Ibid., p. 232

40. Foundation for Documentary Projects, Interview with Zev Yaroslavsky

41. Zev Yaroslavsky, in conversation with the author, Los Angeles, CA, April 21, 2003

42. Zev Yaroslavsky

43. Si Frumkin, in conversation with the author, Studio City, CA, February 25, 2003

44. *25th Anniversary Issue, Outcry*, Bay Area Council for Soviet Jews, San Francisco, CA, October 1992, p. 17

45. Doug Kahn, in conversation with the author, San Francisco, CA, December 14, 2003

46. John Rothmann, in conversation with the author, San Francisco, CA, December 16, 2003

47. *25th Anniversary Issue, Outcry*, Bay Area Council for Soviet Jews, San Francisco, CA, October 1992, pp. 23–27

48. Murray Friedman and Albert Chernin, eds., p. 188

49. *25th Anniversary Issue, Outcry*, Bay Area Council for Soviet Jews, San Francisco, October 1992, p. 26

50. Greg Smith, in conversation with the author, San Francisco, July 2, 2003

51. Murray Friedman and Albert Chernin, eds., p. 191

52. Morey Schapira, in conversation with the author, Sunnyvale, July 5, 2004

53. Murray Friedman and Albert Chernin, eds., p. 190

54. Andy Altman-Ohr, "Former Protesters Celebrate Inside Russian Consulate", *Northern California Jewish Bulletin*, November 26, 1999

55. Gina Waldman, in conversation with the author, Tiburon, CA, August 12, 2003

56. Bob Hirsch, in telephone conversation with the author, August 27, 2004

57. Gina Waldman

58. Clark Mason, "Soviet Dissident Credits Westerners For His Emigration," *Harvard Crimson*, October 30, 1975
Alexander Goldfarb returned to the Soviet Union in the late 1990s to work on a project funded by George Soros to eradicate tuberculosis in Russian prisons. At Lefortovo Prison Goldfarb met former KGB agent Alexander Litvinenko who was awaiting trial on charges of abuse of office. They became friends and in 2000 Goldfarb helped Litvinenko defect to Britain. Goldfarb was Litvinenko's spokesman before his death from radiation poisoning in November 2006.

59. Gina Waldman

60. Caroline Drewes, "At the heart of a human rights struggle," *San Francisco Examiner*, November 21, 1989

61. *25th Anniversary Issue, Outcry,* Bay Area Council for Soviet Jews, San Francisco, October 1992, p. 15

62. "Underground Jewish Art," *San Francisco Chronicle*, August 5, 1976

63. Morey Schapira

64. Gina Waldman

65. Petrus Buwalda, *They Did Not Dwell Alone* (Washington, DC: The Woodrow Wilson Press, 1997), pp. 139–146

66. Morey Schapira

67. Eva Seligman-Kennard, in conversation with the author, San Anselmo, CA, August 24, 2005

68. David Waksberg, in conversation with the author, Palo Alto, CA, March 26, 2004

69. *25th Anniversary Issue, Outcry,* Bay Area Council for Soviet Jews, San Francisco, October 1992, p. 23

70. David Waksberg, in conversation with the author, Palo Alto, CA, March 26, 2004

71. Daniel Grossman, in conversation with the author, San Francisco, September 3, 2004

72. Marshall Platt, in conversation with the author, Foster City, CA, May 10, 2005

73. Murray Friedman and Albert Chernin, eds., p. 195

74. David Waksberg
75. Judy Balint, in conversation with the author, Jerusalem, October 23, 2003
76. Sheldon Wolfe, in conversation with the author, San Francisco, December 17, 2003
77. *25th Anniversary Issue, Outcry,* Bay Area Council for Soviet Jews, San Francisco, October 1992, p. 35
78. Ibid., p. 39
79. Greg Smith
80. *25th Anniversary Issue, Outcry,* Bay Area Council for Soviet Jews, San Francisco, October 1992, p. 40
81. David Waksberg, letter to BACJRR board members, July 21, 1994

CHAPTER SEVENTEEN

1. Lou Rosenblum interviewed by Daniel Rosenblum, September 22, 1996, Transcript edited by Lou Rosenblum, 2004
2. Discussion between Hillel Levine and Lou Rosenblum on control of Soviet Jewry issues by the Israeli Government, Brookline, MA, December 27, 1987
3. Murray Friedman and Albert Chernin, eds., *A Second Exodus* (Hanover, NH: Brandeis University Press, 1999), pp. 229–231
4. Discussion between Hillel Levine and Lou Rosenblum
5. Lou Rosenblum interviewed by Daniel Rosenblum
6. William Orbach, *The American Movement to Aid Soviet Jews* (Amherst, MA: University of Massachusetts Press, 1979), pp. 68–69
7. Si Frumkin, in conversation with the author, Studio City, CA, February 25, 2003
8. Foundation for Documentary Projects, Interview with Zev Yaroslavsky
9. William Korey, in conversation with the author, Bayside, NY, March 1, 2005
10. Foundation for Documentary Projects, Interview with Zev Yaroslavsky
11. Bob and Myriam Wolf, in telephone conversation with the author, April 9, 2004
12. Obituary of Avraham Shifrin, by Michael Sherbourne, March 10, 1978
13. Adele Sandberg, in telephone conversation with the author, January 8, 2004
14. William Orbach, p. 42
15. Robert Wolf, email to the author, April 19, 2007
16. Adele Sandberg, in telephone conversation with the author, January 8, 2004
17. Moshe Sachs, *Brave Jews,* unpublished manuscript

18. Bob and Myriam Wolf, in telephone conversation with the author, April 9, 2004
19. South Florida Conference on Soviet Jewry, press release, June 7, 1973
20. Cathy Lynn Grossman, "500 at Cape Launch Plea for Soviet Jews," *Miami Herald*, July 15, 1975
21. Joel Sandberg, fax to the author, April 23, 2007
22. Bob and Myriam Wolf, in telephone conversation with the author, April 9, 2004
23. Frederic Sherman, "Orphans of the Exodus Fight Soviet Cruelty," *Miami Herald*, February 15, 1976
24. Dear Friends letter, National Conference on Soviet Jewry, March 7, 1977
25. Foundation for Documentary Projects, Interview with Adele Sandberg
26. Robert Wolf, email to the author, April 19, 2007
27. Adele Sandberg, in telephone conversation with the author, January 8, 2004
28. Joel Sandberg, fax to the author, April 23, 2007
29. Wayne Firestone, in conversation with the author, San Francisco, October 8, 2007
30. Micah Naftalin, email to the author, April 17, 2007
31. Andrew Harrison, *Passover Revisited: Philadelphia's Efforts to Aid Soviet Jews, 1963–1998*, (Madison, NJ: Fairleigh Dickinson University Press, 2001), p. 25
32. Ibid., p. 29
33. Murray Friedman and Albert Chernin, eds., p. 42
34. Malcolm Hoenlein, in conversation with the author, New York, July 17, 2003
35. Andrew Harrison, p. 40
36. Toby Shuster, in conversation with the author, Jerusalem, June 19, 2006
37. Andrew Harrison, pp. 36–37
38. Enid Wurtman, in conversation with the author, Jerusalem, October 30, 2003
39. Joe Smukler, in telephone conversation with the author, April 9, 2007
40. Stuart Wurtman, memo to All Councils, January 6, 1976
41. Enid Wurtman, email to the author, July 10, 2003
42. Enid Wurtman, in conversation with the author, Jerusalem, October 30, 2003
43. Morey Schapira, in conversation with the author, Sunnyvale, CA, July 6, 2007
44. Steny Hoyer, "In Remembrance of Irene Manekofsky," *Congressional Record*, September 10, 1992
45. Sid Manekofsky, in conversation with the author, Washington, DC, July 21, 2003

46. Joan Dodek and Ruth Newman, "Washington Jewry's Activities on Behalf of Soviet Jews, 1968–1991", *The Record*, Jewish Historical Society of Greater Washington, 1991, p. 7

47. Ruth Newman, email to the author, July 21, 2007

48. Joan Dodek and Ruth Newman, pp. 7–9

49. Joan Dodek, in telephone conversation with the author, December 9, 2003

50. Ruth Newman, in conversation with the author, Bet Shemesh, Israel, October 21, 2003

51. Terence Flynn, in conversation with the author, Novato, CA, January 24, 2003

52. Naomi Shapiro's father, Lev Shapiro, first applied to emigrate in 1977. The Shapiros were one of the 99 separated families listed in the 1977 issue of the series of books on refusenik published by the South Florida Conference on Soviet Jewry.

53. Terence Flynn

54. Rabbi David Oler, in telephone conversation with the author, July 10, 2007

55. Rabbi David Oler, "Our Soviet Brethren," Proceedings of the 1986 Rabbinical Assembly Convention

56. Rabbi David Oler, in telephone conversation with the author, June 8, 2005

57. Morey Schapira, in conversation with the author, Sunnyvale, CA, July 6, 2007

58. Joan Dodek and Ruth Newman, p. 15

59. Bob Gordon, in conversation with the author, Boston, May 21, 2003

60. Morey Schapira, in conversation with the author, Sunnyvale, CA, July 5, 2004

61. William Orbach, p. 116

62. "Trip of Marge & Bob Gordon, July 6–July 20, 1975, Moscow, Kiev, Leningrad,"

63. Bob Gordon, in conversation with the author, Boston, May 21, 2003

64. "Bob Gordon – Man of Action," Action for Post-Soviet Jewry, invitation to reception at Temple Emanuel, Newton, MA, May 19, 2003

65. Gloria Negri, "Clara Katz: Soviet Émigré Saved Ailing Granddaughter", Boston *Globe*, October 4, 2006

66. Bob Gordon, in conversation with the author, Boston, MA, May 21, 2003

67. Sheila Galland, in conversation with the author, Waltham, MA, May 20, 2003

68. Lynn Singer, in conversation with the author, East Meadow, NY, July 18, 2003

69. Foundation for Documentary Projects, Interview with Lynn Singer

70. John LeBoutillier, "Lynn Singer: Long Island's Voice on Behalf of Soviet Jewry," *Congressional Record*, March 2, 1982

71. Lynn Singer, in conversation with the author, East Meadow, NY, July 18, 2003

72. "Long Island Honors 'Guardian Angel' Ida Nudel," Long Island Committee on Soviet Jewry, press release, June 20, 1979

73. "Join Us at Our Olympic Village in Exile," Long Island Committee on Soviet Jewry, press release, June 12, 1980

74. Lynn Singer, in conversation with the author, East Meadow, NY, July 18, 2003

75. http://www.angelfire.com/sc3/soviet_jews_exodus/English/WhoHelped_s/WhoHelpedLynn.shtml

76. Lorel Abarbanell, in conversation with the author, Chicago, June 23, 2004

77. Joel Sprayregen, letter to Henry Feingold, February 18, 2005

78. Sidney Yates, "Operation Exodus, *Congressional Record*, September 23, 1970

79. Lorel Abarbanell, in conversation with the author, Chicago, June 23, 2004

80. Alexander Lerner, *Change of Heart*, (Minneapolis: Lerner Publications, 1992), pp. 190–191

81. Lorel Abarbanell, in conversation with the author, Chicago, June 23, 2004

82. Lorel Abarbanell, letter to the author, July 12, 2007

83. Lorel Abarbanell, interviewed by Aba Taratuta, Omaha, NE, Remember & Save, July 18, 2004, http://www.angelfire.com/sc3/soviet_jews_exodus/English/Interview_s/InterviewAbarbanell.shtml

84. Pamela Cohen, email to the author, August 2, 2007

85. Marillyn Tallman, in conversation with the author, Highland Park, IL, June 22, 2004

86. Foundation for Documentary Projects, Interview with Pamela Cohen

87. Jewish Women's Archive, http://www.jwa.org/exhibits/wwd/jsp/bio.jsp?personID=ppcohen

88. Harvey Barnett, in telephone conversation with the author, June 9, 2005

89. Marillyn Tallman, in conversation with the author, Highland Park, IL, June 22, 2004

90. Donald Harrison, "Hecht Synagogue: A Fortress of Faith Overlooks Jerusalem," *San Diego Press-Heritage*, May 7, 1999

91. "Chicago Native Explores Changed City After Years in Soviet Union," *New York Times*, July 6, 1989

92. Pamela Cohen, in telephone conversation with the author, June 8, 2005, IL

93. Morey Schapira, in conversation with the author, Sunnyvale, CA, July 6, 2007

94. Pamela Cohen, in telephone conversation with the author, June 8, 2005

95. Murray Friedman and Albert Chernin, eds., p. 234

96. Pamela Cohen, email to the author, August 14, 2007

97. Micah Naftalin, in conversation with the author, Washington, DC, July 22, 2003

98. Pamela Cohen, email to the author, August 14, 2007

99. Murray Friedman and Albert Chernin, eds., p. 221

100. Ibid., p. 238

101. Micah Naftalin, email to the author, August 20, 2007

102. Micah Naftalin, email to the author, March 23, 2007

103. Pamela Cohen, email to the author, August 14, 2007

104. Micah Naftalin, email to the author, August 20, 2007

105. Murray Friedman and Albert Chernin, eds., p. 235

106. Pamela Cohen, in telephone conversation with the author, December 6, 2006

107. Evgeny Lein, *Lest We Forget* (Jerusalem: The Jerusalem Publishing Centre, 1997), p. 248

108. Micah Naftalin, email to the author, April 17, 2007

109. Murray Friedman and Albert Chernin, eds., pp. 235–236

110. Pamela Cohen, in telephone conversation with the author, December 6, 2006

111. Foundation for Documentary Projects, Interview with Pamela Cohen

112. Micah Naftalin, email to the author, August 31, 2007

113. Leonid Stonov, in conversation with the author, Highland Park, IL, June 22, 2004

114. Micah Naftalin, email to the author, August 31, 2007

115. Leonid Stonov, email to the author, May 3, 2007

116. Petrus Buwalda, *They Did Not Dwell Alone*, (Washington, DC: Woodrow Wilson Center Press, 1997), p. 202

117. Leonid Stonov, in conversation with the author, Highland Park, IL, June 22, 2004

118. Murray Friedman and Albert Chernin, eds., p. 235

119. Foundation for Documentary Projects, Interview with Pamela Cohen

120. Leonid Stonov, in conversation with the author, Highland Park, IL, June 22, 2004

121. Micah Naftalin, email to the author, April 17, 2007

122. Murray Friedman and Albert Chernin, eds., pp. 224–225

CHAPTER EIGHTEEN

1. "Sister Rose's Passion", http://www.faithindialogue.org/update/story. cfm?chnl=20&storyid=83
2. Chris Hedges, "Public Lives; She Helped Change a Church's View of Jews," *New York Times*, July 29, 2004
3. "Sister Rose's Passion",
4. Eugene DuBow, in telephone conversation with the author, March 15, 2006
5. Eleanor Blau, "Nixon Asked to Plead for Soviet Jews," *New York Times*, March 21, 1972
6. William Orbach, *The American Movement to Aid Soviet Jews* (Amherst, MA: University of Massachusetts Press, 1979), pp. 108–9
7. Necrology: Sister Ann Elizabeth Gillen, January 14, 1995, Society of the Holy Child Jesus Archives, Rosemont PA.
8. Caroline Drewes, "On the line for Soviet Jews," *San Francisco Examiner*, Dec. 16, 1974
9. A. James Rudin, in telephone conversation with the author, March 23, 2006
10. Paula Herbut, "Nun Says Russians Seized Notes, Film," *Philadelphia Evening Bulletin*, June 30, 1978
11. Ida Nudel, *A Hand in the Darkness*, (New York: Warner Books, 1990), p. 157
12. Anders Jerichow, "A Nun Wants to Give Two Years of Her Life in Siberia," *Berlingske Tidende*, (English translation),Copenhagen, July 17, 1980
13. National Interreligious Task Force on Soviet Jewry, Press Release, Madrid, Nov. 25, 1980
14. Jim Asker, "Religious Persecution Seen as Top KGB Priority," *Houston Post*, Dec. 3, 1983
15. Gretchen Keiser, "Religious Rights A Topic During Russians' Visit," *Georgia Bulletin*, Archdiocese of Atlanta, May 24, 1984
16. Steve Maynard, "Plight of Soviet Jews is Getting Worse, American Nun Says," *Houston Chronicle*, Sept. 13, 1986
17. Judy Turpie, "Project Co-Adoption Sponsored by National Interreligious Task Force on Soviet Jewry, *The Jewish Herald-Voice*, Houston, October 16, 1986
18. Necrology: Sister Ann Elizabeth Gillen, January 14, 1995, Society of the Holy Child Jesus Archives, Rosemont PA.
19. A. James Rudin
20. Eleanor Blau, op. cit.
21. Robert F. Drinan, *Cry of the Oppressed* (San Francisco: Harper & Row, 1987), pp. 134–5

22. James Hitchcock, "The Strange Career of Father Drinan," *Catholic World Report*, July 1996

23. Robert F. Drinan, p. 136

24. Robert G. Gordon, letter to Herb Kavett, July 15, 1980

25. William Orbach, p. 77

26. "Robert Drinan to Discus U.S. War on Terrorism at Bates", News release, January 24, 2002, www.bates.edu/x19855.xml

27. Thomas P. O'Neill, Excerpt from the *Congressional Record*, June 11, 1980, Volume 126, Number 95

28. Doug Cahn, in telephone conversation with the author, April 7, 2006

29. Murray Friedman and Albert Chernin, eds., *A Second Exodus*, (Hanover, NH: Brandeis University Press, 1999), p. 234

30. Shelly Lewis, in conversation with the author, Palo Alto, CA, June 16, 2004

31. Doug Huneke, in conversation with the author, Tiburon, CA, July 23, 2004

32. Marshall Krantz and Peggy Isaak Gluck, "Christians Organize to Aid Soviet Jewry: 1st Time Since '60s," *The Northern California Jewish Bulletin*, May 27, 1988

33. Doug Kahn, in conversation with the author, San Francisco, December 17, 2003

34. Shelly Lewis

CHAPTER NINETEEN

1. Daphne Gerlis, *Those Wonderful Women in Black* (London: Minerva Press, 1996), pp. 129–135

2. Rabbi Awraham Soetendorp, in telephone conversation with the author, October 21, 2004

3. David Selikowitz, in telephone conversation with the author, June 30, 2003

4. Anna Rock, in telephone conversation with the author, July 20, 2006

5. Torsten Press, in telephone conversation with the author, January 12, 2006

6. William Orbach, *The American Movement to Aid Soviet Jews* (Amherst, MA: University of Massachusetts Press, 1979), p. 97

7. http://www.jwa.org/exhibits/wwd/jsp/bio.jsp?personID=ppcohen

8. Daphne Gerlis, pp. 17–18

9. William Orbach, p. 99

10. Daphne Gerlis, pp. 21–22

11. Michael Sherbourne, in conversation with the author, Studio City, CA, April 20, 2003

12. Ida Nudel, trans. Stefani Hoffman, *A Hand in the Darkness* (New York: Warner Books, 1990), p. 65
13. Michael Sherbourne, in conversation with the author, Studio City, CA, April 20, 2003
14. Random House Webster's College Dictionary (New York: Random House, 1991), p. 1133
15. Michael Sherbourne, in conversation with Lou Rosenblum, London, May 15, 1987
16. Rae Sharfman, in telephone conversation with the author, May 19, 2003
17. Michael Sherbourne, in conversation with the author, Studio City, CA, April 20, 2003
18. Daphne Gerlis, p. 20
19. Michael Sherbourne, in conversation with the author, Studio City, CA, April 20, 2003
20. Michael Sherbourne, in conversation with Lou Rosenblum, London, May 15, 1987
21. Michael Sherbourne, in conversation with the author, Studio City, CA, April 20, 2003
22. Daphne Gerlis, pp. 26–30
23. Barbara Oberman, "Skirts Against the Kremlin", *Jerusalem Post*, July 26. 2007
24. Daphne Gerlis, pp. 27–42
25. Ibid., p. 16
26. Ibid., p. 34
27. Ibid., p. 22
28. Zelda Harris, in conversation with the author, Netanya, October 12, 2003
29. Daphne Gerlis, p. 92
30. Zelda Harris, in conversation with the author, Netanya, October 12, 2003
31. Daphne Gerlis, p. 31
32. Ibid., p. 43, 53
33. Ibid., p. 51–52, 177
34. Ibid., pp. 145–147
35. Barbara Portner, in conversation with the author, Netanya, October 12, 2003
36. Daphne Gerlis, pp. 112–116
37. Ibid., p. 59
38. "An Anglo-Saxon Tale: Lady Godiva", http://www.bbc.co.uk/history/ancient/anglo_saxons/godiva_02.shtml
39. Zelda Harris, email to the author, March 12, 2007
40. Daphne Gerlis, pp. 59–62

41. Ibid., pp. 97–107
42. Rita Eker, in conversation with the author, London, October 9, 2003
43. Daphne Gerlis, p. 46
44. Daphne Gerlis, p. 91
45. Evgeny Lein, *Lest We Forget* (Jerusalem: The Jerusalem Publishing Centre, 1997), p. 161
46. Daphne Gerlis, pp. 108–109
47. Ibid., pp. 237–238
48. Wendy Eisen, *Count Us In* (Toronto: Burgher Books, 1995), p. 74
49. Daphne Gerlis, p. 190
50. David Selikowitz, in telephone conversation with the author, June 30, 2003
51. Susan Smith, "An Adoption Agency for Soviet Refuseniks", *International Herald Tribune*, November 2, 1977
52. Patty Pyott, "Recommendations for Future Action by the Committee of 15", internal memo, July 5, 1978
53. Pat Donohoe, "Seventeen Families and Still Counting...", *The Hill*, Western Maryland College, 1985
54. Wolfgang Saxon, "Inna Meiman, Émigré, Dies at 53; Left Soviet for Cancer Treatment," *New York Times*, February 10, 1987
55. David Selikowitz
56. Journal-Souvenir du Comité des 15, January 1993
57. Awraham Soetendorp, in telephone conversation with the author, November 22, 2004
58. Awraham Soetendorp, email to the author, June 24, 2007
59. Petrus Buwalda, *They Did Not Dwell Alone* (Washington, DC: The Woodrow Wilson Center Press, 1997), p. 23
60. Awraham Soetendorp, in telephone conversation with the author, November 22, 2004
61. Felix Corley, "Obituary: Dr. Mikhail Stern", *The Independent*, London, June 24, 2005
62. Awraham Soetendorp, in telephone conversation with the author, November 22, 2004
63. Chana Berlowitz, email to the author, June 13, 2007
64. http://www.afz.ethz.ch/handbuch/bestaend/institutionenAJSArchiv.htm
65. Chana Berlowitz
66. Ruth Bloch, in conversation with the author, Jerusalem, October 22, 2003
67. Seth Jacobson, in telephone conversation with the author, May 19, 2004
68. Ruth Bloch
69. Susanna Merkle, in telephone conversation with the author, February 22, 2007

70. Chana Berlowitz
71. Evgeny Lein, pp. 194–195
72. Ibid., pp. 167–170

CHAPTER TWENTY

1. Morey Schapira, in conversation with the author, Sunnyvale, CA, July 5, 2004
2. Paul Appelbaum, in conversation with the author, Newton, MA, June 28, 2004
3. Michael Dobkowski, Jewish American Voluntary Organizations (Westport, Connecticut: Greenwood Press, 1986), p. 314
4. Morey Schapira
5. William Orbach, *The American Movement to Aid Soviet Jews* (Amherst, MA: University of Massachusetts Press, 1979), p. 103
6. Michael Dobkowski, pp. 315–316
7. Ibid., pp. 317–318
8. Joel Sandberg communication to the author, April 23, 2007
9. Leonard Schroeter, in conversation with the author, Seattle, WA, September 15, 2003
10. Daphne Gerlis, *Those Wonderful Women in Black* (London: Minerva Press, 1996), p. 13
11. Lev Goldfarb, in conversation with the author, Washington, DC, July 20, 2003
12. Victor Borden, in telephone conversation with the author, December 5, 2003
13. Linda Opper, in telephone conversation with the author, March 25, 2004
14. Victor Borden
15. Igor and Inna Uspensky, in conversation with the author, Jerusalem, October 17, 2003
16. Michael Dohan, in telephone conversation with the author, June 11, 2003
17. Victor Borden
18. Jack Cohen, *Confessions of a Jewish Activist* (unpublished memoir sent to the author August 28, 2006)
19. Jack Cohen, "Summary of Origin of CCS," sent to the author October 18, 2006
20. Mark Azbel, *Refusenik* (Boston: Houghton Mifflin Company, 1981), p. 253
21. Jack Cohen, "Summary of Origin of CCS," sent to the author October 18, 2006

22. Jack Minker, letter to the author, December 11, 2006

23. Jack Cohen, *Confessions of a Jewish Activist* (unpublished memoir sent to the author August 28, 2006)

24. Andreas Acrivos, "Benjamin G. Levich 1917–1987," Memorial Tributes: National Academy of Engineering, Volume 5 (1992), pp. 165–166

25. Joel Lebowitz, in conversation with the author, Piscataway, NJ, May 6, 2004

26. http://www.libertynet.org/ccs/histry2.htm

27. Jack Minker, *International Joint Conference of Artificial Intelligence (IJ-CAI-4) – 1975* (unpublished memoir dated June 23, 2005 and sent to the author August 28, 2006)

28. Micah Naftalin, email to the author, August 31, 2007

29. Wendy Eisen, *Count Us In* (Toronto: Burgher Books, 1995), p. 88

30. James Langer, "Journey to an unauthorized scientific meeting," *Physics Today*, June, 1979, pp 9 and 82–83

31. Joel Lebowitz

32. Alexander Lerner, *Change of Heart* (Minneapolis: Lerner Publications, 1992), pp. 194–5

33. Jack Minker, letter to the author, December 11, 2006

34. Neil Bradman, in telephone conversation with the author, August 27, 2006

35. Joel Lebowitz

36. Jack Minker, in telephone conversation with the author, December 19, 2006

37. Igor Uspensky email to the author, October 16, 2006

38. William Korey, *The Promises We Keep* (New York: St. Martin's Press, 1993), p. 196

39. Jack Minker, unpublished, undated memoir sent to the author August 28, 2006

40. Jorgen Bennedsen, Jan Olav Eeg, and Jacob Krarup, "Report of a Visit to Moscow," *Frontiers of Science: Reports from the Final International Session of the Moscow Refusenik Seminar*, Annals of the New York Academy of Sciences, Volume 661, December 28, 1992

41. Yuri Chernyak, Preface to *Frontiers of Science: Reports from the Final International Session of the Moscow Refusenik Seminar*, Annals of the New York Academy of Sciences, Volume 661, December 28, 1992

42. http://www.libertynet.org/ccs/annual2005.pdf

43. Moishe Pripstein, in conversation with the author, Berkeley, CA, October 19, 2004

44. Philip Siegelman, in conversation with the author, Berkeley, CA, August 9, 2004

45. Scientists for Orlov and Shcharansky, "2400 U.S. Scientists Restrict Co-operation with the Soviet Union," Press release, March 1, 1979

46. Nahum Maiman and Andrei Sakharov, Letter to Scientist for Orlov and Shcharansky, March 10, 1979, received by telephone and translated by Michael Sherbourne, London

47. Philip Siegelman, "Paul Flory and His Work," *Freedom at Issue*, March-April, 1986

48. Philip Siegelman, letter to the author, November 22, 2006

49. Philip Siegelman, in conversation with the author, Berkeley, CA, August 9, 2004

50. David Perlman, "Now Scientists Have a Role in Freeze on Russia," *San Francisco Chronicle*, January 30, 1980

51. Scientists for Sakharov, Orlov and Shcharansky, "SOS Background Information," October 16, 1980

52. Scientists for Sakharov, Orlov and Shcharansky, "Progress Report of Recent SOS Activities," February 2, 1981

53. Scientists for Sakharov, Orlov and Shcharansky, Press release, February 17, 1983

54. "'Hostage' Plan Proposed to Help Sakharov's Wife," *San Francisco Chronicle*, August 17, 1984

55. "Dear Colleague" letter from John Kwapisz, Center for Peace and Freedom, Washington, DC, received by Philip Siegelman June 30, 1986

56. Philip Siegelman, in conversation with the author, Berkeley, CA, August 9, 2004

57. Monica Friedlander, "Lab Scientist Wins Human Rights Award for Effort to Help Soviet Dissidents," Lawrence Berkeley Labs *Currents*, July 10, 1998

CHAPTER TWENTY-ONE

1. Report on Brussels Presidium Meeting, American Jewish Committee Archives, IAD 1970s, Box 194, Soviet Union 1979

2. Sylvia Rothchild, A Special Legacy: An Oral History of Soviet Émigrés in the United States (New York: Simon and Schuster: 1985), p. 289

3. Dorit Grossman Perry, in telephone conversation with the author, September 28, 2004

4. Hedva Boukhobza, in telephone conversation with the author, July 24, 2006

5. David Korn, "The New Russian Jewish Immigration to America," *Jewish Digest*, June 1979

6. Hedva Boukhobza

7. David Harris, "Letter from an Ex-HIAS Employee," American Jewish Committee – Publications – David Harris Letters, November 15, 2001
8. David Harris, "Letter from Rome," American Jewish Committee – Publications – David Harris Letters, March 28, 2005
9. Hedva Boukhobza
10. Petrus Buwalda, *They Did Not Dwell Alone* (Washington, DC: The Woodrow Wilson Center Press, 1997), p. 14
11. ibid, p. 21
12. Tom Shachtman, *I Seek My Brethren* (New York: Newmarket Press, 2001), pp. 116–120
13. Wendy Eisen, *Count Us In* (Toronto, Burgher Books, 1995), p. 39
14. Genya Intrator, in telephone conversation with the author, October 31, 2004
15. Murray Friedman and Albert Chernin, eds., *A Second Exodus* (Hanover, NH: Brandeis University Press, 1999), p. 8
16. William Orbach, *The American Movement to Aid Soviet Jews* (Amherst, MA: University of Massachusetts Press, 1979), pp. 64–75
17. Petrus Buwalda, p. 168
18. Fred Lazin, "Refugee Resettlement and 'Freedom of Choice,' The Case of Soviet Jewry," Center for Immigration Studies, June 2005
19. Tom Shachtman, p. 127
20. William Orbach, p. 82
21. Petrus Buwalda, p. 224
22. Hedva Boukhobza
23. Statistical Abstracts, HIAS, New York
24. Shirley Goldstein in telephone conversation with the author, December 12, 2003
25. Leo Adam Biga, "Cream of the Crop: One Woman's Remarkable Journey in the Free Soviet Jewry Movement Part II: Shirley Goldstein, Activist, Humanitarian, Philanthropist," *Omaha Jewish Press*, April 4, 2006
26. Shirley Goldstein
27. "The History of the Matching Grant Program," Office of Refugee Resettlement, http://www.acf.hhs.gov/programs/orr/programs/matchgh.htm
28. Fred Lazin
29. Valery Bazarov, e-mail to the author, January 11, 2007
30. 2001 Census Analysis Series: The Jewish Community in Canada, by Charles Shahar, for UIA Federations Canada, 2004
31. Fred Lazin
32. Gregg Beyer, "The Evolving United States Response to Soviet Jewish Emigration," *International Journal of Refugee Law*, 1991
33. Hedva Boukhobza
34. Gregg Beyer

35. Fred Lazin
36. Hedva Boukhobza
37. Fred Lazin
38. Dorit Grossman Perry
39. Jonathan K. Blum, Gary N. Finder, Adrienne C. Lalak, "Refugee Status for Jews Emigrating from the Soviet Union: The Need for a Congressional Response to the Crisis in Ladispoli," Report to the Subcommittee on Immigration, Refugees and International Law, Committee on the Judiciary, U.S. House of Representatives, March 29, 1989
40. Joshua Phillips, "U.S. Closes Door to Jews and Evangelical Christians From Former USSR Despite Evidence of Persecution," http://www.pacificnews.org/jinn/stories/5.06/990317-refugees.html
41. "Changes in U.S. Consular Practices in Moscow" Fact Sheet, U.S. Department of State, October 2, 1989
42. Gregg Beyer
43. Dorit Grossman Perry
44. Aaron Gershowitz, in conversation with the author, New York, June 6, 2006
45. "Refugee Admissions Program for Europe and Central Asia," Fact Sheet, Bureau of Population, Refugees and Migration, Washington, DC, January 16, 2004
46. Joshua Phillips
47. William M. Cohen, "The Escalation of Anti-Semitic Violence in Russia," Center for Human Rights Advocacy, Boulder, C.O., August 13, 1999
48. "HIAS around the World," *Passages*, Autumn 2005

CHAPTER TWENTY-TWO

1. William Orbach, *The American Movement to Aid Soviet Jews* (Amherst, MA: University of Massachusetts Press, 1979), pp. 117–118
2. Ellen Harris, "Celebrating 30 years of Jackson-Vanik Amendment," ClevelandJewishNews.com, December 28, 2004
3. William Orbach, pp. 118–128
4. William Korey, *The Principles We Keep* (New York: St. Martin's Press, 1993), pp. 54–55
5. William Orbach, pp. 129–132
6. Mark Azbel, *Refusenik* (Boston: Houghton-Mifflin, 1981), p. 300
7. Jerry Goodman in conversation with the author, New York, May 5, 2004
8. William Orbach, p. 133
9. Jerry Goodman
10. Elliott Abrams, "The Last Good Democrat," *The Weekly Standard*, October 2, 2000

11. Foundation for Documentary Projects, Interview with Richard Perle

12. Interview of Glenn Richter, *Remember and Save*, http://www.angelfire.com/sc3/soviet_jews_exodus/English/Interview_s/InterviewRichter.shtml

13. Gordon Zacks, *Defining Moments* (New York: Beaufort Books, 2006). p. 187

14. William Orbach, pp. 134–135

15. William Korey, "The Struggle of Jackson-Mills-Vanik," *American Jewish Year Book*, 1974–75, p. 199

16. Itschak Pukan, letter to Senator Henry Jackson, November 13, 1972

17. Murray Friedman and Albert Chernin, eds., *A Second Exodus* (Hanover, NH: Brandeis University Press, 1999), p. 99

18. William Orbach, pp. 136–137

19. Ibid., p. 138

20. Boris Morozov, *Documents on Soviet Jewish Emigration* (Portland, OR: Frank Cass, 1999), pp. 170–173

21. William Orbach, pp. 138–140

22. William Korey, "The Struggle of Jackson-Mills-Vanik," *American Jewish Year Book*, 1974–75, pp. 215–216

23. William Orbach, pp. 140–141

24. Jerry Goodman

25. Interview of Glenn Richter, *Remember and Save*, http://www.pacificnews.org/jinn/stories/5.06/990317-refugees.html

26. William Orbach, pp. 142–143

27. Richard Lourie, *Sakharov* (Hanover, NH: Brandeis University Press, 2002), pp. 254–265

28. William Orbach, pp. 145–147

29. Anatoly Dobrynin, *In Confidence* (Seattle: University of Washington Press, 1995), pp. 334–335

30. William Orbach, pp. 151–153

31. William Korey, "The Struggle of Jackson-Mills-Vanik," *American Jewish Year Book*, 1974–75, p. 234

32. Tommy Daniels, "The Jackson-Vanik Amendment", Excerpts from Congressional Research Service – The Library of Congress

33. Mark Azbel, p. 381

34. Petrus Buwalda, *They Did Not Dwell Alone* (Washington, DC: The Woodrow Wilson Center Press, 1997), p. 109

35. William Orbach, p. 153

36. Anatoly Dobrynin, p. 269

37. Elliott Abrams

38. William Orbach, pp. 153–154

39. Murray Friedman and Albert Chernin, pp. 118–120

40. Petrus Buwalda, pp. 133–135

41. William Korey, *The Principles We Keep*, p. 116
42. Murray Friedman and Albert Chernin, pp. 214–215
43. William Korey, "Jackson-Vanik: Its Origin and Impact as Russia Nears 'Graduation," *The Harriman Review*, November 2002
44. Murray Friedman and Albert Chernin, pp. 113–114
45. Anatoly Dobrynin, pp. 268–269
46. Ibid., p. 159
47. Andrew Kutchins, "A Turning Point in US-Russian Relations?", Carnegie Endowment for International Peace – Publications, November 20, 2006
48. "Jackson-Vanik Amendment Has Long Been Irrelevant – Kremlin Aide", Johnson's Russia List, Moscow, April 10, 2007, http://www.cdi.org/russia/johnson/2007-85-15.cfm
49. "President Signs Bill to Strengthen Trade Between u.s. and Ukraine," The White House, Office of the Press Secretary, March 23, 2006
50. Adrian Karatnycky, "Ukraine's Orange Revolution", *Foreign Affairs*, March, April 2005

CHAPTER TWENTY-THREE

1. Kathryn Cameron Porter in telephone conversation with the author, December 15, 2006
2. John Edward Porter in telephone conversation with the author, January 10, 2007
3. Kathryn Cameron Porter
4. John Edward Porter in telephone conversation with the author, January 10, 2007
5. http://lantos.house.gov/HoR/CA12/Human+Rights+Caucus/About+the+CHRC
6. Annette Lantos in conversation with the author, San Mateo, CA, August 4, 2004
7. John Porter, email to the author, April 12, 2007
8. Micah Naftalin, email to the author, August 31, 2007
9. John Edward Porter in telephone conversation with the author, January 10, 2007
10. Stuart Gorin, "Backgrounder: The Congressional Human Rights Caucus," u.s. Department of State, International Information Programs, March 26, 2001
11. "1988 Congressional Handbook for Soviet Jewry," Union of Councils for Soviet Jews, Washington, DC
12. Murray Friedman and Albert Chernin, eds., *A Second Exodus* (Hanover, NH: Brandeis University Press, 1999), p. 194

13. *Anniversary Issue, Outcry*, Bay Area Council for Soviet Jews, San Francisco, October 1992, p. 30
14. Foundation for Documentary Projects, Interview with Steny Hoyer
15. Annette Lantos
16. Remarks of Teresa Heinz Kerry to United Jewish Communities Lion of Judah Conference, Washington, DC, October 17, 2004 http://www.ujc.org/content_display.html?ArticleID=128157
17. Murray Friedman and Albert Chernin, eds. p. 179
18. Annette Lantos
19. John Edward Porter in telephone conversation with the author, January 10, 2007
20. Congressional Human Rights Caucus Fact Sheet, 1988
21. "Anti-Semitism in the Soviet Union," Statement of the UCSJ to the Congressional Human Rights Caucus, Washington, DC, August 9, 1988
22. Dear Colleague letter from Tom Lantos, John Porter, James Scheuer, and Jack Buechner, August 5, 1988
23. John Edward Porter in telephone conversation with the author, January 10, 2007
24. Foundation for Documentary Projects, Interview with Steny Hoyer
25. Kathryn Cameron Porter
26. John Edward Porter in telephone conversation with the author, January 10, 2007
27. Annette Lantos
28. Barbara Boxer e-mail to the author, December 13, 2005
29. David Shribman, "No More Business as Usual," *Boston Globe*, December 11, 1994
30. John Edward Porter in telephone conversation with the author, January 10, 2007
31. Tom Lantos, "Mr. Putin, for Democracy's Sake, Tear Down This Wall of Censorship," *Los Angeles Times*, June 11, 2004
32. Congressional Human Rights Caucus – Mission Statement, http://www.ujc.org/content_display.html?ArticleID=128157
33. Evgeny Lein, *Lest We Forget*, (Jerusalem, Israel: The Jerusalem Publishing Centre, 1997), p. 179
34. Marillyn Tallman, in conversation with the author, Highland Park, IL, June 22, 2004
35. *American Jewish Year Book*, 1989, (Philadelphia: Jewish Publication Society, 1989), p. 423
36. John Edward Porter in telephone conversation with the author, January 10, 2007

CHAPTER TWENTY-FOUR

1. George P. Shultz in conversation with the author, Stanford, CA, February 5, 2003

2. George P. Shultz, *Turmoil and Triumph* (New York: Charles Scribner's Sons, 1993), p. 550

3. William Korey, *The Promises We Keep* (New York: St. Martin's Press, 1993), p. 110

4. Max Kampelman in conversation with the author, Washington, DC, June 24, 2004

5. Max Kampelman, "The Ronald Reagan I Knew," *The Weekly Standard*, Nov. 24, 2004

6. Max Kampelman in conversation with the author, Washington, DC, June 24, 2004

7. Murray Friedman and Albert Chernin, eds., *A Second Exodus* (Hanover, NH: Brandeis University Press, 1999), p. 131

8. William Korey, p. 133

9. Jeri Laber, *The Courage of Strangers* (New York: Public Affairs, 2002), p. 122

10. Max Kampelman, "Rescue with a Presidential Push," *Washington Post*, June 11, 2004

11. Max Kampelman in conversation with the author, Washington, DC, June 24, 2004

12. Jack Matlock, *Reagan and Gorbachev* (New York: Random House, 2005), p. 58

13. George P. Shultz, *Turmoil and Triumph*, p. 165

14. Max Kampelman in conversation with the author, Washington, DC, June 24, 2004

15. George P. Shultz, *Turmoil and Triumph*, pp. 170–171

16. Ibid., p. 273

17. Natan Sharansky, trans. Stefani Hoffman *Fear No Evil*, (New York: Random House, 1988), pp. 357–358

18. Petrus Buwalda, *They Did Not Dwell Alone* (Washington, DC: Woodrow Wilson Center Press, 1997), p. 98

19. William Korey, p. 58

20. George P. Shultz, *Turmoil and Triumph*, pp. 121–122

21. Ibid., p. 266

22. Ibid., p. 469

23. Jack Matlock, p. 108

24. George P. Shultz, *Turmoil and Triumph*, p. 530

25. Ibid., pp. 586–587

26. George P. Shultz in conversation with the author, Stanford, CA, February 5, 2003

27. Carolyn Ekedahl and Melvin Goodman, *The Wars of Eduard Shevard-nadze* (University Park, PA: Pennsylvania State University Press, 1997), pp. 103–113

28. William Korey, p. xxix

29. Murray Friedman and Albert Chernin, p. 140

30. George P. Shultz, *Turmoil and Triumph*, pp. 886–887

31. Wendy Eisen, *Count Us In* (Toronto: Burgher Books, 1995), p. 236

32. Wyatt Andrews in conversation with the author, Washington, DC, July 21, 2003

33. George P. Shultz in conversation with the author, Stanford, CA, February 5, 2003

34. George P. Shultz, *Turmoil and Triumph*, pp. 985–986

35. NCSJ Press Release, "NCSJ Mourns Morris B. Abram.," March 16, 2000, www.ncsj.org/AuxPages/abram031600.shtml

36. Ida Nudel, trans. Stefani Hoffman, *A Hand in the Darkness* (New York: Warner Books, 1990), p. 304

37. George P. Shultz, *Turmoil and Triumph*, p. 990

38. Ibid., p. 1095

39. Ibid., p. 1137

40. Excerpts from Secretary Shultz's Acceptance Speech, December 1, 1990, *Outcry*, The Newsletter of the Bay Area Council for Soviet Jews, January 1991, p. 2

41. Carolyn Ekedahl and Melvin Goodman, pp. 136–138

42. Richard Schifter in conversation with the author, Bethesda, MD, June 25, 2004

43. Murray Friedman and Albert Chernin, pp. 138–142

44. Carolyn Ekedahl and Melvin Goodman, pp. 141–142

45. Murray Friedman and Albert Chernin, pp. 144–145

46. Richard Schifter

47. Igor and Inna Uspensky in conversation with the author, Jerusalem, October 17, 2003

48. Petrus Buwalda, p. 214

49. Igor and Inna Uspensky

50. Carolyn Ekedahl and Melvin Goodman, pp. 119–121

51. William Korey, p. 304

CHAPTER TWENTY-FIVE

1. During a press conference on May 12, 1954 Eisenhower originated the "Domino Theory" in answer to a question about the strategic importance of Indochina. He said, "You have a row of dominoes set up, you knock over the first one, and what will happen to the last one is the certainty that it

will go over very quickly. So you could have a beginning of a disintegration that would have the most profound influences." In 1957 he expanded on the applicability of the Domino Theory: "We must recognize that whenever any country falls under the domination of Communism, the strength of the Free World – and of America – is by that amount weakened and Communism strengthened."

2. Carolyn Ekedahl and Melvin Goodman, *The Wars of Eduard Shevard-nadze* (University Park, PA: Pennsylvania State University Press, 1997), p. 159–162

3. http://www.balticsworldwide.com/tourist/lithuania/history.htm

4. http://news.bbc.co.uk/hi/english/static/in_depth/europe/2001/collapse_of_ussr/timelines/late1991.stm

5. Petrus Buwalda, *They Did Not Dwell Alone* (Washington, DC: Woodrow Wilson Center Press, 1997), pp. 211–214

6. Ibid., p. 224

7. Peter Golden, *Quiet Diplomat: A Biography of Max M. Fisher* (New York: Cornwall Press, 1992), pp. 469–472

8. Zale Anis, email to the author, May 18, 2007

9. "Plan to Provide Bus Transportation for Soviet Jews," Action for Soviet Jewry, Boston, June 5, 1990

10. Sergey Broude email to Zale Anis, December 9, 2004

11. Zale Anis, "Update on Alternative Emigration Routes", memo to UCSJ Executive Committee, July 8, 1990

12. Stuart Altshuler, *The Exodus of Soviet Jewry: The Role and Activities of the Union of Councils for Soviet Jews During the Decisive Years 1985–1991*, Graduate School of the Jewish Theological Seminary of America, 2002, p. 287

13. Letter from Judy Patkin, Action for Soviet Jewry, Waltham, MA, September 4, 1991

14. Benjamin Netanyahu, letter to Israel Harel, July 23, 1990

15. Zale Anis, email to the author, May 18, 2007

16. Zale Anis, in telephone conversation with the author, July 9, 2003

17. Zale Anis, "Lack of Sochnut Cooperation on Implementation of Alternative Emigration Routes", memo to UCSJ Executive Board, September 27, 1990

18. Zale Anis, reporting information supplied by Elie Weiss, in telephone conversation with the author, November 10, 2004

19. U. Ariel and Y. Harel, letter to Natan Sharansky, July 12, 1990

20. Harold Hubschman memo "Ride to Freedom Meeting on July 15, 1991," Action for Soviet Jewry, Waltham, MA

21. Zale Anis, email to the author, May 14, 2007

22. Leah Chernobilsky, in conversation with the author, translated by Natasha Ratner, Jerusalem, June 6, 2006

23. Ida Nudel, trans. Stefani Hoffman, *A Hand in the Darkness*, (New York, Warner Books, 1990), pp. 139, 211

24. Leah Chernobilsky

25. Michael Shapiro, in conversation with the author, Sunnyvale, CA, August 13, 2004

26. http://www.ebenezer-ef.org/UK/welcome.htm

27. http://www.restorationfoundation.org/volume_2/23_5.htm

28. Sam Orbaum, "A Friend in Deed", *Jerusalem Post*, December 31, 1999

29. Chris Mitchell, "Christian Ministry Helps Jews Return to the Holy Land", *Christian World News*, June 18, 2004

30. Michael Jankelowitz email to the author, January 12, 2006

31. Peter Golden, pp. 473–474

32. Ibid., p. 475

33. Ibid., p. 468

34. http://www.jafi.org.il/dinitz.htm

35. Joe Obersky, "Simcha Dinitz Dies at 74", Chicago Jewish Community Online, September 23, 2003

36. Stuart Altshuler, pp. 355–384

37. Matthew Dorf, "Jewish Agency Seeks $60 million in Emergency Aid," Jewish News Weekly of Northern California, March 27, 1998

38. http://www.ujc.org/page.html?ArticleID=68069

39. Robert Gottstein, in telephone conversation with the author, June 23, 2005. Gottstein owns the Purely Alaskan Water Company, a producer of bottled water and packaged ice.

40. Hannah Mitson, "The King-Havenner Bill of 1940", *Alaska History*, the journal of the Alaska Historical Society, Volume 14, Spring/Fall, 1999.

41. Robert Gottstein, in telephone conversation with the author, June 23, 2005.

42. Robert Gottstein, letter to the author, June 28, 2005

43. Robert Gottstein, in telephone conversation with the author, June 23, 2005.

44. http://www.kh-uia.org.il/Christian/3.html

45. http://www.ifcj.org/site/PageServer?pagename=whoweare_history

46. Robert Gottstein, in telephone conversation with the author, June 23, 2005

47. Rabbi Yechiel Eckstein, in telephone conversation with the author, June 9, 2005

48. "While the Door is Still Open", 18WD002, International Fellowship of Christians and Jews, Chicago, IL

49. Rabbi Yechiel Eckstein

50. Aryeh Dean Cohen, "Turning to the Gentiles", Jerusalem Post International Edition, January 24, 1998

CHAPTER TWENTY-SIX

1. Miriam Stark Zakon, *Silent Revolution* (Brooklyn, NY: Mesorah Publications, 1992), p. 148

2. Lev Krichevsky, "Ethnicity Line Axed from Russian Passports", *Jewish Bulletin of Northern California*, October 31, 1997

3. Mikhail Chlenov, in telephone conversation with the author, February 14, 2007

4. Natan Sharansky, trans. Stefani Hoffman, *Fear No Evil* (New York: Random House, 1988), pp. 49–51

5. Isi Leibler, "Soviet Jewry – Report on Visit to Moscow (September 20–29th 1987)", pp. 69. 179

6. Eugene Satanovsky, "Organized National Life of Russian Jews in the Late Soviet and Post-Soviet Era: a View from Moscow", Jerusalem Political Studies Review 14: 1–2 (Spring 2002), Jerusalem Center for Public Affairs, http://www.jcpa.org/cjc/cjc-satanovsky-so2.htm

7. Mikhail Chlenov, Biography, Euro-Asian Jewish Congress, http://www.eajc.org/pers_bio_e.php?id=2

8. Daniel Nehmad, "A Decade Later, Group Unites Jews from FSU and Asia-Pacific Regions", JTA News, March 14, 2002

9. Zeev and Leah Shakhnovsky, in conversation with the author, Jerusalem, June 25, 2006

10. Benjamin Fain, in conversation with the author, Tel Aviv, October 28, 2003

11. Daniel J. Elazar, "How Strong is Orthodox Judaism – Really? The Demographics of Jewish Religious Identification", Jerusalem Center for Public Affairs, http://www.jcpa.org/dje/articles2/demographics.htm

12. Benjamin Fain and Mervin Verbit, *Jewishness in the Soviet Union* (Jerusalem: Jerusalem Center for Public Affairs, 1984), p. 11

13. Joyce Klein, *The Shabbat Book* (Mevasseret Ziyyon, Israel: Scopus Films, 1997), p. 40

14. Zvi Gitelman, *A Century of Ambivalence* (Bloomington, IN: Indiana University Press, 1998). p. 240

15. Herman Branover and Avraham Naveh, trans. Mika Tubinshlak, *The Ultimate Jew* (Jerusalem, Israel: Shamir Publishing House, 2003), p. 277

16. Rabbi Naftali Estulin, in telephone conversation with the author, July 1, 2007

17. Rabbi Moshe-Leib Kolesnik in conversation with the author, Ivano-Frankivsk, Ukraine, June 27, 1999

18. "West Ukrainian Jewish Community Supports Summer Programming", Federation of Jewish Communities of the CIS, News, August 5, 2005, http://www.fjc.ru/news/newsArticle.asp?AID=300847

19. Rabbi Moshe-Leib Kolesnik

20. "The Return of Synagogues", The Jewish Agency for Israel, Department for Jewish Zionist Education, http://www.jafi.org.il/education/worldwide/synagogues/part2b.html

21. "Rabbinical Alliance", Federation of Jewish Communities of the CIS, About FJC, http://www.fjc.ru/AboutUs/default.asp?AID=80123

22. History, Federation of Jewish Communities of the CIS, About FJC, http://www.fjc.ru/AboutUs/default.asp?AID=80122

23. Education, Federation of Jewish Communities of the CIS, Departments, http://www.fjc.ru/AboutUs/default.asp?AID=80134

24. Zev Chafetz, "The Missionary Mogul", *New York Times Magazine*, September 16, 2007

25. Rabbi Berel Lazar, Federation of Jewish Communities of the CIS, About FJC, http://www.fjc.ru/AboutUs/default.asp?AID=84605

26. Caryn Aviv and David Schneer, *New Jews: The End of the Jewish Diaspora* (New York: New York University Press, 2005), pp. 39–40

27. Yuri Chernyak, in conversation with the author, Waltham, MA, May 22, 2003

28. Tom Schachtman, *I Seek My Brethren: Ralph Goldman and "The Joint"* (New York: Newmarket Press, 2001), pp. 194–206

29. Yearbook 2005: JDC in the Former Soviet Union, American Jewish Joint Distribution Committee, New York

30. David B. Green, "Moscow Lock Out", *The Jerusalem Report*, December 26, 2005

31. "Goldschmidt Gets His Visa", Jewish Telegraphic Agency, January 17, 2006

32. "Colel Chabad Charity Pure & Simple", www.colelchabad.org

33. "Russian Jewry", www.colelchabad.org/index.asp?id=9

34. Friends of Refugees of Eastern Europe, About Us, www.russianjewry.org/about/

35. Eliyahu Essas, in conversation with the author, Jerusalem, June 13, 2006

36. Miriam Stark Zakon, p. 15

37. Eliyahu Essas

38. Martin Gilbert, *The Jews of Hope* (New York: Penguin Books, 1985), p. 165

39. "Grisha Wasserman – Teacher and Publisher", Shvut Ami, www.shvutami.org.il/people/Wasserman

40. Eliyahu Essas

41. Miriam Stark Zakon, pp. 60–61

42. Ilya Essas (refusenik profile), Long Island Committee for Soviet Jewry, October 1981

43. Martin Gilbert, pp. 1–3

44. Ruth Bloch, "Report of Telephone Conversation with Eliyah Essas," Ak-

tionskomitee fur die Juden in der Sowjetunion, September 18, 1980 to January 22, 1985

45. Ernie Hirsch, in conversation with the author, Netanya, June 18, 2006
46. Alice Markowitz, *Refused* (Tel Aviv, Israel: Technosdar, 2004), pp. 21–41
47. Ernie Hirsch
48. Eliyahu Essas
49. Lisa Schneider, "A Holy Man from Moscow", *Washington Jewish Week*, April 17, 1986
50. Miriam Stark Zakon, p. 153
51. Ibid., p. 148, 156
52. Eliyahu Essas
53. Zeev Dashevsky, in conversation with the author, Jerusalem, June 27, 2006
54. Isi Leibler, "A Contemporary Challenge for World Jewry", Report on Mission to Moscow, October 18–25, 1988, pp. 125–128
55. Zeev Dashevsky
56. http://www.haverim.ru/?la=e&sm=1_5
57. The Lookstein Center, www.lookstein.org/press/042005.htm
58. Lev Utevski, in conversation with the author, Jerusalem, Israel, June 21, 2006
59. Jakov Gorodezky, email to the author, July 26, 2007
60. Lev Utevski
61. Grisha Wasserman, in conversation with the author, Haifa, June 18, 2006
62. Shvut Ami, Grisha Wasserman, Teacher and Publisher, www.shvutami.org.il/people/wasserman
63. Lev Utevski, email to the author, July 20, 2007
64. Shvut Ami, We are world leaders in three areas, www.shvutami.org.il/
65. Shvut Ami, Shimon Grilius – from the Gulag to Jerusalem, www.shvutami.org.il/people/grilius
66. Shvut Ami, Reaching Out in Israel, www.shvutami.org.il/programs/reaching
67. Shvut Ami, Emissaries in the Former Soviet Union, www.shvutami.org.il/programs/emissaries
68. Jakov Gorodezky, in conversation with the author, Brooklyn, NY, March 16, 2005
69. Jakov Gorodezky, email to the author, July 26, 2007
70. Jakov Gorodezky, in conversation with the author, Brooklyn, NY, March 16, 2005
71. Biography of Soviet Jewish Refusenik – Yakov Gorodetsky, Bay Area Council for Soviet Jews, May 29, 1985
72. Peggy Isaak Gluck, "Soviet destroying Jewish leaders, ex-refusenik charges", *Northern California Jewish Bulletin*, June 13, 1986

73. Jakov Gorodezky, email to the author, July 26, 2007

74. Gennady Farber, in conversation with the author, Los Altos, CA, May 18, 2004

75. "Memorial Event Honors Holocaust Victims", Federation of Jewish Communities of the CIS, News, October 14, 2004, www.fjc.ru/newsArticle.asp?AID+212660

76. Boris Kelman, in conversation with the author, Mountain View, CA, July 7, 2004

77. Isi Leibler, "A Contemporary Challenge for World Jewry", Report on Mission to Moscow, October 18–25, 1988, pp. 68–69

78. About St. Petersburg Jewish University, www1.coe.neu.edu/~mnosonov/maz/peu.htm

79. Gennady Farber, email to the author, August 30, 2007

80. Boris Kelman

81. Congregation Beth Am, Los Altos Hills, CA, Émigré Program, www.betham.org/emigre

82. Boris Kelman

83. Gennady Farber

84. Rabbi Richard Block, email to the author, July 19, 2007

85. Inna Benjaminson, in conversation with the author, Los Altos Hills, CA, August 3, 2007

86. Inna Benjaminson, email to the author, October 11, 2007

87. Joshua Shuster, "Area Rabbi Moving to Israel to Lead World Reform Body", *Jewish News Weekly of Northern California*, December 18, 1998

88. Rabbi Richard Hirsch, in telephone conversation with the author, June 20, 2007

89. Richard Hirsch, *From the Hill to the Mount* (Jerusalem: Gefen Publishing House, 2000), p. 85

90. Sid Manekofsky, in conversation with the author, Washington, DC, July 21, 2003

91. Rabbi Richard Hirsch, in telephone conversation with the author, June 20, 2007

92. Richard Hirsch, *From the Hill to the Mount*, p. 87

93. Caryn Aviv and David Schneer, p. 34

94. Zinovy Kogan, email to the author, July 6, 2007

95. Lev Gorodetsky, "10 Years Later, Reform Jews Thrive in Former Soviet Land", *Jewish News Weekly of Northern California*, November 10, 2000

96. Zinovy Kogan

97. World Union for Progressive Judaism, 32nd International Convention, Moscow, June 30-July 5, 2005, pp. 10–13

98. Ibid., pp. 16–17

99. Steve Bauman in conversation with the author, Los Altos, CA, June 5, 2007

100. "Strength Through Unity", World Union for Progressive Judaism Annual Report 2004

101. World Union for Progressive Judaism, Issue #282, October 18, 2007, http://wupj.org/Publications/Newsletter.asp?ContentID=86#RECORD

102. World Union for Progressive Judaism, 32nd International Convention, Moscow, June 30–July 5, 2005, pp. 6–13

103. Alex Kagan, in telephone conversation with the author, July 1, 2007

104. "Report of the Committee for the Formulation of the Jewish Agency Long-Range Policy in the FSU", Jewish Agency for Israel, Jerusalem, June 2004

105. Alex Kagan

106. World Union for Progressive Judaism, 32nd International Convention, Moscow, June 30-July 5, 2005, pp. 14–15

107. Matt Siegel, "With Chabad Struggling in Belarus, Reform Community has Stepped Up," JTA, June 24, 2007, www.jta.org/cgi-bin/iowa/news/article/20070624minskchabad.html

108. http://www.schechter.edu/rus/yachad.htm

109. www.birthrightisrael.com

110. Gidi Mark email to the author October 23, 2007

111. "Report of the Committee for the Formulation of the Jewish Agency Long-Range Policy in the FSU", Jewish Agency for Israel, Jerusalem, June 2004

112. Wayne Firestone, in conversation with the author, San Francisco, CA, October 8, 2007

113. Marcia Neeley, "Jewish Study Flourishes in Moscow", New York *Jewish Week*, November 2, 2007

114. http://www.ort.org/asp/article.asp?id=330

115. Iri Kassel, in telephone conversation with the author, July 15, 2007

116. Jewish Virtual Library, http://www.jewishvirtuallibrary.org/jsource/Society_&_Culture/convert.html

117. Iri Kassel

CHAPTER TWENTY-SEVEN

1. Tom Schachtman, *I Seek My Brethren: Ralph Goldman and "The Joint"* (New York: Newmarket Press, 2001), pp. 229–233

2. "Yearbook 2005 JDC in the Former Soviet Union", American Jewish Joint Distribution Committee, New York, pp. 10–11

3. Tom Schachtman, pp. 239–242

4. "Yearbook 2005 JDC in the Former Soviet Union", p. 8
5. Ibid., p. 15
6. Judy Patkin, in conversation with the author, Waltham, MA, May 19, 2003
7. Mark Levin, in telephone conversation with the author, July 17, 2007
8. Larry Tye, *Home Lands: Portraits of the New Jewish Diaspora* (New York: Owl Books, 2001), pp. 61–63
9. JCRC Boston, "JCRC/CJP Dnepropretrovsk Kehillah Project (DKP) Overview of Projects 2006–2007
10. Nancy Kaufman, in telephone conversation with the author, August 3, 2007
11. NCSJ – Kehilla Projects, Boston-Dnepropetrovsk, http://www.ncsj.org/AuxPages/kh_boston.shtml
12. Larry Tye, p. 87
13. NCSJ – Kehilla Projects, Boston-Dnepropetrovsk, http://www.ncsj.org/AuxPages/kh_boston.shtml
14. Judy Patkin, in telephone conversation with the author, August 3, 2007
15. Betsy Gidwitz, "A Winter Visit to Dnipropetrovsk and Kyiv", January-February 2000, http://www.reportsbetsygidwitz.com/winter_visit_to_dnipropetrovs_Kyiv_05.html
16. Judy Patkin, email to the author, August 28, 2007
17. Sandy Cantor, Shirley Hurwitz, Barbara Karchmer, Judy Patkin, "Trip to Ukraine & Belarus", October 21 – November 6, 2003, Action for Post-Soviet Jewry, Waltham, MA
18. http://www.actionpsj.org/Adopt.htm
19. Yad l'Yad Partnership List, Union of Councils for Jews in the Former Soviet Union, 2005, http://www.fsumonitor.com/yadpartners.shtml
20. Chana Berlowitz, email to the author, June 13, 2007
21. "Hierarchs of Russian Church Asked to Publicly Distance Themselves from Anti-Semites", Union of Councils for Jews in the Former Soviet Union, March 6, 2002, http://www.fsumonitor.com/stories/030702Russia.shtml
22. Mikhail Chlenov, in telephone conversation with the author, February 14, 2007
23. Letter from Leonid Stonov to UCSJ, May 26, 1990
24. Lev Krichevsky, "News Analysis: Communist Resurgence Makes Russia's Jews Uneasy", *Jewish News Weekly of Northern California*, December 22, 1995
25. Leonid Stonov, in conversation with the author, Highland Park, IL, June 22, 2004
26. Yuri Zarakhovich, "From Russia With Hate", *Time*, August 1, 2004
27. Pnina Levermore, in conversation with the author, San Francisco, November 21, 2006

28. http://www.fsumonitor.com/stories/021799aa.shtml

29. http://www.climateoftrust.org/civil.htm

30. Leslie Katz, "Former teen activist for Soviet Jews to head BACJRR", Northern California *Jewish Bulletin*, February 7, 1997

31. Pnina Levermore, email to the author, April 27, 2007

32. Micah Naftalin, in conversation with the author, Washington, DC, July 22, 2003

33. Yossi Abramowitz, in telephone conversation with the author, March 27, 2007

34. Micah Naftalin, email to the author, August 31, 2007

35. "Alexander Nikitin: Case Summary", Union of Councils for Soviet Jews, June 15, 1998, http://www.fsumonitor.com/stories/061598nik.shtml

36. "Strasbourg Court Examines Nikitin Case", Bellona, http://www.bellona.org/english_import_area/international/russia/envirorights/nikitin/26657

37. Leonid Stonov, Official Secrecy Paranoia Damages Democracy", *St. Petersburg Times*, August 18, 2000

38. Leonid Stonov, "Briefing: Human Rights in Russia", Written testimony to Commission on Security and Cooperation in Europe, September 23, 2000

39. Micah Naftalin, "Briefing: Intolerance in Contemporary Russia", Testimony to Commission on Security and Cooperation in Europe, October 15, 2002

40. Lev Krichevsky, "Post-Communist Russia Denies Some Jews Permission to Leave", Jewish Telegraphic Agency, July 4, 1997, http://www.jta.org/cgi-bin/iowa/news/article/19970704BPostCommunistRu.html

41. Foundation for Documentary Projects, Interview with Yossi Abramowitz

42. UPDATED Re: Yossi, http://www.peoplehood.org/?page_id=2

43. Micah Naftalin, email to the author, April 17, 2007

44. Leslie Katz, "S.F. Agency Fights for Uzbek Jew Accused of Murder," *Jewish News Weekly of Northern California*, October 20, 1995

45. Helene Kenvin, email to the author, July 12, 2007

46. "Uzbekistan Report on Human Rights Practices for 1996", U.S. Department of State, Bureau of Democracy, Human Rights and Labor, January 30, 1997

47. "Uzbek Jew Accused of Murder Sent to Mental Hospital", *Jewish News Weekly of Northern California*, January 12, 1996

48. Helene Kenvin, in conversation with the author, Washington, DC, July 20, 2003

49. Helene Kenvin, in telephone conversation with the author, July 8, 2007

50. Daniel Palanker, in conversation with the author, Sunnyvale, CA, December 17, 2003

51. The Caucasus Network newsletter, March 20, 1989
52. Carol Dvorkin, in conversation with the author, San Francisco, August 10, 2004
53. Helene Kenvin, July 20, 2003
54. Helene Kenvin, July 8, 2007
55. Mark Levin, in telephone conversation with the author, January 12, 2007
56. "About NCSJ", http://www.peoplehood.org/?page_id=2
57. Mark Levin
58. Eric Fingerhut, "New NCSJ President Aims to Publicize Needs of Jews Still in Former Soviet Union", *Washington Jewish Week*, January 3, 2007
59. Nathaniel Popper, "David Duke Offers 'Anti-Semitism 101 at a Ukrainian University", *Forward. Com.* November 3, 2006
60. "MAUP, Inter-Regional Academy of Personnel Management", NCSJ, February 2007, http://www.ncsj.org/AuxPages/020207MAUP.pdf
61. "Kehilla Projects", http://www.ncsj.org/kehilla.shtml
62. James D. Besser, "From Freeing Refuseniks to Today's Dimming Democracy, NCSJ Head Sees Renewed Need for American Jewish Activism", Baltimore *Jewish Times*, June 9, 2006
63. Mark Levin, in telephone conversation with the author, July 9, 2007
64. Haviv Rettig, "Jewish Right Organizations Nominated for Nobel", Jerusalem *Post*, February 10, 2007
65. Yossi Abramowitz, email to the author, July 8, 2007
66. Elie Wiesel, in conversation with the author, Boston, September 12, 2005

INDEX

Schlieffer, Solomon, 21–2
Schlossberg, Norm, 250
Schneersohn, Dovber, 12
Schneersohn, Yosef Yitzchak, 11–4, 30, 119
Schneerson, Menachem Mendel, 13, 411, 413, 435
Schnur, Zeesy, 236
Schoenberger, Carl, 327–8
School of Oriental Languages, 144
Schorr, Daniel, 23–4
Schroeter, Leonard, 44
Schudnovsky, Gregory, 317
Schwab, Susan, 368
Schweitzer, Albert, 65, 308
Science, 341
Scientists for Orlov and Shcharansky, 218, 340
Scientists for Sakharov, Orlov and Shcharansky, 327, 339, 342
Sde Boker, Israel, 38
Seattle, 44, 260
Seattle Action for Soviet Jewry, 260
Seattle-Tashkent Sister City Association, 260
Second World Conference of Jewish Communities on Soviet Jewry, 268, 301
Seligman-Kennard, Eva, 257
Selikowitz, David, 316–8
Selma, Alabama, 52, 270, 295–6
Senate Wives for Soviet Jewry, 374
Separated Soviet Families, 269
SERJ, 420–1
Sessler, Andrew, 339
Seton Hall University, 296
SFCSJ, 267–9, 291, 293
Shagalow, Benzion, 16
Shagalow, Yitzchak Elchanon, 14–6, 20

Shakhnovsky, Leah, 408
Shakhnovsky, Vladimir (Zeev), 210, 408
Shalem Center, 222
Shalom Prayer Book, 21
SHAMIR, 28
Shamir, Yitzhak, 140–1, 235, 403
Shammai, 209
Shapera, Peggy, 423
Shapira, Moshe Chaim, 38
Shapiro, Felix, 136, 143–4
Shapiro, Gabriel, 310
Shapiro, Irina, 400–1
Shapiro, Lev, 375
Shapiro, Michael, 400–1
Shapiro, Naomi, 274
Sharansky Unmasked, 223
Sharansky, Avital, 208–9, 212, 214–9, 215, 221–2, 237, 253, 256–7, 272–3, 277, 301, 311–2, 316, 321, 341, 374, 378, 383
Sharansky, Natan, xi, xv, 147, 159, 168, 171, 188, 197, 215–7, 221–4, 232, 237–9, 253–5, 269, 272, 278, 289, 301, 311–2, 315, 317, 319, 321, 324, 366, 374, 392, 398, 403, 407, 430, 447, 449
Sharett, Moshe, 33–4
Sharfman, Rae, 310
Sharm el-Sheikh, 92
Sharon, Ariel, 222
Shayevich, Adolf, 412, 434
Shcharansky, Anatoly (Tolya), 56, 188, 197–201, 205–21, 256–8, 278, 327, 339–343, 380, 382–4
Shcharansky, Boris, 205
Shcharansky, Leonid (Lenya), 205, 213–4
Sheen, Fulton, 297
Shenkar, Ann, 69